On Nabokov, Ayn Rand and the Libertarian Mind

The author gratefully acknowledges the following permissions:

A Contracorriente/Against the Current magazine. For material on Friedrich von Hayek, in Bell-Villada, "Bye, bye Marx, and Welcome to Our Andes and Our Tropics, Herr Doktor von Hayek!", Spring 2004 issue. Reprinted by permission.

Amador Publishers. For Bell-Villada, "Hitler Reconsidered" in *The Pianist Who Liked Ayn Rand: A Novella & 13 Stories* (1998). Reprinted by permission.

The Berkshire Eagle, copyright New England Newspapers Inc. For Bell-Villada, "Larry's Unmodest Proposal" (1985) and "A Day in the Life of a Rugged Individualist" (1995). Reprinted in full, with permission.

Georges Borchardt, Inc. For Louis Begley, unpublished "Introduction" to Vladimir Nabokov's *Speak, Memory*. Reprinted by permission.

Journal of Ayn Rand Studies. For passages from Bell-Villada, "Nabokov and Rand: Kindred Ideological Spirits, Divergent Literary Aims," Fall 2001. Reprinted by permission.

University Press of Mississippi. For selected passages from Bell-Villada, *Overseas American: Growing up Gringo in the Tropics* (2005). Reprinted by permission.

Monthly Review Press. For selected passages from Bell-Villada, "*1984*: Looking Backward at Orwell's Novel of the 1940s" (May 1984) and "No More Munichs! Or, What the Media Won't Tell" (April 1988). Reprinted by permission.

Palgrave Macmillan. For extensive reuse of Bell-Villada, "On the Cold War, American Aestheticism, the Nabokov Problem—and Me." In Kelly Comfort, ed., *Art and Life in Aestheticism*, 2008. Reproduced with permission of Palgrave Macmillan.

Salmagundi magazine. For extensive reuse of Bell-Villada, "Who Was Ayn Rand?" in Winter-Spring 2004 issue. Reprinted by permission of Skidmore College.

North Adams Transcript. For Bell-Villada, "Larry the Libertarian a hardliner on Soviet negotiations," January 25, 1986; "For Larry, the Libertarian, greed can be good, even beautiful," May 7, 1986; and "Arm the Teachers and Students." March 8, 1995. Reprinted in full, with permission.

AlterNet. For Bell-Villada, "Shooting Rampages: An American Tradition," July 26, 2012. Reprinted with permission.

On Nabokov, Ayn Rand and the Libertarian Mind: What the Russian-American Odd Pair Can Tell Us about Some Values, Myths and Manias Widely Held Most Dear

By

Gene H. Bell-Villada

With a formerly suppressed introduction to Nabokov's *Speak, Memory* by the novelist Louis Begley

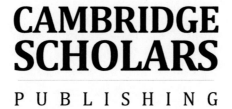

CAMBRIDGE
SCHOLARS
PUBLISHING

On Nabokov, Ayn Rand and the Libertarian Mind:
What the Russian-American Odd Pair Can Tell Us about Some Values,
Myths and Manias Widely Held Most Dear,
by Gene H. Bell-Villada

This book first published 2013. The present binding first published 2014.

Cambridge Scholars Publishing

12 Back Chapman Street, Newcastle upon Tyne, NE6 2XX, UK

British Library Cataloguing in Publication Data
A catalogue record for this book is available from the British Library

ISBN (10): 1-4438-6660-1, ISBN (13): 978-1-4438-6660-6

For Audrey Dobek-Bell, "La Osa."

In memoriam, 1945-2013

Ad ursam, iterum

TABLE OF CONTENTS

Chapter Eleven 129
On Their Russian Side

Chapter Twelve 145
On Their Nasty Side

Chapter Thirteen.. 161
On Their Respective Legacies

Chapter Fourteen 174
On the Libertarian Mind

Chapter Fifteen.. 196
On Guns, Flood Victims, Libertarians, Orwelliana, My Father, and Me

Appendix A 221
An Introduction to Nabokov's *Speak, Memory*
by Louis Begley

Appendix B... 241
My Encounters with Libertarians

Bibliography 264

Index.. 273

PREFACE AND ACKNOWLEDGMENTS

Nabokov and Rand? In the same breath? Casual readers who are literarily inclined will surely balk at the combination. Friends and colleagues have in fact expressed surprise and indeed bewilderment whenever I've mentioned to them the title and initial focus of this volume. And yet I believe that a great deal of intellectual space and common ground is shared by these two Russian-Americans. Hence this book, in which I endeavor to map out those swaths of territory.

It bears noting that I am not the first to take on such a comparison. Back in the 1990s, when the idea for this unorthodox venture was just a gleam in my eye, I was pleased and relieved to find out that D. Barton Johnson, a professor of Slavic languages at the University of California-Santa Barbara, also was pursuing researches on the very same topic.

Each of these Russian-Americans, of course, is a problematical figure, although in divergent ways: Nabokov was the absolute aesthete, Rand the propagandist and ideologue.

In dealing with Nabokov, my ambivalent—nay, conflicted—relationship to him is here fleshed out. I am a genuine admirer of his two greatest works; am less enthusiastic about some of his other writings, a few of which I consider to be either terrible artistic mistakes or bad novels in good prose. And I have found Nabokov the man to be vain and peevish, his views on both politics and art singularly dogmatic and mean-spirited. In the course of my critical and other investigations for this study, it has been a genuine consolation to discover that I was not alone in my reservations concerning the Master, even though those dissenting opinions—from man of letters Edmund Wilson to novelist Paul Russell, and many fine scholars such as Page Stegner, David Rampton, Douglas Fowler, Dean Flower, and philosopher Richard Rorty—have not been paid much heed.

Ayn Rand is another matter. Here, I feel not the least ambivalence. Along with the vast majority of literary critics, I find it difficult to take seriously either her work while rejecting everything it stands for. As a novelist, her character portrayals are propagandistic and one-dimensional, her plots childish and implausible, her ideas simplistic and cruel. And her style is unmemorable, her humor heavy-handed, her tone relentlessly didactic. Moreover, only the Rand faithful and her personality cultists would argue that she was an admirable, caring human being. And yet, "Randianism," one must grant, is a formidable presence and mass phenomenon in today's United States. Not for nothing is a recent book by Gary Weiss entitled *Ayn Rand Nation*. Few other writers with literary aims have achieved the broad level of cultural diffusion and ideological influence gained by Rand with her two, thick novels and her later, non-fiction statements and public appearances. Rand, quite simply, is there; she cannot be ignored.

In my examination of Rand's fiction, I have elected to concentrate almost exclusively on her two major works, *Fountainhead* and *Atlas Shrugged*. They are the source books of her thinking and as such have inspired perhaps millions of young American devotees. By contrast, her first, more realistic novel, *We the Living*, set in Soviet Russia, has exerted minimal sway in U.S. life, while the underlying messages of her experimental play, *Night of January 16th*, or of her second novel, the dystopian *Anthem*, become clear only in the wake of prior acquaintance with the ideas given flesh in the later two tomes. In analyzing her work, I have endeavored to bring out the core and corollaries of Rand's thinking, and also to demonstrate precisely *how* she puts across her preachments—how her characterizations, her plotting, as well as her deliberate omissions all serve to prop up and enhance her ideological agenda. (In the process, I have found it necessary to provide a certain amount of plot summary, given that few Nabokov fans read Rand, whereas the story of Lolita and her mad lover is something like common knowledge among the educated.)

For the record, I anticipate that some Rand devotees will label me a "Rand hater," summoning up the accusation that Bell-Villada "does not understand Rand" and has not even read her writing. These are the standard formulae usually trotted out by Rand believers, who have said those very things about my earlier volume, *The Pianist Who Liked Ayn Rand: A Novella & 13 Stories*, and who have made similar comments about recent major studies of their icon by Gary Weiss, Jennifer Burns, and Anne Heller. Let me thus preempt the Randians in their predictable fits of passion!

My observations on "the libertarian mind" later in this book are aimed at placing my literary investigations within some broader contexts. Since the 1980s, the United States has seen a series of intermittent, grass-roots stirrings on the Right, has felt the ebb and flow of a radical mass movement that is heavily libertarian-inflected. This right-wing upsurge is, arguably, the most notable ideological shift and the most vocal political phenomenon of the past few decades. Prior to 1980, one could assume that the New Deal and its successor programs were firmly, safely in place. That legacy is now being eroded, is in the crosshairs of a constant and relentless libertarian siege. Though the trend does not command a solid majority, it poses an aggressive challenge and can set the terms of engagement and the agenda for its center-to-left adversaries, as well as blocking progressive legislation. Occasionally, through various political maneuvers (for instance, redistricting) or special circumstances such as third-party candidates or the antiquated power of the Electoral College, the movement even attains significant victories from time to time.

Libertarians are not, strictly speaking, fascists, inasmuch as they still believe in and rely on the established mechanisms of democratic governance in accomplishing their ends (although some of its prominent intellectuals—von Hayek, Milton Friedman—did support the Pinochet dictatorship in Chile). Moreover, after Reagan, they have been largely lacking in charismatic leadership. Still, the Republican Party has few remaining moderates and has thus evolved into a monolithic, far-Right alliance, a Right well-imbued with much of the libertarian world-view, of which Madame Rand was the most visible pioneer as well as the most severe exponent. She is to the United States in our time what Chernyshevsky was to late-Tsarist and Soviet Russia in theirs. (See chapter 11.)

Besides literary criticism, *On Nabokov, Ayn Rand and the Libertarian Mind* has an autobiographical component. The book at hand, it should be said, is not my first effort at commenting on literature through a personal lens. My memoir, *Overseas American* (2005), includes a great deal of literary reflection; and, in a recent essay, I examine the work of Jean Rhys and Barbara Kingsolver through the knowing eyes of a displaced individual who, like the two woman novelists (one Caribbean-English, the other American), has lived the largely unacknowledged double experience of a childhood spent outside one's passport country followed by a "return" to a land not fully one's own.[1]

In this work, I expand that autobiographical focus—in various ways and for a variety of reasons. There are many great writers whom I unqualifiedly admire—say, Shakespeare, Jane Austen, Baudelaire, Samuel Beckett, Pablo Neruda, and García Márquez, to name a few. Even though the entirety of these authors' respective oeuvre is uneven, with some titles that are less achieved or less mature than others, their overall artistic worth is not in question. (Granted, French neo-classicists may have rejected the Englishman; traditionalists, Stalinists and Objectivists, rebuffed the

---

[1] See "On Jean Rhys, Barbara Kingsolver, and Me: Reflections on a Problem That Has No Set Name," in Bell-Villada and Nina Sichel, eds., *Writing Out of Limbo*, pp. 411-425.

Franco-Irishman; and anti-leftists, despised the Chilean and the Colombian. Those, however, are matters of the politics of taste rather than of aesthetic appraisal.) Nabokov, on the other hand, presents a highly skewed and uneven picture, while his own critical judgments are quite questionable. Yet many Nabokov specialists and cultists tend to justify most everything about him, or they ignore his less-attractive side—be it his weaker writings, his anti-Freudianism, his blanket dismissal of all abstract thought, his support of McCarthyism, his defense of the Vietnam War, and his unpleasantness both as interviewee and as presenter of his earlier work.

My divided feelings about the high-level Russian-American artificer, I should note, have haunted me since my graduate-school days. One of my first publications for a national magazine was in fact a long, harsh look at Nabokov and *Strong Opinions* in *The Nation* in 1975. Such reservations grew and made their way into portions of my *Art for Art's Sake & Literary Life* (1996). A review of the book in *Publisher's Weekly* (22 April 1996) specifically singled out those sections, speculating that Bell-Villada's "bilious analysis of Nabokov's work is likely to raise some hackles." That sentence, which made its way onto the Internet and Wikipedia, has been cited to me on more than one occasion. For years, then, it has been impossible for me not to view Nabokov as anything but a thorny topic for discussion; and perhaps I found myself in need of a whole new volume such as this in order to play out my own Nabokovian dilemma and, somehow, get it out of my system.

Rand by contrast is an author about whom I harbor no mixed feelings. Her thoughts had already been injected satirically into the narrative and the dialogues of my 1998 novella about the pianist. When actually commenting on an author one dislikes, however, some explanation is due. In the course of this book, readers will note how, in many respects, mine was a difficult childhood, the circumstances and the male parent of which could well be described as "Randian." My father was an American businessman abroad who lived for money-making at the exclusion of all else—whether these be family, parenting, community, culture, learning, entertainment, sports, or even simple physical enjoyment. Moreover, the growth and development of his three children, I realized later in life, were matters of supreme indifference to him. Parental pride and joy were not emotions he was wont to cultivate. Like Rand's emblematic hero John Galt, he worshipped the dollar and felt he owed nothing to anyone except himself.

Hence, to confront the larger, hidden premises that had made possible such an upbringing is worth the trouble and labor, if only for the purposes of catharsis and self-knowledge. Still, I should say that, over the years, I have made the acquaintance of Randians and libertarians who have proved to be amiable souls and appreciative colleagues, and also that (if you please) my quarrel with Rand thought and Rand cult must not, in any way, be taken by them personally.

*

The two Appendices bring to this book an added dimension. They offer diverse hues and flavors. Or, to employ a musical metaphor: changes of rhythm and tempo, like the different movements of a piano sonata or string quartet. An andante cantabile in the case of Begley's essay, followed by a scherzo cum finale giocoso in my concluding spoofs. Some slow lyricism, then some concluding levity.

Novelist Louis Begley's set of ruminations on Nabokov's *Speak, Memory*, in Appendix A, was originally commissioned by Random House as an introduction to their new edition of the Russian-American's memoir. The piece, however, was scrapped at the proofs stage when, according to Mr. Begley, Nabokov's son Dmitri raised some "unspecified objections." For me it has been a personal pleasure to rescue this lovely essay (which I word-processed, line by line, using a copy of those original proofs) from the oblivion of the Boston University archives where it had been housed.

Appendix B is a group of occasional lampoons of libertarian issues that I have published over the past three decades. In some cases they are even more relevant now than when they first saw print. In the end, the satires may sum up my attitude more crisply than does my literary analysis.

*

I wish to express my gratitude to the following individuals and institutions who, in the course of fifteen years, have enabled this book's existence and also helped make it better.

To John Burt Foster, who in 1997 first brought my attention to the comparative studies of D. Barton Johnson on Nabokov and Rand, and who, with Ronald Bogue, gave me the opportunity to present my own ideas on the subject at the 1999 meeting of the Southern Comparative Literature Association;

To D. Barton Johnson, who graciously corresponded with me and then joined me on a panel dealing with the two authors at a special session of the MLA convention in 2000;

To Steve Levin and the Faculty Lecture Committee, who provided a forum for my thoughts as part of the Williams College Faculty Lecture Series in 2001;

To Tomás Eloy Martínez (in memoriam, 1934-2010), fine novelist and journalist from Argentina, who first drew my attention to the shaping influence of Friedrich von Hayek on Latin American neo-liberalism;

To Gordon Bigelow and to Nicholas Birns, who each put together MLA panels on neo-liberalism (2001 and 2008, respectively) on which I could first rehearse my reflections on Friedrich von Hayek;

To Greg Dawes, who invited me to share my ideas on Hayek and his Latin American disciples on the online journal *A Contracorriente*;

To Chris Matthew Sciabarra, libertarian thinker, expert "Randologist," and a likeable man, who gallantly encouraged me to work out my ideas on Nabokov and Rand, and on Randian aesthetics, for his *Journal of Ayn Rand Studies*;

To Zoran Kuzmanovich, who was hospitable to my thoughts on "Nabokov's Obsessions" at the 2002 MLA meeting's panel of the International Vladimir Nabokov Society;

To Robert Boyers, under whose editorial guidance my reflections on Rand's 100th anniversary saw light in *Salmagundi* magazine;

To Kelly Comfort, for commissioning my essay on Nabokov and including it in her collection, *Art and Life in Aestheticism*;

To Ron Morin, for reading an earlier version of the above essay and offering suggestions;

To Louis Begley, novelist, for granting me permission to include his suppressed essay on *Speak, Memory*; for obtaining for me the proofs of the essay from the Howard Gottlieb Archival Research Center at Boston University; and for providing some insider's details about the episode with Dmitri Nabokov;

To Stephen Fix, for sharing with me the anecdote of his students' reactions to *Strong Opinions*;

To Darra Goldstein, for leading me to Paul Russell's novel about Sergey Nabokov;

To novelist Paul Russell, for *The Unreal Life of Sergey Nabokov*, and for some fruitful exchanges on the delicate yet vast topics of Nabokov and his brother, and of Nabokov's multiple prejudices;

To Julie Cassiday, for pointing me in the direction of scholarship on Chernyshevsky;

To Linda G. Senesky, for suggesting a change in the title of this volume;

To Enrique Peacock-López, physical chemist, who elucidated for me the workings of John Galt's magical energy machine and also clarified some of the fallacies and problems in Rand's engineering physics;

To Andrea Pitzer, whose recent book, *The Secret History of Vladimir Nabokov*, opened this writer's eyes, at the very last minute, to another dimension of the novelist's world;

To Williams College, for two generous mini-sabbaticals that allowed me the free time for doing full-time research and writing of this book;

To Rebecca Ohm of the college library, who, with her electronic expertise, dug up some important past documents related to my researches;

To Rachel Kranz, novelist, all-around writer, and ever the genius reader, for a thorough and sensitive job of copy-editing the manuscript and helping iron out its rough spots;

Last but not least, to Audrey, for putting up once again with my ongoing graphomanic compulsions and with the return of our old friend Larry the Libertarian.

Thanks to the help of all of the above, my ideas have taken on book form and improved in the process. Any faults, solecisms, or gaps are my own.

GB-V
Williamstown, Mass.;
Cambridge, Mass., 2009-2013

A NOTE ON PAGE REFERENCES

All references to books by Nabokov and Ayn Rand appear, parenthetically
and abbreviated, within the body of the text. The following editions are
utilized:

Books by Nabokov

Ada or Ardor: A Family Chronicle (A). New York: Fawcett, 1970
The Annotated Lolita (L). Edited, with preface, introduction, and notes by
   Alfred Appel, Jr. Revised and updated edition. New York: Random
   House, 1991
Bend Sinister (BS). London: Penguin Books, 1947
The Defence (LD). Translated by Michael Scammell in collaboration with
   the author.
   London: Grenada Publishing, 1964
Despair (D). Translated by the Author. New York: Vintage International
   (Random House), 1989
The Gift (G). Translated by Michael Scammell in collaboration with the
   author. New York: Vintage International, Random House, 1991
Invitation to a Beheading (IB). Translated by Dmitri Nabokov in
   collaboration with the author. London: Penguin Books, 1963
King Queen Knave (KQK). Translated by Dmitri Nabokov in collaboration
   with the author. New York: McGraw-Hill, 1968
Laughter in the Dark (LD). Translated by the author. London: Penguin
   Books, 1963
Lectures on Literature (LL). Edited by Fredson Bowers. Introduction by
   John Updike. New York: Harcourt Brace Jovanovich, 1980
Lolita (L). (See under *The Annotated* Lolita.)
Look at the Harlequins! (LATH) New York: McGraw-Hill, 1974
The Original of Laura (Dying Is Fun) (OL). Edited by Dmitri Nabokov.
   New York: Knopf, 2009
Pale Fire (PF). New York: Vintage Books (Random House), 1989
Pnin (P). In Page Stegner, ed., *Nabokov's Congeries*, pp. 362-514. New
   York: Viking, 1968
The Real Life of Sebastian Knight (RLLK) .London: Penguin Books, 1964

Speak, Memory: An Autobiography Revisited (SM). New York: Vintage
    International Random House, 1989
Strong Opinions (SO). New York: McGraw-Hill, 1973

Books by Ayn Rand

Anthem (An). New York: New American Library, N.D.
Atlas Shrugged (AS). New York: New American Library, 1959
Capitalism: The Unknown Ideal (CUI). New York: New American
    Library, 1967
For the New Intellectual (FNI). New York: New American Library, 1963
The Fountainhead (F). New York: New American Library, N.D.
Night of January 16th (NJ). New York: Penguin, 1987
Romantic Manifesto (RM). New York: New American Library, 1971
The Virtue of Selfishness: A New Concept of Egoism (VS). New York:
    New American Library, 1964
We the Living (WL). New York: New American Library, 1959 (?)

CHAPTER ONE

THE PAIRING

Ladies and gentlemen, we have before us two iconic figures.

Standing behind podium number one, stage center, his 3" x 5" cards in one hand, a butterfly net in the other, is Vladimir Vladimirovich Nabokov (1899-1977). (APPLAUSE.) And there, standing at the other podium, stage right, is Ayn Rand, née Alyssa Rosenbaum (1905-1982), sporting in her hand a long, swanky cigarette holder and, pinned to her black cape, a shiny, golden dollar sign. (APPLAUSE.) Both of them literary products of pre-1917 Russia as well as mid-twentieth century America.

Their respective magnum opuses first saw light on U.S. soil within a year of one another—*Lolita* in 1958, *Atlas Shrugged* in 1957. Each book surges onto the best-seller lists of its time. Each volume goes on to survive into the twenty-first century, with new editions, special editions, anniversary editions, audio editions, electronic editions, and the like. Each title becomes shorthand for an entire set of experiences, preoccupations, issues: in one case a forced amour, carried on in countless comical motels, between a thirty-something guy and a sassy pubescent teen (his stepdaughter); in the other, the celebration of a genius-inventor-businessman who, via a general strike that he leads with the captains of industry and their equally brilliant allies (scientists, musicians, sculptors, and other luminaries), brings the mighty U.S. of A. to its knees, and who, in a seventy-page, nationally broadcast allocution over radio, defends individual selfishness as *morally right*!

Both these writers, and their writings, have become handy references and sources for popular culture.[1] Each author was interviewed by *Playboy*, Nabokov in 1961, Rand in 1964, both—coincidentally—by Alvin Toffler. Two feature films based on *Lolita* exist thus far, one by Stanley Kubrick (1962), the other by Adrian Lyne (1997). The first was funny, the second was not. Neither of them, alas, could replicate the formal cum verbal wizardry of the prose original. In addition, a couple of Nabokov's middle-

---

[1] For a survey of Nabokov's larger impact, see Suellen Stringer-Hye, "Vladimir Nabokov and Popular Culture."

period Russian works, *Laughter in the Dark* (1933, trans. 1938) and *Despair* (1936, trans. 1937) were brought to celluloid, respectively, by Tony Richardson (1969) and by Rainer Werner Fassbinder (1978), though the artistic results are not among those respected cinéastes highest. Probably the best Nabokov-inspired movie, *The Luzhin Defense* (2001), by the fine Dutch filmmaker Marleen Gorris, came out of what is, arguably, the man's best Russian-language novel, originally by that name (1930), yet known in English simply as *The Defense* (1964), about a brilliant chess player who may be something of an idiot savant. Meanwhile, Jim Jarmusch's sort-of romantic road movie *Broken Flowers* (2005) actually has among its cast a fleeting character called Lolita, who is (what else?) a sexy teen, daughter of the womanizing protagonist's whilom girl friend.

Indeed, within the pulp media's more sordid and sensationalistic news tales, the term "Lolita" is a common enough tag for alleged teen seductresses, even though the notion was not exactly what Nabokov had in mind.[2] As an instance, in the wake of the scandal surrounding Amy Fisher, a 17-year-old who shot and wounded the wife of her lover Joey Buttafuoco, the accused came to be known in the yellow press and on TV as "the Long Island Lolita."[3]

Then there are the passing allusions in pop music. The lyrics to the song "Don't Stand So Close to Me" by Sting and The Police, to take just one instance, tell of a schoolgirl's lustful crush on a male teacher twice her age; its concluding lines note that he "starts to shake and cough/Just like the old man in/That book by Nabokov." (The pronunciation is off, the rhyme is right.) Australian singer and writer Nick Cave in turn credits his discovery of *Lolita* as one of the signal formative experiences of his youth, and, on 4 March 2011, read aloud from its opening pages to an assembled multitude at the first World Book Night in London's Trafalgar Square.[4]

Lolita moreover can help catapult literary essays to best-sellerdom. Nabokov's most famous novel takes up the initial chapter in Azar Nafisi's *Reading Lolita in Tehran: A Memoir in Books* (2000), the subject matter being not so much the Russian writer's wondrous art as the hazards of studying transgressive texts while living in the shadow of a theocratic regime.

Ayn Rand likewise has had her filmed adaptations and pop-culture incarnations. The 1949 film of *The Fountainhead*, directed by King Vidor

---

[2] For a "revisionist" look at this established view, see Elizabeth Patnoe, "Discourse, Ideology, and Hegemony: The Double Dramas in and around *Lolita*."
[3] Ibid., p. 154.
[4] Both cited in D. Barton Johnson, "Nabokov, Ayn Rand, and Russian-American Literature, or the Odd Couple," p. 106.

and starring Gary Cooper, helped further boost sales of the book and enhanced her reputation. And 1999 saw a docudrama, *The Passion of Ayn Rand*, on cable TV, starring such respected actors as Helen Mirren, Julie Delpy, Peter Fonda, and Eric Stoltz. Based on chosen portions of close disciple Barbara Branden's book by that name, it focuses largely on the strange, sordid, years-long affair that Rand conducted with Barbara's then-husband Nathaniel, who was twenty-five years Rand's junior—all with the "consent" of the respective other spouses, whom the great sage had persuaded (as rational individuals! as superior beings!) to accept the twin-triangle arrangement.

Allusions to Rand's work often crop up in film and TV narratives whenever some advocacy of selfishness—virtuous or not—is in the spotlight. In *Dirty Dancing* (1987), the upper-class cad Robbie who gets his working-class girl friend Penny accidentally pregnant has as his bible... *The Fountainhead*, a copy of which he waves about as he declares blithely, "Some people matter, some people don't." An episode of *The Simpsons* features a nursery called the Ayn Rand Day Care Center (ironically, given Rand's contempt for motherhood and total lack of interest in children), and cites the Randian formula "A is A" taken from *Atlas Shrugged*. (The nursery likewise features signs saying "Helping Is Futile" and bans pacifiers, because toddlers should "develop the bottle within.") The advertising agency CEO Bert Cooper of the *Mad Men* office series gives away copies of the *Atlas* tract to his favored employees. A kind of official recognition was also granted writer Rand when, in 1999, the U.S. Postal Service issued a commemorative stamp honoring her as part of its "Great American Authors" series.

Going Nabokov and The Police's pop tune one better, Rand can boast from the Canadian rock band Rush a 1975 song called ... "Anthem"! Its words, which pointedly take issue with "bleeding hearts," indeed advocate living only for oneself and imply that selfishness is, yes, just fine. At that time, the group's lyricist-composer, drummer Neil Peart, was admittedly under the influence of La Rand. Senatorial hopeful Rand Paul, a libertarian, used Rush's music as background to his successful political campaign in 2010, as did far-right-wing radio celebrity Rush Limbaugh over the years to spice up his talk show. The band's attorneys formally sued both the Honorable Dr. Paul and the radio announcer on grounds of copyright infringement.

Would any high-school curriculum require *Lolita* for an English class? Doubtful, for reasons anyone will easily guess. The instructions for the Advanced Placement literature course in fact reportedly counsel its participating teachers against having their young charges study the work.

Teachers blogging on the Web frankly admit that they can't (or at least won't) use *Lolita*. By contrast, Rand's *Anthem* is actually read and discussed in some high-school classrooms—owing presumably to its pamphlet-like plainness and brevity (according to biographer Anne Heller, it has sold some three and a half million copies).[5] Even *Fountainhead* is used on occasion, the notorious rape scene notwithstanding. *Atlas*, though, with its 1,200-page heft, is obviously not easily utilizable. At the college level, by contrast, *Lolita* and other Nabokov fictions have long served as standard fare in advanced undergraduate lit. classes, whereas precious few English professors would so much as consider requiring Rand—and fewer still Philosophy profs, save for the most convinced, extreme, and axiomatic libertarians, who, as Rand herself did, consider her absolutely the greatest thinker of all time!

The late Nabokov enjoys enormous critical, cultural, and academic standing. He lives on in "the canon," albeit somewhere at its edges. Renowned Yale University critic Harold Bloom, significantly, does not include any of the Russian-American master's works in his own best-seller, *The Western Canon* (1994). And Nabokov doesn't even rate mention in respected historian Peter Gay's encyclopedic survey, *Modernism* (2008), presumably owing to the Russian's virulent hatred of Freud, whom both Bloom and Gay have built upon and touted. In contrast with a posthumously triumphant Rand, there is not and probably will not be a postage stamp bearing Nabokov's name. British director Adrian Lyne for his part encountered some difficulty placing his 1997 *Lolita* film in U.S. theatres during that time of child-molestation scandals.[6]

Still, to have read *Lolita* is one step toward being literate and learned in America, even though the novel is less than accessible to U.S. teens, despite its American-teen co-protagonist. The literary-linguistic artifice and the life-experience that sustain it are far too much save for the most sophisticated of adolescents. Fittingly, *Lolita*'s several-hundred laudatory readers' reviews on Amazon.com exhibit a high level of literary culture and a nuanced appreciation for the book's evocative and descriptive powers, its narrative and moral ambiguities, its dazzling prose. Even the scattered one-star dismissals on that website tend to grant the novel its strengths *qua* art.

If bulk sales of books were our chief measure for determining literary worth, then Rand as scribbler would have to be ranked well above her exquisite émigré compatriot. Rand's thick, preachy epics, *The Fountainhead* and *Atlas Shrugged*, along with her half-dozen collections of articles,

[5] Anne Heller, *Ayn Rand and the World She Made*, p. 104.
[6] Stringer-Hye, p. 152.

continue to sell in the six figures every year. Indeed, in the wake of the ominous, 2008 financial panic, sales of *Atlas* actually surged to around 600,000 just in the year 2009! These were purchases generated by word-of-mouth and made by individual consumers—not the result of college-course reading lists or publishers' ad campaigns.

Rand's ardent followers, most of them hooked when in their teens, have numbered in the millions. It's a passing phase, as a nervous mom may note; the kids will usually outgrow their infatuation and become everything from libertarians, Marxists, or New Ageists to plain old centrists and Republicans. Yet there are bright grown-ups who have continued to cleave to the faith. Some convinced Randians hold, or have held positions in the headiest upper reaches of U.S. life. In the best-known case, economist Alan Greenspan showed up at Rand's doorstep in Manhattan when in his mid-twenties and became one of her most devoted acolytes. Even when at the height of his fame and power as head of the Federal Reserve, he gratefully acknowledged his role in her life. Michael Milken, the financier who served time in prison for securities fraud, reportedly had twenty-two copies of *Atlas Shrugged* in his jail cell.

Likewise, John A. Allison IV, retired CEO of the BB & T bank in North Carolina, is a devout Randian who publicly extols selfishness, and has his bank donate $5 million per year in support of teaching and researches to propagate Randthought. Other vociferous Randians include hedge-funder Clifford Asness; the CEO of the Whole Foods chain, John Mackey;[7] Rex Tillerson, the chairman and CEO of ExxonMobil, whose favorite book is *Atlas Shrugged*;[8] Eddie Lampert, CEO of Sears; and the 2012 Vice-Presidential candidate Paul Ryan, who, in 2005, explicitly said, "The reason I got involved in public service..., if I had to credit one thinker, one person, it would be Ayn Rand." Finally, in September 2013, Senator Ted Cruz, Republican of Texas, as part of his crusade against President Obama's Affordable Care Act, conducted on the Senate floor a twenty-one-hour filibuster in which, among other things, he "read long excerpts from the novels of Ayn Rand, one of his literary heroes."[9]

Rand has been a favorite of U.S. politicians for some time. The very witty Gore Vidal remarked in 1961 that, when he ran for a seat in the House of Representatives, Rand was the only writer whom people in Washington knew about or would talk about.[10]

---

[7] Andrew Martin, "Give Him Liberty, but Not a Bailout," *New York Times Sunday Business*, August 2, 2009, pp. 1, 6.

[8] Steve Coll, "Gusher: The Power of Exxon Mobil," p. 28.

[9] Jeffrey Toobin, "The Absolutist," p. 38.

[10] Gore Vidal, "Comment," *Esquire*, July 1961.

Rand's sway at the mass level, or at least the effectiveness of her fan base, was dramatically demonstrated in two revealing polls from the 1990s. In a 1991 survey, sponsored by the Library of Congress and the Book-of-the-Month Club, readers chose *Atlas* as the book that had most influenced them, after the Bible. And in a later poll conducted by Modern Library asking for votes on the best 100 English-language novels of the 20th century, some 400,000 readers responded as follows: numbers 1 and 2, *Atlas* and *Fountainhead*; numbers 7 and 8, *Anthem* and *We, the Living*. In a corresponding poll for the best 100 works of non-fiction, Rand's *The Virtue of Selfishness* topped the list. In a separate survey of the imprint's editorial board, consisting of eighteen highly respected authors and editors, not a single novel by Rand cropped up. *Lolita*, by contrast, was #4.

Randianism, nonetheless, exists. There is the movement, still a grass-roots presence via the Objectivist Clubs whose posters bedeck the campus bulletin boards each year. And there is the 1997 film *Ayn Rand: A Sense of Life*, a glowing, sans-blemishes fairy tale made under the auspices of a Randian financier from Bermuda (his name: Monroe Trout, something out of Scott Fitzgerald or Sinclair Lewis) and an Oscar nominee under the Documentary category the next year. (When I saw the movie at a multiplex art house in Boston, the hush among the audience was church-like. Subtitle of the picture could well have been *A Sainted Life*.)

On the other hand, there's *Atlas*, the movie—or rather the multiple aborted attempts at a movie. One proposal, in 1972, fizzled out because Rand insisted on full control over any such screenplay. She herself later began a script but left it only one-third complete when she died in 1982. A couple of planned TV miniseries, by NBC in 1978 and by the Turner Network in 1999, were abandoned in the wake of organizational shuffles at each firm. Finally, in 2010, a high-tech investor by the name of John Aglialoro put up funding for a movie trilogy. This time the obstacles came from casting: no glamorous female stars could be found to assume the role of super-heroine Dagny Taggart. The eventual troupe for the film was made up of unknowns, with American-Canadian thespian Paul Johansson directing and also playing the part of a shadowy hero John Galt. Its release, on Tax Day, 2010, was greeted with largely negative critical reception, except for glowing reviews in—where else?—the Randian journal *Reason* and the business bi-weekly *Forbes*. The movie showed at a total of 465 screens out of a possible 37,000 and lost over $10 million. Both as art and as entertainment, the film was a stiff and stillborn thing.

For *Part 2: The Strike*, the entire cast was changed and TV director John Putch took over the reins, with only the cinematographer, Ross Berryman, remaining from the original crew. Although this time the movie appeared on twice as many screens, its box-office receipts were yet lower, and the reviews even more negative, than for its predecessor. The product came and went, largely unnoticed except among hard-core libertarian audiences at such venues as Heritage Foundation and Cato Institute. Given its bulk, didacticism, and outdated technology (railroads!), *Atlas* may well be unfilmable...

Cinematic disasters aside, Randian history has all the morbid if fascinating features of a religious sect, as expertly anatomized by Canadian journalist Jeff Walker in his important muckraking study, *The Ayn Rand Cult* (1999). Like all guru-centered cults, Randism has had its fair share of eager acolytes, passive followers, and loyal dissidents who have somehow been linked or witness to the rivalries, the infighting, the excommunications, the quarrels over fine points of doctrine, and the creepy sexual intrigues. Rand herself achieved some notoriety as a nasty little dictator who demanded total dedication and, conversely, who ruthlessly quashed any hints of doubts as to her rightness. It's a bizarre tale that is beautifully evoked in Mary Gaitskill's disturbing, seriocomic novel, *Two Girls: Fat and Thin* (1991).

But Randianism also exists as a consistent and rather simple set of beliefs, a theology one readily grasps after some time spent with its scriptures. "Objectivism" is how the founder dubbed her system. At its core is the idea that selfishness is good, greed is admirable, and altruism is evil—indeed, as she says in her essay "Theory and Practice," altruism is "a doctrine of the hatred of man" (C, 148). (*The Virtue of Selfishness*—those are her very words! A more complete title for her book would be *The Virtue of Selfishness and the Evilness of Caring about Others*.) Unfettered capitalism is thus in Rand's view the only true moral system in history. The successful businessman is the ideal hero of our time. The sign of the dollar is an icon to be worshiped and flaunted. Conversely, generosity and compassion have no place in the world according to Rand. In a letter from the 1940s she singles out competence as "the only thing I love or admire in people. I don't give a damn about kindness, charity, or any of the other so-called virtues." Or, as Dominique Francon, the gorgeous and cold-hearted heroine-cum-bitch of Rand's *Fountainhead* reflects at one point with lofty sarcasm, "Compassion is a wonderful thing. It's what one feels when one looks at a squashed caterpillar" (F, 274).

Having ambitious claims as a total philosophy, Objectivism also posits a theory of knowledge. For Rand, the external world is to be grasped only through man's highest faculty: reason. (*Reason*, not incidentally, is the name of the libertarian magazine, founded by a Randian.) Rand's and Randians' formulaic paeans to rationality often sound like sloganeering, though admittedly the tradition goes back to the French Revolution and its anti-clerical, anti-religious struggles. Rand herself was aggressively atheistic. Still, despite Randroid fixation on the term "epistemology" and their own mega-word (take a deep breath) "psychoepistemology," she and her friends have little to say about messy, more complex and elusive ways of understanding such as experience or intuition. Darwin and Einstein, to cite just a couple of examples, were not exactly pure rationalists.

Feelings, meanwhile, are secondary, or dangerous, or simply shouldn't count for much. Within our range of human faculties, emotion for Ayn Rand is a no-no as a path to wisdom, let alone as a means to a good life. As she herself thundered in her 1964 *Playboy* interview, whosoever chooses to live for family and friends rather than for "creative work" is an "emotional parasite" and, what's more, is "immoral."[11] She adduces no figures, but those immoral parasites easily number in the billions, world-wide. They presumably include the field workers who've picked your table grapes and the Salvadorans who now mow many a front lawn in Long Island—all for the sake of their wives and kids back home or right here in the U.S. Could anything under the sun be more morally repellent?

Rand thought. Randspeak. Randcult. They're very much an American phenomenon. Though she has some fans scattered about the U.K., the (white) British Commonwealth realms, and Scandinavia, her oeuvre is something scarcely known beyond the U.S. coastal shores and southern borders. Over the past couple of decades I've chanced to mention La Rand to well-read Europeans and Latin Americans. Almost invariably her name draws a blank. And when I proceed to summarize for them her cherished ideas and values, my interlocutors generally find such notions puzzling, strange, and kind of wacky.

*

I first heard about *Lolita* in Caracas, Venezuela, from my male classmates at the American School in that South American metropolis. To our sex-obsessed young souls and longing libidos, *Lolita* was rumored to be the latest, big "dirty book," the successor to *Peyton Place*. Several in my social group had already gobbled up the notoriously scabrous small-town saga by a New Hampshire scribbler of French-Canadian origin named Grace Metalious.

I too had imbibed from Peyton, mainly because I'd found the novel sitting in the two-shelf library of my father, an expatriate entrepreneur from Kansas who, a few years earlier, had ditched my Asian mother in

---

[11] Alvin Toffler, "*Playboy* Interview: Ayn Rand," p. 37.

Puerto Rico for a sexy Cuban, name of Mary (rounded hips, dyed-blond hair), and who, in the process, had stealthily taken possession of—"abducted," perhaps—my brother and me. (Other books of his that I casually plucked from those twin shelves included mass-market paperback editions of business novels by one Cameron Hawley—*Executive Suite* and *Cash McCall*; Sloan Wilson's best-seller and then-cultural icon, *The Man in the Gray Flannel Suit*; stories by Graham Greene; some early Orwell; and a sensationalist novel about a child murderess entitled *The Bad Seed*.)

My mother later would inform me, when I rejoined her a couple of years later in New Mexico, that Dad had always found the light versifier Ogden Nash too arty for his tastes.

Meanwhile, there were no Spanish books gracing that meager, lone bookcase—our stepmother Mary didn't read. *Lolita*, for its part, was still unavailable in paperback, and for other reasons was inaccessible to young minds. To us whelps, the idea that erotic experience could be evoked via indirection, artifice, and high art would never have crossed our still-green minds.

As for La Rand, I never had occasion to encounter so much as her name until my last couple of years as a music student at the University of Arizona. Her axiomatic doctrines were a favored reference point for a few pop ideologues and sages who hung around the student cafeteria, huffing and puffing cigarette fumes as they gabbed at great length over their coffee cups.

About that same time my junior-year roommate, a fellow musician and aspiring musical scholar, devoured *Lolita* (the American edition of the book was only four years old then, and it had somehow crossed his path). He was particularly baffled by, but also taken with, the strangely named author's odd lexical items: *solipsized, solecisms, phocine*. Thanks to my Latin American background I had previously learned the definition of *solecismo* in a Cuban high school class; vaguely sensed that *phocine* resembled *foca*, the Spanish word for "seal"; and was acquainted with *solipsism* from philosophical lectures and casual vocabulary study.

My years of adolescence and my twenties were times of enormous confusion for me (quasi-madness, really), with much catching up to do—personal, cultural, emotional, and more. Both Rand and Nabokov seemed like alien entities (which, in fact, they literally were). I could never have imagined that some sort of complex, conflicted yet compelling relationship with these two figures—she the pure didacticist, he the recherché wordsmith—was in my long-term future…

CHAPTER TWO

ON THE BIG BOOKS THEY WROTE

Both Nabokov and Rand left their mark on the larger culture with a couple of thick volumes that sold on a grand scale and grew into publishing phenomena. Those prose artifacts also became representative of certain values, certain unwonted ways of seeing our modern, American world.

Their key works came only after years of early struggles to earn a reputation through their writings.

*

Nabokov arrived in the United States in 1940 with fluent English, the happy result of resident childhood tutors on his Russian estate, and of his B.A. from the mighty University of Cambridge. Under the pseudonym "Sirin" he already had to his credit ten Russian books that had gained him *succès d'estime* among émigré literati in Western Europe. These works would also provide some precarious extra income from foreign translations. Shortly after his American arrival, the sheer luck of an emerging friendship with man of letters Edmund Wilson helped our recent immigrant publish a few stories in *The New Yorker*.

Lolita was Nabokov's third novel in English. Before that, *The Real Life of Sebastian Knight* (1941) and *Bend Sinister* (1947) had been bringing him critical attention but low sales, along with *Conclusive Evidence* (1951), an initial version of his autobiography *Speak, Memory*.

Nabokov reportedly came within a hair of burning the manuscript of *Lolita*, but his wife Véra dissuaded him from so drastic a move. The story of the gestation, publication, and canonization of *Lolita* is a long one, a legend unto itself that need not concern us at this point. Without *Lolita* in print and its strange subsequent fame, however, Nabokov as author would certainly be a more marginal, even an obscure figure today. Yet in *Lolita*'s wake, every novel previously penned by him would become the vivid harbingers of a twice-displaced master artificer's literary razzle-dazzle, the telling forerunners to the twin saga of Humbert Humbert and his less-than-willing paramour. Already in his second novel, *King Queen Knave* (1928), for instance, we are struck by the twenty-something author's uncanny talent for telling about sex purely by hints and quite comically, just as, in *Despair*, we marvel at his ability at capturing the voice of a deluded psychopath. (Not surprisingly, the names of Hermann in *Despair* and Humbert in *Lolita* share in common several letters and phonemes.)

Despite these predecessors, *Lolita* by itself is something of an artistic miracle. In the hands of a Naturalist author—a latter-day Zola or Dreiser, say—so sordid a subject would have generated a correspondingly sordid novel, with an implicit yet foreseeable moral to it. In Nabokov's atélier the tale becomes a wondrous artifact, a thing of self-reflexive, multifaceted beauties. The moralizing role is assigned to John Ray Jr., Ph.D., a psychologist who in his "Foreword" describes protagonist Humbert Humbert as *"horrible..., abject, a shining example of moral leprosy" and worse* (5). All of which, in terms of everyday mores and ethics, is simply true. Yet nothing in *Lolita* is ever "simply". Dr. Ray's piece is of course a spoof on the invented experts' prefaces that, until the 1960s, would "present" pornographic novels to the reader—a formulaic way of imparting "redeeming social value" to such fare in legal prosecutors' eyes. The front matter also serves to inform us about Dolores Schiller/Lolita's death in childbirth, and the divers destinies of the other characters— information usually reserved for a novel's final pages.

The first-person account that follows, the novel itself, is H.H.'s purported defense to be read before the jury, an apologia for his misdeeds sexual and homicidal. The book thus exists as a hall-of-mirrors-type montage of texts-within-texts. This distancing artifice is further compounded by Humbert's narrative voice and its key traits. First, he is very funny. His confession bristles with jokes, puns, conceits, alliterations, self-deprecating jabs, and amazingly succinct summaries. (About his mother's death: "picnic, lightning." About his first marriage bonds: "These burst.") (10, 27)

H.H., besides, is crazy. He himself admits it, and alludes to his previous stays in sanatoriums. He is hence ipso facto "unreliable," and so we're inclined to judge him as less   depraved than demented. The certifiable madness of a wrongdoer, by definition, puts him outside the realm of ordinary humanity and its laws. Furthermore, it must be emphasized, Humbert comes to *love* his Lolita to distraction—a sentiment he declares on numerous occasions, especially towards the end. About the only subject on which Humbert repeatedly waxes lyrical concerns either Lo or his love of Lo. Some of the paeans he pours out to her are truly gorgeous effusions of prose poetry, in the venerable tradition of love verse

addressed to one's beloved. Finally, in his last visit to Lolita, now Mrs.
Schiller, Humbert all but proposes, asking her to join him so that "we shall
live happily ever after" (278). In an odd sort of way, such feelings
potentially redeem H.H. in the reader's eyes, or at least make his motives
more complex, his actions less than merely heinous or evil.

Humbert's transgressiveness, moreover, is somewhat mitigated by the
character (in both senses of the word) of Dolly Haze herself. It is not H.H.
who deflowers her: she has already had sexual relations with camp mate
Charlie Holmes. Those relations, moreover, were hardly the awkward
fumblings of a pair of novices, according to Humbert's report.

> All at once, with a burst of rough glee…, she put her mouth to my
> ear…and she laughed…, and tried again, and gradually the odd sense of
> living in a brand new, mad new dream world, where everything was
> permissible, came over me as I realized what she was suggesting. I
> answered I did not know what game she and Charlie had played. "You
> mean you have never—?"—her features twisted into a stare of disgusted
> incredulity… I took time out by nuzzling her a little. "Lay off, will you,"
> she said, with a twangy whine, hastily removing her brown shoulder from
> my lips. (It was very curious the way she considered…all caresses except
> kisses on the mouth or the stark act of love either "romantic slosh" or
> "abnormal".)
>
> "You mean," she persisted, now kneeling above me, "you never did it
> when you were a kid?"
>
> "Never," I answered quite truthfully.
>
> "Okay," said Lolita, "here is where we start."
>
> However, I shall not bore my learned readers with a detailed account of
> Lolita's presumption. Suffice it to say that not a trace of modesty did I
> perceive in this beautiful hardly formed young girl whom modern co-
> education, juvenile mores, the campfire racket and so forth had utterly and
> hopelessly depraved. She saw the stark act merely as part of a youngster's
> furtive world, unknown to adults. What adults did for purposes of
> recreation was no business of hers (133).

Later, a woman lodger at a hotel asks Humbert, "Whose cat has
scratched poor you?' (164)—an indication, presumably, that Lolita is
rough in bed. Lolita is thus wiser about sex, and has had a far more active
pubescence, than H.H. could even have imagined in his proper European
adolescence or in his truncated idyll with Annabel Leigh. And of course
there's Lolita's concurrent, secret amour with Clare Quilty, the intimate
details of which remain elusive both to Humbert and ourselves.

In this regard, Nabokov's nymphet looks ahead to the promiscuous,
somewhat anomic sexuality that would become commonplace among
certain sectors of American pre-adult life. Today's press has its share of

reports about teens and even pre-teens who look upon sex as "no big deal." Although prophecy was the least of Nabokov's concerns as a novelist, his evolving portrait of Lolita has its uncannily prescient side.

During the few occasions on which Dolly Haze surfaces as a character in her own right, she proves to be a fairly typical suburban brat who's bored with school and prefers comic books to literature. As H.H. pointedly notes:

> Mentally, I found her to be a disgustingly conventional little girl. Sweet hot jazz, square dancing, gooey fudge sundaes, musicals, movie magazines and so forth—these were the obvious items in her list of beloved things...If some café sign proclaimed Ice cold Drinks, she was automatically stirred...She it was to whom ads were dedicated: the ideal consumer... (148)

In addition, the relatively scarce samples of Lo's language that filter through Humbert's prose are the recognizably slangy yet limited patterns of American teen-speak. Hence, save for her magnetic sexual aura ("she radiated...some special languorous glow which threw garage fellows, hotel pages, vacationists [etc.] into fits of concupiscence"—159), Lo comes across as an unremarkable young WASP-American, as relayed via the Old-World refinements of H.H.—himself a parody of the cultured European, for whom Lo's speech may well seem exotic. Lolita, then, while not necessarily a negative figure, is at least an ordinary one—except for the extraordinarily monstrous situation that she has had the misfortune to fall into.

In the way it is assembled, *Lolita* furnishes a prime instance of the dynamic of "the dehumanization of art," as described by philosopher José Ortega y Gasset in his influential volume by that name. For the Spaniard, what characterizes the modern arts is their focusing their sights not on the garden outside the viewer's window, but on the windowpane standing between viewer and viewed. Or to put it in more recent terms: the medium—literally the intermediary, that which is in the middle—becomes the message.

In Nabokov's case, the medium is his prose style; the story told is in the telling; and the "windowpane" is his verbal and architectural wizardry. During his American phase, the author took the Flaubertian search for the *mot juste* to heroic extremes, writing his novels on 3" by 5" cards, never moving on to his next card until the one he was crafting was complete. The elaborate web of words and texts that constitutes *Lolita*—a totally autonomous sphere in which pedophilia, rather than a moral issue, is but one element within a vast pattern—stands far removed from any "human" issues or concerns outside of and beyond it. (Pedophilia is "dehumanized," as it were.) The intricate dynamic between all-American teen Dolores and dandified European H.H. (with the latter's coruscating prose as medium) constitutes the main event. To merely label Humbert a "child molester" and Lolita his "victim" would be inappropriate, a violation of the specially constructed, rarefied world in which Nabokov's novel exists. (In fact I've yet to encounter such loaded terms systematically applied in any mainstream academic commentary on the book.) As Oscar Wilde might have declared in an updated preface to *Dorian Gray*, "There is no such thing as a moral or immoral book *about pedophilia*. Books are well-written or badly written, that is all." Or, "*Child molestation* and virtue are materials for art."

Lolita attained national, then global fame, if often for the wrong reasons. (Many purchased copies probably went unread.) In time it became a prized item in the so-called "post-Modern" canon. Scholars combed its complex texture for hidden meanings and allusions, and Alfred Appel Jr., a Princeton academic, gave its fans the highly useful *Annotated Lolita*. In many ways, it is an indispensable read for anyone claiming to be a well-read person today.

*

Like Nabokov, Ayn Rand was a Russian émigrée who grew into an American—nay, an arch-American, a hyper-American—author. She came to the United States in 1926 at just twenty-one years of age, with scant knowledge of the language or of Anglo-American culture. She stayed at first with an aunt and uncle in Chicago. Once in her new land she started to write almost maniacally, working hard on her new tongue, single-minded in her pursuit of fame and fortune from her obsessively typed plots and prose. From early on, even before her transatlantic crossing, she had decided on the spondaic pen name whose origins remain as yet obscure. For years the idea was floated about that the "Rand" portion came from her Remington Rand typewriter. Subsequent researches show, however, that that brand of machine did not even exist before a business merger in 1927.[1] As regards "Ayn," on occasions she would mention a supposed Finnish author's name as its provenance, but a casual online search reveals no such recognized literary figure. The best conjecture thus far, raised by a biographer, is that the word may be a variant of "Ayin," a childhood nickname utilized by her Russian parents, itself based on "an affectionate

---

[1] Heller, p. 55.

Jewish diminutive meaning 'bright eyes.'"[2] As happens with many an aspiring *littérateur*—Nabokov included—Rand put in some years producing works (the play called *Night of January 16th*; the realist novel *We, the Living*; the dystopian fantasy *Anthem*) that achieved publication but drew only passing attention and went largely nowhere.

Already in the mid-1930s Rand was doing preliminary sketches for *The Fountainhead*.

By 1940 her agent was sending out portions of the work-in-progress for consideration. A dozen major houses turned it down; how it finally saw print is a small publishing legend of its own. Archibald Ogden, a junior editor at Bobbs-Merrill, read the sample chapters. On that basis he envisioned a great book. Mixed reports from in-house readers, though, led to rejection orders from on high. In response, Ogden wired the company head in Indianapolis: either accept this manuscript, or I quit. The boss gave his bold employee the go-ahead for a contract but warned him that "THE BOOK BETTER BE GOOD." Despite poor reviews when it came out in 1943, *Fountainhead* built up a gradual following that grew further in the wake of King Vidor's 1949 movie. Rand herself wrote the final film script on condition that not one word be altered—an audacious demand to which movie mogul Jack Warner surprisingly acceded.

Fountainhead enjoys special renown for two features, even amongst those who haven't so much as leafed through it. For starters, there's Howard Roark (whose very name opens the book), the first of those god-like heroes that would in time people the Objectivist pantheon. A brilliant, thoroughly original genius architect (modeled after Frank Lloyd Wright), Roark spends twenty years facing a constant battle against stodgy traditionalism and villainous mediocrity: at the "Stanton Institute of Technology" in Boston (MIT?), with its classical training; in the staid and stupid professional milieu of New York; with architecture critics or charity dames who preach the social gospel; and against meddling bureaucrats and do-gooders who dare to alter his creations—the latter dunderheads causing him to blow up and reduce to rubble a public-housing project that he had designed on the sly for pathetic loser Peter Keating. (Some today might call it "terrorism.") Roark thenceforth becomes an object of moral opprobrium and vilification throughout New York City. BUT ... at his criminal trial, before a packed courtroom, Roark delivers a grand-scale, world-historical-philosophical oration against "the sacred cow of altruism" and in defense of independent creators such as himself. And, dear reader, the twelve-man jury—seven of whom are regular, working-class guys—

---

[2] Heller, 56.

acquits him! How the courtroom spectators, the city-dwellers, and the press respond to this verdict is something Rand leaves conveniently unstated ...

Then there's the book's soft-porn contents, its male-female liaisons narrated in the prose style of romance novels and that exude what at the time was considered steamy sex. In the "love"-plot's most notorious scene, Roark (he's almost never called "Howard," except in dialogue), temporarily unemployed as architect, is relegated to hard labor at a stone quarry in rural Connecticut, where he's subjected to endless taunts by Dominique Francon, an icy, upper-class brat. One night, though, Roark shows up at Dominique's swanky country house and proceeds scornfully to toss her onto the bed, whereupon—"in the act of a master taking shameful, contemptuous possession of her" (210)—our hero violates her without uttering a word. And, reader, she adores it! Next morning, a blissful Dominique, the dominatrix now tamed, goes around chirping repeatedly to herself, "I've been raped... I've been raped..." (212). In case of any lingering doubts as to the nature of that encounter, toward the end of the book Dominique will confess defiantly to Gail Wynand, her second husband, "He [Roark] didn't ask my consent. He raped me" (665).

On an immediate, initial level, the first half of *Fountainhead* can perhaps be read in the light of a certain twentieth-century Modernist sub-genre that tells of the free inventive spirit in revolt against authority, tradition, censors, faith, and (in H.L. Mencken's word) the booboisie—a pattern famously pioneered in Joyce's *Portrait of the Artist as a Young Man*. (That the theme as filtered through Rand becomes vulgarized and debased, and that she most probably never read Joyce, are not of great importance here.) Had Rand died prematurely in 1950, she might well have subsequently been seen more as an advocate of a pop-individualist ethics and aesthetics than as the militant crusader for unbridled capitalism into which she later evolved. Ironically enough, Rand—much like the Soviet tastemakers and commissars she was fleeing—loathed most Modernist art, music and literature, much preferring 19th-century models like Hugo and Dostoevsky, along with light operettas. Her avant-garde Roark, then, is a grand exception to her preferences.

Among Rand's works, *Fountainhead* is the first to dramatize her visionary doctrine of an endless clash between a high, inspired selfishness and a low, degrading altruism. The strictly economic and political side of Rand thought, however, is not yet explicit and only begins to emerge in the book's final 100 pages, where such New Deal practices as subsidized housing come under attack (and explosion). Research by biographer Jennifer Burns has singled out the extent to which Rand intended her

Fountainhead "to be philosophical and abstract, not rooted in historical circumstance".[3] Hence there are neither Russians nor Communists to be found anywhere in the book. Moreover, on the advice of her friend and fellow conservative novelist Isabel Paterson, Rand purposely excised such names as Lenin, Hitler, and Stalin from the manuscript version of the climactic speech by Roark, thereby dispelling any whiff of topicality from his lengthy courtroom lecture.

The hidden philosophic subtext of *Fountainhead*, on the other hand, is Nietzsche, from whom Rand imbibed intensely during the writing of the novel. Indeed, an earlier version of the manuscript featured quotations from *Beyond Good and Evil* as epigraphs to each of the four parts of the work, and, as Burns points out, the text itself contained "several direct allusions to Nietzsche."[4] The aphorisms and allusions were later dropped, partly in support of Rand's lifelong bid to be perceived as an absolute original, sans precursors or literary debts, in her vision.

Fountainhead's cast of characters all fit within this pop-Nietzschean ideological schema.

First and foremost, we have Roark the conquering hero. His steelworker father having died when he was just a boy (no mention of a mother), Roark has since labored as "electrician, plumber, plasterer" (201) and can stroll, fearlessly and with ease, on high-up planks and naked beams— building trades all of which he, as a teenager, thoroughly mastered! Curiously, though, we never find out how Roark as bambino was supported during early childhood (orphanages? foster homes? an inheritance?)—the reason being, of course, that Rand wishes to portray him as entirely self-made, without outside help or shaping influences of any sort. Presumably, Roark also attended public schools at some point, though Rand would not have wanted to acknowledge his being the beneficiary of government-funded education. Moreover, it is never made clear how Roark, as an orphan, has managed to attend the (presumably private) Stanton Institute; perhaps he was on scholarship, though, alas, we are never thus informed ...

Throughout the novel, Roark is characterized as having "no sense of people" (65); as never noticing other people; as admitting that he can't "handle people;" as lacking such a sense and possessing "no organ to acquire it with" (152). Frankly unconcerned with other people's suffering, he simply states, "I'm not kind" (82) and tells an architectural committee, "I don't cooperate, I don't collaborate" (506). In his courtroom defense

---

[3] Burns, *Goddess of the Market*, p. 43.
[4] Ibid., p. 87.

Roark declares, "I am a man who does not exist for others" (678). Roark's personal equanimity is absolute and unflinching; during his many setbacks he never feels anger or discouragement, never falls prey to resentment or hate. When Roark eventually starts achieving success and runs an office with staff workers, he is a "cold, unapproachable, inhuman boss" who neither takes his employees our for drinks, nor inquires about their families, nor even smiles at them. And yet, somehow, much like Dominique in the wake of her rape, this frigid aloofness of Roark's breeds, in the narrator's own words, "an immense feeling of self-respect at the office" (301). In sum, dear reader, yes, indeed, precisely the sort of head honcho and the kinds of working conditions we all yearn for...

These traits are all set forth as positive, for "Howard Roark, Architect," represents the perfect hero according to La Rand, a free individual needing no one else and capable of doing anything, dependent all along on his own reason and creativity. His being both a rapist and perhaps even, by nature, clinically *autistic*, are, in fact, virtues. He is, in a word, the man without faults.

About the only major, male character approaching Roark in human perfection is Gail Wynand, an early orphan, too, a product of city street gangs and completely self-educated (thanks to his use of the government-supported New York Public Library). As an accomplished adult, he possesses "an air of consummate elegance" and a face that "belongs to ancient Rome; the face of an eternal patrician" (384). Now he owns a vast news empire ("twenty-two newspapers, seven magazines, three news services, and two newsreels"—386), including the *Banner*, a yellow-press tabloid, in the offices of which much of the secondary action in *Fountainhead* unfolds.

Gail Wynand, a world-wide pleasure-boater and compulsive womanizer, later in the book enjoys a close friendship-of-equals with Roark, even as he unknowingly shares with him a love of the same girl, none other than Dominique, the woman he will in time marry. What eventually brings about Gail's tragic downfall is that, through his own staff of salaried writers, he has been giving the unwashed masses the "collectivist" myths they wanted, rather than standing up for his individualist principles. Alas, he loses his great love, the statuesque Dominique, to a superior, puissant Roark.

Although at first browse *Fountainhead* may feel like and look to be a realist novel, much of it, as we are seeing, qualifies as fantasy. (An academic literary theorist who chooses to read Rand's work might class it as "romance," along the lines of medieval chivalric tales or dime-store Westerns.) Diva Dominique, in this regard, embodies, so to speak, the adolescent male fantasy whereby, as the phrase goes, "women just want to be raped!" She is also the classic femme fatale, with "an air of cold serenity and an exquisitely vicious mouth," and whose eyes give off "a sense of cold cruelty" (104). In conversation she often insults people to their faces, and at one point she calmly tells her future first husband, Peter Keating, "This is the first time I've ever been kind to anyone" (243). Like Roark, who's never had a friend, Dominique never had and never will have a girl friend. As the daughter of the rich, famous architect Guy Francon, she is sublimely bored, and in her regular columns for Gail's *Banner* she skewers her targets without much believing anything she writes.

Rand's heroine exemplifies the most implausible sorts of human psychology. Following her ecstatic rape at the hands of Roark, Dominique will begin encountering her pleasure-giving assailant in New York circles, and throughout the book she nurtures a secret love for him. In fact, she eventually carries on a clandestine affair with her ravisher, even as, in her *Banner* reviews, she lambastes Roark's building designs! Then there are her two initial marriages. Spouse no. 1 is Peter Keating, a monumental foil to Roark and fundamentally a nullity, for whom La Dominique—being the daughter of the man who is first his boss and then his business partner—represents a social triumph, a catch. For some strange reason, though, it is *she* who ends up asking for his hand in marriage! During their twenty months of near-silent matrimony, Dominique will never once initiate ordinary conversation with Peter and will keep her body absolutely still during their sex acts together. About Keating she once admits to Wynand, "I despise him … I think he's a third-rate architect," yet she sticks with the nuptial knot because, well, "It amuses me" (429).

Next, Dominique ditches nonentity Peter for wealthy libertine Gail, he now "desperately in love" with her beauty (512). The magnate nevertheless wants her hidden away in a sumptuous "prison" in rural Connecticut: his mansion, specially designed for him by … Roark. And how does Dominique feel? Well, she doesn't love Gail either, yet goes along with it all as she leads the luxurious existence of a pampered trophy wife. Meanwhile, deep in her heart (?) her one true love is Roark, Roark, Roark! And so, with the fall of Gail and the acquittal of Roark at his trial for blowing up the housing project, Dominique dumps Spouse no. 2. And on the book's penultimate page, at a construction site, where a skyscraper commissioned by Gail Wynand is being built by "Howard Roark, Architect," she identifies herself to the superintendent as "Mrs. Roark." Thus begins Dominique's lofty ascent as she is literally hoisted up towards the very top platform of "New York's greatest building" and reaches the pinnacle, where "there was only the ocean and the sky and the figure of Howard Roark." *"The End"* (687)

The title of *Fountainhead* was a last-minute afterthought. The original handle under which Rand's big book had long been abirthing was *Second Hand Lives*. The joltingly judgmental, vaguely Nietszchean phrase reflected the author's abiding scorn for all those who 1) aren't high geniuses, 2) depend on others, and 3) evince the unpardonable sin of altruism. However, her editor at Bobbs-Merrill, Archibald Ogden (who had already rescued the novel from rejection), felt that such a title gave priority to the villains in black hats rather than to the heroes on white horses. Agreeing with him, Rand first thought of *The Mainspring*, but another book already bore that name. The word "fountainhead" was plucked from a thesaurus. Still, in this regard, it bears mention that virtually *every* character in the book who is *not* in the august, embattled company of Roark plus his half-dozen equals is, is, in fact, a contemptible "second-hander." As far as sheer numbers are concerned, in *Fountainhead*, the second-handers have it.

The prime instance of those lowly second-handers is Peter Keating, who starts out as Roark's housemate and slightly older fellow undergraduate at "Stanton." Keating has been student-body president and captain of the track team, and, as the book opens, is set to graduate at the top of his class, whereas Roark on that same day is expelled from Stanton for insubordination. Peter has a warm smile, is polite and eager to please, and likes people—he "needed his fellow men" (31). However, he is excessively attached to his mother, a woman who—sickening thought, is it not?—has scrimped and saved in order to put her son through college, and who in her many letters to him in New York will proffer constant advice about clothes and women. Peter's warmth is superficial, however, and once he joins Guy Francon's firm he becomes a calculating careerist and climber, elbowing out rivals and indirectly causing the death of Francon's senior partner. For deep down, his outstanding academic record notwithstanding, Keating is a most pedestrian and unoriginal architect, and twice he has Roark secretly design major projects in his name. Peter even stoops so low as to pressure his then-wife Dominique to sleep with Gail in order to get from the press baron a building commission. In time Keating's personality deteriorates, his mother comes to live with him, and he abjectly admits to Roark, "I'm a parasite" (568).

If Peter is a second-hander beneath contempt exemplar, Ellsworth Toohey is the second-hander as arch-villain cum professional advocate. Clever, precious, and shrewd, Toohey is first introduced in the most unflattering terms as a slight man with "little feet", a "thin little body," a "narrow chest," "ears that flared up ... like the handles of a bouillon cup" (220), and a "thin neck... like that of a plucked chicken" (248). As a child he showed "all the earmarks of a sissy" (289), and was pushed around and beat up by bully Johnny Stokes, the latter a kid with "able fists," "healthy body," and "startling good looks" who somehow "seldom opened a book" yet could write a masterly essay and knew more than the teachers (288), as opposed to poor Ellsworth, who had to work hard to be the model pupil that he was. Nicknamed "Elsie" for a while, Toohey in his teens flirted briefly with religion, then discovered socialism.

A regular columnist for Gail's *Banner* (and as a character a composite of urban sociologist Lewis Mumford, leftish journalists Heywood Broun and Clifton Fadiman, and in particular British Labourite Harold Laski), salaried scribe Toohey is on contract to write whatever he wants. His articles enjoy a huge mass following, and time and again he expresses his passion for "the common people" and the "little people," airs his concerns about "injustice, unfairness" and "the cruelty of society toward youth" (238), and advocates "selflessness" as a solution. Further involved with assorted philanthropies, charities, and "radical publications," Toohey also holds a post as lecturer on "Art as Social Symptom" (214), and he positively compares the caves and camp fires of primitive man with the skyscrapers and neon lights of our time because, as he explains in a little exchange with Dominique, "I am a humanitarian" (274).

However, Toohey's true, Machiavellian colors come forth toward the end of the novel when, in a long, private peroration delivered to a distraught Keating at the latter's home, the scribbler frankly confesses that what he ultimately seeks to achieve is (in a one-liner) "Power, Petey," and that among his studied techniques for doing so are:

Make man feel small. Make him feel guilty. Kill his aspiration ... Preach selflessness ... Kill man's sense of values ... Enshrine mediocrity ... Altruism is of great help in this ... [Man] must *believe* ... We don't want any thinking men (628-30).

He is frankly aiming for

a world of obedience and of unity ... A world where the thought of each man will not be his own ... A world with its motor cut off and a single heart, pumped by hand. My hand—and the hands of a few, very few other men like me (631).

The aspiring dictator spells it out in "a single word—collectivism" (632). And indeed, in his pursuit of collectivist power, Toohey will soon attempt to stage a coup at the *Banner*, a move that is thwarted when owner Gail Wynand simply shuts down the newspaper. End of Toohey's career.

In addition to Keating and Toohey, for whom the first two of the book's four sections are named, *Fountainhead* is populated by, is indeed crawling with, dozens, nay, legions of minor "second-handers." Among them one may cite the charity ladies with quaint names like "Mrs. Wayne Wilmot;" guilt-ridden rich people with funny names like "Horton Stoddard;" mediocre writers with a social conscience, who bear funny names like "Lancelot Clokey," "Alvah Scarret," and "Trinky Halloway;" traditionalist architects likewise humorously baptized e.g. "Ralston Holcombe;" Lois Cook, an ugly, greasy, sallow, unkempt, best-selling author, committed to ugliness in her tastes and all her activities; ordinary folks on holidays; and many, many more.

The prize for "second-handedness" probably goes to Catherine Halsey, niece of Toohey, who appears initially as Peter Keating's early sweetheart and his first fiancée, pre-Dominique. In her youth Katie is characterized as anemic, "heavy and colorless" (228), and somewhat pitiful. Later in life, after being dumped by Peter, she becomes a social worker. (Rand has a special animus against social workers—see my chapter 12, "On Their Nasty Side.") And—the second of two strikes against her!—she is employed "in Washington," which, for Rand, is always a bad sign. Now, as she bumps into a deteriorated Keating on the street and joins him at a diner, she wears "flat, brown oxfords" and is obsessed with diet foods and "proper nutritional balance" (590). And at her job, we are told by Rand's less-than-neutral narrative voice, Katie can "issue orders, but not big orders or cruel ones; just mean little ones—about plumbing and disinfectant" (589).

Family and family ties get a consistent and relentlessly bad rap throughout *Fountainhead*, are depicted as the hapless, malign breeding grounds for future "second-handers." While Roark and Wynand, being orphans, have had the good fortune to be spared that sorry fate and thus to be self-made, other characters are not so lucky. Peter Keating, we have seen, is weakened by his all-too-loving and too-supportive mother. Catherine at age seventeen wants a job but, alas, lives with her uncle Ellsworth, who won't allow her to work because he is against child labor. Toohey, in turn, having been born "a blue baby," was his mother's "idol;" the good woman was "almost disappointed when he survived without becoming an actual cripple" (287), though she continued to hope that he might become a "saint" (288). After Mrs. Toohey died, Ellsworth's Aunt Adeline, she of the "horse ... face," took his mom's place and raised him, and he of course was sickeningly affectionate to her. Even the fleeting character Jessica Pratt, a member of Ellsworth's charmed circle, has dedicated her life and "sacrificed everything" in order to bring up her baby sister Renée after the two were orphaned at an early age; she is thus portrayed as a scheming little monster, so unselfish that she "would have everybody who refused to be unselfish *shot*" (549, 548; emphasis added).

*

The Fountainhead, with its equal-parts mixture of hero worship and fierce misanthropy, generated a steady flow of gushy fan letters. Rand in time met with some of her youthful correspondents. From among them there took shape a shifting but close-knit circle of ten or so star-struck disciples who adopted the casually ironic group name "the Collective." Meeting at Rand's New York apartment on Saturday evenings, the group provided company and support as a kind of "family," along with a loyal readership and weekly feedback for the work-in-progress *Atlas Shrugged*, on which she was to spend thirteen years. As a best-selling author, she now had her pick of publishers. Responding to a friendly courtship from Bennett Cerf, who found her doctrines abhorrent yet saw in the book a potential money-maker, Rand sold the manuscript to Random House. "I am challenging the cultural tradition of two and a half thousand years," she confidently asserted.[5]

Rand had already characterized herself in a 1944 letter as "the chief living writer of propaganda fiction,"[6] and in a letter to Gerald Loeb, characterized her own novels as anti-Communist propaganda.[7] In this regard, *Atlas* is essentially an anti-Communist tract in the form of a 1080-page novel. But it is propaganda fiction with a difference. Just as *Fountainhead* had eschewed all reference to contemporary names or current events, *Atlas* is set in an indeterminate future and never once alludes to "Russia," "Communism," "Socialism," "Soviets," "Party," "Stalin," or "Marx." Nor is the menace that of a military kind: no Cold-War fantasies here about Red Army troops seizing an idyllic American village or landing on the White House front lawn. Indeed, the Communist threat has largely triumphed. Most of the world now consists of "People's States"—the People's State of England, of Germany, of Norway, even of Europe; and the People's State of Mexico, of Guatemala, of Argentina, and even of South America; the People's State of India; et cetera. (One thinks of those "Red Tide" maps in the more hysterical anti-Communist

[5] Heller, p. 275.
[6] Claudia Roth Pierpont, "Twilight of the Goddess," p. 70.
[7] Cited in Heller, p. 31.

short features.) And all over the planet, the masses are starving under these vaguely sinister entities. Only the USA, as it turns out, is not yet a People's State, though the intent is underway in a hostile Washington D.C.

What has brought about this disaster, however, is not a Communist movement but rather the efforts of humanitarian altruists and other professional do-gooders who invoke concepts such as "the public good," "the underprivileged," "social conscience," "self-sacrifice," "the plight of the working man," and "the meek, the weak, the sick, and the humble." Yet there is hope stirring against this foul, manipulative monster. "Who is John Galt?" Such are the words that open the novel. Accompanied at times by a shrug of the shoulders, the query has become widespread across the USA, a kind of proverb expressing puzzlement or frustration. Two-thirds of the story will be spent in search for an answer to that intriguing riddle...

In the meantime we have Dagny Taggart, heiress to and Vice-President of Operations of Taggart Transcontinental, and the book's heroine, who struggles to keep the railway going in the face of altruistic government meddlers, vicious labor unions, and her bumbling, again altruistic brother James. And we also have Hank Rearden, successful steel magnate and sole inventor of a brand-new alloy called Rearden Metal. A man desirous since childhood only of making a buck, Rearden is set upon implacably by, again, government do-gooders as well as his despicable wife, mother, and brother, all moochers. Well, Dagny and Hank become lovers; and as they drive together across the U.S. they will encounter, in an abandoned Wisconsin factory, a super-motor with a special coil, accompanied by a manuscript. And simply by looking at it they both realize that its creator

> tried to invent a motor that would draw static electricity from the atmosphere, convert and create its own power as it went along.. It's the greatest revolution in power motors since the internal-combustion engine ... Who'll want to look at Diesel? Who'll want to worry about oil, coal or refueling stations? (275)

The engine, we are told, will provide "an unlimited supply of energy." Luckily, Dagny has an engineering degree, for only a trained engineer could have understood the device simply from a casual looksee.

[Here, dear reader, a digression is due. The chief provenance of static electricity, by far, is lightning from storm clouds. Otherwise there are no sparks large enough from ordinary friction on land surfaces (say, from rubbing woolens, or from shuffling rubber-soled shoes on a carpet) to generate massive amounts of energy. One wonders, then, how and where the motor's maker has located a continuous source of lightning discharges. Moreover, the energy contained in a lightning bolt is so huge that the motor would have to sustain inordinately high temperatures—about 54,000 degrees F (or 30,000 degrees C), a full six times hotter than the surface of the sun. The ultimate idea, then, is to control and channel the energy received by a lightning rod, a goal that thus far has remained beyond man's reach.]

So, returning to *Atlas*: Some fifty pages later, Dagny pays a visit to Dr. Robert Stadler, a man who at one time was the nation's greatest scientist but who, alas, has sold his soul to the altruistic government. Dagny shows him the manuscript and photographs of the motor. And Dr. Stadler exclaims,

> "But this is extraordinary!... He arrived at some new concept of energy ... He discarded all our standard assumptions ... He formulated a new premise of his own and he solved the secret of converting static energy into kinetic power." (336)

[One more digression, dear reader. Rand here, it seems, confuses three concepts: "static electricity," "static energy," and "potential energy." The first is, quite simply, the accumulation of an electronic charge that, in search of neutrality, seeks release, a discharge—as obtains, once again, in a storm cloud. "Potential energy," a wholly different kettle of fish, refers to the energy inhering in any given object, due either to the position of the body relative to others, or the arrangement of the particles within the system.][8]

Meanwhile, over the next 300 pages the country steadily deteriorates as altruistic Washington imposes its will with arbitrary directives, and as more and more businessmen simply vanish in response. Dagny eventually takes a series of trains out West to confront some company problems, but the railroad has become dysfunctional, again the result of altruistic governmental initiatives. As a last resort, at a Colorado airfield she rents a monoplane (yes, she is a pilot, too), takes off into the wild blue yonder, and accidentally crash lands in a remote Rocky Mountain valley. There, in a chapter called "Atlantis" (presumably in echo of Sir Francis Bacon's utopian narrative, *The New Atlantis*), she encounters a wondrous refuge where the nation's top geniuses are On Strike! As Dagny receives the guided tour, she will meet, one by one, Atlantis's leading inhabitants: strong, attractive yet regular-guy industrialists and inventors (along with a sculptor, a composer, and a writer) all of whom had found themselves oppressed and looted by those convoluted, subhuman, dictatorial altruists

---

[8] I am grateful to my friend and colleague, Enrique Peacock-López, Professor of Physical Chemistry at Wiliams College, for elucidating this matter to me.

(of course). Hence their Olympian withdrawal to this "Utopia of Greed" (another chapter title) where the verb "to give" is banned, help is not expected, and everything is done for cash payment.

"Galt's Gulch" is how the place is unofficially known to its dwellers, after none other than John Galt, he of "Who is John Galt?" fame, the superhuman hero who, we find out, has inspired and led this venture. It is Galt who first finds Dagny in her plane wreck, and this is how she perceives her savior:

> She was looking at … a face that bore no mark or pain or guilt. The shape of his mouth was pride, and more: it was as if he took pride in being proud. The angular planes of his cheeks made her think of arrogance, of tension, of scorn—yet the face had … a look of serene determination and of certainty, and the look of a ruthless innocence which would not seek forgiveness or grant it. It was a face that had nothing to hide or to escape, a face with no fear of being seen or of seeing... It seemed to her for a moment that she was in the presence of a being who was pure consciousness—yet she had never been so aware of a man's body. The light cloth of his shirt seemed to stress, rather than hide, the structure of his figure, his skin was suntanned, his body had the hardness, the gaunt, tensile strength, the clean precision of foundry casting, he looked as if he were poured out of metal, but some dimmed, soft-lustered metal, like an aluminum-copper alloy, the color of his skin blending with the chestnut-brown of his hair, the loose strands of the hair shading from brown to gold in the sun, and his eyes completing the colors... (652)

In other words, Galt is male perfection incarnate, a figure surpassing heroes from the big screen and epic lore. (Beauty, intelligence, strength, serenity, sheer will…) He's also, just incidentally, the genius who had fashioned the mysterious motor found by Dagny and Hank, and which mighty Galt has chosen not to share with a nation thoroughly sick and infected with you-know-what. The motor instead provides most of the Gulch's energy needs at minimal cost, supplemented by oil extracted from mountain shale, a process that the gathered geniuses have easily, and independently, mastered.

In the course of Dagny's becoming acquainted with the world of Galt's Gulch, she comes across these words, inscribed in granite above the door of the central powerhouse:

I SWEAR BY MY LIFE AND MY LOVE OF IT
THAT I WILL NEVER LIVE FOR THE SAKE OF ANOTHER MAN,
NOR ASK ANOTHER MAN TO LIVE FOR MINE. (680)

The motto is an oath to be taken by all valley residents. Not only that, but the stark declaration possesses magical powers. When John Galt faces the door and pronounces the motto, even as he reaches the concluding word, the portal (Sesame!) opens slowly... The axiomatic pledge will serve, moreover, as the resounding final sentence in the book's climactic chapter (which took Rand over two years to write) entitled "'This Is John Galt Speaking,'" a seventy-page peroration in which Rand's philosophy of history, knowledge, ethics, and life in general is spelled out in stentorian, often scolding tones. Aside from the repeated attacks on "jungle witch-doctors" and assorted "scum," the speech also states to the national audience, "Do you ask what moral obligation I owe to my fellow man? None—except the obligation I owe to myself" (948).

There follow yet a hundred more pages (!) of confrontations, arguments, intrigues, a gunfight, and even a scene in which John Galt is tortured in front of government altruists and Dagny's brother James. Galt steadfastly refuses to speak, and never is he more noble than under torture:

> His naked body looked strangely out of place in this cellar.... The long lines of his body, running from the ankles to...the straight shoulders, looked like a statue of ancient Greece, sharing that statue's meaning, but stylized to a longer, lighter, more active form and gaunter strength, suggesting more restless an energy—the body, not of a chariot driver, but of a builder of airplanes. (1059)

Then, in a scene worthy of a Hollywood action drama, Galt is rescued by Hank Rearden and Dagny, and they all head back to their mountain retreat. Shortly thereafter, on the last page, Rand's giants, like Zarathustra, decide to stride down from their mountain top.

And Galt says, "We are going back to the world."

And Rand says, "He raised his hand and over the desolate space he traced the sign of the dollar."

The sexuality in *Atlas* also merits a brief look. While there is no repeat of the famous rape scene in *Fountainhead*, male-female sexual relations in this vast soap opera are consistently depicted in brutal, abusive terms that come quite close to out-and-out violation. In the first session between Hank and Dagny, he tears her clothes off and addresses her with a tone of "contemptuous triumph" (240). The morning after, he admits to Dagny the contempt he feels for her, telling her that she's "as vile an animal as I am." (242). During a later such encounter Hank will rip off Dagny's clothes "in the manner of an owner undressing a person whose consent is not required" (348). Similar language is employed when it is John Galt's turn to have his way with Dagny hundreds of pages hence.

Early on in the book, Francisco D'Anconia, a rich Argentine playboy and Dagny's former lover, slaps our fair heroine on the face, and she feels "pleasure from the dull, hot pain in her cheek" (100). (The word "pleasure" is thrice invoked in this passage.) Generalizing on the matter, in a long discussion further on between Francisco and Hank, the South American asserts with apodictic certainty, "Sex is the most profoundly selfish of all acts, an act which [a man] cannot perform for any motive but his own enjoyment—just try to think of performing it in a spirit of selfless charity!" (460) And indeed, throughout *Atlas*, sex is never warm and tender, never loving or caring, but is habitually tinged instead with violence and control, with coldness and outright sado-masochism. Neither "eroticism" nor least of all "*love*-making" are terms that one could ever employ to characterize the power-obsessed sex scenes in *Atlas Shrugged*.

*

Lovers of Rand fiction invariably agree with or accept her teachings; they admire the work for its content, not its art. Curiously, those who are put off by Rand's strident   sermons are equally indifferent to her literary side. This is not one of those complex cases in which you reject an artist's repugnant world view yet can admire their artistry—as progressives at times do with, say, T. S. Eliot or Ezra Pound, D. W. Griffiths or Leni Riefenstahl. *Fountainhead* in this regard qualifies as a competent, commercial, middlebrow novel, neither better nor worse than dozens of such titles cranked out by trade houses year after year. A suspenseful page-turner with a serviceable if not stunning prose style, it has able plotting and an impressive command of snappy, wise-guy sorts of American dialogue and street corner speech (skills Rand learned in Hollywood), along with a highly charged eroticism, albeit of a particular type. Story and doctrine, moreover, are ably integrated, though of course what cultists revere is the latter. These modest virtues compensate for the book's principal vice: namely Rand's "allegorical" tendency to make every character into an ideological or moral type, a mouthpiece for this philosophical position or that. Oh, yes, and, as we have been seeing, unlike you and me, dear reader, as people her cast members are, all of them, either heroic or villainous, grand or puny, awesome or just awful.

Sometimes Rand pulls her vices and virtues together to create a readable, if florid, fiction. In *Atlas*, however, her vices win out. This is a narrative inordinately made up of relentless speechifying and counter-sermonizing, the contents of which are thoroughly predictable and lacking in subtlety of any sort. The big brown book of Chairman Rand's thought is, quite simply, a very bad long novel that nonetheless has moved and inspired countless true believers out there, and still does. It became the fantastical, race-neutral *Gone with the Wind* of pitiless adolescents, tin-ear ideologues, and illiterate entrepreneurs, potential or actual, while Galt's oath grew into the proud motto of many a John Galt wannabe around our college and corporate corridors. Rand, incidentally, admired Margaret Mitchell, even mentioning her in the same breath with Victor Hugo.

Sales aside, *Atlas* failed to garner the intellectual prestige and respect Rand so hungered for. She had fondly hoped with her writing to bring about big changes in American life; more, La Rand and her circle of friends actually expected *Atlas* to spark a revolution in the streets. There followed a brutal reality check when the book was widely excoriated in the press, even in William F. Buckley's *National Review*, in a lengthy attack written by none other than senior anti-Communist Whittaker Chambers. And so, while Rand's acolytes eagerly gorged and guzzled, the rest of America shrugged.

Rand now fell into a blue funk. Never completing another novel, she turned instead to writing articles for a series of journals churned out by members of "the Collective," and also had a passing phase as syndicated columnist for the *Los Angeles Times*.

*

In the mid-1960s, when I moved out to Berkeley, California, I was discovering and slowly absorbing the great books: the canon, the old masters, the sacred-secular texts. From the standard, mass-market verse anthologies edited by Oscar Williams or Louis Untermeyer, I'd tear out pages bearing my favorite poems, carry them around with me and, during spare moments, learn the lines by heart. But I also was becoming aware of the then-new stuff by the then-living. Samuel Beckett, for instance... I'd plop his *Waiting for Godot* into my Harvard green book bag whenever heading to the split-level, espresso-serving Caffé Mediterraneum on Telegraph Ave., where I'd commit whole dialogues and speeches to memory. And his novel *Molloy* had me transfixed; I gobbled it up in a couple of sittings at my Dwight Way apartment, chuckling silently at the extensive joke sequences surrounding Molloy's bicycle and his sucking-stones. The day after finishing *Molloy*, I felt like a different person. (To my delight years later, during a casual visit to Berkeley in 2008, I came upon a "Beckett's Pub" on Shattuck Avenue, with a portrait of the Irishman's gaunt, creased visage poised in the foyer, greeting new arrivals.)

And then there were the Latin Americans. For months I steeped myself in Pablo Neruda's hallucinatory surrealist verse, with its Dalí- and Magritte-like images, and imbibed its existential angst and anger; or I savored the spare humor and understated wit of his "Elementary Odes" devoted to such mundane subjects as artichokes and onions, elephants and house cats. I first dipped into Borges's short stories, feeling both baffled and amazed by the metaphysical conundrums of "The Babel Library" and "The Aleph." And I discovered and delved into Cortázar's recent novel *Hopscotch*, with its verbal experiments and its random, aleatory shape, something unprecedented in literature.

Meanwhile there was also Nabokov, whose formal artifice and unique prose style had me, for the time being, hooked, infatuated. I read *Lolita* maybe three times and carried around photocopies of some of its key pages in my shirt pocket for casual sampling while waiting at a bus stop or a cafeteria queue. I don't know how many times I   grinned at the episode of Valeria and her lover the Tsarist taxi driver, who leaves a liquid souvenir of himself in cuckolded Humbert's toilet bowl…

Over the next three decades my readerly relationship with Nabokov would   expand, become more complicated and evolve finally into a deep ambivalence. Of course, *Pale Fire* soon astonished me with its sheer artifice, its spectacle of a verbal juggler throwing about the weightless bricks of an invisible, floating architecture. Ditto for the hard, sharp, gem-like prose of his best short stories. As the years went by, I slowly devoured, in his own Englishings, Nabokov's highly uneven, pre-1940s Russian fiction. I followed up and kept up with his subsequent, highly flawed or severely limited American books, and began taking note of Nabokov the public figure. And I gradually become acutely aware of my divided feelings about the man and his mind and his temper and his work. In these pages I hope to trace and come to terms with a sometime Nabokovophile's profound discomfort and unease.

As for Rand, at the time she existed to me only as something remote and negative. I was vaguely aware that her writings celebrated the businessman both as hero and as victim, and that sufficed to me then to regard her with indifference. Having endured a father who (as we shall be seeing) was an obsessive entrepreneur as well as an unpleasant, destructive, sinister spouse and parent, my motivation to plow through books that extolled his kind was, to put it simply, nil. From time to time rumors reached me of a Rand club around the Berkeley campus whose adepts joyously proclaimed that society should do nothing to aid the less-than-fortunate. Though the Randian youths would never have confessed to it in such brutal terms, they presumably meant that the poor, the orphaned, the unemployed, the maimed, the sick, the racially excluded, and the otherwise deprived should best be let to, well..., die... kick the bucket... rest in peace... no hard feelings, 'bye 'bye...

Lest this inference appear too extreme, I quote herewith a sharply worded letter that, in 1957, a young Alan Greenspan published in the *New York Times Book Review*, in rebuttal to a hostile review of *Atlas Shrugged* by Granville Hicks.

> *Atlas Shrugged* is a celebration of life and happiness. Justice is unrelenting. Creative individuals and underwriting purpose and rationality achieve joy and fulfillment. *Parasites who persistently avoid either purpose or reason perish as they should.*[9]

Thus spake the then-whelp who would later become America's most influential Randian. "Perish" does mean "die."

Now flash-forward to 12 September 2011, at a presidential candidates' debate over the CNN channel. TV host Wolf Blitzer, when questioning libertarian hopeful Ron Paul, brings up the hypothetical case of a healthy 30-year-old who has opted not to have medical insurance, but to whom something terrible happens and then spends six months in intensive care. Blitzer now asks Dr. Paul, "Congressman, are you saying society should let him die?" Scattered voices in the Tea Party-dominated live audience shout "Yeah!" in response. Enthusiastic applause follows.

I am reminded of the official slogan "¡Viva la muerte!" ("Long live death!") that was adopted by the nationalist Spanish Legion around 1900, and that, in 1936, was intoned by Francoist troops in the early stages of Spain's civil war.

Oh, yes, Dr. Paul's reply was to let churches and charities handle the needs of the uninsured (that old libertarian chestnut). Given Rand's and Randians' absolute loathing of religion and charity, in the absence of such entities one gathers that their solution is indeed to let such contemptible beings die...

---

[9] Quoted in Jerome Tuccille, *Alan Shrugged*, p. 71. Emphasis added.

CHAPTER THREE

ON THE ODD PAIR'S GROWTH
AND DEVELOPMENT

Nabokov's youthful years seem in every respect to have been inscribed in some ancient fairy tale. First, there was the palatial vastness and sumptuous beauty of his parents' country estate, Vyra, located south of St. Petersburg, and also their spacious, multistoried town house on 47 Morskaya Street in what was at that time Imperial Russia's embassy row. A permanent staff of fifty servants—including butlers, gardeners, chauffeurs, footmen, doormen, coachmen, a gamekeeper, a night watchman, and a nurse—took care of the family's day-to-day needs. Nabokov's highly cultured father had at his disposal a private librarian, and his dinners he would order via a written menu.

The family's roots could be traced as far back as 1380. Two lions rampant adorned its coat of arms. Through government and military positions its members had long been intimately imbricated within the Imperial system. Vladimir's grandfather Dmitri had served as Minister of Justice, while his uncle Sergey was Master of Hounds to His Majesty the Tsar.

At home, boy Vladimir had a personal valet, and was bathed by attendants. An activity so mundane as his going to bed was a glorious, sumptuous nightly ritual (SM, 86). On turning seventeen, young Vladimir was bequeathed by his maternal uncle Vasily Rukavishnikov an estate valued at several million dollars. Nabokov père was strongly against the inheritance, which in any event was soon lost to the Bolshevik takeover.

The father, V.D. Nabokov, qualifies as a remarkable individual for his time and place. Despite his lofty station he was a committed liberal activist who wished for Russia a British-style constitutional monarchy. He wrote passionately against capital punishment and anti-Semitism, penned an article sharply criticizing the role of the police in the 1903 Kishinev pogrom, and even spent three months in prison for his dissident activities. A man of cosmopolitan culture, he was fluent in English, French, and German; knew hundreds of lines of Russian verse by heart; could boast an extensive collection of French literature; and was a fine tennis player to boot. His record of service to his nation's better side was truly outstanding. In 1906 he served for a year in the Russian Parliament. During the February 1917 revolution he actually helped draft the Romanovs' abdication proclamation, and then was invited by Kerensky's provisional liberal government to be its justice minister. During the family's post - 1917 exile in Berlin, he figured prominently as a leader in expatriate circles and edited the émigré daily *Rul'* ("Rudder").

Even the circumstances surrounding the tragic death of Nabokov *père* have their positive, noble side. On 28 March 1922, in Berlin's Philharmonia Hall, fellow Russian liberal and constitutional democrat Paul Milyukov was delivering a lecture to an audience of 1500 people. Suddenly, a Russian monarchist (and future fascist) sprang up from the public and charged ahead with the intent of assassinating the speaker.

Statesman Nabokov now lunged onstage and wrestled the gunman to the floor. At that point, a second thug moved in on the mélée, shooting V.D. Nabokov fatally in the back.

A hero's death, then, incurred while successfully saving the life of a political and ideological comrade, who himself suffered no wounds.

Having so towering a figure as a parent will inevitably carry great weight in shaping an elder son's developing soul. And, even without some acquaintance of Nabokov the man, it is all too easy for us seasoned adults to speculate on the long-term impact of such a father's horrific yet complex death on a 22-year-old's psyche. That very night, Nabokov penned in his diary an extensive entry reflecting in depth on the incident; thereafter he would seldom allude to it publicly. Indeed, it rates only about a half-dozen scattered lines in his *Speak, Memory.*

Not only that, however. Unlike what often happens with the children of powerful progenitors, boy Vladimir was blessed with model parents who gave him a personal life and a home existence that were all but utopian. Rather than attend primary school, boy Vladimir was educated on the family estates by a series of private tutors, foreign and domestic, who imparted, to him and his four siblings, fluency in French and English (among other things). The developing youngster was also given instruction in boxing and fencing, and became proficient in both. Later in life, his pugilist skills would prove quite useful to him in a couple of public altercations.

In addition, a growing Vladimir was fully encouraged in his earliest passions: literature and lepidoptera. The Nabokovs allowed their son free rein in his love of butterflies, and saw nothing wrong, unmanly, or less-than-healthy in his lonely pursuit of, and constant trilingual readings in so arcane a subject matter. Nabokov's mother, Elena, would leave books lying around in his bedroom, and she praised and copied out his youthful verse efforts. She was also personally sympathetic to his visual gifts and his strong inclination toward synesthesia, his "visual hearing." As French scholar Georges Nivat observes, Nabokov's parents gave him an "excellent, diversified, luxurious, and well-thought-out education."[1]

Above all, the boy received from Vladimir Dmitrievich and Elena Ivanovna a profound sense of self-confidence, self-esteem, and self-worth. From the start he was raised with the notion that his existence on earth, and his development as a human being, truly *mattered*.

Oh, yes, one more fact: in his memoirs, Nabokov notes in passing that as a child he was never once spanked…

*

Whenever I read of Nabokov's upbringing, I feel a deep, sad envy. Envy not at all those riches—wealth and high luxury have but the slightest interest for me. What sparks my jealousy is his boyhood idyll and its contrast to my own less-than-paradisial home circumstances, lived first in Haiti (my birthplace), and then successively in Puerto Rico, Cuba, and Venezuela. I also envy Nabokov for having had a father who was a positive, admirable figure.

My mother, Carmen Villada, a Filipina-Chinese woman from Hawaii, had gotten pregnant with me in 1941. Meanwhile my dad Gene, a roving businessman from Kansas, had spirited her away from her native Honolulu with much sweet talk about their both striking it rich in the Caribbean.

And he did not want her to give birth to me.

How do I know this? Following Carmen's death from lung cancer in 1984, I came across her private papers; among these was a diary that she'd kept in 1953, when her wayward husband, my dad, had secretly put her away in a mental asylum (he Rochester, she Bertha Mason), a forced reclusion that was cut short after a week or so thanks only to the intervention of a family friend who happened to be a brain surgeon.

In her diary pages Carmen reminisces and reflects on her early years as my father's wife, and then writes simply, "I couldn't go through with the abortion." She further notes that on the day of my not-so-welcome birth, dad spent his time lifting weights and drinking with his buddies on the

---

[1] Georges Nivat, *"Speak, Memory,"* in Vladimir Alexandrov, *The Garland Companion to Vladimir Nabokov*, p. 674.

beach. He thus seems to have had no involvement with my first entering the world.

Over the next twelve or thirteen years, in Puerto Rico, dad was supremely indifferent to my brother Kanani (born there three years later) and to me. More often than not Gene Sr. was away on business, to the point where a pained Carmen complained to him just once in a letter, "You treat your family like a hotel." And in the literally hundreds of letters he did write to her from all over the Caribbean and El Norte, he never once makes reference to his two sons. I mean not once. Zero.

At our Catholic school near San Juan, the Colegio Espíritu Santo, Kanani and I regularly earned top grades. I can recall no words of praise from my father, no attempts on his part at encouraging our academic bent, no sense of pride or joy in having two gifted children. Moreover, as a result of my intently listening to classical music over the local public radio station, I was showing a marked interest in and love of the art, and by my tenth year I could sing whole portions of the Haydn, Mozart, Beethoven, and Brahms symphonies from memory. I yearned for music lessons, desperately wanted to learn to play musical instruments. Yet unlike Nabokov's father, my dad showed no interest in fostering my talent, citing cost as an obstacle. He did drag Kanani and me to his factory one summer, though, for the purpose of teaching us mechanics—an activity for which my talents were most meager. On another occasion he handed us a box of transparent plastic rain hats from his import-export business for us to sell door-to-door. Much like my mechanical training, our efforts at salesmanship did not go far...

Among my few personal outlets for music was to set aside my weekly allowance for the purchase of classical recordings. At some point, however, dad disallowed even those modest acquisitions as "too specialized." In mid-1955, a couple of years after he had deserted my mom, his two sons, and his infant daughter Valerie for a sexy blonde Cuban, my brother and I were spending the summer in Caracas with the newlyweds. In the furnished apartment that they had rented in the middle-class El Bosque neighborhood was a spinet piano. Though my stepmother Mary loathed and reviled what she dubbed that "música de muertos" ("dead people's music") of my LPs, she nonetheless marveled at my uncanny ability to pick out on the piano keys the melodies that streamed out from the small table-top record player. "This boy needs music lessons!" she once remarked, in amazement to my entrepreneurial pa.

Although dad mumbled some vague assent, no music lessons materialized. Instead, he backed out on his previous parental agreement to return us to our mom in Puerto Rico and flew Kanani and me to distant

Cuba, dropping us off at a military school, where we were to spend two
years of our ever-more-confused lives as boarders, off and on.

Following that martial adventure, from 1957 to 1959 my brother and I
cohabited with dad and Mary in Caracas, where the man managed to add
passing insult to ongoing injuries. As was my wont, every day I'd study
diligently in my bedroom. One evening he stood firmly at the doorway,
glaring, and with righteous indignation, he barked, "Why d'you spend so
much time studying? *Why don't you play a musical instrument or
something?"* (Emphasis added.)

Kafka, as someone once remarked, was a realist author.

Later, in my twenties, when my father and I were starting to air our
many differences and   experience some bitter adult clashes, I finally asked
him outright why he had never gotten me music lessons in childhood. To
which he replied, "Well, why didn't *you* show some *initiative* and get
lessons on your *own*?" (Emphasis added.)

The model he upheld for me was Mike Todd, the flamboyant movie
impresario and the latest of the multiple husbands of actress Liz Taylor,
who had recently died in a plane crash. And dad said unto me, "By his late
teens, Mike Todd had made a fortune. And what have *you* done?"
(Emphasis his.)

So I envied Nabokov. Or at least I would do so when I got to know
more about him.

*

The young Rand—born Alyssa Rosenbaum—grew up not in aristocratic
pomp and splendor, but at least in fortunate, bourgeois comfort. Like
Nabokov she first saw light and was raised in St. Petersburg, where her
father Zinovy, who held a pharmacy degree from Warsaw, had a thriving
practice in his own drugstore. The family of five were Jewish yet
cosmopolitan and secular. They occupied a spacious apartment on a main
thoroughfare downtown, the Nevsky Prospekt, where Alyssa and her two
sisters benefited from language tutors, a cook, a nurse, and a Belgian
governess to assist them in their physical and educational needs. As was
the custom among the Russian elite, the Rosenbaums took their vacations
at summer resorts on the Crimean peninsula. And at age nine, Alyssa and
her kin traveled in Austria and Switzerland. In a small-world coincidence,
little Alyssa was a schoolmate and a close childhood friend of Nabokov's
younger sister Olga, and a not infrequent visitor at the Nabokov clan's vast
town house.

Alyssa's intimate home life, though, was not the family idyll we've seen in Nabokov's case. Recent biographical researches portray Rand's mother Anna as "a tyrant"[2] who openly admitted to never wanting children and who "hated caring for them and did so only because it was her duty."[3] One sees here a direct line from flesh-and-blood Anna Rosenbaum to fictive Lillian Rearden, the nasty, tyrannical wife of brilliant industrialist Hank Rearden in *Atlas*. Indeed, the few times family existence crops up in Rand's work, it is a place not for warmth, affection, and support, but a horror show where pettiness and manipulation thrive. "I did not like being attached to a family," Rand's admiring disciple Barbara Branden quotes her mentor as saying.[4] In this regard Rand differs from those traditional conservatives for whom Family is the prime social unit. (For example, the motto of pro-fascist Vichy France was *Travail, Famille, Patrie*—"Work, Family, Fatherland.") Instead of participating in "family-values" conservatism, Rand belongs rather to that American individualist ideal of starting life from scratch, sans ties, sans roots of any kind.

Rand's experience of her mother presumably motivated a little anecdote that is a favorite of the biographical literature. While in middle school, Alyssa at some point found herself captivated by a classmate, a smart, popular, attractive, and self-assured girl. One day Alyssa walked up to this source of fascination and inquired what mattered most to her. "My mother," the girl replied—whereupon Alyssa walked off in scorn. In Rand's own words decades later, "I had thought she was a serious girl…but she was just conventional and ordinary, and she didn't mean anything as a person. It was really like a fallen idol."[5]

Rand's response is exclusively hers; she seems incapable of broadly interpreting the nameless classmate's answer. Let us speculate: Perhaps the mother was the young classmate's only truly loving relative. Or perhaps a widow. Perhaps the father, if not deceased, was cruel, or abusive, or indifferent, or irresponsible. Perhaps the mother strongly encouraged and supported the youngster's academic bent. Of course we'll never know. But in the adult Rand's absolute view, anyone who cared about filial and family ties was contemptible. Indeed, an acquaintance once heard Rand say that she was "absolutely, *violently* against" birth families.[6]

---

[2] Heller, *Ayn Rand and the World She Made*, p. 4.
[3] Burns, *Goddess of the Market*, p. 10.
[4] Barbara Branden, *The Passion of Ayn Rand*, p. 34.
[5] Ibid, p. 26. Heller, pp. 19-20. Neither of these biographers chooses to comment on this story.
[6] Heller, p. 225

Alyssa grew up alienated and lonely. At school she was intensely shy. In her teens she would actually write in a composition, "childhood is the worst period of one's life."[7] The girl hid in her books, notably *The Mysterious Valley* by one Maurice Champagne, a colonial romance that depicts a dashing imperial hero named Cyrus. Nine-year-old Alyssa developed a lifelong crush on this tall, long-legged adventurer, a British proto-Rambo who overcomes every Asian ordeal and merely laughs at the evil Rajah's would-be torturers. Alyssa also cultivated a predilection for operettas, perhaps because of their happy obliviousness to human suffering.

These tastes would remain with her as an adult, influencing her thought and fiction. The haughty heroine of her first novel, *We the Living*, bears the name "Kira," the Russian feminine form of "Cyrus." Noble, mighty Cyrus also served as inspiration for Rand's triumphant male heroes. John Galt, who gallantly resists torture in *Atlas Shrugged*, is old Cyrus writ large to world-historical stature. Moreover, the future thinker Rand would systematically dismiss all ordinary suffering—whether physical or spiritual—as a topic of scant interest. She did outgrow her love of operettas and come to prefer military marches and romantic Rachmaninoff over other kinds of music.

The youthful Alyssa already showed a tendency to worship conventional good looks and vested power. On a trip to London she was quite taken with its parade of tall, slender, English blondes. (One thinks of the legendary infatuation, depicted in Philip Roth's earlier fiction, of male, Jewish young bloods with willowy, flaxen-haired *shiksas*.) Rand's heroes are all handsome, reflecting her professed aesthetic philosophy: "I fully believed that appearance showed character, that my type of face necessarily showed a good character, my type of man."[8] Hence, in the world of Rand, beauty equals virtue, much as is the case in romance novels.

Similarly, a teenaged Alyssa admired feudalism "because it represented a 'pyramid of ability,' with noble, if not necessarily gifted, men and women at the top."[9] Already at that age Alyssa saw Robin Hood as a villain. Years later, in *Atlas*, she would place a minor character who is a reverse Robin Hood, stealing from the poor to give to the rich.

Alyssa went on to attend the tuition-free Petrograd State University. Later Rand would claim to Barbara Branden that she had graduated "with highest honors"—a retrospective invention, apparently, inasmuch as the

---

[7] Burns, p. 11.
[8] Barbara Branden, p. 81.
[9] Heller, p. 36.

only grades given there at the time were "pass, fail, and retake."[10] She then matriculated at the newly founded—and also free—State Institute for Cinematography, where she published pamphlets on an Italian actress and on the Hollywood system. By age twenty-two she had idealized California's distant movieland and nourished dreams of becoming a screen-writer, seeing forty-seven films in 1924 and 114 of them in 1925.

*

Other than from my mom, there was little general warmth or caring in our "family" fold. Many grown adults, I've since learned, are given to fondly looking back, in private or in company, at the blissfully happy times they'd once lived, as youths, with close kith and kin. Of such moments I knew previous few. From my childhood in Puerto Rico, ages 2 to 13, I cannot recall with nostalgia any instances of us being gathered at the dinner table, enjoying and savoring a home-cooked meal together. "We are family:" those are not words I recall hearing from my father. When we all would sit around for a game of Monopoly or Scrabble, dad played to win and then made fun of mom if she lost. (As a result I cannot play board games today.) Nor had I any sense of being a protective older brother to my kid sibling Kanani. If anything, I'd mock him, oftentimes in public. In this regard I was simply falling in line with our own larger "family" pattern. Likewise, whenever I chanced to come home crying after having been taunted, abused, or roughed up out in the street, my dad would do nothing—neither confront the culprit kid, nor urge me to fight back, nor teach me cagey tactics or coping mechanisms. (Nabokov may not have been fully conscious of his sheer luck in being provided boxing lessons by his father.)

Our mother loved us, Kanani and me, quite deeply, as she later did our baby sister Valerie, born in 1953. Her hundreds of letters to my father from the 1940s and early 1950s are chock-full of affectionate references to us, tender anecdotes about her two sons' growth and progress. Yet she found herself lacking in broader supports, what with her own parents and blood-kin on the farthest side of the planet; she herself on an alien island; and, as an Asian, looking "different" and thus being twice-foreign among Americans and Puerto Ricans both. Meanwhile, my father had her tending to his business on a daily basis, doing all of the clerical work and essentially serving as the sole, unpaid secretary for his import-export ventures in every manner of products—cattle, liquor, military wear,

---

[10] Ibid, p. 47.

fountain pens, what have you—as he hopped all over the Caribbean. It's worth passing mention that, for his start-up investments, he had depended in part on her personal savings. For some reason he wouldn't let her learn to drive, a fact that kept her even more isolated from the world outside the home...

This state of affairs and its tenuous family ties lasted until circa 1954, when dad deserted my mother in San Juan, had her temporarily locked up in a mental hospital, got a divorce in a Cuban court (putting him out of the reach of U.S. law), promptly remarried his mistress *la Cubana*, plopped Kanani and me into a military school in Havana, and set up a new household with his bride in distant Venezuela. His daughter Valerie he had scarcely set eyes on; and he would send mother just the barest in child-support payments. Later, in 1957, when the political situation in Cuba started to take on an alarming cast, dad flew us on to Caracas, where my brother and I moved into the apartment that he, his wife Mary, and their infant son Hal occupied. There, Kanani and I were more or less under orders to stick to our own back bedroom and not entertain friends anywhere else in the house. Over the next two years our grades at the local American schools were at best erratic at best and on occasion catastrophic. Much of our free time we spent out on the city streets. Through an odd series of circumstances I even spent three nights in jail.

Our teachers, sensing that something was wrong, offered what help they could. One of them, Mrs. Thelma Buckley, who had Kanani as a ninth-grade pupil, even made tentative offers to our mother to adopt him (which mom politely but graciously declined). My English teacher, Katherine Williams, happened to be my next-door neighbor and often heard me singing along with the classical radio broadcasts. When she found out about my musical interests, she got me piano lessons, free of charge, and allowed me to use her grand piano for practice. Were it not for her, I might never have learned to play piano or been able to become a music major in college.

My father I never had much liked. Perhaps from early on in my life I'd already intuited in him some lack of desire to have me or raise me. Our rocky relationship was further complicated during my university days when he "got religion" and took to regaling me with Bibles, writing letters with a view to converting me to his new-found evangelical creed, and trying to persuade me to enlist in the expanding U.S. crusade in Indochina. Tensions mounted; we argued, quarreled. At long last I broke with the man when, in January 1968, he added slander and insult to past injury. To wit: on the final, chilly night of a visit to me at Harvard, as we sat in his rented car, dad softly, soothingly claimed that my mom had had an affair with the family doctor, and further suggested that my sister Valerie was actually not his daughter.

Next day I sent him a curt note, and months later a longer one, in which I terminated our few ties. I told him that I would return his communications unopened and that I hoped, someday, to put him in a book. (He eventually replied with a telegram, saying, "HAVE NOT WRITTEN NOR WILL I EVER AS PER INSTRUCTIONS HATE FILLED LETTERS STOP GOOD LUCK WITH YOUR HATE FILLED BOOK.") I never saw him again. We did, however, have a few less-than-pleasant letter exchanges in the 1990s, when he raised the stakes and confidently asserted that my brother Kanani was not his biological child, either.[11]

Following his first slander, I spent many years fleeing, disregarding, or otherwise scanting family ties as well as any other deep emotional commitments or responsibilities. Inasmuch as, to me, the family life had signified mostly pain, I could not conceive of it as a locus of affection, bonding, fulfillment, support, security, harmony, peace or what have you. In a strange way, I was replicating a certain "Randian" pattern, if more out of self-protection than ideological conviction.

Occasionally I'd catch a glimpse of another reality. When living for a while in Binghamton, New York, for instance, I had a young neighbor who worked as an engineer at the local branch of IBM. John once casually mentioned certain colleagues of his who refused to show up at the office on weekends, seeing those two free days as time to be spent with their families. At the time I was puzzled and surprised to hear about fathers who actually *wanted* to be with their kids!

Luckily my marriage to Audrey in 1975 helped me to slowly put my phobias behind me. Some years into our life together she would remark, "Gene, you don't seem to have any family stories!" She, by contrast, having been raised amid dozens of relatives, is a living repository of such tales, which she shares freely. I, on the other hand, seldom talked family. A couple of decades later, though, I realized I actually did have family stories, only they happened to have been, for the most part, bad stories. Painful, hurtful stories.

In *The Ayn Rand Cult*, Jeff Walker's important book that deftly anatomizes the Randian movement, there is an entire subsection called "Do Children Exist?" Walker's answer to the startling question, on the consensus of several other commentators, whether partisan or non-, comes

---

[11] I deal with the larger context of this incident, and its aftermath, in my memoir, *Overseas American*, p. 208-212.

quite close to a "NOOOO." In those pages, Walker takes a look at several Randian scribblers, Rand herself included, all of whom, via some contorted intellectual acrobatics, set forth their reservations about, or even opposition to, having and raising kids. Final word in that section is granted to Henry Scuoteguazza, an account engineer and professed Objectivist, who admits, frankly and somberly, "Loneliness is all too often the Objectivist trademark... [T]he typical Objectivist is single, or if married, has no children. Too many Objectivists are lonely. They have a difficult time getting married, staying married or having children... For a philosophy that champions the bold fearless hero and heroine, there is an astonishing number of timid young bachelors and desperate aging spinsters. Of all the phenomena I have witnessed, this has to be the saddest."[12]

Whenever I encounter, over the Internet, some angry, smug, and lengthy posting by a self-professed Objectivist somewhere, I imagine precisely that sort of reclusive Randian, cocooned in their righteous rage and absolutely certain in his/her right-minded rancor. In their imaginations they might identify with "bold, fearless" Randian heroes Howard Roark or John Galt. Yet they seem much more akin to Dickens's Miss Havisham, or to Travis Bickle, the cooped-up, companionless, hermit-like taxi driver played by Robert de Niro in the film by that name.

Hiding and existing in, and solely for, one's Olympian hatreds, is no way to live. I see it in the ravings of lonesome Randians. I know because I've been there, from other motives both personal and political. And I feel ever relieved at having found my way out of such a mental morass.

---

[12] Cited in Walker, *The Ayn Rand Cult*, pp. 114-115.

CHAPTER FOUR

ON THEIR IMMIGRATION STORIES

Emigrants from the USSR. Immigrants to the USA (with Nabokov spending time in U.K., Germany, and France along the way).

The respective life-trajectories of Rand and Nabokov were crucially shaped by this geopolitical, twin fact and its long-term effects, its myriad implications.

Already in 1924, as a nineteen-year-old student at the just-founded state film school in St. Petersburg, Alyssa Rosenbaum was entertaining plans to find her way to Hollywood. She was working at her script-writing, a skill she wished to eventually apply within a new and remote California film industry, notwithstanding her as-yet zero knowledge of American English. Providentially, an aunt and uncle in Chicago offered to sponsor Alyssa for a six-month stay in the United States. Alyssa's mother, seeing an opportunity for the ambitious young woman, sold off the family jewels in order to pay for her eldest child's transatlantic fare. And so, in January 1926, Alyssa boarded a series of trains to Riga, to Berlin and Le Havre. In February, a French ocean liner took her to New York City; from which she proceeded by train to Chicago.

Rand's new-found relatives in the lakeside city found her self-absorbed and difficult, to say the least. She took no interest in family meals, seldom referred to mutual relatives back in Russia, and in fact hardly spoke, responding in monosyllables to their friendly queries. A freshly arrived Alyssa talked exclusively about what she herself was going to achieve in life. Already doing practice writing, she'd regularly begin her creative typing around midnight, unconcerned about the clickety-clack that kept everyone else awake. As a result of Alyssa's non-stop nocturnal noise and (so to speak) "eccentricities," she was moved about from one blood-kin's household to another. Meanwhile she had already settled on her double-barreled pen name.

By pure chance, Alyssa's cousin Sarah Lipton owned a movie theater. During her six months in Chicago, Alyssa saw 138 films there, free of charge on a family pass, and became especially taken with Cecil B. DeMille's epic blockbusters. In time she was ready to follow her bliss and go seek fame and fortune in Hollywood. Not saddened at her departure, her relatives raised money for her train fare to Los Angeles and provided $100 in pocket money—a sum today worth thousands. Her Chicago movie-theater cousin had enough authority to arm her with a letter of introduction to the DeMille Studio.

In L.A. Rand headed straight to that studio, where there occurred an encounter that has become legend. The details vary according to version, but roughly: At the front gate she saw Cecil B. himself, sitting in his roadster. She approached the man and introduced herself as an admirer from Russia. On a whim, the magnate waved her into the car and drove her to the shooting site of *King of Kings*, a Biblical extravaganza about the life of Christ. On different occasions he would also give the young novice advice about film-making—camera angles, setting up a scene—as well as four days' worth of entry passes. He eventually employed her for a stint as an extra.

For housing, Rand settled into the Studio Club, a privately subsidized dormitory with YWCA backing, reserved for female aspirants to the movie life. Biographer Heller raises the possibility that DeMille's wife, who was a member of the Club's board of directors, might well have had a hand in moving Ayn up on the waiting list and helping her to secure one of its rooms early on.[1] As often happens with struggling immigrants, at times Rand could not keep up with her $10-a-week rent payments. Hence, at one point she received a $50 donation from a Miss Williams, who wished to provide aid for "the neediest girl in the club."[2] Moreover, during her leaner years out West, her Chicago relatives would often loan her emergency money. One cousin, Minna Goldberg, would later remember Rand gratefully saying, "I'll never forget you. I'll get you a Rolls-Royce and a mink coat."[3] Even at the height of her glory, however, Alyssa-turned-Rand never repaid her uncles, aunts, and cousins for the essential if modest survival money they'd once dispensed to her—let alone giving them gifts of luxury cars or animal furs.

After *King of Kings* finished shooting in January 1927, Rand's connection with DeMille got her a job in the mogul's screen writing department. Over the next year she summarized novels and plays and assessed their possibilities for the screen. She also wrote tentative scripts and scenarios of her own, absorbing the Hollywood technique of building up suspense toward a narrative climax. Then, after a series of shake-ups in

[1] Heller, p. 62.
[2] Burns, p. 24.
[3] Heller, pp. 60-61.

the industry—the sale of DeMille Studios to MGM, the shift to talkies, the Depression—Rand was laid off. She went on to work in movie-related white-collar positions such as file clerk and wardrobe supervisor. During the next two decades she would labor, off and on, as a free-lance script-writer, sometimes evaluating screenplays on a per-hour basis and meanwhile crafting about a dozen of her own, though only three of them (one of which was her script for *Fountainhead*) made it to the screen. At the same time she was writing many apprentice short fictions, picking up the skills of the genre from then-popular writers such as Sinclair Lewis and O. Henry.

What we may call the literary education of Ayn Rand is, in many respects, an unusual journey. Most authors now considered canonical have served their apprenticeship first as writers for student rags, then surviving through work-for-hire in journalism or editing, or in the hand-to-mouth world of bohemia, getting on via the occasional publisher's advance or magazine fees (a book review, a story), or in teaching, or at a variety of odd jobs—or from some mix of all of these. And of course there was once the vibrant if precarious culture of "little" magazines, where many writerly aspirants found a kind of spiritual home, an artistic incubator in which to grow, a small stage on which to gain visibility. Hollywood, by contrast, figured in the lives of seasoned literary professionals—Fitzgerald, Faulkner, etc.—largely as a way of making some ready cash, not as training for the production of novels.

Rand's trajectory is markedly different. Her university studies in Soviet Russia were largely behind her. As an adult immigrant the only known, paid employment she would ever know was within the Hollywood film world, a special domain in which the order of business consists primarily of suspenseful plots populated with quickly sketched, fairly simple characters (these played mostly by gorgeous thespians), and conceived for popular appeal and mass sales. It is a milieu, moreover, where dreams are sold, where good is always portrayed as triumphing over evil, and where a positive hero always prevails (much as in the more primitive, heavier-handed narratives of top-down Soviet mass culture). Thanks to her day-to-day professional experience with Hollywood and its overall concerns, the newly arrived Rand acquired a much-prized, first-hand acquaintance with a major, new segment of U.S. popular culture, language, and mythmaking, itself launched by immigrants. These aesthetic elements she would eventually fuse with her secret Nietzscheanism and with a defense of unbridled capitalism, thereby creating a uniquely American form of Hollywood-inflected novelistic propaganda.

Weeks into her L.A. phase, on the shooting set of *King of Kings*, Rand took note of a handsome young movie extra of Ohio working-class origins named Frank O'Connor. She pursued him, indeed stalked him (some sources claim she had already stalked DeMille, too). With occasional interruptions, a romance between them burgeoned. Meanwhile, Ayn continued to renew her visa. In April 1929, just as the extensions were about to run out, she married Frank. As her wedding was held in the same month in which she was due to depart from the U.S. and return to Russia, friends of the groom believed without exception that Frank was doing his sweetheart the favor of resolving her immigrant status.

By all accounts Frank was a passive, easy-going, nice-guy type. For the next fifty years he would put up with Rand's many manias and caprices—with disquieting results. Although in the 1940s he built up a thriving practice and local reputation as a florist in the Los Angeles area, Rand convinced him to abandon his business so that they could move to New York (and, secretly, so that she could be near her admirer Nathaniel Branden). The culmination to their strange marriage came in the 1950s and '60s in Manhattan, where Rand—now a famous author and cult figure—conducted a lengthy amour with Branden, by then her right-hand man in the Objectivist movement. Their spouses grimly accepted the twice-weekly trysts at Ayn and Frank's apartment as a rational choice between two superior beings. Nathaniel's wife Barbara did live to include this bizarre tale in her authoritative biography of the priestess, but the affair contributed to Frank's slow destruction, driving him to drink. He died a broken man in 1979, still married to a Rand whom he reportedly no longer much liked.

Yet another major cultural force that furthered Rand's development as a writer was the various friendships and alliances she sought out and cultivated with a wide range of pro-business writers of her time, among them Channing Pollock, Isabel Paterson, Albert Jay Nock (author of a 1935 polemic tellingly entitled *Our Enemy, the State*), and Rose Wilder Lane (who collaborated with her mother Laura Ingalls Wilder on the *Little House on the Prairie* series), to cite only a few. As thinkers these fiercely anti-New Deal scriveners are largely forgotten today. Their chief legacy is, arguably, their having served as "angels" to Rand, who in turn would never acknowledge their vital role in fostering her career.

A number of business leaders also took the budding Rand under their wing. In the 1940s, for instance, DeWitt Emery, the owner of a small stationery factory in Ohio and head of the National Small Business Men's Association, was an enthusiastic supporter and publicist for Rand's efforts. Anti-New Deal outfits with neutral-sounding names like the Committee for Constitutional Government and the American Economic Foundation recruited her for debates and forums and helped place one of her manifestoes in *Reader's Digest.* In a kind of mutual courtship, she even met with high-ranking individuals from DuPont, Con Edison, the Los Angeles Chamber of Commerce, and the National Association of Manufacturers. Though *Anthem* had already appeared in England, it had yet to find a U.S. publisher, and in 1946 the short book was first issued by a small, pro-business press called Pamphleteers, Inc.

Pro-business writing, needless to say, did not originate with Rand or with her immediate cohorts. Indeed, when she arrived in the U.S. in the mid-1920s, there already existed a substantial body of pro-business literature that reflected the dizzying—and illusory—prosperity of the times. Jeff Walker ably traces this trend in his seminal book, *The Ayn Rand Cult*, pointing out that authors such as Charles Fay and Ben Hooper openly praised selfishness as a positive force and frankly advocated the writing of novels that would celebrate capitalism. Walker also suggests that a spokesman for the National Association of Manufacturers with the telling name of John Gall (!), and moreover a lawyer for Rand, might well have directed Rand to that mother lode of pro-business thought.

While the film industry shaped Rand's sense of narrative, served as her writing school and as her initiation into American life, the more ideological culture of popular, pro-business writers, along with certain anti-New Deal businessmen and their powerful organizations, offered Rand role models as well as providing literary patronage and an intellectual home for her thinking side. They helped an ambitious Soviet émigrée grow into the most renowned American pro-business novelist, mythographer, and propagandist of the latter half of the twentieth century—and beyond.

*

Nabokov's emigration/immigration story is far more varied and complex, is uneven, disjointed, and multiple. In the end he too ended up an American literary icon, but of a completely different sort.

As they fled the Red Army's presence in Petrograd, young Vladimir and members of his family boarded trains south to the Crimean peninsula, where they remained until 1918. Then they all set sail for a three-week port of call in Greece, went on again by sea to Marseilles and proceeded by land to Le Havre, traveled by steamer to Southampton, and finally if temporarily settled in London. As would happen with Rand's mother Anna Rosenbaum, Madame Nabokov also sold off some family jewels, in this case to help defray the costs of Vladimir's British education. By October 1919, the twenty-year-old exile was enrolled at Trinity College, Cambridge. In that luscious and idyllic setting he read French and Russian literature, played soccer and tennis, and spent time with fellow Russian expatriate students. Already a compulsive scribbler since his early teens, by 1921 he had settled on the pseudonym "Sirin" (the name of a bird from Russian folklore), in order to differentiate himself from his father. Vladimir Sirin was how Nabokov was to be known throughout his years of European exile.

Following graduation from Cambridge in 1922, Nabokov left for Berlin, where his father and family had already resettled early on. At its height the Russian émigré colony there would number in the low six figures. Economics and geography both dictated this demographic. Life in Germany was cheaper than in Paris or London, and of course it was the world capital situated closest to Russia. During the 1920s a thriving literary community was to burgeon in that setting; as Brian Boyd notes, Germany in 1924 was home to some eighty-six Russian-language publishers. Among them were two enterprises founded by none other than Nabokov *père*, via a partnership with the prestigious German house Ullstein: a publishing firm called Slovo ("Word"), and a Russian daily by the name of *Rul'* ("Rudder").

In that alien milieu, Nabokov set up shop as a young free-lance Russian writer, producing fictions long and short as well as verse and plays, all in Russian, and doing such standard, bread-and-butter scribbling as book reviews, along with the very Nabokovian activities of devising chess problems and crossword puzzles (in Russian, too). His precarious literary income he supplemented via private tutoring about town in French and English, plus tennis and pugilism. With his gradually growing reputation, Nabokov-Sirin would receive invitations to give readings of his work at cafés and soirées, and even in auditoriums, where on occasion his sole name on the announcement was enough to fill all the available seats. By the 1930s, he had managed to stretch out his meager earnings with translations of his fiction into the English, French, and German. Although over the next eighteen years he would endure countless false leads, dashed hopes, and disappointments—the lot of most journeyman artists— Nabokov still became known among his compatriots as *the* leading exiled writer of his generation.

Owing to his striking good looks and aristocratic bearing, the young Nabokov would enjoy with the opposite sex a degree of success so extreme that it shades into libertinism. During each of his family's brief stays in both the Crimea and in Greece he managed to juggle three love affairs at once; he also carried on several amours while a student at Cambridge. In 1923, however, at a charity ball in Berlin, he met Véra Slonim, the exiled Russian-Jewish daughter of an émigré lawyer and timber exporter. The couple were engaged within a year, took marriage vows at city hall in 1925, and had their only child, Dmitri, in 1934, whereupon Vladimir discovered the joys of parenthood, reportedly becoming a model father.

The marriage would become a legendary love-bond lasting more than five decades, its sole odd feature being that Vladimir and Véra always slept in separate bedrooms. Their lifelong union was darkened just once, early in 1937, when Nabokov plunged into a steamy, off-and-on affair with Irina Guadanini, a lively, blonde divorcée who was also an exiled Russian. The writer seriously considered leaving Véra for Irina, but, following months of agonizing on all sides over the matter, man and wife and young son were eventually reunited on the beach in Cannes. The liaison with Irina was the last real threat to the marriage, though Stacy Schiff in her biography of Véra tells of an occasional, innocent flirtation carried on by Professor Nabokov with a Wellesley College student or two in the 1940s.

The 1930s were a dark decade in other ways for the Nabokov family. With the Depression, publishing outlets died out, among them *Rul'*. Though the family got by on the supplementary wages brought in from various clerical jobs held by Véra, and though they never went hungry, their economic situation came fairly close to "Destitution," as a chapter in Brian Boyd's biography is called. And of course with the Nazi régime in power since 1933, things were less than tenable for Nabokov's Jewish wife and their half-Jewish child. Meanwhile the émigré Russian population in Berlin was thinning out, moving on to wherever it could. As early as 1936, Nabokov himself was frantically writing letters to fellow countrymen in England and the U.S., seeking academic jobs as a professor of Russian and even preparing literary lectures for possible future use.

Late in 1937 the Nabokovs left Germany permanently for expatriate status in France, where as aliens they were nonetheless banned from working. In 1940, as the German war machine steamrollered across Europe, Nabokov sought ways to flee to America. The prospect of a summer-school teaching job at Stanford University in 1941 provided the legalities and a further incentive for a transatlantic relocation. With help from fellow emigrés, Nabokov secured passage for three on the U.S.S. *Champlain*, chartered by an American Jewish refugee organization; and on 19 May 1940 they set sail from the port of St. Nazaire to New York City. The Nazi takeover of France was just four weeks away.

Nabokov had spent a total of fifteen years living and writing in Germany, and had even published three Russian-language novels with German casts of characters and German goings-on. And yet, as is often pointed out, despite his natural cosmopolitanism and gift for languages, he never learned German, other than the practical, day-to-day survival phrases—although, as is also sometimes noted, the pattern may well have been not just individual but one broadly shared among expatriates. ("Little Havana" in Miami, for instance, is home to many émigré Cubans whose knowledge of English is minimal.) Nabokov's justification for this linguistic lacuna was that he did not want German interfering with his literary Russian.

Subsequent scholarship, however, suggests something much deeper: to wit, Nabokov simply *disliked* Germany and Germans. In a 1937 letter to a friend, he writes, "I have always been unable to abide Germany, the swinish German spirit."[4] Similarly yet more pointedly, in *The Gift*, its positively portrayed hero Count Fyodor despises Germans for their "love of fences,...mediocrity; for the cult of the office;...for the lavatory humor and crude laughter; for the fatness of the backsides of both sexes;... for cruelty in everything, self-satisfied, taken for granted."[5] And in 1942, at the height of the Russo-German eastern front, Nabokov in a letter to Edmund Wilson frankly yearned that Russia would "defeat or utterly abolish Germany—so that not a German be left in the world."[6] The first volume of Brian Boyd's monumental life of Nabokov bears the subtitle *The Russian Years*. Fifteen of those years, however, were spent in Germany. And yet it would be scarcely possible to imagine an equivalent study, by Boyd or any other scholar, entitled *Nabokov: The German Years*.

The life that Nabokov led in the United States, and his relationship to his New World home, was to be the polar opposite of his long sojourn in Germany, the latter a time of economic drift and cultural isolation, further complicated by his deep lack of regard for the host country and its natives. In America, by contrast, he already knew the language, indeed loved it (and worked at it, too), a fact that gave him a ticket of entry and a wide mobility never available to him while stationed in Berlin. Not to mention the access to local literati: Settling briefly first in New York and then for the better part of the decade in the Boston area, within months Nabokov was making contact with some of the leading lights of the U.S. literary and academic scene, and was also getting to know the people, the day-to-day

---

[4] Cited in Rampton, *Vladimir Nabokov*, p. 195.
[5] Cited in ibid., p. 94.
[6] Karlinsky, *Dear Bunny, dear Volodya*, letter 21, p. 53.

mores, and the general look and landscape of his adopted land. It is thus quite understandable that he once said to a European interviewer, "America is my home now... The intellectual life suits me better than any other country. I have more friends there, more kindred souls there than anywhere."[7]

As early as October 1940, Nabokov made the acquaintance of Edmund Wilson. At that time the dean of American letters was pursuing a personal interest in Russia, its language and literature. Hence the friendship that developed between the two writers—their huge egos notwithstanding—suited them both. Soon Wilson was getting the recent immigrant paid book-reviewing assignments for *The New Republic*. Eventually Wilson also brought the novelist into the *New Yorker* fold, a tie that would lead to many of Nabokov's short stories being accepted by what was then and remains today America's most eminent commercial-literary magazine. So highly regarded was Nabokov's work by the journal's editors that in time they made with him a coveted "first-reader" agreement for his new manuscripts. In time Nabokov also met Edward Weeks, the legendary editor of *The Atlantic*, a venue in which around ten of the novelist's shorter works would see print as well.

Moreover, again in 1940, Nabokov's friend Mikhail Karpovich, an historian of Russia at Harvard, was to introduce the novelist to Harry Levin, then just starting out on a path that would make him one of America's most prominent, campus-based literary critics, and who just happened to be married to an émigrée Russian woman. Finally, Nabokov was soon laboring as an—initially unpaid—researcher at Harvard's Museum of Comparative Zoology, pursuing major work in lepidopteral taxonomy that in time would earn him a modest annual stipend for his efforts.

Before his transatlantic departure, European friends and acquaintances had warned Nabokov about an ignorant and uncultured U.S.A. And indeed there had long existed this notorious side of American culture: the money worship, the aggressive know-nothingism and provincialism, the Babbittry and philistinism that many a U.S. author had previously criticized, satirized, or deplored in their writing. In this regard, Nabokov was fortunate to have been spared extended exposure to or entrapment by that stereotypical and less-than-attractive side of American ways. Instead, he became friendly with some of the most learned, sophisticated, and cosmopolitan spirits that the American republic had to offer. Perhaps owing precisely to his early acceptance within this rarefied milieu, he

---

[7] Boyd, *Vladimir Nabokov: The American Years*, p. 22.

could find American vulgarianism somewhat exotic and "exhilarating" (to quote the eloquent afterword to *Lolita*) rather than repellent or disquieting, as other European emigrés indeed did.

And there was his new, emerging, occupational status. For the first time in his forty-one years of existence, Nabokov would now hold regular, salaried jobs as a college professor, first at Stanford summer school in 1941, then as an instructor at Wellesley College in 1941-42, the latter a temporary post that nonetheless went through several renewals throughout the rest of the decade. Further boosting his status as a newly minted American writer was the Guggenheim Fellowship he was awarded in 1943, to write fiction full-time, for a year, at his leisure—the first such official honor in his life. Though the Nabokovs' economic situation was still far from secure, at least they were no longer living hand to mouth, book to book, on the edge of genteel poverty, as had been the case in Germany and then in France.

Finally, by 1948, the Nabokov threesome would attain stability when, through the agency of the eminent French scholar Morris Bishop, the novelist was appointed a tenured associate professorship at Cornell University. In that post, where Nabokov remained for eleven years, he first taught tiny classes in Russian language and literature, then gained special prominence when he began imparting his legendary, elective lecture class on "The European Novel," a course offering that would routinely show enrollments in the low hundreds—and grow steadily. Nabokov, we have since learned, never took his teaching commitments all that seriously, seeing them less as a vocation than as a regular paying job—and, at times, as a burden. Moreover, rather than commit himself permanently to a fixed address, he and his family lived from year to year in houses that they'd sublet from faculty colleagues who were away on sabbatical.

America's highest-quality academic enclaves nevertheless gave Nabokov not just a livelihood, but professional purpose and human dignity. In that setting, he built up a direct knowledge of day-to-day American life and its educational mores that he would put into several of his American-based novels. He also rode buses in order to overhear American speech, and talked with young girls at social gatherings so as to capture their American gestures and phraseology. Hence, whereas in his "German" novels the host country had existed as a rather shadowy and abstract entity, and his German characters speak a dialogue that probably no real-life Germans ever spoke, his American locations, by contrast, show a palpable and recognizable texture.

By the same token, Nabokov's new access to America's superb libraries—with their splendid collections and open stacks—and his direct experience with the world of professional scholarship eventually allowed him to undertake his mammoth, annotated translation of Pushkin's *Eugene Onegin*, as well as the dazzling, ground-breaking spoof of academic erudition that is *Pale Fire*. (The two works in some sense feed on each other, each one being made up of an initial poem followed by a plethora of endnotes.) And of course there were—yet another "first" in Nabokov's life—the paid summer vacations! The far-flung butterfly trips!... Those cross-country wanderings took the Nabokovs through the vast landscapes, myriad small towns, and quirky motels that were still new even for native-born Americans, many of whom had just purchased their first motor cars, too, and that would be deftly reimagined in *Lolita*.

Much of *Lolita* was in fact written on the road, in the countless motel rooms where Véra and Vladimir spent countless nights. The 450-page manuscript was completed during the academic year, on 16 December 1953. Its fortunes have since become legendary, and have been covered in detail by scholars more knowledgeable than myself. Here, though, are the general outlines.

Lolita was rejected by five major U.S. publishers, who, given the prevailing puritanical ethos of the time, feared the possibility of punitive fines, high court costs, and even imprisonment. Nabokov's good friend Edmund Wilson, moreover, frankly disliked the manuscript—the start of tensions that in time would sour their relationship. As a last resort, the author settled on having the book issued by Olympia Press, a notorious Parisian publisher of erotica. The novel drew no initial reviews in its Olympia version, but when Graham Greene at the end of 1955 listed it in the Sunday *Times* as one of the three best books of the year, the process of wide recognition for *Lolita* was unleashed. (One might well speculate on the fate of the work had Greene *not* published his opinion.) High-level condemnations of the book came in reaction to Greene's praise. Across England, France, and the U.S., official bans and protracted legal battles gave the book increased visibility, prompting many clandestine sales in those same countries. With the whiff of scandal, 100,000 copies were quickly sold. The anti-censorship forces eventually triumphed. G. P. Putnam's bought the U.S. rights to the volume while the Literary Guild book club chose it as a main selection. By 1957, Nabokov was famous, even a cult figure among the literati. By 1959, he was also a rich man.

In a curious irony, a realignment of ideological forces in the U.S. cultural sector helped keep *Lolita* afloat and less vulnerable to attack. With the onset of the Cold War, a concomitant suspicion of any "social" conceptions in the arts, and the triumph of the New Critics in the expanding academic sphere, literature was now regarded as an almost

exclusively formal matter, a self-contained world in which background
and content carried relatively less weight. A more complex, mid-century
version of "Aestheticism" had triumphed within the United States, and
hence positive endorsements of *Lolita* as strictly a work of art, by the likes
of e.g. Elizabeth Janeway, Lionel Trilling, and Harry Levin could, in such
a climate, openly thrive.

Meanwhile, success bred success. By 1958, the renowned American
cinéaste Stanley Kubrick had purchased the movie rights to *Lolita*. And in
1960, Nabokov would briefly follow in the footsteps of his compatriot
Ayn Rand when he spent six months in Beverly Hills, all expenses paid by
studio funds, as he composed on commission the screenplay version of his
best-selling, romantic road novel. Fame, however, brought with it its costs.
Constant media attention, along with a host of other interruptions, were
making it difficult for Nabokov to write in peace. And so, in 1959 he
resigned from his Cornell teaching position; following a couple of years'
peregrinations on both sides of the Atlantic (including that Hollywood
stint), Vladimir and Véra finally settled into the Hotel Montreux Palace in
Montreux, Switzerland, owing in part to the town's proximity to Milan,
where son Dmitri was at the time pursuing a career as an opera singer at
La Scala.

It was Nabokov's fifth and final emigration (after England, Germany,
France, and United States), although by choice in this instance. And of
course it was the place where he breathed his last, in 1977. In that idyllic
Alpine setting, finally free from economic worries or day-to-day conflicts,
Nabokov established a routine of writing on a full-time basis, while also
supervising the ongoing translations of his Russian works into English. In
the process, he came up with one more great novel in his adopted
language, *Pale Fire*, a book in some ways even more original than *Lolita*.
Its innovative format helped generate a line of literary inheritors that
includes D. M. Thomas's *The White Hotel* and A. S. Byatt's *Possession*.

Concerning the business side of his life's work, Nabokov now felt less
than satisfied with his deal with G. P. Putnam's. He thus moved to
McGraw-Hill, where he came under contract to provide ten future books
for the mammoth publishing conglomerate. Hence, for the first time in his
life, Nabokov was doing writing-for-hire on a grand scale. The lack of
regular contact with everyday life, however, in some ways worked against
him as he put out a bloated, self-indulgent, self-congratulatory book like
Ada, or the often vain, petulant, and ill-humored interviews gathered in
Strong Opinions, or the unabashedly narcissistic swansong, *Look at the
Harlequins!* Although *Ada*, riding on the crest of *Lolita* and *Pale Fire*,
soon hit the best-seller lists and served as a major book club's pick of the

month, much of the critical reception was hostile, and many bought copies
probably sat on suburban night tables, barely dipped into. Sales of all of
Nabokov's books thereafter proved disappointing.

                                        *

In retrospect, I now believe that among the reasons for the initial appeal of
Lolita to me in my student days was its immigrant, outsider's "take" on
mainstream U.S. life. Humbert, after all, is an educated European who
arrives in postwar America and for whom everything about the place—the
schools, customs, highways, the motels, housewives, youngsters both male
and female, as well as suburbia and the well-scrubbed medium-sized
towns—are surprisingly exotic, striking, and new. Today, owing to the
plethora of images from glossy magazines, movies, TV, and the Internet,
the American "look"—its spaces, settlements, human types, and
fashions—has become a familiar enough sight to millions world-wide. In
the 1950s, however, these subjects were a recent, still-emergent phenomenon.
Lolita's USA is not the dazzling, outsized, mythologized America of New
York City skyscrapers or Hollywood film stars (neither of which appear in
the book), but of everyday, white, middle-class life, without the social and
political clashes that would rock the nation in the 1960s.

     The narrative voice in *Lolita*, moreover, captures the uneasy
enthrallment with which many an unattached and restless foreigner can
respond to American girls aged early teens and upward. These young
lasses and their personal freedoms, their casual mores and lack of
formality, their combined brashness and innocence, not to mention their
shapely limbs, up-front sexiness, and apparently intuitive sense of their
sexuality—all of this can prove quite captivating to a male-with-a-roving-
eye who has been raised in a more restrictive, tradition-bound society,
where early-to-late adolescent female eroticism assumes other, more
stylized forms of conduct and expression.

     In another instance, the fascination that foreign men can feel for
American women gets some lively play in *Journey to the End of Night*
(1932), the notorious classic novel by Louis-Ferdinand Céline. Early on in
the book, its French protagonist and narrator, Bardamu, has an American
lover actually called … Lola (!), a Red Cross worker whom he has met
while a soldier on the front lines in World War I. Of her he reminisces,
"Her body was an endless source of joy to me. I never tired of caressing its

American contours" (49).[8] Later in the novel, Bardamu sails to New York, where he soon lands there a temporary job as "flea-counter" for one Major Mischief, whose unnamed daughter occasionally drops by wearing short tennis skirts, and of whom he observes, "Finer legs I've seldom seen …, a vision of budding young flesh, an absolute challenge to happiness, an exclamation of promised delight" (90). And while strolling in Manhattan, the hero is smitten at the sight of "a sudden avalanche of absolutely lovely women!" Of these female apparitions Bardamu waxes lyrical: "[W]hat suppleness, what grace! What unbelievable delicacy of features! What daring tints—always, invariably successful! Every possible masterpiece of face and figure among the many blondes! And all these brunettes, these red-heads, too!" (193) In their effusive style, Bardamu's rhapsodies are surprisingly similar to Humbert's own outpourings when he first catches a glimpse of a half-dressed Lolita, kneeling on a mat on Mrs. Haze's lawn.

Although my younger brother Kanani and I carried U.S. passports and had parents who were both U.S. citizens, the two of us had scarcely set foot in the United States prior to my seventeenth year. Outside of textbooks and classes, first at a bilingual, parochial school for Puerto Rican kids and later at standard American schools in Caracas, our scant familiarity with American life had come largely from movies and comic books along with the black-and-white TV shows that arrived with two weeks delay via the medium of kinescope. Kanani and I were in fact foreigners, "Americans" stationed in Puerto Rico, Cuba, and Venezuela who'd somehow never known the nation known elsewhere as "America," and who had spent only a few days in our "home country" as tourists in Florida.

My acquaintance with the American opposite sex was correspondingly limited. After all, my own mother—who was ethnically Filipina-Chinese and had grown up in colonial Hawaii—was American only by virtue of her birth and education. Her appearance and family background were East Asian, and much of her world view had more Asian traits of feeling than I then realized; indeed her passport classed her as "Mongolian," the commonly employed racial term at the time. In Puerto Rico she had her American women friends whom I'd meet socially, but otherwise I'd hardly known American females, let alone young ones, before my junior year in high school. Prior to that, I'd entertained but the vaguest notions about *las*

[8] Louis-Ferdinand Céline, *Journey to the End of Night*, trans. John H. P. Marks. Page references from this book will be placed in parentheses in the body of the text.

americanitas, mostly through the mythical depictions found in wholesome teen comics such as *Archie & Veronica* and *A Date with Judy*.

Meanwhile, my adolescent Hispanic playmates held ideas about American male-female relations that were, at very best, fanciful. A friend named Paco, who once, sitting side by side with me on the curb, had given me my first lesson in Spanish sexual vulgarisms, had spent some time in New York. He could therefore discourse with some authority when reporting to me that, you know, actually, up there, thirteen-year-olds *chingan* (roughly equivalent to the "f" word though not as strong). Later, at the Cuban military school, a shy, heavyset dorm mate called Feliciano earnestly and whisperingly confided to a few of us as we sat around during rest period that "los *dates*" were, in reality, meetings for young couples to carry on secret sex romps ...

I was awed yet incredulous at these communications, knowing full well that *Archie & Veronica* and other comix had never even suggested such unspeakable goings-on. Readers with long enough memories may remember an analogous urban legend that in the 1960s took hold among American college-age male youths, many of whom "knew" that, in Sweden, there was free love! ... that a Swedish girl would go to bed with you at the drop of a hat!... Many of us fantasized about visiting Stockholm, needless to say.

Those free flights of the imagination among my Latin cohorts, I now realize, were inevitable in a Hispanic culture in which teenagers out alone on dates were something unheard of, in which the presence of chaperones was still the norm with young couples, and in which the slightest kissing and petting, let alone premarital sex, were completely off-limits. The absolute chastity of a female person's body was her prized possession. Even less-than-virginal lips could be cause for scandal. The Hispanic cult of virginity, moreover, is capable of bringing forth violence, as depicted in such works as García Lorca's *House of Bernarda Alba* and García Márquez's *Chronicle of a Death Foretold*.

I still remember my first attendance in Caracas at what, I later found out, was known as a "make-out party." In my former experiences in Puerto Rico and Cuba, a get-together for Latin teens consisted of moderate drinking (not getting soused), social chatting, and very decorous (if at times vigorous) dancing. Cheek-to-cheek was about as close as one might get. So, that September 1957 I arrived, in coat and tie, at the house party of a friendly gringa classmate in a gringo neighborhood, ready for what I'd previously known. By 9 o'clock, however, the lights had been dimmed; couples were slow-dancing in tight embrace; others were smooching in a corner; yet another twosome was sprawled out on the couch. Naturally, the handsome, Anglo-Saxon-looking guys had the pick of the prettiest ladies. The Latinos—and that included yours truly—were largely left out.

It took me at least two or three years to adapt to this shift in erotic mores. I'll say it again: Latina damsels at that time simply did not engage in passionate kissing with boys. And even though, for the American girls, "going all the way" was still an unusual step, the gringas at our Colegio Americano simply *knew* about matters of bodily contact and corporeal pleasure. In this regard they were well ahead of their Latina schoolmates— the latter frankly disdainful of the *Americanitas*, seeing them as slutty little tramps who let guys manhandle them at will. Hence, when I later became an eager devourer of the great books old and new, I could vaguely, unconsciously respond to Humbert's amazement at a Dolores Haze and at her classmates whose experiences had been simply unimaginable to him in his teens.

In 1959, following my graduation from high school, Kanani and I left Venezuela and an untenable home situation to join up with our mother and her Chicano boy friend and future spouse, Estevan Romero, in New Mexico. Our first full exposure to the US of A was a five-day journey on highways stretching from Key West to Santa Fe. We spent our nights not in comically named motels, but on a successive series of Greyhound buses. As, wide-eyed, we crossed much of a continent, we were amazed at the geometrism of the U.S. roads, the sense of endless space and shifting vanishing points, and the trusty efficiency of the transport. We also felt somewhat disconcerted at the cold impersonality of the human ambiance.

Our biggest shock came in response to the forced racial segregation that we were to see throughout the Southern states. This was not a way of life that had been revealed in the comic books, TV shows, and movies from which we'd learned about "our" country. Indeed, we felt a personal dilemma when faced with signs saying "WHITE BATHROOM" and "COLORED BATHROOM." Did our yellow-brown, Asian skin qualify as "white"? Or were we "colored?" Over the next few days we'd venture cautiously into the white-designated areas, though our initial concerns were not unfounded. Indeed, during a lunch stop in Little Rock, Arkansas—at the time a nerve center for violent, anti-integrationist militancy—my brother was stealthily followed into the bathroom by a trio of white roughnecks. They stood about in silence as he did his number-one business. As he departed the urinal, the threesome surrounded him threateningly. Thinking fast, he addressed them in rapid-fire Spanish, sashayed toward the door without having washed his hands, and left the courageous warriors somewhat nonplussed.

Thanks to the efforts of my high-school English teacher, Mrs. Williams, I had been awarded a tuition-and-fees scholarship at the University of Arizona. As a result of that chance grant, in the desert town of Tucson I was able for the first time to live my long-standing dream of becoming a musician. In addition I enjoyed the benefit of a few caring professors in music and the humanities. For some years previously I'd imagined campus life as an endless round of dormitory rap sessions dealing with the great books, the big ideas. There certainly was some of that, but there were also such things as fraternities, which shocked me with their overt racism, philistine anti-intellectualism, and sexism, not to mention their loud parties and their occasional street thuggery, of which I was, on occasion, a minor victim. I also remember my sophomore-year roommate, a tall, lanky sort with a blond brush cut and a couple of pimples in his sunken cheeks. His D plus grade average had earned him suspension from his fraternity, yet he still thought of non-frat people as "rinky-dink." He'd routinely employ the "n" word when alluding to blacks; would refer to Venezuela and other countries where I had lived as "those Mexican countries;" and spoke of Arabs as "camel jocks," my first time hearing that pejorative term for Arabs. He found my love of classical music laughable, and when I had friends visiting the room, he'd introduce himself by saying, "Hi, Seymour Butts here!" or "I'm Dick Bender!" (I came to be known humorously as "the man with the crude roommate.") Such, then, were among my initial encounters with the less savory side of American campus culture.

Later on, in my move to UC-Berkeley, I was once again able, because of good grades, to have my out-of-state tuition waived, keeping my fees to a modest $100 per semester. From then on I had the good fortune to spend four amazing years at one of the nation's richest, most vibrant intellectual environments, where students of all ages really did sit around the Terrace and the Bear's Lair, bandying their thoughts about literature, culture, society, and even classical music.

It was at Berkeley, moreover, where I became aware of "politics" in its broadest sense—not just as the work of professional lawmakers and government officials but as the whole network of relations and activities in society. It was at Berkeley that I got my first real political education, largely via the wide array of activists' tables at the Telegraph Avenue gateway to the campus. I spent many an afternoon standing about at that open forum, listening intently to arguments from all points in the ideological spectrum. The Civil Rights movement was in high gear in the South and elsewhere, and it was then, around those tables, that I first encountered the curious arguments to the effect 1) that racial discrimination is a problem best left to the local and State governments to work out, 2) that Federal legislation to bring about racial justice would only make matters worse, being the first step toward totalitarian dictatorship, and 3) that there's nothing more sacred than a businessman's right to reject a customer he does not like. For some reason, I never heard any rebuttal noting that, in the South, white restaurateurs were being *forbidden* to serve black customers, even if they so desired. Though I only dimly realized it at the time, I was encountering the standard formulas of the libertarian right and hard-line Randians who, four or five decades hence, are among the subjects of this book.

At Berkeley, too, I started to learn about the hidden, more sinister underside of U.S. foreign policy, particularly the numerous armed interventions and CIA-sponsored military coups d'état throughout Latin America and elsewhere, and of course the expanding, murderous war in Southeast Asia. At one point I even spent a few days on street corners hawking copies of the *Vietnam Observer*, a short-lived anti-war tabloid weekly. A preoccupation with the American imperialism of which I am a product—my white father having beguiled an innocent, Asian, colonial college girl in the Pacific, then taken her across the globe to the American "lake" as part of his overall business schemes—remains with me to this day.

Still fresh in collective memory was the 1957 Russian launching of Sputnik, the world's first communications satellite (which both Rand and Nabokov denied had really happened). In response to that upset propaganda victory for the Soviets, the United States found it necessary to start competing with them in the physical sciences and aerospace, as well as in foreign languages. Before that development, scientists in American pop culture had been portrayed either as creepy crackpots (the "mad scientist" cartoon figure) or as impractical klutzes who couldn't cope with everyday reality. Now, suddenly, government-supported scientific research was being presented in the mass media as a noble, forward-looking enterprise. At the time, though, I had no idea that the spectacular growth in U.S. science was ultimately part of an ideologically motivated race for prestige between the two then-superpowers.

Yet Sputnik would ultimately impinge upon my own intellectual life as well. Among the secondary results of the U.S. push to "catch up" with the Soviets was a generous infusion of Federal aid for the learning and teaching of foreign languages, in particular of those dubbed "critical" languages—Spanish, Russian, and Vietnamese among them. Meanwhile, a set of personal and academic circumstances compelled me to seek a transfer to some, to any other major university on the East coast. In time I was accepted by Harvard, on a three-year fellowship funded by the august-named National Defense Education Act (NDEA). Thus did a pioneering, Soviet aerospace machine serve as the prime mover for Federal legislation that would furnish a living stipend to an entire generation of budding scholars (myself included), as we undertook advanced study in languages "critical" to American interests.

Once settled in the Boston area I naturally took advantage of the myriad attractions of that metropolis. I can thus fully understand Nabokov's enchantment with and his sheer luck at having drifted into an association with some of the highest-level intellects in his new land, in a region of considerable cultural density that offered him some modest income to boot. (Sheer luck for both of us...) Though I was working toward a degree in Romance languages, I continued to dip freely into the world's classics, including more of Nabokov's oeuvre and a reread of *Lolita*. By the same token, I found it difficult to respond to American fictions placed squarely in those suburban enclaves where Humbert first settles—e.g. the novels of John Updike, whose insider optics on that geography I found alien and baffling. During those years I also came to know American and foreign left-wing traditions and texts when I shared an apartment with four Asian-Studies graduate students; they were deeply immersed in anti-war politics, to which movement I contributed my modest, evolving prose skills. (One of my roommates, Tom Engelhardt, has since become a prominent critic of U.S. empire in books and on his online magazine, Tomdispatch.)

Around that time there occurred the ugly break with my father, described above in chapter 3. Shortly thereafter, I finally, foolishly reciprocated my love to an icy-blooded girl friend (in some ways a female version of my dad), who had spent months attempting to convince me that I was "perfect" for her and had said "I love you" more than once. She'd had a past history of jilting her boy friends; she jilted this one just a few weeks after he'd declared himself. (She later served as one of the models for Livie Kingsley, the villainess of my novel, *The Carlos Chadwick Mystery*.) Subsequently, I chose to bury myself in my books, entering into an "angry recluse" phase that lasted well into the 1970s.

After my studies at Harvard I went on to hold a series of jobs at excellent academic institutions, and to live for a while in Paris and Madrid. Throughout all those experiences I was regularly scribbling away on Latin American, U.S., British, and European literature while eking out my own narratives and satires, and slowly working out my complex set of identities. Knowing that I qualified neither as fully "American" nor completely "Hispanic," I had long ago realized that I was, by default, a cosmopolitan, and that I therefore had no recourse but to build on precisely those confusing though nourishing foundations.

What finally helped me give shape to those dilemmas was writing my memoir, *Overseas American: Growing Up Gringo in the Tropics*, which took me nine years and some thirteen drafts to complete. Along that scrivening journey I happened upon the existence of an entire body of scholarship about individuals whose histories resembled mine. As it turns out, a 1950s sociologist by the name of Ruth Hill Useem had coined the term "Third Culture Kids" to designate those children who, due to their parents' career duties abroad, have grown up outside their passport nation and who, when returning "home" to their official culture, felt less than fully at ease in what was simply the latest country where they've resided. In time, other writers on the subject minted the term "Hidden Immigrants" to denote those supposed "returnees" to a nation-state they haven't much lived in, yet who have attended American schools overseas and speak standard, idiomatic American English. Through a series of lucky accidents, the publication of my memoir led to a commission from a British house to gather a collection of thirty essays and a poem on the subject, which was entitled *Writing Out of Limbo: International Childhoods, Global Nomads, and Third Culture Kids*, co-edited by myself and Nina Sichel, a fellow overseas American raised in Caracas.

I therefore share with Nabokov and Rand the experience of immigration to the USA, albeit with a very different sort of trajectory and, unlike them, with several identities to disentangle. Rand, for her part, elected to forget, negate, occlude her Russian antecedents as she fashioned herself into the most renowned propagandist for American business and its values. Nabokov, by contrast, reconstructed his luxurious and idyllic Russian past in *Speak, Memory* and made of it a visible literary reality, part of his rite of passage to a new role as American artist and artificer.

Like both of these writers, I am an immigrant of sorts, albeit a "hidden" one. In my teaching and writing I have endeavored to live each of my backgrounds and combine from them the best of both. On the other hand, having experienced via my father the worst of American culture—the imperialism and chauvinistic jingoism, the philistinism, the individualist delusions and greed—I had no choice but to reject the man and his negative, destructive legacies, private as well as public, personal as well as political. Figuring out my relationship to America is thus a project that is still ongoing and continues through this very work.

CHAPTER FIVE

ON WHAT THEY EACH STOOD FOR

Nabokov and Rand were both intellectual absolutists. Dogmatists they were, each in his and her own way: extremists who brooked no disagreement, no compromise, no nuance, no vision or position outside their own. And they granted no concession, however minimal, to points of view differing even slightly from those they represented.

Radicals, one might conceivably say. Others (their fans) would argue that he and she were simply being true to his/her principles.

Of course, what is principled to some may be dogma to others, just as one man's terrorist is another man's freedom fighter. The dividing line between rigor and rigidity, between purity and presumptuousness, is not always a clear-cut one.

*

As any reasonably educated American reader knows, Rand believed in the *morality* of the free, selfish individual—be he architect, inventor, or businessman. (The latter two are conjoined in *Atlas* and oftentimes in the non-fiction.) Conversely, any interference with these superior beings' endeavors she viewed as objectionable and indeed *im*moral. The notion permeates virtually every page penned by this truculently ideological scrivener.

Where does this mindset come from? Personal experience plays a crucial role. In a virulent, dialectical reaction to the state socialism of which the Rosenbaums were economic victims, Rand would summarily reject any philosophic conceptions that inclined to the "social" or the "humane." Accordingly, both her fiction and her essays show an unrelenting hatred of trade unions, socialists, the New Deal, labor laws, family ties, charitable works, and anything tainted with the sin of caring about others. Whenever a Rand character is introduced as being "from Washington," you can be sure he's either a tyrannical, obtuse New Dealer or an evil crypto-communist. And anytime a Rand character invokes family responsibilities or the general welfare, they (oftentimes a she) are

portrayed as manipulative, vicious, or just plain dumb. Significantly, there
are almost no children to be found in Rand's work, other than in her
economic arguments in favor of child labor, given that parenting is, ipso
facto, an altruistic task. Besides, having a ten-year-old tot give philosophic
speeches on selfishness or altruism, whether pro or con, might come off as
a bit forced, stilted, absurd...

Still, being by bent a thinker, Rand was well aware of the attractions
offered by Marxism as a means of explaining historical and cultural
change. Moreover, she felt deeply discomfited, nay, embittered, by the
circulation of Marxist ideas and the acceptance of the Soviet régime
among intellectual and creative circles in Los Angeles and New York.
Accordingly, she envisioned the need for a comparably broad,
encompassing, anti-Marxist, explicitly pro-capitalist alternative. Her entire
life's work would be marked by this singular motive. It's not by chance
that each of her grandiose fictions has as its climax a protracted speech, in
which Roark or Galt sets forth an entire philosophy of history, starting
with the savage, cave-dwelling brutes of our dark past and leading us by
steps to the bright utopia of man's free, capitalist future.

Countering the pernicious collectivist tide are those great heroes whom
Rand made no secret of seeking to glorify. They're mostly tall, square-
jawed, handsome (of course), stouthearted, fiercely independent, Anglo-
Saxon, and alone. Men of absolute genius, they are unfailingly right about
everything. Their enemies, by contrast, are despicable sub-humans who
live "second-hand lives"—a typically Randian phrase of scorn, and
indeed, as we have seen, the originally proposed title for *Fountainhead.*

If much of this smacks of Nietzsche's cult of the *Übermensch* and his
contempt for "the herd," it's not coincidental. Recent scholarship has
noted the depth of the influences from the German philosopher on the
Russian-American pop-philosophaster-to-be. The first book reportedly
purchased by the immigrant Rand was an English translation of *Thus
Spake Zarathustra*. Young Alyssa, Burns notes, "devoured" Nietzsche as a
student, and her journals are filled with allusions to him.[1] His ideas,
moreover, were very much in the air in the Russia of her time. D. Barton
Johnson observes that, during Alyssa Rosenbaum's youth, the best-selling
novelists in her native land were Anastasia Verbitskaya and Mikhail
Artsybashev, authors whose "ideological potboilers featured socially and
sexually emancipated heroes and heroines spouting half-baked
Nietzscheanisms."[2]

---

[1] Burns, 16, 25.
[2] D. Barton Johnson, "Nabokov, Ayn Rand, and Russian-American Literature," p.
105.

Rand in her own fiction writing would continue with this tradition. In the first, 1936 edition of *We, the Living*, her only novel with a Russian setting, the human masses are seen as "'mud to be ground underfoot, fuel to be burned,'" for the sake of those who are gifted'.[3] In the wake of Rand's subsequent fame, later editions of the book either softened or suppressed the Nietzschean rhetoric. Still, his influence remains there. *Anthem*, in turn, is written in an aphoristic prose style—her one and only departure from straight exposition—that can only have been modeled after *Zarathustra*. Later she would rely on the Teutonic maverick thinker in characterizing her *Über*-architect Howard Roark, and her initial notes for *Fountainhead* are sprinkled with aphorisms from *Beyond Good and Evil*. Indeed, in its early drafts the manuscript featured direct quotations out of that work, serving as epigraphs to each of the four parts of Rand's own "ideological potboiler" (as it is sometimes dubbed.) Again, the epigraphs were dropped in publication.

During Rand's apprenticeship phase her pop-Nietzscheanism had actually been even more extreme. In 1928, in Los Angeles, she penned a novella, "The Little Street," based on the true-life, sensational crime trial of William Hickman, a twentyish fellow found guilty of strangling and dismembering a twelve-year-old girl named Marion Park, and who even bragged about it once he'd been apprehended. When describing Hickman himself in her notes, Rand praises "his disdainful countenance" and "his immense, explicit egoism." Lamenting the attacks on him in the press, she nonetheless reflects, "A strong man can eventually trample society under his feet. That boy [Hickman] was not strong enough."[4]

The fictive protagonist of "The Little Street," Danny Renahan, is described in Rand's working notes as having "the true, innate psychology of a superman." He is, in her view, a "man who really stands alone, in action and in soul," who has "no social instinct or herd feeling" and "does not understand,... *has no organ for understanding*, the necessity, the meaning of importance of other people."[5] This is precisely the kind of language she would later utilize for characterizing Howard Roark in *Fountainhead*. In her unpublished novella, then, Renahan/Hickman is the true victim, while the victimizers are the courtroom jurors and spectators, characterized as "human herds...who have but one aim: to ruin all individuals and individuality."[6] Rand's avowed aim here is "to show that

---

[3] Heller, 140.
[4] Ibid, 70.
[5] Burns, 24-25. Emphasis in the original.
[6] Heller, 70.

humanity is petty. That it's small. That it's dumb, with the heavy, hopeless stupidity of a man born feeble-minded." [7]

Needless to say, as she evolved, Rand would prudently evade the artistic risk of portraying a boastful child murderer in a sympathetic light. Still, one can trace a direct line from Nietzsche's brand of utopian advocacy to that of La Rand in her later years. The following passages from *Beyond Good and Evil* now seem like springboards, templates for Randthought, although the German's aphorisms have a richer, more poetic style than does the Russian-American publicist with her simplistic, tub-thumping prose.

Regarding selfishness, Nietzsche notes:

> At the risk of annoying innocent ears I set it down that egoism pertains to the essence of the noble soul... The noble soul accepts this fact of its egoism without any question-mark, also without feeling any severity, constraint, caprice in it, but rather as something that may be grounded in the primal law of things:—if it sought a name for it, "it is justice itself." (265)[8]

And where does this egoistic hero belong? Nietzsche states early on:

> Every superior human being will instinctively aspire after a secret citadel where he is *set free* from the crowd, the many, the majority, where, as its exception he may forget the rule "man." (26)

> The very notion of social, human ties, and caring about others, meanwhile, is up for questioning:[9]
> ... the feelings of devotion, self-sacrifice for one's neighbor, the entire morality of self-renunciation must be taken mercilessly to task and brought to court. (33)

Nietzsche's utopia, as is well known, consists of an aristocracy of superior beings, to which a society must sacrifice itself and submit:

> The essential thing in a good and healthy aristocracy is... that it does *not* feel itself to be a function...but as their *meaning* and supreme justification... Its fundamental faith must be that society should *not* exist

---

[7] Burns, 25.
[8] Friedrich Nietzsche, *Beyond Good and Evil*, trans. by R. J. Hollingdale. Quotations will be identified by the number of the aphorism.
[9] In this regard it is worth noting that, like Rand, Nietzsche never had children, nor does he allude to them at any point. And of course feeling nothing but contempt for women, he never married. Rand's marriage to Frank O'Connor, for its part, was a largely nominal relationship.

for the sake of society but only as foundation and scaffolding upon which a select species of being is able to raise itself to its higher task and in general to a higher *existence.* (258)

And what of those who are not so fortunate? Nietzsche observes:

Among men, as among many other species, there is a surplus of failures, of the sick, the degenerate, the fragile, of those who are bound to suffer; the successful cases are ... always the exception. (62)

In this aphorism, Nietzsche takes religions to task for siding with "the *sufferers,*" and adds—not without a sinister and prophetic touch—that those creeds have "preserved too much of that *which ought to perish.*" So lamentable a practice of preserving "everything sick and suffering" has led to the "*corruption of the European race*" (all emphases in the original).

As we might recall, a younger Alan Greenspan, in his defense of *Atlas Shrugged,* asserted that "Parasites perish as they should." Hence we see here a precise and identifiable line of succession from Nietzsche to Rand to Greenspan, even with the same verb.

The *Überfrau* never owned up to her debt to Nietzsche, in keeping with her self-conception as a completely original thinker; and she publicly repudiated his anti-rationalist and relativist tendencies. Actually, the only philosopher Rand claimed to respect was Aristotle; most other thinkers (including Descartes, Kant, and Wittgenstein) did not, in her view, believe in objective reality—though she'd also scarcely read them, as some close fans have since granted. Whatever the case, Nietzsche's aphoristic irony and wit were well beyond this solemn didacticist to whom humor reportedly seemed both strange and pointless. (What humor there is in Rand's fictions is of the unintentional, campy variety.)

Moreover, by the late 1930s, Rand may have sensed the dangers in claiming Nietzsche as an influence once Nazi culture had selectively adopted him as its preferred, semi-official philosopher. Still, much like Nietzsche, the empress cared mostly about "the great and the exceptional," not to mention the struggles of Greatness against fools, looters, and assorted other *Untermenschen* who deny Greatness its due. Throughout *Atlas Shrugged* the only victims we see are rich businessmen, who suffer more than all the "so-called underdogs" put together (as Rand herself puts it). Nevertheless, at the end, Rand's victorious Superbeings emulate wise Zarathustra and go down from their Rocky Mountain heights into "the world."

*

Rand's views are well known, even to those who shun her work. Fewer casual readers, by contrast, are as precisely aware of Nabokov's absolute, aloof aestheticism, his extreme version of Art for Art's Sake. For Rand, the egoistic doctrine was everything; the ideology precedes her writing and her fictive art (such as there was). Not exactly so for Nabokov in his two best and best-known American works, or even in a surprisingly touching and humane earlier book like *The Defense* (1930). Nabokov, moreover, didn't fully "go public" with his ideas until the international success of *Lolita* made him desirable copy for interviewers, and also rendered "salable" his former Russian novels, to which he now added his combative prefaces.

Before we look at Nabokov's aesthetic doctrines, a quick glance at the America in which he was setting up shop should prove helpful.

With the onset of the Cold War, aestheticist doctrines rapidly gained prominence in high-culture circles in the United States. The triumph was a bit paradoxical. After all, the U.S. had previously been perceived—both at home and abroad—as a land of Babbitts and cowboys, "of gum-chewing, Chevy-driving…philistines."[10] The shift nonetheless has been recognized and documented over the last three decades.

In the visual arts, Abstract Expressionism took center stage as the art world's most esteemed style, with critic Clement Greenberg as its chief spokesman.[11] Realistic art was marginalized, to such an extent that, "in 1952, some fifty American artists, including Edward Hopper [and] Charles Burchfield…attacked [the Museum of Modern Art], in what came to be known as the 'Reality Manifesto,'" for "coming to be more identified in the public eye with abstract and non-objective art."[12]

In classical music, a daunting and ever-more complex twelve-tone system, also known as "atonality" and "dodecaphony," won out as the most prestigious of idioms, notably in the universities. The founder of the method, Arnold Schoenberg, had actually taught at UCLA in 1936-45, where their music building was subsequently named after him. Yet another segment of American composers followed in the footsteps of Stravinsky's "neoclassical" phase, the Stravinsky of *Soldier's Tale* and the two symphonies, and, again in the hospitable setting of the campus and the conservatory, they built on the legacy of this less forbidding branch of musical avant-gardism.

In the case of literature, the change was more complex. The novel, still a market-driven genre, saw a withdrawal from Modernist experimentation

---

[10] Frances Stonor Saunders, *The Cultural Cold War*, p. 19.
[11] Serge Guilbaut, *How New York Stole the Idea of Modern Art*, pp. 94-98, 168-72.
[12] Saunders, p. 265.

and a corresponding return to traditional realism via Bellow, Malamud, and Updike, though now without the broad societal vision of the nineteenth-century European masters, and also without the social conscience of Steinbeck in *The Grapes of Wrath* or Mailer in *The Naked and the Dead*. The focus was more on the individual consciousness, on existential subjectivity[13] —a kind of "solipsist realism." The outstanding exception to this trend, as we shall see, was Nabokov.

It was in literary studies that the post-War aestheticist "turn" came through with special clarity. Between 1945 and the late 1960s, New Criticism became the dominant paradigm for examining poetry and fiction in the classroom and in academic journals. There's an irony in the triumph of the New Critics. In their original incarnations as Fugitives and Agrarians in the 1920s and 1930s, these men of letters were ardent neo-feudal nostalgists who celebrated the ante-bellum South (slavery and all). The group, however, had also included practicing poets on the order of John Crowe Ransom, Robert Penn Warren, and Allen Tate, who, as did many poets since 1830, profoundly disliked an industrial capitalism that they viewed as inimical to their art and values.

By the 1940s, however, the Agrarian-New Critics had abandoned their retrograde social project, even as they and their followers became the regnant literary voice on U.S. campuses. Their hegemony is symbolized by the widespread use, during that era, of Brooks and Warren's *Understanding Poetry* (1940) in undergraduate courses, and Wellek and Warren's *Theory of Literature* (1949) in graduate seminars. Eventually, New Criticism's well-focused formalism would be complemented by the grand system of Northrop Frye's *Anatomy of Criticism* (1957), where the Canadian theorist nonetheless still saw literature as being shaped by itself rather than by external factors.[14]

The New Critics and their kin in some measure won by default. Nineteenth-century historicism—itself the product of bourgeois progressivism—was an exhausted model and lacked the verbal tools for dealing with the more elaborate, hermetic products of Modernism. In addition, the McCarthyist repression had not only purged the academy of individual Marxists but had succeeded in exorcising all left-wing discourse from respectable debate. To apply "social" criteria to literature was considered suspect and would have endangered any young scholar's career. During the years of New Critical hegemony, form mattered most, while content and background counted for little.

---

[13] Morris Dickstein, *Gates of Eden*, pp. 25-50.
[14] Northrop Frye, *Anatomy of Criticism*, p. 97.

The reasons for these discourses victorious were ultimately political
and ideological. The Soviets' military victory over the Nazis, and the
control they went on to exert over Central Europe, had generated among
ascendant U.S. conservatives a backlash against anything deemed
"socialistic" or "social." In the culture wars that ensued, the general
aestheticist position would function as a reverse mirror to the doctrines of
the Soviets and of their allies on the Western Left. Where Soviet
commissars rejected "formalism" and literary experimentation, American
academics welcomed those very tendencies. Where the Soviets dismissed
abstract art as "decadent," New York celebrated it. Where musical avant-
gardism was viewed as dangerous in the USSR, the Ivy League campuses
gave it free rein. And where Soviet aesthetics stressed content and
background at the expense of form, American critics made form their sole
criterion, relegating other concerns to the sidelines.[15] To put it in Ortega y
Gasset's terms: while the Soviets wanted to see the garden outside,
America's Cold War intellectuals preferred contemplating the windowpane
in between.

These cultural shifts gained further strength and legitimization from
U.S. arts policies consciously adopted in certain ruling circles. The
financial élites of New York purposely set out to foster art and artists that
were not "socially" minded or engaged. Jackson Pollock had actually
studied with Mexican muralist (and avowed Communist) David Alfaro
Siqueiros, while Adolph Gottlieb and other Abstract Expressionists had
done time as Marxist activists. With the Cold War gearing up, however,
they would put their leftist sins behind them. Meanwhile, Nelson
Rockefeller, after his disastrous sponsorship of a mural created by Diego
Rivera, became one of the nation's major supporters of non-figurative art
and reportedly had some 2,500 abstract canvases, many of which served as
perfect décor for the family's Chase Manhattan Bank buildings.[16]

In addition the CIA, via international conferences, dummy foundations,
and other means, actively (but covertly) encouraged aestheticism and
avant-gardism in the arts. The agency funded music festivals that featured
twelve-tone composers and was supportive of abstract-painting exhibits.
Through its front, the Congress for Cultural Freedom (CCF), the CIA
provided the full budget for the influential British monthly *Encounter* and
also partly supported well-respected little magazines in the U.S., including
Hudson Review and *Partisan Review*. The CCF, moreover, sponsored in
1952 an International Exposition on the arts in Paris, where Allen Tate,

---

[15] I deal with these shifts at greater length in my *Art for Art's Sake and Literary
Life*, 251-56.
[16] Saunders, p. 258.

now reconstructed as a Cold-War liberal, delivered a lecture in which he made no mention of the alleged virtues of the old slave South, and defended the right to free speech instead. In yet another, somewhat bizarre instance, "the CIA...commissioned a translation of Eliot's *Four Quartets* and then had copies air-dropped to Russia."[17]

*

Nabokov too believed in Lit. for Lit.'s Sake, in beauty all pure, in an art that possessed no connection to society, humanity, ideas, politics, or current affairs. (In practice, as we shall see shortly, things were a bit more complicated.) For a random sample, I cite his *Playboy* interview with Alvin Toffler: "A work of art has no importance whatever for society ... I don't give a damn for the group, the community, the masses."[18]

Nabokov's view is thus a latter-day avatar of Oscar Wilde's humorous, apodictic aphorism that concludes his "Preface" to *The Picture of Dorian Gray*: "All art is quite useless." (And so, Long live useless art!) Significantly, the first major study of the author in English, by Page Stegner, bears the title *Escape into Aesthetics: The Art of Vladimir Nabokov* (1966).

As we have seen with Rand, such a set of dogmas does not spring from nowhere. Nabokov, after all, began and developed as an émigré Russian author. As the scion of wealthy, cultured, displaced gentry, he had many reasons to despise Soviet rule and all it stood for. Not least of those reasons was the Stalinist doctrine of social usefulness in art, an official line that had historical roots in the theories of such nineteenth-century liberal critics as V. Belinsky and Dobrolyubov. In choosing the absolute aestheticist stance, Nabokov was, in a dialectical way, differentiating himself from an entire Russian legacy as well as repudiating its allies on the Western left.

Nabokov's aesthetic stance first achieved broad visibility in his essay, "On a Book Entitled *Lolita*," published initially in the *Anchor Review*. The piece was then added as an Afterword to the 1958 edition of the novel put out by Putnam, and has since become a standard feature in subsequent printings. There, in no uncertain terms, Nabokov declares his supreme value:

---

[17] Ibid., p. 248.
[18] Nabokov, *Strong Opinions*, 33.

For me a work of fiction exists only insofar as it affords me what I bluntly
call *aesthetic bliss* ...[emphasis added]. There are not many such books.
All the rest is either topical trash or what some call the Literature of Ideas,
which very often is topical trash coming in huge blocks of plaster that are
carefully transmitted from age to age until somebody comes along with a
hammer and takes a good crack at Balzac, at Gorki, at Mann (314-15).

The position is set forth in this quasi-apologia with a certain wise
serenity, sans any of the harshness of later pronouncements; it is thus
justly renowned as his most oft-cited reflection in that respect. Still, the
passage contains the germs of his later attacks on any author who stands
outside that blissful aesthetic. "Topical trash," for instance, would become
a key yardstick-in-reverse: For Nabokov, all literature dealing with current
affairs, without exception, would be so adjudged, especially if it deals with
such overtly political subjects as slavery or war. By extension, any fiction
and literary criticism concerned with social issues or with ideas was
"topical trash," too.

As the Russian-American emerged into a public figure, these views
took on an obsessive, monomaniacal cast, and ended up filling the pages
of his thick tome *Ada* (as we shall see later).

In a supreme sort of irony, however, the man who allegedly despised
the Literature of Ideas wrote at least two novels of ... ideas. The concept
to which he gives fictive flesh in both cases is, not surprisingly,
aestheticism, along with its struggle against socially or historically
engaged writing (the latter often depicted via caricature).

The first such instance, *The Gift* (1938), would turn out to be the
author's farewell novel in his native tongue, not to mention his bid at a
major statement within the tradition of Russian literature. Its fourth,
penultimate chapter features a biography of Chernyshevsky, the
nineteenth-century pamphleteer whose novel, *What Is to Be Done?*, would
serve as the basis for Socialist Realist doctrine. In Nabokov's interpolated
essay, purportedly written by his protagonist—a budding poet and
committed aesthete named Fyodor Godunov-Cherdyntsev—the entire
philosophy of Chernyshevsky, including the latter's social view of art, is
taken apart and found wanting, while Chernyshevksy himself is made to
come across as a pathetic fool.[19] The fictional poet who penned the
broadside, not accidentally, is an aristocrat, a Count, whose second
surname, Cherdyntsev, was the name of a real, by-then extinct Russian

---

[19] Richard Rorty, the American philosopher who much admired Nabokov,
nonetheless observes in his essay "The Barber of Kasbeam" that, by comparison to
Lolita, "*The Gift* is *didactic*, a set of illustrations from some general ideas." P. 161.

noble family. In preparing for the writing of *The Gift*, Nabokov actually wrote his friend Nikolay Yakovlev in Riga asking him to obtain this genealogical information.[20]

The Real Life of Sebastian Knight (1941), Nabokov's slim first novel in English, came out shortly after *The Gift* and can thus be read as a sort of sequel, an ideological companion, to the thicker Russian tome. Among its characters is a mediocre hack named—presumably with ironic intent—Goodman, who serves Nabokov as a whipping boy with which to mock historically-minded literary critics, and who more or less inherits the role allotted to Chernyshevsky in the previous book. The unnamed narrator—a stand-in for Nabokov—pokes fun at Goodman's earnest concern with the ideas of "our time," with "Post-War unrest" and with his notion that, "The War had changed the face of the universe." (In a 1934 letter to Khodasevich, Nabokov himself had vented his hatred of the terms "postwar" and "modern era," and frankly boasted about not reading newspapers.)[21] Not accidentally, Goodman has his office on Fleet Street, the standard symbolic location for journalism, trashy or not.

By contrast, the book's eponymous hero, whose surname "Knight" once again carries obvious implications of nobility, represents the aristocratic writer who stands at a superior, smirking distance from collective ills such as mass hunger, joblessness, and world war. Sebastian Knight here thus corresponds to the young Count, poet, and aesthete who served as Nabokov's positive figure in *The Gift*. Straw man Goodman predictably deplores Sebastian's "aloofness" toward a world filled with "economic depression," "unemployment" and faced with "the next super-great war" (52) as well as his "absolutely refus[ing] to take any interest whatsoever in contemporary questions" (97). *Sebastian Knight*, significantly, was composed in the late 1930s, when hunger and war fever were widespread. At one point its nameless narrator blithely brushes off the anti-fascist Popular Front (along with anti-Semites) as "idle idiots" (258).

The fictional authors in these two novels of ideas correspond in many ways to La Rand's high and mighty heroes. Like Roark, Galt, et al., they too are handsome men of genius and fortitude, "nobles" in both the moral and the social senses of the world, set upon by "social" demands on the part of lesser breeds—Goodman in the case of Nabokov, Toohey in Rand. And of course they exemplify Nietzsche's conception of the Superman,

---

[20] Boyd, *Vladimir Nabokov: The Russian Years*, 404.
[21] Ibid, 409.

even if Nabokov's readings of the philosopher's work were sporadic and occasional at best.

In addition to its presence in these two frankly ideological fictions, Nabokov had previously inserted his pro-aestheticist polemic in a most unlikely setting: namely, his psychological thriller *Laughter in the Dark* (1933; Russian original *Kamera Obscura*), a sordid account of a skin-crawling, often cruel ménage à trois. (According to David Rampton, it is the Nabokov work with sales second only to those of *Lolita*.)[22] In this book, the debate is farmed out among several male characters. First, there is Albert Albinus (Kretschmar in the Russian), an art dealer yet "not a particularly gifted man" (5), who, in the course of the narrative, also turns out to be a pitiful fool—not least because the fellow believes in a literature that engages "social problems" (86). Among his friends is one Baum, characterized as an "author ... with strong Communist leanings" (82).

Albinus's love-rival, casual opponent, and eventual nemesis is a memorable trickster called Rex (Horn in the original; the English has obvious overtones of royalty), a handsome, charming, dapper, but also evil sort: Among the things he likes doing is watching a blind man sit down on a freshly painted park bench, or pouring oil over live mice and then putting a match to the creature, or, simply, fooling people. Unlike Albinus, however, "this dangerous man was, with pencil in hand, a fine artist indeed" (92) who, fittingly, makes the claim that "'an artist must let himself be guided solely by his sense of beauty'" (117). Hence, much like Count Godunov-Cherdyntsev, and like Sebastian the Knight, regal Rex represents in no uncertain terms the noble aestheticist position.

The debate first surfaces at a dinner hosted by Albinus; among his guests are Baum and Rex. We read that the "Communist" writer has just finished composing a novel set in the then-British colony of Ceylon (today's Sri Lanka). His book, Baum states, will deal with "'the exploitation, the cruelty of the white colonialist. When you think of the millions—'" "'I don't,' said Rex" (85).

The sadistic painter's curt, blithe-lofty response—inevitably associated with Nabokov—elicits a sympathetic giggle from Margot (orig. Magda), the shallow floozy who is the shared mistress of the two male protagonists.

A more complex exchange occurs two thirds of the way through the novel. During a stay in France Albinus pays a visit to Udo Conrad, characterized by the omniscient narrator as a neglected major author who, sadly, has not received his due. (Of Udo Conrad, the "Communist" Baum had lamented previously over dinner, "he has a contempt for social

[22] Rampton, *Vladimir Nabokov*, 25.

problems which, in this age of social upheavals, is disgraceful" [86].) This invented Conrad therefore corresponds to Fyodor in *The Gift* and to the eponymous Sebastian Knight, though in a less vocal way, he being but a fleeting, minor character. The drift of the Albinus-Conrad conversation is first suggested thus:

> "I didn't know you were in France," said Albinus. "I thought you usually dwelt in Mussolini's country."
> "Who is Mussolini?" asked Conrad (138).

Here, then, Nabokov depicts as a positive figure, and presumably a great artist, a grown man of the pen who is blissfully ignorant of the then-dictator of Italy.

Further on in the encounter, Conrad makes the following, familiarly Nabokovian assertion:

> [i]t is not literature in the mass that matters but the two or three real writers who stand aloof, unnoticed by their grave, pompous contemporaries. All the same it is rather trying sometimes. It makes me wild to see the books that are being taken seriously (139).

Conrad's aestheticist stance is now disputed by Albinus, who, like the future straw man Goodman, invokes "post-war unrest"—a phrase that in turn leads to a monosyllabic retort by the Nabokovian man of genius:

> "No," said Albinus, "I'm not at all of your mind. If our age is interested in social problems, there's no reason why authors of talent should not try to help. The war, post-war unrest—"
> "Don't," moaned Conrad gently. They were silent again (139).

With a single, impatient command, the Nabokov spokesman dispatches everything that Albinus's argument stands for... [23]

This literally anti-social, formalist-aestheticist vision was to permeate the lectures that Nabokov delivered yearly in his course at Cornell on "The European Novel." Throughout those lessons, Professor Nabokov purposely shunned all questions of social or historical background and scanted any notion of literary movements or "schools." In a bumptious letter to his then-friend Edmund Wilson, the novelist frankly brags about his classroom approach to Dickens: "In discussing *Bleak House*, I

---

[23] As Rorty himself notes, "[Nabokov] never quite brings himself to say that artists should not pay attention to social evils or try to change them. But he is churlish about any given attempt to do so, and often on wildly irrelevant grounds." P. 147.

completely ignored all sociological and historical implications and unraveled a number of … thematic lines and the three main props of the structure."[24]

Indeed, Nabokov's posthumously published version of the lecture finds "the sociological side" of Dickens to be "neither interesting nor important," and he turns a blind eye to such key Victorian aspects as the juridical machinery or the battles in defense of children's rights—what the Olympian pedagogue summarily derides as "child labor and all that" (LL, 68, 65). As philosopher Richard Rorty pointedly observes, "Nabokov has to pretend, implausibly, that Dickens was not, or at least, should not have been, interested in the fact that his novels were a more powerful impetus to social reform than the collected works of all the British social theorists of his day."[25]

Actually Nabokov's position was not all that unusual in academic literary studies at the time. As we have noted above, the triumph of the New Criticism on U.S. campuses during the Cold War had led to a common practice of examining works of fiction and poetry in isolation from their social and historical settings. The Russian-American high priest simply took this tendency to the utmost extreme, becoming as dogmatic and uncompromising in his views as were the Soviets with their state-imposed doctrine of Socialist Realism.

*

There is a side of me that can understand and even sympathize with the "escape into aesthetics" of an artistic purist like Nabokov. During my Caribbean childhood and adolescence—a time of family desolation, geographic dislocation, and military-school confinement, among other things—listening to and reading about classical music served me as a vivid personal refuge, a self-contained alternative to a daily life that largely lacked any sort of meaning or caring or solid human ties. Yet though as a pubescent I could sing many symphonic works by heart, I knew nothing about the European cultures where they had come from.

---

[24] In Karlinsky, *Dear Bunny, Dear Volodya*, letter no. 219 (18 November 1950), p. 282.
[25] Rorty, 147. He further observes, "With equal irrelevance, [Nabokov] dismisses the chapters about Sir Leicester and Lady Dedlock, considered an 'indictment of the aristocracy,' as of 'no interest or importance whatsoever, since our author's knowledge and notions of that set are extremely meager and crude'" [LL, 64-65] It is impossible not to see class interests on the part of Nabokov the outspoken aristocrat in this statement.

One afternoon in Cuba, during recess, I had my ears glued to the school radio console, intently listening to a broadcast of Beethoven's Symphony number Five.

Two erudite, white-smocked male teachers (all my teachers were male) were standing about, casually taking in the piece. And as the finale surged to its climax, I heard the elder-statesman prof remark to the younger one, "Yes, it's a music that well reflects the era when it was written." His colleague nodded in assent, "Sí, sí."

Such a response to a disembodied classic was new to me—I'd never heard or seen anyone speak of ol' Ludwig (or indeed, any composer)—in those terms. So alien did I find the interpretation that I felt a resistance surging deep inside of me. I wanted to inform the learned scholars, "No, no, gentlemen, you've got it wrong. It's all just music, 'pretty music'" ("*música bonita*," my personal phrase back then).

The passing encounter was probably my very first glimpse of the long-established debate between aestheticism and historicism. Significantly, I came down firmly on the aestheticist side.

Fast-forward to the late 1960s and '70s, my years as a somewhat confused literature student at Berkeley and then at Harvard. The aestheticist vision at the time was still riding high; and we young scholars-in-training were expected to assimilate the view. At Harvard graduate school I would have as a teacher an eminent critic, a smaller version of Nabokov at Cornell, who would teach Latin American novels dealing with revolution, dictatorship, and war as if they were strictly formal, verbal artifacts. Any look at the social phenomena as represented in those texts he considered to be "external," irrelevant, and unsuitable for discussion.

It's not that I thought this approach mistaken or wrong—just incomplete. There was no *logical* reason for one to exclude the other. The clash rather originated in the fact of two warring ideological camps. As my way of getting a handle on the dilemma, in the mid-1970s I embarked on a broad historical investigation of the problem, in which I traced the idea of aestheticism to its Enlightenment origins and then told of its diffusion over two centuries and across three continents. Two decades later I published *Art for Art's Sake and Literary Life: How Politics and Markets Helped Shape the Ideology and Culture of Aestheticism, 1790-1990*—and felt much relieved to put the debate behind me.

To my amazement, however, the study was a finalist for the 1997 National Book Critics Circle Award, and, a few years later, was translated to Serbian and Chinese. Interestingly, when I asked both of the translators, Vladimir Gvozden and Ta-tao Chen, what might have drawn them to so obscure a volume, both came up with essentially the same reply: My general overview, but especially my chapter on Latin American aestheticism—said the two of them—were directly applicable to some analogous movements that, in the early 20th century, had cropped up in Serbia and Taiwan. I was pleasantly surprised to find out that I'd managed to provide some means of understanding a cultural product with world-wide reach and local manifestations.

Aestheticism, then, wasn't only Nabokov preaching in *The Gift* or holding forth in his lectures at Cornell. The species had evolved over time, with many variants, in a variety of environments, struggling for existence against a range of adversaries...

*

Unlike many an intellectually restless student, I never went through a youthful Nietzschean phase, though I did in time read all of his major works as part of my job in the man-of-letters trade. Granted, as an obsessive, late-adolescent atheist, I could sympathize with his best-known aphorism, "God is dead!" (sighted scrawled even on the occasional campus bathroom wall in the 1960s). And his irreverent wit and impatience with academic pedantry spoke to this greenhorn scribbler who was then trying to get beyond the arid bounds and vested limits of established discourse. Nietzsche's total vision, moreover, was sufficiently broad-ranging and eclectic that I would often hit upon a phrase that resonated within me, such as "We are punished for our virtues" or "Madness is something rare in individuals—but in groups, parties, peoples, ages it is the rule." Finally, I felt assured that the commonplace, post-war association between Nietzsche and the Nazis seemed well refuted in his clearly stated loathing for anti-Semitism, Prussian nationalism, and mass movements as a whole.

On the other hand, Nietzsche's personal cult of the Superman, his converse contempt for ordinary folk, and his strange, perverse misogyny were repellent to me. In later years I also would learn of the ill health that plagued most of his existence and brought him chronic physical suffering, as well as his final decade of clinical insanity. There was a double irony here. First, a thinker who frankly advocated letting the sick and the "sufferers" *perish* was at the same time being supported by his academic pension, granted precisely *because* of his illness, even as he was being sustained and nursed by his mother Franziska, his sister Elisabeth (i.e. two women) and his close friends, without which he would either have *perished* or joined the contemptible "sufferers" out on the streets or in a state asylum. Second, Nietzsche's later, total isolation and his disconnection from the most common societal practices, along with his inexorable descent into madness, inevitably raise doubts about the ultimate validity of his philosophical system. Can a man—however brilliant—on the edge of psychosis ever be considered a reliable narrator, thinker, or imaginer?

The formative influence of Nietzsche on numerous writers (G.B. Shaw, H.L. Mencken, Georges Bataille) and movements (segments of Nazism, Existentialism, French Structuralism) stands as a matter of public record. Regarding La Rand, however, it is only thanks to recent biographical volumes that she has emerged as the visionary, megalomaniacal German metaphysician's most ardent, vocal, yet secret U.S. acolyte. (If surprisingly few readers have known of Rand's Russian origins, fewer still know about the Nietzschean connection.) Her "Objectivist" devotees, moreover, would be loath to admit, let alone celebrate, the Nietzsche-Rand tie, given the inherent clash between the philosopher's frank irrationalism and his Russian-American disciple's purported cult of "Reason," not to mention the unsavory dangers of being linked with somebody who was certifiably crazy…

Well aware of the subterranean sway exerted by La Rand on far-right U.S. attitudes, in the late 1980's I set out to write a piece of fiction depicting the seductive allure of Rand's views to young American minds. In preparation for the task I duly read through most of her oeuvre, raiding it for representative and juicy quotes. Concurrently I drafted a novella tentatively entitled "Abortive Romances," in which I placed those abundant citations on the lips of my youthful characters. The story tells of a naïve Chicano jazz pianist and music student, José/Joe, who gets involved with Jennifer, a sorority coed who happens to be ardently "Randian." They enjoy a brief fling; she uses him as her accompanist for her violin performance, after which she ditches him for not treating her roughly enough nor being sufficiently "strong"—and evokes wise Rand as her sage inspiration. In response, Joe devours Rand's works over the summer, is thoroughly converted, and proceeds to apply Randthought to every last aspect of his existence. Following graduation from college in Tucson, he moves to Los Angeles, starts a career as a jazz artist, carries on a brief, ugly liaison with yet another slinky, true-believing Randian beauty, name of Nancy—and his life goes downhill thereafter.

The story comes brimful of real-life Randianisms, imbedded as they are in the dialogue, in the narration, and in Joe's letters to his brother. (For the form, I took as a model Goethe's *Sorrows of Young Werther*.) Deciding to call attention to the gist of the thing, I eventually retitled the work "The Pianist Who Liked Ayn Rand" and placed it in a book stories under that handle.

Several dozen rejections later, the volume was issued by Amador, a small publisher of progressive and experimental fiction located in Albuquerque, whence my novel, *The Carlos Chadwick Mystery*, had formerly come out. The newer book got minimal press attention outside of a positive review in *Publisher's Weekly*. With "Randian" readers on Amazon.com, however, it touched a raw nerve, eliciting angry comments from select faithful who accused me of being a "Rand-hater" and "virulently anti-Rand," and who berated me for not "understanding" their high priestess. Those reactions, I'd find out in due time, are the standard, formulaic ripostes by devout Randians to any commentator who is less than worshipful of their diva. Tellingly, the negative, single-star comments on Rand biographies by Jennifer Burns and Anne Heller resort frequently to the epithet "Rand-hater," and assert condescendingly that these two scholars (tsk, tsk) simply "don't understand" the greatest thinker in the history of the world.

On the other hand, a libertarian novelist and screenwriter called Thomas Sipos praised my story both on Amazon and in a small newspaper, saying, "The novella will resonate with libertarians. Many of us have seen, or read of, or heard of real-life versions of Bell-Villada's characters. (I had a high-school classmate who turned 'Randroid' for a few years.)"

And so, given these extremely varied responses, I can safely feel that, in my novella about young "Randians," I have illuminated an important little corner in U.S. ideological and cultural life.

CHAPTER SIX

ON THEIR WAYS OF KNOWING

As do their fellow human beings, every author has a distinctive way of apprehending the world they live in and then dealing with it, conveying it through words. Dickens was thus primarily a man of feeling, as is his fictive art, in some cases notoriously so. Keats and Neruda in turn are master poets of the individual sensation—visual, aural, even tactile and gustatory. Pope and Shelley, George Eliot, Thomas Mann, and Sartre perceive human existence through the lenses of their ideas, an all-around intellectualism, their inclination philosophical. Poe, Borges, Cortázar, and most sci-fi authors, appropriately, tend to bring the imagination to bear upon their respective, visionary universes.

Not surprisingly, Rand's way of seeing, knowing, and writing is through thinking and reasoning. Via ideas, or rather via *an* Idea—hers. In person she loved to engage people in logical volleyball exchanges, and she was given to confronting newly met acquaintances and raw recruits with the pointed exhortation, "Check your premises." Much of her fiction and essays, along with many reports of her life, bring to mind the hair-splitting disputations of medieval scholiasts and argufiers; and her current, perpetually blogging acolytes on the Internet can easily resemble Swiftian or Rabelaisian caricatures of that lofty sort of disputatiousness.

Fittingly, many of Rand's youthful admirers have been science-and-math wonks, whiz kids with a considerable gift for abstract cerebral schemes but whose knowledge of emotions and understanding of human ties is at best slight. Around MIT (perhaps the world center for science and tech) the student Objectivist group in the 1960s was a prominent voice in the marketplace of ideas; they published an alternative newspaper bearing the pitch-perfect name of *Ergo*. It has sometimes been said that the thinking type, the idea person, is an easy target for humor and parody: think Sherlock Holmes; think of Lucky's lecture-monologue in *Waiting for Godot*. In certain ways the rationalism of Rand can approach such self-parodic levels, too: think of John Galt's seventy-page lecture-monologue in *Atlas Shrugged*.

As we saw in chapters 1 and 2, Rand presumed to be a grand, totalizing big thinker, complete with a theory of knowledge, a system of ethics, and a philosophy of history, as well as an implied aesthetic. Vast is her horizon—yet the specific content of her cosmos, quite meager. For all its sometime celebration of science and scientists and engineers, Rand's writing demonstrates little if any fascination with the details, the concrete, sensuous phenomena, of our world. Even the famous motor that can alter our existence, invented by mighty Galt in *Atlas*, is a shadowy and obscure artifact, as is its inventor. In Rand's novels, everything—and I mean absolutely *everything*—is subsumed to the rationalistic schemata of her crusading mind.

By the same token, in all of Rand's prose there are virtually no portions memorable for their literary qualities—no moments lyrical or melodic, eloquent or descriptive, touching or moving in any way. Whatever quotable passages exist in Rand are so because of the shock value of the outrageous arguments therein trumpeted (as well as the subjacent values and hatreds therein implied)—and naught else. Quite simply, there is little of *beauty* in Ayn Rand, save for the seductive beauty of the system itself, so alluring to the young, the susceptible, the incompletely educated, and the unhappy.

The lack becomes especially clear in Rand's free-standing essays, items she began producing only—at the prompting of her disciples—in the wake of the colossal critical failure of the almighty, hefty *Atlas*. In those thought pieces, conceived and written directly in her sermonizing voice—sans fictional characters, imagined dialogues, or novelized contexts to give them drama or spice—the style and tone are combative, one-dimensional, humorless, preachy, and often shrill. Absent from Rand's "essays" (seldom classed by that generic rubric) is the slightest sign of grace, charm, delicacy, elegance, understatement, humanity, irony, or wit. They show all the nuance and subtlety of a sectarian political leaflet, which in certain ways they resemble. The tradition founded by Montaigne will not be including Ayn Rand among its ranks in the near future.

For all her principled repudiation of the emotions, Rand was in many ways profoundly driven by, indeed in the thrall of, a singular, all-encompassing emotion: namely, hatred of the Communism that had expropriated her family wealth, and, by extension, of anything that smacked of social concern, charity, or altruism in whatever form, including family affection. Not accidentally, the countless negative reviews that greeted *Atlas Shrugged* often noted the element of hate that pervaded the would-be magnum opus. As a corollary, I would venture to speculate that La Rand's grand paeans to "reason" served in many ways as an *ex post facto* rationalization and sublimation of her deep-seated, irrational hates. In her many public appearances, moreover, Rand was hardly a model of cool-headed rationality. Whenever a questioner from the audience dared to politely disagree with her, she would notoriously lash out in a mad fury, subjecting the audacious dolt to verbal invective and venom.

Rand's emotional core came especially to the forefront during the extended break-up stages of the adulterous, consensual, overlapping-triangles affair with Nathaniel Branden, her right-hand man. In 1968, as the facts were gradually being leaked to her about the long-standing secret liaison between Branden and Patrecia Gullison, a beautiful young model and aspiring thespian, Rand exploded and, in a series of bitter confrontations with him, unleashed on her erstwhile lover an unrelenting and unforgiving attack. "You bastard! You nothing! You fraud! You contemptible swine!" she screamed at the younger man, her visage contorted with hate. In another climactic meeting, immortalized in the 1999 TV docudrama *The Passion of Ayn Rand*, she summoned Branden to her Manhattan apartment and had him sit on a chair in the foyer, where, with rage and odium, she reviled him at length. Finally, she slapped him across the cheek thrice and, as she threw him out, cursed him and wished impotence on him for the next twenty years. Signficantly, throughout these scenes and during their public aftermath, the woman of reason steered clear of any suggestions of sexual jealousy or abandoned lover's pain and, rather, construed Branden's straying-away and betrayal in terms of the younger man's incapacity to appreciate her high values and standing...[1]

*

Nabokov's own way of knowing is a vastly different story. Perhaps his salient and most dazzling form of intelligence, both as individual and as artist, is his virtuosic eye for detail, his uncanny ability to conjure up the look of things with vivid accuracy and high poesy. (If Rand is the hedgehog who knows **One Big Thing**, and wants the whole world to know it, Nabokov is the wily fox who knows many, many little things, and quietly disdains those contemptible breeds who do not, cannot, simply see them.) This visual gift, along with a special bent for synesthesia—apparently inherited from his mother—was a strength that his loving parents greatly valued and encouraged in the boy Nabokov. And of course his photographic recall, coupled with his verbal precision were traits that

---

[1] For a full account of these episodes, see Heller, pp. 264-72.

would serve him well in his scholarly labors describing and classifying butterflies.

This unusual knack would manifest itself in various and, at times, curious ways during the course of his life. In high school at Tenishev, for an essay that he wrote on Gogol's *Dead Souls*, he received a low grade for totally disregarding the novel's social content, its landowners et al., and saying that what most mattered was "General Betrishchev's crimson wedding gown."[2] Years later, Evgenia Zalkind, a writer and, under the name Evgenia Cannac, a translator of the author into French, would recall how, during their émigré days in Berlin, Nabokov could look at a picture for a couple of minutes and then, with eyes closed, recite every last detail of the image.[3] As a Cornell professor he applied this epistemology in his literary judgments and teaching, and expected his students to share in his extreme eidetic capabilities. Hence a typical—and, to the students, unforgettable—exam question of his was, "Describe the wallpaper in the Karenins' bedroom."[4] Or he might have them list the contents of Anna Karenina's handbag.[5]

Nabokov the writer naturally excels at visual description, at capturing the unique particulars of an experience of the eye. Much of his most beautiful prose consists of the verbal painting of a scene. Here is an almost random excerpt, from approximately his seventeenth year, in *Speak, Memory*:

> I recall one particular sunset. It lent an ember to my bicycle bell. Overhead, above the black music of telegraph wires, a number of long, dark-violet clouds lined with flamingo pink hung motionless in a fan-shaped arrangement; the whole thing was like some prodigious ovation of color and form! It was dying, however, and everything else was darkening, too; but just above the horizon, in a lucid, turquoise space, beneath a black stratus, the eye found a vista that only a fool could mistake for the spare parts of this or any other sunset. It occupied a very small sector of the enormous sky and had the particular neatness of something seen through the wrong end of a telescope. There it lay in wait, a family of serene clouds in miniature, an accumulation of brilliant convolutions, anachronistic in their creaminess and extremely remote; remote but perfect in every detail; fantastically reduced but faultlessly shaped; my marvelous tomorrow ready to be delivered to me. (SM, 213).

---

[2] Boyd, *Vladimir Nabokov: The Russian Years*, pp. 128-29.
[3] Ibid, p. 278.
[4] Boyd, *Vladimir Nabokov: The American Years*, p. 358.
[5] Schiff, *Véra*, p. 198.

The passage manages to bring in six different hues: black, violet, pink, turquoise, and cream, along with the general "darkening" as the minutes tick by. There are also a variety of different shapes: the bicycle bell, the musical staves of the telegraph wires, the long clouds in fan-like form, the vast sky, the stratus and the other, smaller clouds on the horizon. In the hands of a verbal master, a sunset becomes a literary experience.

Every virtue can have its downside, however; and such is the case with Nabokov. John Burt Foster observes that the novelist's mental constitution is "radically empirical and individualizing," to the point where "he dismisses abstract thought of *all* kinds."[6] Indeed, Nabokov's distaste for "thinkers" (always in quotation marks) was another of his recurrent tics, and to some degree in those recurrent attacks he was making an asset out of a liability. But I would take Foster's point a bit further and speculate that the Russian-American novelist seemed to suffer from sort of metonymic disorder whereby he could see every detail yet could scarcely understand abstract thought, let alone produce it. About the only philosopher he appears to have much knowledge of is Bergson, and when he ventures into his own abstract reflections in *Ada* and elsewhere, the results come uncomfortably close to hifalutin, arrant nonsense.

In the brief Part Four of *Ada*, protagonist Van Veen inserts his personal essay called "The Texture of Time," a phrase that had actually been the working title of the novel itself. Here is a sample passage:

> The direction of Time, the ardis of Time, one-way Time, here is something that looks useful to me one moment, but dwindles the next to the level of an illusion obscurely related to the mysteries of growth and gravitation. The irreversibility of Time (which is not leading anywhere in the first place) is a very parochial affair: had our organs and orgitrons not been asymmetrical, our view of Time might have been amphitheatric and altogether grand, like ragged night and jagged mountains around a small, twinkling, satisfied hamlet... The scene is Eocene and the actors are fossils. It is an amusing instance of the way nature cheats but it reveals as little relation to essential Time, straight or round, as the fact of my writing from left to right does to the course of my thought.[7]

And so on and so forth. By contrast with the earlier-cited sunset description, with its precise details and sculpted specificity, here, the neologisms and extended metaphors in Nabokov-Van Veen's meditation on Time only compound the passage's essential meaninglessness and obscurity, not to mention its self-assured smugness.

---

[6] Foster, *Nabokov's Art of Memory*, p. 50.
[7] Nabokov, *Ada*, p. 408.

*

To sum up: Rand was a thinking "type," and her dominant intelligence was logical and rationalistic, rather than empirical, intuitive, or feeling-based. This trait alone will not guarantee high quality in the thinking that permeates her total oeuvre, which is more appropriately thought of as philosophic kitsch. (As Matei Calinescu points out, "ideological art... can be better described in terms of kitsch.")[8] Her "system," however, gained (and today still gains) the sympathies of certain American businessmen—who have encouraged and supported (and still support) the Randian mission, at times materially—as well as of pro-business intellectuals.

In her writings, moreover, La Rand taps into a set of broad myths and prejudices running deep in U.S. life. Individualism; "self-reliance;" suspicion of both government and society; and the multiple cults of the entrepreneur, the outlaw, the free-wheeling pioneer, the inventor, and of wealth in general—these are all recognizable, long-standing components of the American psyche. They have been variously noted by objective observers of the U.S. scene going as far back as de Tocqueville. It is these myths that Ayn Rand builds on, which helps account for the well-nigh exclusive popularity of "Randianism" on U.S. soil. In other countries, by contrast, such issues as family, community ties, political parties, spiritual values, historical traditions, and active government carry too much weight for so atomistic and individual-centered an ideology to take root.

Moreover, among the developed nations the U.S. is an exception in that its high schools do not impart, let alone require, philosophy as an academic subject. Hence, for many an American adolescent mind, Rand is the first secular "philosopher" they will have encountered. An impressionable teen with a taste for general ideas can easily be led to believe that Ayn's axiomatic, unlearned disquisitions are Philosophy itself. Such youngsters' lack of exposure to e.g. Plato, Aristotle, Aquinas, Descartes, Locke, Hume, Kant, Marx, and Mill, even in the form of brief excerpts or *Cliff's Notes*-type summaries, may well prevent them from seeing La Rand as a minor figure and self-fashioned amateur in the 2,500-year cavalcade of acknowledged Western thinkers.

Finally, as demonstrated in the classic study *The Liberal Tradition in America* by Louis Hartz, Americans are "natural Lockeans." The ideas of John Locke hold sway over the American mind to a degree that no philosophy has dominated any other country in history. The seventeenth-century Englishman's thought and even his phraseology are imbedded in

---

[8] Matei Calinescu, *Five Faces of Modernity*, p. 206.

the nation's founding documents, and such basal premises as limited government and the central role of private property are inscribed in the American population's collective psyche without most people even realizing it. (There is even a right-wing think tank in North Carolina called The John Locke Foundation.) Randthought, then, is within a deeper U.S. tradition rather than outside it. As Gary Weiss points out, Rand "articulated what was already in the American consciousness."[9]

Rand's fiction is essentially propaganda for a set of doctrines that are part of the ideological air Americans breathe. Thanks to the plot-writing skills she picked up as a writer in Hollywood, she knew how to produce novels that would articulate conventional pro-business notions, yet make them seem radical and revolutionary, rather than part of past history. Few serious authors or critics, of course, would adjudge works of simplistic propaganda to be "literary," however, and despite her mass following, Rand's grand oeuvre has no standing as literature, no more than do such formulaic genre works as Stalinist tractor-dramas, Catholic hagiographies, or pulp fictions about cowboys winning the West from savage Indians.

Nabokov, by contrast, was not at all a thinker, and his own attempts at thought, when not schematic or simplistic, are unusually murky, delusional, and inept. In a sense, though, Nabokov's temperament is also "American" in its empirical focus on individual fact and in its gut mistrust of general ideas. Nabokov did produce his own ideological, semi-propaganda novels, as we've seen, in *The Gift* and *Sebastian Knight*, but those publicist fictions today are read almost solely by the Nabokov faithful. (*Bend Sinister* also comes close to political propaganda, we shall note in chapter 10.) Luckily for him, the aestheticist position won the battle of ideas in America during the Cold War, and he could thenceforth concentrate on crafting his twin American masterpieces—*Lolita* and *Pale Fire*—rather than continuing to slug it out with his left-wing, intellectual adversaries of old.

---

[9] Weiss, *Ayn Rand Nation*, p. 116.

CHAPTER SEVEN

ON THEIR LITERARY LOVES AND HATES

Every author has literary favorites, preferences reflecting his/her own personal vision and aesthetic practices. American absurdist playwright Edward Albee, not surprisingly, singled out Samuel Beckett as his master dramatist. Argentine fantast Jorge Luis Borges gravitated toward the sci-fi fare of H. G. Wells and the more fantastical tales of Robert Louis Stevenson. Conversely, many an author will be wont to reject, in lesser or greater degree, those ways of writing that differ from their own. Hence James Joyce had no use for the conventional sorts of novels that are aimed at and conceived for the seasonal book trade. Borges, in turn, was simply uninterested in psychological fiction or garden-variety social realism.

Such patterns emerge clearly in our Russian odd pair's sets of tastes. In the case of Nabokov, however, the opinions take on an obsessive and quasi-pathological cast. His relentless potshots against Freud, to be examined in chapters 8 and 9, achieved special notoriety during his two decades of fame and after. Equally maniacal, though, are his sweeping and unforgiving attacks on hundreds of major literary figures. In Nabokov's general view, almost *all* writers, living or dead, are second-rate or even worse. (The "canon-bashers" of the 1980s had nothing on Nabokov's heavy-artillery barrages.) Such virulent hates, moreover, made their way into his fiction, notably *Ada*, of which more later.

History shows few precedents for this sort of extreme judgmentalism. Nabokov is perhaps outdone only by the aging Tolstoy's *What Is Art?*, a withering broadside against virtually all established music (Beethoven's Ninth included), painting, and literature (Shakespeare's plays included), largely on the grounds that they were conceived for the upper classes and could not move a Russian peasant's soul. In addition, like many a traditionalist of the time, Tolstoy indicts Impressionism, Symbolism, and the entire avant-garde as nonsensical and obscure. Playwright G. B. Shaw, for his part, had an ongoing feud with Shakespeare, and crazy Antonin Artaud furiously dismissed all existing theater to date as "bourgeois." It is to this outlying, cranky clique that Nabokov belongs.

The novelist's admiring critics either ignore this side of him, or they consider it puzzlingly harsh. The eminent Slavic scholar Simon Karlinsky, for instance, refers merely to "the *unpredictable pattern* of [Nabokov's] rejections of other writers."[1] But, as I have noted elsewhere and shall again demonstrate, there is little that is "unpredictable" in these attacks, though they did become indiscriminate and near-total in Nabokov's later years.

First, the Social. As we've seen, Nabokov had no truck with "social" conceptions of literature of any kind. Correspondingly, he loathed all fiction that has a social focus or that looks at a society and its divisions, its sub-groups, its practices good and bad, its history. Hence in his dustbin we find such contemptible social observers as Balzac (the new French bourgeoisie), Conrad (British imperialism), Faulkner the "corncob chronicler" (the U.S. South, the Civil War, white racism),[2] all Naturalists of any stripe (Zola, Upton Sinclair), leftists (Brecht), and any works that deal with the horrors of mechanized warfare (Remarque's *All Quiet on the Western Front*, Barbusse's *Le feu*, even Picasso's "Guernica").

Tolstoy provides an interesting case study in this regard. Nabokov required Tolstoy's tale of adultery *Anna Karenina* in his Cornell classes on the European novel, and placed it in his minuscule library of books worth reading. On the sweeping social drama *War and Peace*, by contrast, he was strangely and conspicuously silent, and subsequent biographical researches reveal why. Brian Boyd reports that, in 1958, Nabokov reread the work and found it "childish and dated, a mere historical novel, not worth continuing."[3] Similarly, Stacy Schiff notes that both Vladimir and his wife Vera thought *War and Peace* to be "a very childish piece of writing."[4] In Nabokov's uncompromising view, a war novel cannot be a good novel.

On Solzhenitsyn, Nabokov was similarly mute. He never saw fit to praise either the novels of his Russian contemporary or the nonfiction works the latter wrote about the evils of Soviet dictatorship. At the same time, neither did Nabokov find fault publicly with his celebrated compatriot's frankly "social-realist" and publicist art, presumably out of a sense of anti-Soviet solidarity. Still, biographer Boyd points out that, in private, Nabokov expressed "grave reservations about Solzhenitsyn's artistic gifts." The biographer cites from Nabokov's private diary on *The*

---

[1] Simon Karlinsky, "Introduction" to *Dear Bunny, dear Volodya*, 19. Emphasis added.
[2] Faulkner, says Nabokov to Edmund Wilson, is "necessary in a social sense, but it is not literature." Karlinsky, letter 187 (21 November 1948), p. 240.
[3] Boyd, *Vladimir Nabokov: The American Years*, 362.
[4] Stacy Schiff, *Véra*, 228.

Gulag Archipelago: "His [Solzhenitsyn's] style is a kind of juicy journalese, formless, wordy, and repetitious, but," he grants, is "endowed with ... oratorical force."[5]

Next, Ideas, especially general ideas, which, for Nabokov, were anathema. His hostility, as we've noted, seems to have been motivated by a deep-seated incapacity to deal with them. Following this pattern, any philosophically inclined novelist of ideas is for Nabokov a no-no. Thomas Mann's narrative art thrives on showing ideas at work—and thus he is out. The same goes for Camus ("second-rate") and George Eliot (a "plaster idol"). Dostoevsky falls into this category as well, and perhaps also T.S. Eliot ("a fraud and a fake"),[6] who came close to getting a doctorate in philosophy, and who was probably the most intellectual and idea-oriented of recent lyric poets.

As we saw in connection with *The Gift* and *Sebastian Knight* and portions of *Laughter in the Dark*, Nabokov was himself not exactly above writing novels of ideas, so long as the idea propagated was that of aestheticism. As Borges once stated, those who object to setting forth doctrines in literature usually mean doctrines that differ from their own.

Finally, writers who lack Style and Structure. For Nabokov, formal and stylistic perfection was what most mattered—perhaps the *only* thing that mattered. And indeed, his best work dazzles readers (even those who may not like his aesthetic) with its verbal inventiveness, its rigorous, complex design. On the other hand, history knows of many major writers whose prose style lacks polish and whose sense of architecture is less than solid. We read these authors for other reasons: for their plots, their ideas or their fanciful notions; for the types of human beings they portray, or for the broad human experiences they convey. In addition, we may feel fascinated by and even sympathetic to the personality, sensibility, soul, and character of such authors themselves.

Writers and artists of this sort Nabokov also consigned to his public wastebasket. For him, Cervantes's *Don Quixote* is a "crude romance," and he condemns the Spaniard for alleged "cruelty." (This from the man who wrote *Laughter in the Dark*.) In addition, Dostoevsky, Céline, and van Gogh are grouped into this pitiful "human interest" bunch, and Stendhal is dispatched as "that novelist for people who like their French prose plain."

As the years progressed, Nabokov's list of hates grew longer, as well as seemingly irrational and arbitrary, though probably motivated in some measure by sheer competitiveness. Writing to Edmund Wilson he

---

[5] Boyd, 570 and 648.
[6] Karlinsky, letter 205 (17 April 1950), p., 263.

dismisses Henry James as a "complete fake" and also a "pale porpoise"[7]—
an alliteration as amusing as it is meaningless." Others at whom he lets fly:
the Greek tragedians, Molière, and Henry Fielding (*Tom Jones* is "drab").
He did praise Beckett's "lovely novellas" in an interview, yet dispatched
the Franco-Irishman's dramatic works as "wretched plays in the
Maeterlinck tradition" (SO, 172), and elsewhere he also likened Borges,
with implied faint praise, to Anatole France. Given Nabokov's own
distaste for "school" labels, comparisons of this kind doubly qualify as
cheap shots.

The exquisite Russian-American's enemies' list further expands within
the covers of *Ada*. This thick book is one of a kind in the history of fiction,
for among its salient tics are its relentless, bilious, high-handed attacks on
other authors. I cannot think of any other work of prose narrative that takes
on as its sub-agenda so grandiose a demolition job. Hence Faulkner and
Mann are conflated as "Faulknermann," Steinbeck becomes "Old
Beckstein," and Malraux and Henry Miller put in cameo appearances as
"Le Malheureux" and "Heinrich Müller," respectively. There are several
swipes at Eliot, reinvented as "Milton Eliot" and as "K. L. Sween"
(playing on the Sweeney poems), purported author of the poem *The
Waistline*. Borges is now rebaptized "Osberg," a creator of "pretentious
fairy tales." Nabokov turns on both Robert Lowell and W. H. Auden,
fusing them into "Lowden, a minor poet and translator."[8] One wonders:
what have both Lowell and Auden done to deserve this?

While most of Nabokov's academic devotees tend to remain silent
about this unattractive side of their master, some scattered voices have
seen fit to criticize his facile potshots. Page Stegner, in the very first full-
length study of Nabokov, in 1966, frankly characterizes the novelist's
"arrogant and intolerant" views as mere "invective" and "name-calling,"
and notes as one of Nabokov's major weaknesses as literary critic a
proclivity for "settling a score rather than judging the work."[9] David
Rampton likewise sees Nabokov's incessant verbal volleys as little more
than "glib dismissals, not argument."[10]

Sometimes Professor Nabokov's summary verdicts could impinge on
his classroom pedagogy. Brian Boyd provides the following revealing
anecdote about Nabokov's clash with a male student of his at Cornell:

---

[7] Karlinsky, letter 249 (10 August 1952), p. 308.
[8] Cited at length in Douglas Fowler, *Reading Nabokov*, 185 ff.
[9] Page Stegner, *Escape into Aesthetics*, 42 and 134.
[10] David Rampton, *Vladimir Nabokov*, 12.

In mid-March [1957], Nabokov was lecturing in his survey of Russian
literature when a student rose to his feet and requested that he be allowed
to talk about Dostoevsky for a class period if Nabokov would not.
Afterwards Nabokov stormed to the English department office, quite
apoplectic with rage, and demanded the student be expelled. He was not.
Instead the student began to boycott Nabokov's classes in protest against
his treatment of committed writers. Often reluctant to credit the
intelligence of those who disagreed with him, Nabokov for the remainder
of the term noted in his diary whether the "idiot" was present or not in
class: only six times out of twenty. The young man, a star student, one of
the brasher young fiction writers in Cornell's creative writing program,
received an F on the exam. He went to Arthur Mizener and M. H. Abrams
to complain. Convinced that Nabokov was overreacting, they asked him to
reconsider the grade. He would not.[11]

It is an incident that shows Nabokov in the less–than-flattering role of
carrying on, albeit on a tiny scale, his Russian homeland's despotic
traditions. Or, at the very least, his unwillingness to listen to other viewpoints
than his own—and his near-hysterical response to being challenged.

Nabokov's list of salvageable authors could be counted on the fingers
of two pairs of hands. Among his fortunate few, predictably, are the
acknowledged practitioners of high Modernism: Flaubert, Kafka, Joyce,
Proust, Bely—and himself. (When lecturing at U. S. campuses, he was
wont to discreetly insert his Russian pen name "Sirin" as he recited the roll
call of literary grand masters.) At the same time, in his own theory and
practice he diverges from those greats and their desire to convey deeper
truths about their worlds and about human existence. For Nabokov, artifice
is all, and "reality" belongs in quotation marks. Curiously, he derided the
stream-of-consciousness technique as artificial, presumably because of its
psychological, subjective emphasis.

For genuine artistry among living French authors Nabokov singled out
Alain Robbe-Grillet and also declared *La jalousie* a great novel.[12] During
their lifetime, of course, Robbe-Grillet and the practitioners of the *nouveau
roman* drew considerable attention among literary circles and were
frequent figures on the campus lecture circuit. Their ideas and works
served as prime instances of a deliberate, programmatic exclusion of
human content from fiction—not to mention a general coldness. Today the
movement stands at best as a notable if failed experiment as well as an
artistic dead end.

---

[11] Boyd, *Vladimir Nabokov: The American Years*, 308.
[12] Schiff, 249.

*

One of Ayn Rand's stated mentors, oddly enough, was Dostoevsky, whose personal religious outlook would obviously have had no appeal for her. Rather she singles out "his superb mastery of plot-structure" and her former compatriot's "merciless dissection of the psychology of evil" (RM, 53). Rand thus learned from his techniques of suspense and then reversed the moral terms, depicting instead the psychology of evil altruists. Moreover, though she doesn't state it, her affinity for the author of *The Brothers Karamazov* is as a novelist of ideas. Dostoevsky's greatest works are in some degree Platonic dialogues between moral or philosophic stances, with entire chapters sometimes representing one position or another. This trait is, indeed, among the reasons for Dostoevsky's appeal to passionate young students who are just discovering the world of ideas yet lack the life experience to grasp the day-to-day realities unfolded in the capacious works of, say, a Tolstoy.

Rand, conversely, loathed Tolstoy because "his philosophy and his sense of life, are not merely mistaken but evil" (RM, 55)—even if in almost the same breath she praises the mystico-religious Dostoevsky. Moreover she never really states what Tolstoy's "philosophy" is. Does she mean his historical determinism? His celebration of family ties? His unusual feel for the texture of the quotidian? His utopian socialism? His Christianity? Perhaps all of these. Still, just as Nabokov did with other authors, she condemns *Anna Karenina* as "the most evil book in serious literature" (RM, 104), with no explanation or arguments as to why. Similarly, Shakespeare is anathematized by Rand as the alleged father of Naturalism (RM, 103). She inveighs against the latter school because it depicts society as determining people's fates (RM, 104). Rand likewise attacks the Greek tragedians and, again, the evil Shakespeare for the philosophical sin of determinism.

Aside from these extensive hates, most of Rand's discussions of literature are rather conventionally focused on the agreed-upon past masters such as Dostoevsky and Hugo. On modern writers, in most of whom she perceives "the mannered artificiality of a second-hander" (RM, 52), she has, by contrast, little to say. In a marvelous instance of projection, she snipes at Mann's *Magic Mountain* for featuring (of all things) "lengthy and abstract discussions of ... ideas" (RM, 63)—a phrase that fits her own big tomes to a T. (One is reminded of Nabokov objecting to *Don Quixote* on account of its "cruelty.") Otherwise we can safely say that such contemporary authors as Joyce, Proust, Kafka, Faulkner, and Woolf meant nothing to La Rand. In her own tautological words, "Except for the exceptions, there is no literature (and no art) today" (RM, 108). Not surprisingly, as Barbara Branden points out more than once in her pioneering biography, Rand was never a dedicated reader and, while in New York, she scarcely took advantage of the city's offerings in music and ballet. Significantly, a pair of Randian disciples, Michelle Kamhi and Louis Torres, coauthored and published in the year 2000 a volume on aesthetics that in great measure consists of a wholesale denunciation of the entire Modernist canon. Their title, *What Art Is: The Esthetic Theory of Ayn Rand*, clearly takes as its template Tolstoy's *What Is Art?* Ironically, given Rand's contempt for Tolstoy, they share in Tolstoy's general dismissal of virtually all contemporary literature, painting, and music.

Rand's roster of worthwhile recent authors is even more exiguous than Nabokov's, though of a different kind. The writer on whom she lavished praise the most was the maker of hard-boiled pulp fictions, Mickey Spillane, who in the 1940s and '50s, along with his most famous novel *I, the Jury*, were almost household words. (Thanks to a few TV series, his tough-guy detective, Mike Hammer, is today better known than is its creator.) In a syndicated piece for the *Los Angeles Times*, Rand lauded as Spillane's signature traits his "plot ingenuity and moralistic style" as well as his portrayal of the struggle between "good and evil." To Rand, the literary neglect suffered by Spillane was the result of "vicious injustice on the part of the 'intellectuals.'"[13] In the same vein, Rand saw fit to defend Margaret Mitchell, and she classes *Gone with the Wind* as comparable to *Les Misérables* (RM, 58).

The author whom Rand most esteems, however, is Ayn Rand. Her literary essays come chock-full of allusions to her own book titles, and the abundant citations from her own works can take up entire pages, even multiple successive pages. As her recent biographers have noted, with the passage of time, Rand's writing and the Rand cult became increasingly "self-reflexive."

*

In my days as a rebellious grad student and greenhorn instructor, there were a few years in which I truly believed that realist narrative, built as it was around linear plot and well-rounded character, had outlived both its cultural purposes and its artistic usefulness. Head over heels at the time with Beckett's minimalism, and swept away by the new wave of Latin Americans (Borges, Cortázar, García Márquez, et al.) as well as by such

---

[13] Heller, 311.

American fabulists as Pynchon, Coover, Barthelme, I saw no reason to learn about writing from past masters. In addition, my being a musician (however incomplete), coupled with my ethereal bent, had made me a rather unobservant sort, clueless as to the details of day-to-day existence—which are, of course, the nuts and bolts of narrative realism.

Not that I went as far as the "to hell with the classics" crowd. I still thought that the ancient Greeks, most of Shakespeare, the humorist Cervantes and the rest of the lot were really the best we've got (apologies, dear reader, for the double rhyme). I was in some way love-struck by Jane Austen's intelligence and wit, and had scant sympathy for the snippy classmates who brushed her off as prissy and irrelevant. (I wouldn't have traded her for, say, Djuna Barnes, as a fellow student once suggested.) But in my spirit of contestation I sincerely felt that authors of her ilk had had their day, and that newer, bolder, and much improved ways of writing about our current condition were upon us.

In my early thirties, though—dare I say?— I rediscovered realism. One decisive push in that phase was my marriage to Audrey, with her innate bent towards traditional storytelling. Over the first decade or so of our life as a couple we would read together dozens of books by the old masters: Balzac, the Brontës, George Eliot, Trollope, Wilkie Collins, Henry James, along with Tolstoy's *Karenina*, Jane Austen's lesser-known works, and a host of others. My spouse was my co-learner and, in part, she was my teacher of realism and its beauties. Thanks to our joint reading program, this humble literary scribbler's understanding of both life and literature were much deepened. Such are the benefits of the married life...

Still, even in my days of headiest rebellion it would never have occurred to me to consign hundreds of authors to the trash heap simply because I disagreed with their aesthetic or their subject matter. In this regard I always found Nabokov's brand of dogmatism to be as repugnant as that of the Soviets and their fellow-travelers or successors abroad. Aesthetic intolerance can turn as narrow, hidebound, and pernicious as is the political or sexual or religious kind. Many are the ways of "doing" literature. Those ways come and go. They each have their exits, their entrances, their dramatis personae—their acknowledged masters, their journeymen, their tinkerer-craftspeople, their incomplete geniuses, their flashes in the pan, their disappointments, and yes, their second-raters and mediocrities. Yet rather than feeling outraged at the mediocrities, I am far more often overcome by a certain sadness when encountering a touching poem or short story, a subtle movie, a dazzling art installation, or a rousing piano sonata that at most will reach a few hundred souls … and then pass into oblivion.

The Greats are the greats. There are some whom not all of us can thoroughly like or understand, due to our personal prejudices, temperaments, or backgrounds. But although the greats are there for us to admire, I can at the same time respect a small, well-crafted piece of work that, within its limits, does its best with its chosen materials and conveys something special of its own.

For some ten years, Audrey and I attended Montreal's World Film Festival at the end of the summers. From Friday through Monday we would take in as many as six movies per diem. We viewed feature films from Portugal, Catalonia, Romania, China, Mexico, among others, as well as from obscure corners of the U.S. And what often struck me about most of those products was their high artistic quality, along with the near-certainty that, following a few weeks in the theatres, they would pretty much be gone, vanish, become footnotes to history. There were also countless short subjects that, at very best, could hope for a TV screening in their home countries once their brief and rarefied festival life was over. The experience served as a reminder of just how much good art is being made around our world, and how little of it will attract the audience it may well deserve.

Owing to this outlook, I never could have felt in the least sympathetic to Nabokov's total and uncharitable nastiness toward any literature that did not assume his specially valued form of aestheticist Greatness...

CHAPTER EIGHT

ON THE MATTER OF THINKERS, REVISITED

Yes, thinkers again.

Few literary authors qualify as thinkers. Most of them function not within the ethereal realms of higher thought but down in the more concrete workshops of imagery, rhythm, and rhyme, of setting, characterization, description, and plot. Some, as in the case of Nabokov, can be quite gauche when it comes to abstract, intellectual exposition. They may have doctrines, beliefs, prejudices, but for most authors that is all.

On the other hand, there have been imaginative writers for whom ideas are natural territory. Milton wrote political theory, as did the great Spanish poet Quevedo and of course Rousseau, who was an effective novelist, thinker, and even opera composer. Coleridge and George Eliot were well-versed in the German thought of their time. Matthew Arnold is as highly regarded for his cultural reflections as for his eminently quotable verse. Sartre and Camus each made their mark in both thought and fiction. Brecht and Dos Passos, being committed leftists, knew their Marxist theory. And T. S. Eliot actually completed an entire Ph.D. dissertation on the British idealist philosopher F. H. Bradley. These are exceptional rather than typical cases, however.

Ayn Rand was, by temperament, a thinker who wrote narratives filled with long stretches of abstract discussion. She turned to straight essay-writing only in the wake of her profound disillusionment with the hostile reception given her would-be magnum opus, *Atlas Shrugged*. Rand is a thinker, though, only in the same way that, say, Dale Carnegie or Norman Vincent Peale are thinkers. Like those two American epigones, she pushed a pop doctrine of self-help, novelizing it with broad swatches of intrigue and sex, and her fiction and non-fiction belong within that line of U.S. commercial genre-writing, a mass market literature that continues with Rhonda Byrnes's massive, 2006 best-seller, *The Secret*. (Some representative samples from the latter: "Your thoughts are the primary cause of everything." "Expect the things you want." "Prosperity is your birthright."

"Visualize checks in the mail."[1] Think this way, dear reader, and everything will turn out just right!)

About Rand's epistemology, there is nothing new. Her focus on reason is as old as philosophy itself. Her moral system, we saw in chapter 4, is essentially a popularized, vulgarized, and stealthily Americanized distillation of Nietzsche. And her grand conception of history is little more than the standard, official, Euro-American, post-Enlightenment narrative about Western Man's triumphal emergence out of primitive tribalism, naked savagery, and religious superstition into the glories of technological progress and individualism. Most of the rest amounts to filler and local color, along with her personal narcissism and dislike of family elevated to the status of a universal principle.

Rand's work reveals few signs of any dialogue with the thinkers of the past, and of course the crucial, formative Nietzschean content is carefully hidden from view. The one philosopher whom she regularly invokes is Aristotle, owing, presumably, to the ancient Greek's belief in an external world. Plato, by contrast, she condemns as "the father of Communism." In Rand's view, as noted earlier, most other thinkers (including Descartes, Kant, and Wittgenstein) did not believe in objective reality—though she'd scarcely read them, as some close friends eventually conceded, following her demise. Instead, she picked up on a few formulaic, even false notions of their thought by chatting with those of her followers who did have a working knowledge of the tradition. At one point she also whipped up among her cultists a curious anti-Kant campaign; hence for a spell one frequently saw conventions of Randians wearing buttons saying "Kant" with the diagonal slash cutting through the hated Teuton's name. In keeping with her cavalier treatment of other philosophers, she once wrote a review of John Rawls's *A Theory of Justice* without so much as having skimmed the Harvard professor's book, consulting the reviewers instead.[2]

So we have in Ayn Rand an unusual case: a writer considered, by herself and by her many followers, as the greatest philosopher of all time—yet who had at best a casual, selective dilettante's knowledge of the field of philosophy. She was, in Jungian terms, a thinking type, but a "thinker" in only the broadest and most charitable possible sense of the word.

*

---

[1] Rhonda Byrne, *The Secret*, pp. 33, 93, 109, and 111, respectively.
[2] Walker, *The Ayn Rand Cult*, pp. 100 and 224.

Nabokov was wont to employing the word "thinker" as a pejorative and often consigned it to the irony of quotation marks to boot. The tag "Fake thinkers," for instance, crops up just after "Freud, Marx" in fictive poet John Shade's long list of hates—hates that just happen to be Nabokov's, too—in line 990 of his poem "Pale Fire." But as we saw earlier, Nabokov's recurrent animus against thinkers, real or fake, might actually have grown out of certain intellectual incapacities on his part.

Nabokov's hatred of one particular thinker, Freud, is the stuff of legend. The rancor was long with him; as early as 1925, in a talk in Berlin, he attacked the Austrian. Most of his later novels contain a potshot or two either at the original psychoanalyst or at psychoanalysis in general. And in most of the prefaces added to the English translations of his earlier Russian works he vents his fury at "the Viennese quack" or applies some other angry epithet. Similarly, early in his memoir *Speak, Memory* he snipes at "the vulgar, shabby, fundamentally medieval world of Freud" (*SM*, 20). He also fulminated freely at Freud in his Cornell lectures; in a passage from his archives, cited by Brian Boyd, the novelist reports with glee that, in 1952, a female student actually got up and walked out on the class when he launched into his "Viennese quack" routine.[3]

Not surprisingly, Jeffrey Berman, in his book *The Talking Cure: Literary Representations of Psychoanalysis*, dedicates an entire chapter to Nabokov. As the author observes, "Nabokov's virulence is astonishing and unsoftened by time. The invective is bitter, mirthless, and unprecedented."[4] Moreover, Berman rightly notes, few of Nabokov's critics have shown themselves to be disturbed by his rabid ravings, and many in fact accept or even agree with it.[5] Berman also observes that, from the Russian's frequent fumings, one would never know that Freud was a victim of Nazism who had to take refuge in England and whose four sisters died in concentration camps.[6]

What is conspicuously absent from Nabokov's strident anti-Freudianism are any counter-arguments or even any concrete references to his works. He seems to believe that Freud is nothing more than sex-and-Oedipus, and appears oblivious to the Austrian's contributions toward shedding light on such matters as the unconscious mind, underlying human instincts, sexuality both infantile and adult as a factor in human development, and the role of parental, filial and sibling emotions in the shaping of a child's long-term psyche. Instead he concentrates his firepower on the feeblest

[3] Boyd, *Vladimir Nabokov: The American Years,* p. 221.
[4] Berman, *The Talking Cure*, p. 213.
[5] Ibid., p. 214.
[6] Ibid., pp. 218-19.

specimens of Freudian lit-crit. Among his precious few attempts at "debate" with psychoanalysis is a brief endnote by Charles Kinbote in *Pale Fire*, wherein the annotator quotes Erich Fromm's rather forced Freudian interpretation of the Little Red Riding Hood story and then says simply "Do those clowns really *believe* what they teach?" (PF, 271; note to line 929)

Nabokov, I believe, had certain deeper, personal motives for despising Freud and also Marx, an issue I shall discuss in my next chapter. Based on his biographies, however, I would venture to speculate that the Russian novelist did virtually no reading of these thinkers' work. As early as 1966, Page Stegner flatly stated that "[Nabokov's] fiction demonstrates no extensive knowledge of Freud."[7] As with Rand, whose knowledge of the philosophic canon came to her only via hearsay, I will be so bold as to infer that Nabokov likewise picked up bits of pieces of Freud that were in the air and were becoming commonplace in American intellectual discourse, especially on the campuses. The same goes for Marx, which in his time had become debased by Bolshevik sloganeering—probably the only Marxism that Nabokov had ever encountered. The notion that Marxian thought had also entered the vocabulary of social science, and that such topics as economic causation, social stratum, and class conflict were part of a widely accepted type of historical analysis, were simply beyond Nabokov's limited ken.

Nabokov was not above making similarly rash pronouncements in scientific fields about which he knew nothing. In private he expressed reservations about Darwin's view of evolution as a struggle for existence and flirted with a theory of quasi-intelligent design of his own eccentric making.[8] In an interview he admits to ignorance of physics yet takes a potshot against "Einstein's slick formulae" (*sic*; SO, 116), though his early biographer Andrew Field suggests that the novelist's distaste for the renowned scientist might well have been motivated by a distaste for Einstein's left-wing politics.[9] Similarly, in his valedictory novel, *Look at the Harlequins!*, the author has his narrator take a swipe at a place called "Neochomsk" and "the about-nothing land of philosophic linguistics" (124-25). How much Nabokov knew about linguistics is a matter for investigation, but one can feel fairly sure that he would have had no truck with Noam Chomsky's dissident politics.

Nabokov pushes his own anti-Einstein stance to the heights of pompous absurdity in a long paragraph in *Ada*, in which, as with other

---

[7] Stegner, *Escape into Aesthetics*, p. 43.
[8] Boyd, p. 37.
[9] Field, *Nabokov: His Life in Art*, p. 199.

contemptible figures, Einstein is rebaptized as "Engelwein." Van Veen in his essay on "The Texture of Time" declares thus:

> At this point ... I should say something about my attitude to "Relativity." It is not sympathetic. What many cosmogonists tend to accept as an objective truth is really the flaw inherent in mathematics which parades as truth. The body of the astonished person moving in Space is shortened in the direction of motion and shrinks catastrophically as the velocity nears the speed beyond which by a fishy formula, no speed can be. That is his bad luck, not mine—Time, which requires the utmost purity of consciousness to be properly apprehended, is the most rational element of life, and my reason feels insulted by those flights of Technology Fiction. One especially grotesque inference, drawn (I think, by Engelwein) from Relativity Theory—and destroying it, if drawn correctly—is that the galactonaut and his domestic animals, after touring the speed spas of Space, would return younger than if they had stayed at home all the time (411-12).

Suffice it to say that Einstein never made so preposterous an inferential leap about travelers moving at the speed of light and coming back younger than when they departed. Such notions are rather the stuff of sci.fi. fantasies in comic books and pulp magazines. Once again, as with Freud and Marx, the Russian-American artificer builds his snide caricature not on the ideas themselves, but on the bastardized, vulgarized, folk offshoots that circulate in the commercial press.

Both Rand and Nabokov mocked or attacked major figures in thought and science, with little or no knowledge of them. Being coddled celebrities, they presumed to know it all, much in the way of pampered adolescents. Had they engaged in such flagrantly ignorant, unfounded, scurrilous ranting in a high-school classroom, they would have earned an easy F. It is not a pretty picture.

CHAPTER NINE

ON DETERMINISM VS. BEING SELF-MADE, LIKE MR. BOUNDERBY & OTHERS

Among the unstated reasons for Rand's and Nabokov's hostility to such thinkers as Marx and Freud is their own profound and resolute *anti*-determinism. In their view, a human being is, potentially at least, an absolutely autonomous entity. As the two Russian-Americans saw it, there are ultimately no forces, inner or outer, that shape a person. There are no instincts, there is no unconscious, there is only free, conscious will. In her *Playboy* interview, Rand flatly denied the existence of irrational, biological drives. As she put it, "To begin with, man does not possess any instincts."[1] By the same token, society is no factor in human choice. Again Rand, in her talk entitled "The Objectivist Ethics," says, "there is no such entity as 'society,' since society is only a number of individual men" (VS, 14-15). Nabokov, for his part, never expressed his notions in such bald and brash terms, but many of his passing statements add up indirectly to a similar blanket denial of any biological or social causation whatsoever.

The flipside of the Russian pair's anti-determinism, conversely, is the high value they assign to any individual who is, as it were, self-made—including the self-made individuals Ayn Rand and Vladimir Nabokov. Thus, those contemptible souls who allow themselves to be shaped by their environments lead "second-hand lives" (Rand's phrase) or rate scarcely higher than corpses (Nabokov's metaphor). Standing behind these larger assumptions is a hidden series of reasonings, to wit: 1) Whereas, under Communism, there is much control and little freedom, and 2) in America and in the West, by contrast, there are fewer controls and much more freedom, 3) ergo in the West, there are no determining factors, no social forces shaping human beings. It never seems to have occurred to the Russian-Americans that their hatred of Communism was itself a product of their experience of Communism. Their simplistic anti-determinism does

---

[1] Toffler, *Playboy* Interview, p. 39.

not allow for the emergence of oppositional forces in human development and history.

Hand in hand with Ayn Rand's absolute anti-determinism goes her personal cult of the free-standing individual who allegedly depends on no one. The motto of John Galt and the concluding words in his seventy-page manifesto readily sum up this position. Citing again: "I swear—by my life and my love of it—that I will never live for the sake of another man, nor ask another man to live for mine" (AS, 993). The declaration would become the proud motto of many a would-be John Galt around U.S. college and corporate corridors.

Similarly, in Rand's epilogue to the novel, she briefly describes her development as a writer, and in her second paragraph she proudly proclaims, "No one helped me, nor did I think at any time that it was anyone's duty to help me" (1085). This is a wondrous claim, the most charitable interpretation of which is that wealth and position may have been blurring Rand's selective memory at the time. We have already seen the enormous amount of *help* that Rand received from her mother (those jewels that paid her passage to the U.S.), her Chicago relatives (free room and board, money, a train ticket, a letter of reference), the Studio Club in Hollywood (subsidized housing), Cecil B. DeMille (that fateful ride), her husband Frank (green card and much more), the advice of novelist Isabel Paterson (who suggested that she clear the manuscript of *Fountainhead* of all topical references), her courageous editor at Bobbs-Merrill (who stuck out his neck for her). And that's just for starters. At that Studio Club, where she lived for three years, she often got behind in rent payments but was never kicked out. In the 1930s, when times were tough, a friend named Albert Mannheimer lent her $500. The list goes on and on; as Jeff Walker pointedly and eloquently notes, "In these and so many other respects Rand was the beneficiary of the charitable impulses of others. Once she had exhausted their use to her, she wrote novels and essays which downgraded such impulses and deprived them of justification."[2] In the 1,000-plus pages of *Atlas Shrugged*, then, there is at least one crucial and objective falsehood.

Meanwhile, as a corollary to her denial of biology as a determining force, Rand generally saw physical disease rather as the (deserved) consequence of an individual's philosophic errors and "bad premises." Flagrantly defying the medical researches of her time, she sported a long cigarette holder, smoked like a turbine, and exhorted the same of her young followers as an expression of their individual liberty.

---

[2] Jeff Walker, *The Ayn Rand Cult*, p. 244.

The goddess of fire eventually contracted pulmonary cancer. While under treatment and in convalescence she alienated many of her friends, making their lives miserable with her endless monologues about her terrible, suffering state. In the words of Anne Heller, "She was an obstreperous patient."[3] Moreover, her lung surgery was paid for by Medicare, without which she would have probably ended up in bankruptcy. (So much for the creator of mighty bulwark John Galt, who will ask no man to live for him.)

During recovery and the aftermath, she would not allow the news of her dread illness to leak out. And although she did personally give up smoking, she refused to announce the decision and continued to hold steadfast to her view that there was no proven link between tobacco and cancer.

Self-help. The self-made man. These are among the most treasured folk ideas in the American civil religion. They predate Rand and would have remained as a force with or without her, but she brought to them the combined allure of "science," theory, and sexual intrigue. How valid are such notions, though?

The first chapter's title of *Atlas* asks, "Who Is John Galt?" The enigmatic query functions as a kind of proverb that recurs throughout the book and will be answered in the course of the narrative. In reply, I've a question of my own, to wit, "Who Is Mr. Bounderby?" Readers of Dickens's *Hard Times* will recall Josiah Bounderby, the comically bumptious "banker, merchant, manufacturer and what not," a self-styled "self-made man" (13) who boasts at length about his rags-to-riches story.[4] At every turn Bounderby harps on his mother and grandmother, two wicked women who abandoned him as a child. And he dwells repeatedly on "the gutter I had lifted myself out of" (121) with "nobody to thank but myself" (14).

Towards the end, however, Bounderby's mom accidentally shows up. Before some gathered guests the good woman innocently remarks that little Josiah was raised by loving parents who worked hard to further his education. Moreover, mum and dad eventually apprenticed their boy to "a kind master" who did much to "lend him a hand" (248).

Bounderby becomes a mite sheepish thereafter...

Meanwhile, once again, who was my father? And how does he fit into this picture? As we have seen in chapter 3, the self-made entrepreneur depended on my mom's savings for his initial investments and then on her

---

[3] Heller, p. 392.
[4] Charles Dickens, *Hard Times*. Page references from this work will be cited parenthetically within the text.

unpaid secretarial labors for the daily running of his Caribbean businesses. Meanwhile, every deal he made was supposed to be the Big One that would set him up for life. Among his favorite books at the time was Napoleon Hill's *Think and Grow Rich*, one of the classics of the American self-help genre. After some thirteen years of this arrangement, however, he abandoned my mother for the blonde Cuban.

What interests me for our purposes, though, is not my father's special virtues as a father and spouse but his world-view. His twin obsessions were money and "self-reliance." Among his last written statements to my mother was, "Everything I have I've earned by the sweat of my brow." Ironically, it was my mother's death and my subsequent discovery of the hundreds of letters written by the couple to each other that allowed me to understand the vast extent of the self-made man's mythmaking, the degree to which Bell Sr. had leaned on his wife's initial finances and on her unsung labors in order to sustain his enterprises. Even after the divorce, when he moved into manufacturing, he always latched on to assorted godfather figures who supported his ambitions. Mr. Self-Reliance relied not on himself alone.

Given La Rand, Mr. Bounderby, my dad, and what I know about them, I have grown deeply skeptical of anyone who boasts, "I made it on my own. Nobody helped me." Self-made manhood, in my view, is a reigning myth that is best scrapped, if only because every successful man has been helped by someone, perhaps by many someones—whether parents, teachers, relatives, friends, colleagues, romantic partners of either sex, or even casual strangers, not to mention government-funded entities such as schools, roads, water supplies, sewage disposal, the postal system, and the G. I. Bill, and more recently, space satellites and the Internet, all brought to you by the friendly Feds. If a person's success was in business, surely there were also employees, whom we sometimes refer to, let us not forget, as "the help." By way of analogy, try to imagine an Army officer proclaiming, "I took Normandy Beach on my own! No one helped me!" Or a baseball club owner bragging, "I won the World Series on my own! No one helped me!" Such notions seem absurd, inconceivable, and yet we readily accept comparable rhetoric from individuals in banking or manufacturing or other less glamorous or less media-worthy walks of life—and from Ayn Rand, Inc.

*

Nabokov, for his part, in his annual Cornell lecture on *Madame Bovary*, regularly and swiftly dispatched "environment" as "by far the least important" of the forces that shape a human being (LL, 126). In a more caustic comment toward the end of *Speak, Memory*, while considering his infant son Dmitri, the novelist speculates on every child's desire "to reshape the earth, to act upon a friable environment," and then adds the parenthetical observation, "unless he is a born Marxist or a corpse and meekly waits for the environment to shape *him*" (SM, 302).

In the light of that observation, let us look back again at Nabokov's own history. Thanks to the resident tutors provided by his father, he picked up fluent, idiomatic English and French, languages in which he would later write. His head-start in English especially allowed him the means to master its prose style without his having to go through the beginning and intermediate learning stages as a grown adult. His boxing lessons, also a gift from Nabokov *père*, gave the young man a significant resource in a violent world—a skill he utilized on occasion. His parents of course encouraged him in all his activities and talents—lepidopteral, literary, athletic, synesthetic. And just as Rand's mother sold her jewels in order to pay for daughter Alyssa/Ayn's emigration to America, Nabokov's mum sold her gems to defray the costs of her eldest son's studies at Cambridge.

Most important of all, the affectionate, supportive *environment* in which Nabokov was raised would help build in him the supreme self-confidence that, throughout his life, was to bolster his sense of self-worth as a person and a writer. As biographer Boyd tellingly notes, "A loving family had provided Nabokov with an unexampled serenity of mind" that would sustain him during the long, lean years.[5] Still, it is not improbable that, much like his anti-determinist compatriot Rand, Nabokov might have disagreed with my characterizations, instead construing his unusual self-confidence and serenity as somehow self-willed, dependent on no external, environmental inputs. Meanwhile, it's worth noting that, when Nabokov's finances were at destitution levels, Nabokov, like Rand, received loans and gifts from friends, including a bestowal of 2,500 French francs sent to him via cable in 1939 by the admiring composer-pianist Rachmaninoff.

Nabokov's lifelong marriage to Véra Slonim is, for many Nabokovophiles, a textbook example of a near-perfect union. In their history as a couple, one sees an astounding intellectual, cultural, and spiritual compatibility. Stacy Schiff, Véra's biographer, describes it as "one of the great love stories" and quotes novelist William Maxwell as saying, "It was as close a marriage as I was ever present at."[6]

[5] Boyd, *Vladimir Nabokov: The American Years*, p. 6.
[6] Schiff, *Véra*, pp. xii and xi, respectively.

Yet the import of Nabokov's marriage goes even deeper than that, down to the most practical, day-to-day details. The confidently independent novelist also leaned on Véra for many of his most basic needs. Like Rand, he never learned to drive an automobile, and for getting about in America he depended on his spouse, who also changed flat tires and scraped the winter snow off the windshield. When the couple would go grocery shopping in Ithaca, Véra would cart and unload the filled-up bags while Vladimir notoriously remained sitting in the passenger's seat. The same pattern obtained with suitcases during their travels, which she toted for the two them. Véra also typed all of his longhand manuscripts and handled all his business mail. On his way to classes at Cornell, she would carry his briefcase, open the door for him, and then sit at the podium throughout the length of the lecture. She helped him read and grade student papers as well.

In this regard, one can safely say that Nabokov was not "a born Marxist or a corpse who waits meekly for the environment to shape *him*." To cite William Maxwell once again, "He would have been nowhere without her."[7] Or as Marc Slonim, the professor of Russian and occasional literary journalist, said, "very few women aside from Véra would be able to tolerate Nabokov's monomaniacal approach to literature."[8]

In addition, in the 1950s, Nabokov sent his early teen-aged son Dmitri to a private boarding school in New Hampshire. The decision, which would cost the Cornell professor a full third of his modest academic salary, was aimed at protecting the boy from "the hooligan argot of public-school playgrounds."[9] One cannot but admire so caring an act of parental sacrifice and love, while at the same time note its obviously contradicting Nabokov's staunch denial of environmental influence on a child.

In sum, this is why I believe that Nabokov's animus against Freud has less to do with any specific details of the Austrian's system than with the broader fact of Freudianism as a species of psychological determinism. In one of the few instances in which he actually engages Freudian arguments in something like debate (rather than merely resort to his curt, Soviet-style slogans and fierce invective), Nabokov raises the following possibility:

> The Freudian faith leads to dangerous ethical consequences, such as when a filthy murderer … is given a lighter sentence because his mother spanked him too much or too little—it works both ways (SO, 116).

---

[7] Ibid., p. xii.
[8] Ibid., p. 87.
[9] Boyd, *Vladimir Nabokov: The American Years*, p. 131.

The scenario raised here is completely hypothetical, a fantastical and grotesque caricature of both Freud and the U.S. justice system. To my (admittedly scanty) knowledge, no defense has been made or could be made of an accused criminal on such grounds; indeed it would be rightly greeted in court with disbelief and derision. Nor would leniency be granted in the wake of such absurd legal reasoning. So far-fetched a notion is on a par with Nabokov's similar dismissal of Einstein (discussed in my previous chapter), an equally wild extrapolation, built on a similarly erroneous premise. But, to elaborate on my earlier statement: Nabokov's anti-Freudian fury was directed not so much at Freud himself as at a larger cultural phenomenon—namely, the Freudianism that took shape in the 1940s as the dominant form of determinism within U.S. intellectual and clinical circles, just as had happened yet more crudely with Marxism under Soviet rule in Russia. One wonders what Nabokov would have made of other, even more deterministic theories such as behaviorism, sociobiology, neuroscience, and evolutionary psychology. Freud for Nabokov was merely a convenient target, the most visible one.

Yet another aspect, itself psychological, of Nabokov's endless tempest-in-a-samovar against a "Viennese quack," merits our close attention. Freud, as we know, is very much the scientist—and the poet—of our hidden, innermost drives, of our invisible and submerged psyche. It is not for nothing that Freud in his work occasionally credits the poets and novelists with having intuited the unconscious long before he himself did. (There is much in Dostoevsky or in Nietzsche, for instance, that looks ahead to Freud's most fundamental insights.)

In this regard, Nabokov appears to have been a writer and a man with virtually no inner demons, no second thoughts, no regrets to cope with. He would thus feel no kindred sympathy for a science of spiritual inner conflict like psychoanalysis, or for authors such as Dostoevsky or Sartre, in whose narratives a good man's inward anguish can take center stage. Not for him something so impalpable as the dark night of the soul... Nabokov did, in his forties, begin to entertain some guilt over the earlier ill treatment and rejection he had dealt his younger brother Sergey, a homosexual and outspoken anti-Nazi who died in a German concentration camp near Hamburg. That, however, is about the only recorded case of Nabokov's express regret. As philosopher Richard Rorty speculates, "Nabokov seems never to have suffered a loss for which he blamed himself, never to have despised, distrusted, or doubted himself."[10]

---

[10] Rorty, "The Barber of Kasbeam," p. 155.

In sum, Rand and Nabokov shared common intellectual and ideological ground in their absolute negation of any hint of determinism, whether biological or social. Rand denied that instincts and society exist precisely because she wished to believe that men are—or at least should be—completely free to acquire wealth without acknowledging the help of others. In the case of Nabokov, an obsessive loathing of Marx and Freud was in reality a pronounced, extreme symptom of his much larger, indeed total rejection of environmental influences. Interestingly enough, as far back as 1948, Edmund Wilson in a friendly letter to the novelist, wondered how he, Nabokov, could study butterflies in their habitat, yet also "pretend that it is possible to write about human beings and leave out of account all question of society and the environment."[11] No subsequent critic, to my knowledge, would ever see fit to challenge Nabokov's negationist dogma as did Wilson in this passage—a uniquely insightful moment in the history of Nabokoviana that stands alone.

---

[11] Karlinsky, letter 186 (15 November 1948), p. 238.

CHAPTER TEN

ON POLITICS AND SOCIETY

Rand's and Nabokov's political views, and their respective visions of society, are remarkably congruent, though they may differ in their details and emphases. Each of the Russian-American pair had relatively little to say about current affairs or public policy, and most of what they did say tended to be subsumed to their own all-encompassing, singular mental obsession. For both, Communism (broadly defined as "the social") was the supreme evil, and anything that even hinted at such a possibility was suspect. After 1945, both also claimed to have been as much against fascism and Nazism as they were against Communism. The written record on this matter, however, raises serious doubts, as we shall see.

First, Rand. Surprising though it may seem, there is in her work not a single known, major anti-fascist statement either prior to or during the Second World War. In 1940 she threw herself into active support for Republican candidate Wendell Willkie, who in his presidential campaign was still assuming a specifically "isolationist" stance (though he later altered his position). Rand, as her biographers Barbara Branden and Anne Heller each note separately, stood thoroughly opposed to U.S. involvement in the war against Nazism in Europe. (Branden, incidentally, refers to the 1930s as "the Red Decade;" and in her comments on the Eastern front she blames Stalin rather than Hitler for the unimaginable horrors of that conflict, despite the German initiation of the attack and the resultant twenty million Soviet dead.) When, following the massive German invasion of Russia in June 1941, Alexander Kerensky sided tactically with Stalin, La Rand declared the exiled Russian liberal head of state an enemy.[1] And even though Russia—and its Jewish population—were prime victims of the Nazis, Rand herself remained silent on the war (in which, she would later find out, her mother, a sister, and a cousin had died, the latter two as a direct result of Nazi bombings). Rand was far more concerned about Soviet "fifth columnists" in the U.S. than about the slaughter going on across the Atlantic. Somewhat disingenuously,

---

[1] Heller, p. 130.

however, from 1945 on she would claim to be *equally* against Nazism and Communism as instances of "collectivism," even though the biographical record does not support such a self-characterization. Indeed, in a letter to DeWitt Emery in 1941, commenting on Communism and Nazism, she writes, "And of the two, Communism is much the greater menace to this country. Anyone who doesn't realize this is tainted with a great big dose of New Deal germs."[2]

Later, during what is inaccurately known as "the McCarthy era," Rand became directly involved with the blacklist and purge of Hollywood leftists. She attended most of the meetings of a powerful anti-Communist organization, the Motion Picture Alliance for the Preservation of American Ideals (MPA), and met with its executive board in preparation for the House Un-American Activities Committee's hearings on the film industry. She wrote the group's pamphlet, entitled "Screen Guide for Americans"; she testified before HUAC in 1947 (where she advocated policing of perceived Communist content in films); and in her journals she argued that Communist Party membership was a criminal offense.

In the ensuing years Rand described herself as opposing racial bigotry and Jim Crow laws, yet, like all run-of-the-mill conservatives back then, she also opposed any Federal action to redress the situation, thus sharing space with the "states rights" racists of the era. On Vietnam, she at first did not publicly or specifically speak out in favor of the action. However, in her constant likening of the Soviet Union to Nazi Germany, and her repeated insistence that "free" countries have a right to intervene against dictatorships (meaning left-wing or Marxist regimes), she was indirectly lending support to the conflict. As the Vietnam ordeal dragged on she eventually turned against the war on grounds that it was allegedly being fought for "altruistic" reasons. She did see a threat of Nazism in America—from the Kennedy Administration; in response to this perceived menace she penned "The Fascist 'New Frontier,'" a 1963 essay that, in the wake of the assassination of the president in November, was prudently suppressed by Random House. Finally, she condemned the environmental movement in no uncertain terms and also saw feminism as simply another form of "collectivism."

In sum, Rand's day-to-day opinions, and year-to-year positions, scarcely differed from those of the typical, garden-variety conservatives of her time—or ours.

What sets Rand apart from her standard-issue right-wing coevals is the alternative vision that she dreamt up, fleshed out, and built up to as one of

---

[2] In Michael S. Berliner, *Letters of Ayn Rand*, p. 60.

the climactic episodes to *Atlas Shrugged*. In that thick novel she starts out by depicting a corporation, the Taggart Transcontinental railroad, in a state of collapse due to—what else?—the altruistic policies of the company leadership, along with government intervention and labor union meddling. As a prime example, James Taggart, the firm's wimpish heir and current president, snobbishly criticizes someone for being "a greedy bastard who's after nothing but money" (17) and, conversely, he extols "the human element" and "friendship" (27) as values far more meaningful than mere material profit. Similarly, company officers and "scabby little bureaucrats" talk of "shar[ing] the burdens of everybody else" (49); they invoke such notions as the "social impact" and the "public welfare" (173); and they hope to free science from "the rule of the dollar" (178) and to provide help to an "underprivileged nation" such as the "People's State of Mexico."

There is, in retrospect, a curious irony in Rand composing a novel in the 1950s, albeit set in a vague future, that tells of the American railways led to rack and ruin by government actions and insufficient greed. In fact, during that very decade it was the process of "automobilization" that actually began altering the transportation profile of the United States. It was a combination of cheap and abundant petrol, suburban housing development, expanded motorcar use and dependency (especially in the newer, Western states), and massive construction of Federal highways that inexorably pushed rail transport in the United States to the margins and to its currently backward, quasi-Third-World levels of service and technology.

Rand's dystopian diagnosis of the decline of the railroads is thus counter-factual—nay, false! Meanwhile, during those very same years, the state-operated railway firms in Europe took to building speedy, comfortable trains that have continued to evolve, long ago surpassing their U.S. counterparts. So much for the historical "reason" and accuracy of Rand's vision.

Atlas, meanwhile, depicts in Part 3, Chapter 1, that famous "Atlantis": La Rand's top-secret Rocky-Mountain Utopia. Here in "Galt's Gulch," the nation's very greatest minds—captains of industry, along with inventors, artists, doctors, and jurists—have withdrawn and, under the mighty John Galt's leadership, gone on strike, leading to the malfunction and collapse of the entire U.S. economy. In this rarefied enclave, giving is strictly banned, inasmuch as everything exists on a fee-for-service basis: the market at its most pure. There are no specialists among these superior beings. Here is a world in which an aircraft industrialist has a hog farm; a judge raises cattle and poultry; a woman writer sells fish (question: where does she find fish in the Rockies?); a classical composer-pianist is also a railroad mechanic; a truck driver is a petroleum engineer; and a sculptor works as a chemical engineer. In perhaps the most charming mix of professions, a philosopher runs a roadside diner. Still, one does not actually *see* these *übermenschen* performing such wondrous tasks and selling their wares; we are merely told that they do them ("Tell, don't show" describes Rand's literary method), begging the question of how any of these tasks get done without an army of workers to actually feed the hogs, muck out the cattle stalls, clean the fish, make parts for the railroad engine, dig the oil wells, or wash the dirty dishes...

Neither is there any mention of who does the daily cooking and domestic duties in the Gulch—save when slinky, fiery Dagny Taggart is contracted by hero John Galt to perform for him such culinary labors (again, for a fee), but also so that our heroine may derive erotic, sensual pleasure from watching the much-esteemed leader consume the foods prepared by her own hand.

"Some of us have wives and children," Galt says once in passing. In the entire book (and, to my knowledge, in all of Rand's oeuvre), there is exactly one pair of paragraphs depicting such a family, an unnamed couple with two sons, ages 7 and 4. In the first of these paragraphs, the children are extolled at great length as "fearless," "joyous," "innocently natural" (730) and filled with curiosity. And why be they such paragons of perfection (like John Galt himself), these two? Because their mother, the owner of a bakery, has elected to come to the Gulch and "bring up my sons as human beings." Yet we are never given any concrete information as to *how*, in the mom's dual-career arrangement, her kids were and are and will be raised. During her everyday baking duties, one asks, who has changed the diapers and wiped the boys' behinds? In raising and educating the twosome while she's at the store, are there nannies, babysitters, paid tutors? Grandparents, aunts, and uncles, incidentally, cannot lend a hand because—as the mother-cum-baker informs visitor Dagny—"families or relatives are not allowed to come here" (730), unless they take up John Galt's oath of *not* living for others.

Conversely, while the baker-mom is with the kids, doing the hard work of watching over them and instructing them, who runs the bakery? Who orders the food ingredients, prepares the dough, bakes the loaves and pastries, markets the product? There is no mention of managers or other employees. Later on, when the boys reach high-school age, is the proud, happy, but very busy mother-baker prepared to enlighten them in the laboratory sciences and in higher math? In foreign languages? In physical education? And is all this to be done free of charge as an altruistic, "giving" relationship? If it is not, then, will the offspring pay mom and pop for the rearing services? Are loan credits accumulated over the two decades-plus of their upbringing?

In this utopia, by the same token, there appear to be no old folks, no infirm people. What happens when one of those rugged individualists suffers a disabling stroke? Or contracts Alzheimer's or (why not?) lung cancer, as Rand eventually did? (Presumably they don't, ever.) Will those old and infirm simply be left to "perish," if we may recall Nietzsche's and Alan Greenspan's wisely philosophic prescription for disposing of the sick, the sufferers, and the non-creative sorts? Oh, and then, who, among the gathered geniuses, will serve as mortician, embalmer, or gravedigger?

And again, in the matter of mundane upkeep, who does the back-breaking work of harvesting the crops, slaughtering the cattle, sweeping the streets, cleaning the toilets? Is it the sculptor? The classical composer? Perhaps something resembling Mao's Cultural Revolution is what helmswoman Rand has in mind here.

*

Nabokov in his lifetime made few general statements about politics. Probably his only capsule creed can be found in the *Playboy* interview: "It is classical to the point of triteness. Freedom of speech, freedom of thought, freedom of art. The social or economic structure of the ideal state is of little concern to me" (SO, 35). Despite this latter claim to the contrary, however, Nabokov's spokesman and alter ego in *The Gift*, his poet-aesthete Count Fyodor Godunov-Cherdyntsev, does speculate on what he calls "*my* kingdom, where everyone keeps to himself, and there is no equality and no authorities" (G, 370).

This is about as "libertarian" a stance as one will find in Nabokov, and it is of a piece with the totality of his world-view. Indeed, Count Fyodor's general outlook much resembles that expressed by John Galt in his mammoth radio address, where at one point Rand's hero declaims: "Do you ask what moral obligation I owe to my fellow man? None—except the obligation I owe to myself..." (948). For just as Rand is concerned solely with the rights of superior architects, inventors, and businessmen to achieve greatness and wealth, and the devil take the rest, Nabokov cares exclusively about the rights of exquisite literary artists to write great art, and the devil take the rest.

Nabokov, like Rand, claimed to be equally opposed to fascism and Communism. And also as with Rand, this retrospective stance is not entirely accurate. Whereas Nabokov and his birth family had immediately fled the Bolsheviks, Nabokov the adult and paterfamilias, with his Jewish wife and half-Jewish son, managed to remain four years in Hitler's Germany, the threesome not leaving for France until 1937. Indeed, Stacy Schiff, in her biography of Véra, asks pointedly, "Why did they stay?"[3] It should be noted that, during the initial phases of the Nazi régime, although Jews were being denounced, discriminated against, and fired from jobs, as an ethnic group they were not yet being subject to large-scale internment or state-sanctioned murder. (The Nuremberg laws were not enacted until 1935, and what became known as the Holocaust was scarcely even in the planning stages until the war began.) The only German groups being herded en masse into concentration camps, starting in 1933, were leftists— first Communists, then Socialists. Western conservatives, as we shall see shortly, by and large accepted and even praised these measures as positive. In the case of Nabokov there is no record as to how he felt about the Nazis' anti-Communist repression, though presumably he would not have been opposed to it. (After all, in the 1950s, he and Véra were in favor of McCarthyism.)

Still, unlike Rand, the immigrant Nabokov showed no hatred of the New Deal, though it's quite possible that he knew and understood next to nothing about the Roosevelt reforms. By the time the Nabokovs arrived in the U.S. in 1940, FDR's programs had become institutionalized, and the vicious polemics over government intervention in the economy had been overshadowed by the spread of military conflict in Europe. Also, in contrast to Rand's unwavering "isolationism," in the wake of the 1941 Nazi assault on Russia, Nabokov personally sided with the Soviets in the war. To cite again his letter to Edmund Wilson on 18 July 1941, in which the novelist actually says, "My ardent desire [is] that Russia, in spite of everything, may defeat or rather utterly abolish Germany—so that not a German be left in the world."[4] Later, in the 1960s, Nabokov would casually praise President Johnson for passing the Civil Rights Act— legislation loathed then and still loathed today by Randians and libertarians alike.

Nonetheless, once he had settled into U.S. life, Nabokov had little to say either about fascism, eliminationist anti-Semitism, or Nazi extermination policy (other than hinting at it very obliquely in the short stories "Conversation Piece, 1945" and "Signs and Symbols"),[5] while his hatred

---

[3] Schiff, p. 67.
[4] Karlinsky, letter 21; p. 53.
[5] Of course there is the matter of Pnin and his earlier beloved Mira Belochkin, who was Jewish and perished in a concentration camp. On the topic of Jewish-Gentile relations in Nabokov, see Maxim D. Shrayer, "Jewish Questions in Nabokov's Art and Life."

of Communism would remain unrelenting and unmovable. In this regard, the prize-winning American novelist Louis Begley, himself a Polish-Jewish survivor of the Holocaust, in an introduction to a new edition of *Speak, Memory* commissioned by Random House in the 1990s, gently chided Nabokov for "how little [he] says in this volume about ... what it was like to live in the thirties in Berlin with a Jewish wife and a half-Jewish child."[6] Begley further makes passing reference to Nabokov's "turned up nose" and "aloofness" vis-à-vis contemporary politics.[7] Presumably in response to these rather friendly and quite mild criticisms, however, Nabokov's son Dmitri intervened in the publishing process, claiming that Begley had "accused [Nabokov] of being scandalously soft on Hitler." Dmitri, by his own admission, ordered editorial changes. Begley refused. Dmitri, the novelist's executor, had the piece suppressed from the volume. Later, at a Nabokov centenary conference held at Cornell in 1998, Dmitri boasted briefly to the gathered Nabokovians, "The introduction did not appear."[8] (I have rescued the essay and included it in Appendix A of this volume.)

Despite Nabokov's touted belief in free speech, he and his wife—like Rand—agreed with the McCarthyite accusations about Communists controlling the upper reaches of U.S. life and approved the blacklists and firings that followed. In private the couple defended Senator McCarthy himself; Véra even became involved in public exchanges in which she expressed her support for the purge of China expert Owen Lattimore from the State Department for his allegedly "advan[cing] the Soviets' hold on China".[9] The novelist, for his part, mocks in *Pnin* the occasional *anti*-McCarthyite professor—thus indirectly reflecting his own pro-McCarthyism.

Nabokov had next to nothing to say about the Khrushchev reforms—the so-called "thaw"—or about the relative loosening of life under the Communist dictatorship. For him, the hated system was ever the same and unchanging. He argued that the Soviets had never really sent men into outer space but had rather pulled off some sort of radar trick, "cosmic propaganda."[10] Later, he doggedly defended the U.S. war against what—always the punster—he referred to as "Sovietnam." (His scattered comments on that conflict were astoundingly ignorant.) He severed all ties with Harvard professor Roman Jakobson over the latter's academic visits

---

[6] Louis Begley, "Introduction" to *Speak, Memory*, p. xv. I am grateful to Mr. Begley for providing access to the unpublished galley proofs for his essay.
[7] Ibid., p. xix.
[8] The episode is mentioned in Dmitri Nabokov, "On Returning to Ithaca," p. 281.
[9] Schiff, p. 192.
[10] Boyd, *Vladimir Nabokov: The American Years*, p. 402.

to Moscow—where the eminent linguist shed joyful tears at seeing his native city once again—and dubbed Jakobson "a Communist agent."[11] Nabokov and Véra honestly believed that the vicious, scurrilous literary politics surrounding the world success of Pasternak's *Doctor Zhivago* were actually part of a larger "Soviet plot."[12] And he even saw with suspicion the publication of Solzhenitsyn's early novels in the West as a calculated result of "KGB compliance."[13]

Nabokov comes fairly close to Rand and other libertarian-minded writers in denying the existence of society and in negating the validity of social analyses of any sort, both in literature and in general. In this regard, his cloistered upbringing—the lavish environment of his youth—goes a long way toward explaining this extreme, asocial point of view.

Besides growing up in the bosom of enormous privilege, Nabokov spent the first dozen years of his childhood blissfully, magically cut off from the rest of the Russian social order. His entire early schooling took place via those resident, English- or French-speaking tutors. Not until age twelve did he so much as set foot into a formal classroom. When the wealthy pubescent finally enrolled as a day pupil at the Tenishev School in Petersburg, he did not readily fit in, and saw the move as a needless separation from his beloved family life. He loathed the egalitarian ethos of the institution where, as Boyd points out, he had "passed from the position of unqualified favorite to simply one among many."[14] Students as well as teachers resented young Vladimir for his easy command of French and English words, his arriving at school by chauffeured luxury car rather than by trolley, and his refusal to join groups or to lay hands on the wet soap and towels in the boys' lavatory.

In *Speak, Memory*, Nabokov dedicates an entire chapter to his resident private tutors. Yet he assigns a mere *two pages* to his years of study at the Tenishev School. The critic Zenaida Shakovskaia notes the book's "snobbish egocentrism" and "class pride," and especially Nabokov's "nearly total ignorance of other social words."[15] This ignorance would persist throughout the novelist's life and would be made by him into a badge of honor, a principle, a virtue. In this regard, when Nabokov started out as a student at Cambridge University, he was surprised that the college

---

[11] Ibid., p. 311.
[12] Ibid., p. 372.
[13] Ibid., p. 648.
[14] Boyd, *Vladimir Nabokov: The Russian Years*, p. 87.
[15] Cited in Georges Nivat, "*Speak, Memory*" in Vladimir Alexandrov, p. 677.

porters could issue orders to him and even impose a fine on the handsome young émigré for treading on the lawns.[16]

Nabokov's incomprehension of and hostility toward any social thinking whatsoever comes through especially clearly in a 1956 letter to Edmund Wilson, in which the novelist harshly criticizes the critic for seeing "social phenomena" in Chekhov and for singling out groups such as "kulaks," "rising serfs," and the "new industrial middle class" in his discussion of Chekhov's short stories and plays. In this particular case one might split hairs and argue, along with Nabokov, that social categories are less than relevant in literary commentary, and that—in his own words— only the "specific detail" matters.[17] However, in his farewell novel, *Look at the Harlequins!*, Nabokov's narrator cum alter ego, Vadim Vadimovich, takes things further and essentially dismisses social class and its concerns as non-existent: "In my set, in my world, in the opulent Russia of my boyhood, we stood so far above any concept of 'class' that we only laughed when reading about 'Japanese Barons' or 'New England Patricians.'" [18] I have already pointed out how the opulent young Nabokov had virtually no contact with the broader Russian society before starting school at age twelve. One gathers that the more elderly Nabokov still believed, as Vadim does, that, in pre-1917 Russia, classes did not exist.

Nabokov's incapacity to deal with sociopolitical topics on any terms other than his simplistic schema comes especially to the fore in his second least-achieved novel, *Bend Sinister* (1946), which portrays the takeover of a nameless East European state by operatives of the Ekwilist (i.e. "Equalist") Party, a "party of the Average Man." Here, as well as in his lengthy short story "Tyrants Destroyed," Nabokov all but implies that tyranny comes into being because one evil, mediocre, and egomaniacal individual, who happens to hate intellectuals such as the hero Adam Krug, so wills it. (This is just a notch above those high-school sophomores who believe that the evil house painter Hitler came to power by screaming at the German masses.) Nothing here about such factors as social movements, geopolitical maneuvers, factional divisions, class conflict, rival security forces, collective scapegoats, militaristic ideology, suppression of unions, and the like—the mere existence of which Nabokov would have pooh-poohed anyway. Instead the author resorts, as he often did in his literary judgments, to facile name-calling—referring regularly to the dictator Paduk as "the Toad"—and also making the tyrant physically grotesque ("blotched complexion," disfigured lip, blackheads—BS, 123) and, of all

---

[16] Boyd, *Vladimir Nabokov: The Russian Years*, p. 167.

[17] Karlinsky, letter 276 (29 February 1956), p. 331.

[18] Nabokov, *Look at the Harlequins!*, pp. 29-30.

things, a homosexual. Given that Nabokov's own brother Sergey, a flesh-and-blood homosexual, had died at the hands of the Nazis, there is something disquieting about this literary choice. To add to the disingenuousness, Nabokov in his 1963 Preface denies that *Bend Sinister* is at all a political novel, claims that it is rather about its suffering hero, Professor Krug and his young son who is tortured to death.

Despite his own disavowals, the many devotees of Nabokov, son Dmitri included, like to see *Bend Sinister* as an indictment of both fascism and communism. There is nothing in the work itself, however, that points to such a twin target or double referent. Real-life Nazism—if I may belabor the obvious—made no claims to bringing equality and "leveling" for everybody, as do Nabokov's "Ekwilists." On the contrary, in the Nazis' world-view and ruling practice, there were the Master Race (*das Herrenvolk*) and then the slave peoples (Jews, Slavs, gypsies, cripples, homosexuals) who were destined for slaughter. In addition, an encompassing, aggressive, nationalist ideology was aimed at superseding all social division among German ethnics across Europe. None of this racialism is to be found in the Russian novelist's inept attempt at a dystopian fiction. What ideology we read about is vaguely Marxist ("a lurid interplay of class passions," "dialectically unfair"—*BS*, 68, 69), never race-based. (As Boyd severely remarks about what he himself terms this, one of the "less successful" of Nabokov's works: "The plot has its poignancy, but it remains too meager in proportion to the self-consciousness and obscurity that surround it.")[19] Ultimately, *Bend Sinister* is little more than a single-minded anti-Communist tract cloaked in precious, well-crafted prose. The book serves as prime, and poor, instance of a genre Nabokov claimed thoroughly to despise: namely, publicist fiction.

Once again, it was Edmund Wilson who demonstrated masterful insight into the limitations of *Bend Sinister*, in a 1947 letter written to his then-friend Nabokov, shortly after publication of the book. I quote Wilson at length:

> You aren't good at this kind of subject, which involves questions of politics and social change, because you are totally uninterested in these matters and have never taken the trouble to understand them. For you, a dictator like the Toad is simply a vulgar and odious person who bullies superior people like Krug. You have no idea why or how the Toad was able to put himself over, or what his revolution implies. And this makes your picture of such happenings rather unsatisfactory. Now don't tell me that the real artist has nothing to do with the issues of politics. An artist

---

[19] Boyd, *Vladimir Nabokov: The American Years*, p. 105.

may not take politics seriously, but, if he deals with such matters at all, he ought to know what it is about.[20]

Nabokov never claimed to be a political analyst or thinker—a species of intellectual he most probably would have held in contempt. Hence we can disregard the political puns and sloganeering of his interviews on these grounds. When he chooses to write a patently political novel, however, his gaping holes in this area inevitably become manifest—a flaw to which Wilson's words bear eloquent witness.

The late twentieth-century Latin American novelists—García Márquez, Carpentier, and Vargas Llosa, among others—have done a much better artistic job of depicting the inner dynamics of *their* region's dictatorships. In García Márquez's *The Autumn of the Patriarch*, for instance, we see at work such crucial factors as the primal role of British and then U.S. imperialism, the use of populist agitation, the armed support provided by a loyal presidential guard, the tyrant's personal skill at fomenting division among his officers, his uncanny intuitive abilities with people and at spotting secret enemies, his sexual manias, his attachment to his mother, and his myriad inner certainties, delusions, and child-like charms. García Márquez in his final chapter even succeeds in evoking pity for his aging and incontinent autocrat. None of this complexity is to be found in the predictable, one-dimensional portrait presented by Nabokov's deeply flawed book.

Bend Sinister was Nabokov's last novel with a specifically Central/East European setting. It was also his final exercise—following immediately after *The Gift* and *Sebastian Knight*—at fashioning fiction with a publicist agenda and a political or didactic slant. His years as an immigrant in America, along with the stability he was to find in U.S. academic life, would eventually free his novelistic imagination to discover and then reshape entirely new places, new people, new ways of being.

*

Being myself a product of the rebellious 1960s, I came of age at a time when all kinds of official, center-right, U.S. orthodoxies were coming into question. Among those ruling orthodoxies about which I began having doubts was the theory of "totalitarianism," according to which fascism and communism were one and the same system. And as I devoured hundreds of history books over the next decade or so, I couldn't help noting that, under Nazism, German industry had remained thoroughly in private hands

[20] Karlinsky, letter 160 (30 January 1947), p. 210.

and had even prospered, and also that, from 1930 to 1945—from the streets of Berlin to the Russian expanses and back to Berlin's streets once again—Communists and Fascists had clashed in fierce battles, these among the bloodiest in history. That such vast blocks of historical truth were being systematically and conveniently obscured by so neatly symmetrical a formula seemed, to me, simply shocking. In the dominant, sanitized version presented in most U.S. textbooks and media, Nazi anticommunism was conspicuous by its absence, fascists were communists rather than brutal mutual antagonists, and the Eastern Front had scarcely taken place. Such an official vision, in due time, had trickled down and essentially become a kind of broadly shared "folklore." Consequently, as historian Peter Novick observes in *The Holocaust in American Life*, surveys show that as few as 49 per cent of Americans are aware that the Soviets were one of the Allies in the Second World War. In other words, 51 per cent do *not* know of the Russian role in defeating Nazism.[21]

Among the sources I consulted in the course of my researches was none other than Hitler's *Mein Kampf*, where the Führer's maniacal anticommunism comes through loud and clear. While the most poisonous prose of Germany's future Chancellor is reserved for the Jews, his diatribes against "the grinning, ugly face of Marxism," I observed, come in a not-too-distant second. Leafing through the index to *Mein Kampf* I saw roughly the same number of entries —about six dozen apiece—for "Marxism," "Communist Party," and "Social Democracy" as for "Judaism," "Jewish Art," and "anti-Semitism." Before his coming to power, Hitler's chief rivals in the German political arena were the Communist and Social Democratic parties, both of which commanded huge electoral blocs and, in their combined numbers, far surpassed the Nazis. And significantly, I noted, one of the twenty-seven long subsections in *Mein Kampf* bears the title "The Struggle with the Red Front." Repeatedly Hitler states his prime concern with "the question of destroying Marxism" and calls for no less than "a war of annihilation against Marxism."[22]

That war soon came, and was swift, ruthless, constant, and open-ended. Within weeks of his accession to power in January 1933, Hitler used the Reichstag fire as a pretext to ban the German Communist Party, confiscate its property, and have its functionaries and deputies interned by the thousands at Dachau. In each country that later fell to German military might, I couldn't help but note, anti-left reprisals were routine. With the takeover of the Czech Sudetenland in 1939, for instance, "20,000 Social

---

[21] Peter Novick, *The Holocaust in American Life*, p. 232.
[22] Adolf Hitler, *Mein Kampf*, pp. 153 and 680.

Democrats … were rounded up and sent to concentration camps" by the German security police. And in the 1941 Soviet invasion, Einsatz units had orders to execute all Communist functionaries along with male Jews, "second-class Asiatics," and Gypsies.[23]

Indeed, the wholesale extermination of the left was to be the largest single *non-ethnic* persecution under the Nazi Reich. Its absence from "normal" American treatments of that era reflected yet another disquieting pattern that, via bits and pieces, I saw taking shape: namely, that ruling circles in the West had by no means felt displeased with Hitler's war of annihilation against Marxism. Indeed, beginning with as far back as the rise of Mussolini in the 1920s and continuing through Hitler's and Franco's seizure of power in the 1930s, the business classes and the conservative press varyingly accepted, defended, acclaimed, and in some cases even profited from the rise of fascism in Europe.

The pattern began with Mussolini's seizure of power in 1923, which was greeted with favorable editorials in *Barron's*, *Nation's Business*, and *The Wall Street Journal* (the latter seeing in the Duce a "New Columbus" who had made Italy into a "New World of will and work"). From historian John P. Diggins's seminal study *Mussolini and Fascism*, I found out that most of the U.S. press and its business allies saw the Duce's government as a bulwark against the Red Menace. The *Saturday Evening Post* praised fascism for its "commercial revolution" and its having "turned red terror into white fear," while William Randolph Hearst extolled the Duce's "astonishing ability" and "public service." Lewis Pierson of the Irving National Bank perceived in Mussolini's régime "the ideals of individualism" and the "inviolable rights of property and contract;" James Emery, the counsel of the National Association of Manufacturers, noted that the Duce had saved Italy from "the blighted hand of radical socialism;" and Thomas W. Lamont of J. P. Morgan became a propagandist for Mussolini and secured for his régime a $100 million loan. Richard Child, the U.S. Ambassador to Rome, remarked that "I believe in the least possible government … and so does Mussolini." As for the antifascist opposition, Secretary of State Frank B. Kellogg shrugged them off as "Communists, socialists, and anarchists."[24]

The advent of Nazism, to my astonishment, had also drawn favorable reviews from civilized Britain's conservative press, which was extremely anti-Soviet and regarded the Hitler régime as a buffer against Marxism.

[23] Laurence Thompson, *The Greatest Treason: The Untold History of Munich*, p. 262; Karl Dietrich Bracher, *The German Dictatorship*, p. 424.
[24] John P. Diggins, *Mussolini and Fascism: The View from America*, pp. 27, 31, 32, 48, 64, 145-46, 157, 266, and passim.

The *Daily Mail* dismissed reports about Nazi tyranny as the ravings of "old women of both sexes." The *Mail*'s publisher, Lord Rothermere, feared a Communist invasion of England and directed staff writers to depict Bolshevism as a greater threat to British interests than Nazism.[25] This sort of information was easily available in Franklin Reid Gannon's *The British Press and Nazi Germany 1936-39*.

At first, the view of Hitler from America had scarcely differed. From my own archival researches in the bowels of Harvard's Widener Library, I read that Miles Boulton of the *Baltimore Sun* had denied Nazi atrocities and claimed that Jewish persecution had been grossly exaggerated.[26] Going Boulton one better, pop novelist Kenneth Roberts in the *Saturday Evening Post* had ridiculed the "erroneous ideas" and the "hysterical" writing that "spoke disrespectfully of Mr. Hitler." To his delight, Roberts found a trip that he took to Germany to be "less eventful than entering the Harvard Stadium for a Dartmouth game." He thought Germany's villagers "by far the kindest, the most obliging, the most contented … and the gayest in Europe," and was quite taken with the "clump-clump-clump" of the marching Hitler Youth, an organization to which he dedicated two lengthy, "balanced" articles.[27] The *Post*'s editorial policy, it bears noting, was completely opposed to diplomatic *recognition* of the USSR ("it would be folly"), but also to any stand against Hitler's Germany, though it judiciously conceded that "certain policies of the Nazi government seem extreme."[28]

Along similar lines, I was also to encounter, in the *New York Times Book Review* of 15 October 1933, a lengthy look at an English translation of Hitler's *Mein Kampf*. The piece, penned by James W. Gerard, a U.S. Ambassador to Berlin from 1913 to 1917, offers a fairly knowledgeable précis of Germany's history going back to the Thirty Years' War. The author, who shows an in-depth understanding of the German nation's past, toward the end of his review praises Hitler for the very same reasons that the Führer was being given high marks by other Western non-Nazis— notably, in Gerard's own words, because of "[Hitler's] destruction of communism" and for "his protection of the right of private property," as well as "his curbing of parliamentary government, so unsuited to the German character." These measures, Ambassador Gerard observes, "are

---

[25] Franklin Reid Gannon, *The British Press and Germany 1936-39*, pp. 13, 25, 26, and 32.

[26] Cited in *New York Times*, March 26, 1933, p. 28.

[27] Kenneth Roberts, "Hitler Youth," *Saturday Evening Post*, 26 May 1934, pp. 8-9 and 98-104, and 2 June 1934, pp. 23 and 30-38.

[28] *Saturday Evening Post*, editorials, 3 June 1933, and 9 June 1934.

all good."[29] Indeed, the only fault he finds with the regime is its "persecution ... of the Jews," a policy that he laments and to which he dedicates four eloquent paragraphs. In sum, its official anti-Semitism aside, well, ultimately, the Hitler dictatorship, in the 1933 reviewer's eyes, did not seem all that bad. (Out of historical interest, the *Times* reprinted the review in its 6 October 1996 issue.)

During the time of my investigations, the biography of Henry Luce by W. A. Swanberg came out to much fanfare, revealing a less savory side of the legendary co-founder and president of *Time-Life* and thereby sparking a great deal of debate (plus hostile reviews in his own magazines). *Time*, Swanberg's book revealed, had regularly minimized Nazi terror, praised the "greatness" of Hitler's oratory, and indulged German remilitarization with a blithe remark that "Germany has been naughty but is not to be spanked." Luce's newsweekly also regularly derided prominent anti-Nazis and labeled the French Popular Front leader as the "Jew Léon Blum," a "rabble-rouser" who "is fired with religious fanaticism; he hates Nazis as they can only be hated by one who is a Socialist, a Frenchman, and a Jew."[30] In France, of course, "Better Hitler than Blum" was the most famous slogan of the nationalist Right, many of which would then go on to collaborate with the occupying Germans or the Vichy régime.

Luce himself, Swanberg showed, had been enthusiastic about European fascism throughout most of the 1930s. In a 1934 address to the Chamber of Commerce of Scranton, Pennsylvania, he had proclaimed that "the moral force of fascism, appearing in totally different forms in different nations, may be the inspiration for the next general march of mankind." Early in 1938, moreover, he actually visited the Reich and, in an unpublished report on his travels, glowed with pleasure at the Nazi régime. He was enraptured that "in Germany there is no 'soak the rich' ideology," for indeed, "the extraordinary thing about Hitler ... is that he has suspended the class war." Having seen the many busy theaters and the motorbikes in the streets, Luce would conclude that the German people "did not seem to be slaves. Their chains are not visible." Nazi Germany, Luce believed, was much "misunderstood."[31]

Luce and his magazines, moreover, were not the only American conservatives holding such beliefs at the time, as I kept finding out. Many of Luce's contemporary business leaders frankly praised the Hitler regime as advantageous to their interests. In October 1933, General Motors

---

[29] James W. Gerard, review of *My Battle* by Adolf Hitler, *New York Times Book Review*, October 15, 1933.

[30] W. A. Swanberg, *Luce and His Empire*, pp. 128-30.

[31] Ibid., pp. 109 and 154-56.

President William S. Knudsen returned to New York from Germany and informed reporters that the Nazi régime was "the miracle of the twentieth century." Similarly, in December 1936, James Mooney, head of GM in Europe and in charge of the Opel works, told an American diplomat that "we ought to make some arrangements with Germany for the future," and later met with Nazi Finance Minister Hjalmar Schacht to discuss prospects for joint commerce between the two countries. Walter Teagle, President of Standard Oil of New Jersey, became a director of the American branch of I.G. Farben, and throughout the Second World War there was to persist between the two firms a Byzantine relationship involving patents and export licenses.[32] Along the same lines, Sosthenes Behn, the colorfully sinister founder and president of International Telephone and Telegraph, enjoyed good relations with top Nazis. One ITT German subsidiary was headed by a man who would later become an SS general. Another ITT firm bought a 28 per cent share of the Focke-Wulf aircraft company in 1938.[33]

The value of U.S. business interests in Nazi Germany has been estimated at $475 million in 1941 dollars.[34] The sheer size of these commercial ties seemed staggering to me—as well as the memory hole into which the facts about them had fallen.

By the standards of conventional economics, moreover, capitalism in the Third Reich was a success story—the most prosperous in Europe at the time. No wonder, then, that those American business leaders had seen in it the future, and believed that it *worked!* From 1933 to 1937, German corporate profits quadrupled; managerial income rose by 50 per cent; and in the period from 1939 to 1942, German industry expanded as much as it had during the preceding fifty years.[35] Just from the dates I could infer the reasons for such spectacular growth: the armaments boom, the use of slave labor, and the pillage of resources from conquered lands. And even though some years later, at the Nuremberg Trials, U.S. Supreme Court Justice Robert Jackson would state that, "It has always been the position of the United States that the great industrialists of Germany were guilty of crimes charged in the indictment quite as much as the politicians, diplomats, and soldiers,"[36] the German businessmen who had been indicted for war crimes nevertheless served mostly light sentences or got off scot-free. All

---

[32] Charles Higham, *Trading with the Enemy*, pp. 32, 163, and 166.
[33] Ibid., pp. 94-95. Anthony Sampson, *The Sovereign State of ITT*, pp. 27-33.
[34] Higham, p. xvi.
[35] Richard Grunberger, *The 12-Year Reich*, pp. 179 and 203; David Schoenbaum, *Hitler's Social Revolution*, p. 155.
[36] Eugene Davidson, *The Trial of the Germans*, p. 7.

this was available in the history books that I was consulting—volumes that, I realized, had had minimal effect in the public arena of the postwar United States.

Needless to say, with the Japanese bombing of the Pearl Harbor naval base in December 1941, the German declaration of war on the United States some days after, and the national mobilization that followed, such "balanced" U.S. discussion of the merits of fascism came to an abrupt end. Nevertheless, for American industries the Reich still remained a directly profitable venue for their business operations. Throughout the European war, Standard Oil continued to ship aviation fuel to the Axis powers; Ford trucks were built for German occupation troops in France; GM's Opel division developed propulsion systems for Messerschmidt fighters and provided the Wehrmacht with most of its tanks; and ITT's German firms furnished the German military with switchboards, telephones, radar equipment, artillery fuses, Focke-Wulf aircraft, and much, much more.[37]

Not surprisingly, these production plants inevitably became prime targets for Anglo-American aerial bombardment during the war, and most were severely damaged or destroyed. And so in 1967 the U.S. government awarded GM $33 million in tax exemptions to compensate for these losses. ITT received $27 million, "including $5 million for damage to Focke-Wulf plants on the basis that they were American property bombed by Allied bombers."[38] As for me, whenever I'd share these facts with friends in casual conversation, they would laugh in amazement. To us it all seemed like a satire, something dreamt up by a modern-day Jonathan Swift. And yet it was all true.

*

In my chapter 4, I looked into Rand's extensive and fruitful ties with prominent anti-FDR publicists and pro-business intellectuals during the 1930s. As we've seen, in her staunch "isolationist" position and her virtual silence on the evils of Nazism, Rand was essentially falling in line with American conservative opinion of the time. Just as the eventual doctrine of "totalitarianism" would later serve to flatten and obscure an enormous twenty-years' war between fascism and communism (right vs. left) into a single, static system, and moreover would provide ideological cover for those who had defended Nazism at its height, similarly, Rand's alleged rejection of "collectivism" would help make her appear anti-Hitler, too,

---

[37] Ibid., pp. V, 99, and 175.
[38] Ibid., p. 177. Sampson, p. 46.

not merely anti-Soviet. Her opposition to fascism, though, turns out to have been a personal myth and a handily retrospective fiction.

My own readings in the history of Nazism, and on the praise the regime had garnered from well-placed conservatives, were driven largely by a burning desire to get beyond the cloud of unknowing, the opaque veil of reigning American myths. In time, however, the knowledge prompted from me a satire of my own, a Borges-style mock-review of a volume by one Will McPazzo, entitled *Hitler Reconsidered: An American Conservative Takes a Second Look at the Third Reich and Finds More than a Few Things to Recommend*, which piece I would include in my book of stories, *The Pianist Who Liked Ayn Rand*.[39] In the piece, after summarizing McPazzo's positive spin on some of the information I've set forth above, I cite what he sees as negatives—among them, dear reader, the most repellent feature of Nazism: **price controls**! To a deeply concerned McPazzo, Germany's businessmen "actually deserve to be memorialized along with the other victims of Nazism," inasmuch as those high industrialists had "suffered more than all of the world's so-called underdogs put together," the latter a near-literal quotation from wise old Rand herself. Rand, in fact, had given in 1961 a lecture provocatively entitled, "America's Persecuted Minority: Big Business."

McPazzo, accordingly, takes a "balanced" view of the concentration camps, on one hand repudiating as "emotional, not rational" the "primitive, quasi-African collectivism" that had led Germany to treat Jews not as individuals but as members of a group. As McPazzo once reflected on the TV show *Firing Line,* "Groups don't exist, societies don't exist, I would even say that Jews do not exist. Only individuals do." On the other hand, McPazzo also finds silver linings in Hitler's camps, noting that "professional Communists" from all over Europe, including 3 million Red Army soldiers, also died in the camps (in his words, "And I'll drink to that, by jingo!"). So did half a million Gypsies, "notorious for their criminal element" and hence their slaughter represents the Nazis' way of being, as McPazzo says, "tough on crime." And so indeed did thousands of homosexuals, whom Ayn Rand had also considered "disgusting," "immoral," and "repulsive," and whom Norman Podhoretz, the renowned editor of *Commentary* magazine and highly vocal neo-conservative publicist, had singled out in 1977 as a chief cause of an "appeasement morality" toward the Soviets. These very Soviets, McPazzo notes, had in 1944 embarked on a war of westward expansion and invaded Germany

---

[39] In Bell-Villada, *The Pianist Who Liked Ayn Rand*, pp. 187-192.

"without provocation" even as the liberal West had stood idly by and acquiesced in an act of "naked conquest"!

In 1989, I wrote the piece as satire. Today if feels like reality. The spoof is to be found in Appendix B of this volume.

CHAPTER ELEVEN

ON THEIR RUSSIAN SIDE

A truth worth restating at the risk of belaboring the obvious: Nabokov and Rand were both Russians. They each immigrated to the U.S. as fully grown adults, Rand at 22, Nabokov at 40. Hence, culturally and otherwise, they'd both been fully shaped by their Russian backgrounds, and in Nabokov's case by his émigré, European-Russian background as well. They thus brought with them a host of Russian preoccupations, topics, issues, concerns, debates, and not to mention manias, which they then subliminally adopted and fused with the American works and public statements by which they would be respectively defined.

Nabokov of course identified himself first and foremost as a Russian author who had consciously chosen to reinvent himself as an American one. He never repudiated his Russian roots and indeed evoked them with loving, lyrical nostalgia in his memoir, *Speak, Memory*. Nabokov's first novel in English, *Sebastian Knight*, actually deals with a fictional Russian novelist and aesthete. The experience of Russian immigration lies at the heart of his academic novel *Pnin*. And in *Pale Fire* and *Ada*, Mother Russia is transformed into a shadowy, remote, quasi-science fiction entity. *Lolita*, then, stands out more as a special case, a dramatic exception, with its strictly American setting and heroine. Only two of its characters— Humbert's first, Polish wife Valeria and her lover, the Tsarist cab driver— are Slavic, and their brief, fleeting role is as that of passing, farcical relief in what is an American tragicomedy.

Though Rand published no work in her native tongue (other than occasional pamphlets that she wrote while enrolled at Soviet film school), as an author she too was a Russian turned American. By contrast with Nabokov, however, she had little to say about the country of her origins, other than to disparage it in talk-show appearances as a land of "mysticism," and even to say that she loathed everything Russian. Russia is notably absent from her fiction in the years following the publication of her first novel, *We the Living*. So successful was she at effacing her Russian past that many educated Americans—believers and detractors both—were not, and still are not, aware of Rand's Russian-immigrant stock.

Only with the posthumous, admiring yet warts-and-all biography, *The Passion of Ayn Rand* (1986) by close disciple (and member of her inner circle) Barbara Branden, did the Russian youth and upbringing of the priestess-to-be receive an extended initial look. And only with the groundbreaking studies in the 1990s by Chris Matthew Sciabarra and D. Barton Johnson, who first started digging up and reconstructing the Russian and then Soviet education of young Rand, did we begin to realize how profoundly *Russian* a writer Ayn Rand is. (Not accidentally, Sciabarra's book bears as subtitle *The Russian Radical*.) And of course the recent biographies by Jennifer Burns and Anne Heller have fleshed out Rand's Russian years, filling a long-standing lacuna. Such latter-day insights would not have been possible during Queen Ayn's reign, when her born-again Americanism and her vaunted image of self-fashioning from scratch were myths too potent to be challenged by past history. Besides, the paladin of individualism was wont to suing any authors who dared feature her pen name in their book or article titles.

Both Rand and Nabokov, however, are Russian in profound and sometimes hidden ways. As writers, for starters, they stand squarely within their country's tradition of the novel of ideas. It is a recognized feature of nineteenth-century Russian literature that its authors strove to integrate general ideas (and perhaps even ideologies) into their plots and narratives. Faced as they were with the backward condition of their country—economic, political, intellectual, legal—and the various political schemes to deal with that condition, novelists under Tsarism saw those diverse plans as part of the human landscape and purposely gave them flesh, blood, and voice.

In fact, few classic novelists have brought ideas into play in their fiction to the extent that the Russians did. The entire opening section of Dostoevsky's *Notes from Underground*—fully half of the book—is an extended essay on the large issues of rationalism and modernity, and on the possible relationship of those notions to Russia. Many a young university student around the world has been drawn into the passionate intellectual debates that lend drama to *The Brothers Karamazov*, a novel that moreover features an entire philosophical essay on the invented legend of the Grand Inquisitor. Even that great down-to-earth realist Tolstoy felt compelled to include those long discourses on historical determinism that punctuate and indeed bring an end to *War and Peace*. And the social project of protagonist Nekhlyudov in Tolstoy's later novel

Resurrection is motivated by his reading of maverick economist Henry George.

The Russian novelists, then, while not being "thinkers" in the strictest sense of the word, certainly channeled their narrative art into representing thought and thinkers. In so doing, they oftentimes fell into what the noted intellectual historian Aileen Kelly describes as the "habit of taking ideas and concepts to their most extreme, even absurd conclusions." In their "search for absolutes" as well as in their "radical denial of absolutes," Kelly further argues, the Russian intelligentsia "embodied the thirst for absolutes in a pathologically exaggerated form."[1] Kelly's words well characterize our Russian odd pair—Rand in her absolute advocacy of capitalism and her total hatred of social altruism (both in theory and in actuality), Nabokov in his absolute aestheticism and equally absolute denial of "the social" (both in lit. and crit., and in the world).

Rand's two "big" books, of course, are novels of ideas writ very, very, very large. In fact, writ huge! They come, as we noted earlier, permeated by a kind of vulgarized Nietzscheanism, wherein a superior individual rises above the demands of "the herd." *Atlas* consists to an inordinate extent of debates between intellectual and ideological positions, in a somewhat debased exercise in Platonic dialogue. Both *Atlas* and *Fountainhead* culminate in lengthy orations, one of them before a jury, their functions reminiscent of the courtroom speeches placed by Dostoevsky at the high point of *Karamazov*. Rand, then, wrote what were essentially Russian novels with American settings.

*

It may seem odd to place Nabokov within the context of the Russian novel of ideas. And yet, as we have been seeing in the course of this essay, both *The Gift* and *Sebastian Knight* are instances of precisely that. The thick, earlier, Russian volume contains his—or rather, protagonist Fyodor's— interpolated essay on Chernyshevsky. The later book, Nabokov's first in English, features long, discursive passages in the form of mini-reviews of the eponymous novelist's fictive works, or else simple denunciations of the ideas of Sebastian's pitiful doubters such as Mr. Goodman. Such debates also creep into *Laughter in the Dark* (cited at length in chapter 5), while the early short novel *The Eye* contains a passing refutation of what he sees as Marxist theory.

---

[1] Aileen Kelly, Introduction to Isaiah Berlin, *Russian Thinkers*, pp. xvii and xxiii.

The trend continues in his old-age years. The original working title of *Ada* was *The Texture of Time*, a phrase that, in turn, is the handle of a philosophical essay occupying Part Four of the novel. The proud narrator of *Ada* lauds his own article as "a difficult, delectable and blessed work" meant to "purify my own notions of Time." The disquisition itself consists of beautifully crafted metaphors and lyric phrases, all of them brought together into a piece consisting of arrant, rambling, high-sounding nonsense—that, or mere banalities in fancy garb. The touted essay—Nabokov at his worst—includes the fictive author's totally inept and ignorant "refutation" of Einstein. As noted earlier, in spite of the Russian-American's professed contempt for "thinkers," he himself was to try his hand repeatedly as a novelist of ideas—always falling flat in the process.

*

The figure of Nikolai Chernyshevsky (1828-1889) especially plays a role in the work and world view (and for Rand, the life) of our Russian-American pair, albeit in a complex, dialectical, zig-zagging fashion. Chernyshevsky, of course, is little more than a name to educated Westerners; they know mainly that the title of his didactic novel, *What Is to Be Done? From Tales about New People* (henceforth abbreviated occasionally as *WIBD*) was appropriated by Lenin for one of his best-known political pamphlets. On the other hand, anyone involved with Russian literary culture is well aware that, both as writer and as legend, Chernyshevsky was a force to be reckoned with. His early atheism and utopian socialism look ahead to major debates and conflicts in Russia. His life is significant in its own right—his twenty-two years' imprisonment (first in the Peter and Paul Fortress in Petersburg, then in Siberia); the writing of his crude novel; the series of fortuitous miracles that saved the manuscript from censorship, destruction, and oblivion; and the author's eventual death from his long ordeal. All of these, in sum, constitute a story in its own right.

　　The son of a small-town Orthodox cleric, Chernyshevsky in time abandoned his religious roots yet retained a kind of evangelical zeal in his social and moral outlook. His 1855 Master's thesis, "The Aesthetic Relation of Art to Reality," called for a strictly utilitarian approach to the arts, assigning to them the task of strictly describing reality, the latter, in his view, always being superior to any type of art or artifice. Eventually he abandoned academia and drifted into political and economic journalism. His hard-hitting articles for *Sovremennik* (*Contemporary*) drove away the more moderate Turgenev and Tolstoy from the journal's pages even as those pieces helped to nearly double its list of subscribers. With his imprisonment for subversion on trumped-up charges, Chernyshevsky was officially banned from publishing articles. The polemicist thus turned to writing fiction as an alternative vehicle for his ideas. The almost immediate result was *What is to Be Done*, his first novel, 400 pages long and churned out in just four months, between December 1862 and April 1863.

The book bears all the marks of the neophyte who wrote it, along with the great haste in which he spewed it forth. As a novel, *What Is to Be Done?*'s merits are slight. Indeed, its most compelling parts are its *non-*novelistic episodes, those that either unfold utopian visions or depict clashes of ideas. Yet, to our surprise today, Chernyshevsky in his muddling-through fashion accidentally anticipates the Modernist technique of juggling time frames as he shifts from present to past to future; moreover, in certain recurring passages addressed to his "perspicacious reader," he also looks ahead to postmodern metafiction.

This aside, *What Is to Be Done?* qualifies as a thoroughly rough, inchoate, undisciplined hodgepodge in which major actions are often barely fleshed out, characters enter and exit with scant preparation, and entire chapters consist of uncontrolled speechifying. The author's narrative skills, truth be told, are meager indeed. As Fyodor, the protagonist of Nabokov's *The Gift* rightly remarks, "the art of literary portrayal... for [Chernyshevsky] was unattainable" (218).

Still, the enormous sway of *What Is to Be Done?* as a social and intellectual document in Russian life cannot be overestimated. Without once mentioning the Tsarist system and its array of archaic, feudal values, the book is a total critique of that system and, via novelized examples, sets out to suggest some wide-ranging alternatives. As the subtitle of the work indicates, *WIBD* has as its subject matter the "New People" who are building a better future for Russia.

First, the woman question. The female protagonist, Vera Pavlovna Rozalskaya, marries a medical student, Dmitry Sergeich Lopukhov, without the consent of her parents—an act then deemed a felony under Tsarist law. Next, she launches a successful cooperative of women seamstresses, and toward the end she even embarks on the study of medicine. The members of her sewing cooperative live in happiness, cleanliness, and luxury, receiving a high income because "they work for themselves, they are the real owners" (383)[2]. *WIBD* moreover depicts a

---

[2] Nikolai Chernyshevsky, *What Is to Be Done?*, trans. Michael Katz. Page references will be cited in parentheses in the text.

situation of complete equality for women, even in romantic ties, as we shall see shortly.

The two male protagonists, (Vera's husband) Lopukhov and Alexander Matveich Kirsanov are both medical doctors who are in contact with Professor Claude Bernard and other major researchers in France, thus representing the role of progress through Western science. Moreover, all three of the major characters are cited, in positive terms, as being egoists. Of Kirsanov, we are made to imagine him saying "Every man is an egoist and so am I" (234). About Lopukhov the narrator notes, "As an egoist he always thought of himself first, and about others when there was nothing left of his own to think about" (249). And Vera in a letter notes to her anonymous Berlin correspondent, "we three are the greatest egoists the world has ever known" (323). Although surprising to find in the work of a utopian socialist, their shared cult of egoism is nonetheless their way of putting family controls and Christian morality behind them, and expressing an almost Romantic belief in the power of individual creativity, vision, and will.

In addition, there shows up a minor character, Rakhmetov, whose impact is well out of proportion to his passing role in the book. A descendant of great aristocratic wealth, he spurns his background, has become an ascetic, and is in the process of building up his physical strength through manual labor and weight lifting. He also reads for days at a stretch in order to improve his mind, hardly sleeps, and subjects himself to such punishments as sleeping on a bed of nails. His one indulgence is to eat mostly raw beef as a means of keeping up his energies. Rakhmetov is, in brief, "an extraordinary man," a kind of secular saint who rejects all established privilege and ordinary human ties for the sake of pursuing an unspecified ideal. A fleeting presence, Rakhmetov vanishes from the book's pages as quickly and mysteriously as he had appeared.

Rakhmetov also shuns emotion, particularly jealousy, which, in his view, "shouldn't exist in a developed person. It's … a false feeling, a despicable one, … the result of regarding a person as my own property" (305). Emotions are dealt with frequently in such abstract, theoretical terms frequently in this novel. Equality between the sexes, accordingly, is extended to the emotions that men and women hold for each other.

And so, halfway through the novel, Vera realizes that she does not really love her husband… Distraught, she confesses to him that she's in love with his best friend Kirsanov instead. Lopukhov, rather than succumb to jealousy, is pleased for her and says, "So what, my dear? Why should that upset you?" (262) Hence, in order to facilitate the potential couple's fulfillment, Dmitry departs, leaving Vera free to can join up with

Kirsanov. In time Vera receives a letter reporting Lopukhov's suicide in Berlin, a fact enabling her to marry her new love. (These are all seen, of course, as the decisions of rational, egoistic beings.) Years later, however, there shows up a traveler named Charles Beaumont, who has lived, among other places, in the United States (a symbol of modernity). In reality, though, he is Lopukhov, refashioned under an assumed name! The new man now marries Katerina Vasilievna Polozova, a close friend of Vera's, and the two couples become next-door neighbors, going on to share a rich social existence together, living happily ever after as they host parties for younger visitors...

A high point of the book is a twenty-page subsection in chapter 4, bearing the title "Vera Pavlovna's Fourth Dream." An exalted vision of a utopian future, it vividly unfolds before the reader a vast system of rural cooperatives in which the land is fertile, machines do much of the work, and people do whatever they please, living and working in a series of crystal palaces all made of aluminum (a new metal at that time). Everywhere there is elegance; there are no bad memories, "no danger of grief or need, only the recollection of free or willing labor, of abundance, goodness, and enjoyment" (377). The sixth and final chapter of *What Is to Be Done?*, exactly one page in length and called "Change of Scene," is a highly coded reference to what Chernyshevsky saw as the upcoming revolution.

Its glaring deficiencies as literature notwithstanding, *WIBD* had an enormous impact on the Russian reading public, both during the old régime and the aftermath. To cite Nabokov's fictional writer Fyodor once again: "it was read the way liturgical books are read—not a single work by Turgenev or Tolstoy produced such a mighty impression" (G, 277). Hence, taking their cue from Vera Pavlovna's sewing enterprise, every manner of cooperative ventures actually cropped up throughout the Russian empire. Many a male youth endured stomach problems from following Rakhmetov's exclusively raw-beef diet. In emulation of Chrenyshevsky's hero, Lenin lifted weights every day. Later, the Soviet régime singled out Rakhmetov as a positive model for Soviet man. Chernyshevsky's Master's thesis was actually the subject of hundreds of Soviet dissertations.

In Chernyshevsky, then, we are faced with not just a literary phenomenon but a major constituent in the cauldron of intellectual dissidence under Tsarism, a cult figure whose tragic life, moral commitments, and singularly amateurish bad novel are the stuff of legend. Moreover, the man's genuine and estimable qualities of integrity, compassion, and desire for justice earned him respect even among those who disagreed with him ideologically.

Chernyshevsky thus exists as a dominant presence within the Russian cultural mind, and it was precisely that presence that Vladimir Nabokov set out to demolish in his own thick novel, *The Gift* (1937-38). In his "Foreword" to the 1962 English translation, Nabokov, now a renowned Russian-American author, observes that the true heroine of his book is not its female protagonist Zina "but Russian literature" (ii). And fittingly, Nabokov's novel singles out Chernyshevsky as a deplorable, even a destructive force in the panorama of Russian literature.

In that same initial paragraph of his Foreword, Nabokov recounts that his fictional Fyodor's "Life of Chernyshevsky," designed to be interpolated as the entirety of chapter 4, ended up suppressed when the novel first appeared serially in *Sovremenniye Zapiski*, in Paris, "a pretty example of life … imitat[ing] the very art it condemns" (i), as he notes. In justification, the fictive editor Vasiliev informs Fyodor that he finds it objectionable "to lampoon a man whose works and suffering have given sustenance to millions of Russian intellectuals" (207). (Though the journal is real, Nabokov has invented the editor and presumably novelized the incident.) Moreover, Fyodor in his long essay takes issue with the entire notion and tradition of social usefulness in literature, and (as David Rampton notes) heaps scorn on other such venerated figures as Belinsky, Dobrolyubov, and Pisarev.[3] In real-life, émigré Paris, this would not, could not have sat well with the editors of a journal founded by members of the Social Revolutionaries—an exiled, left-wing party that, prior to 1917, had rivaled the Bolsheviks in mass support. (Within the pages of *The Gift*, the essay does come out soon thereafter as a short book from another publisher. In the real world of 1951, it was restored as Chapter 4 in an émigré Russian edition issued in New York.)

And yet … Nabokov-Fyodor's book-essay is certainly less than acceptable on a number of other grounds. His/their so-called "*Life* of Chernyshevsky" has few of the expected trappings—clear exposition; straight, chronological narrative; in-the-round portraiture—of a traditional biography. For instance: the birth and baptism of baby Nikolai are not reported until the *final* page of the text! Highly opaque, the work is well-nigh inaccessible to anyone lacking in previous acquaintance with the purported subject matter and his background—or, in turn, with the in-the-flesh, established author (Nabokov) standing behind the invented, budding author (Fyodor). The account itself is exceedingly mannered, precious, and

---

[3] Rampton, pp. 84-85.

filled with supercilious sarcasm. (Adam Ulam, the respected Russian scholar, describes it as "venomous").[4] The essay-book also has its share of academic pedantry: for example, it includes two full pages of fastidious discussion of Russian poetic prosody (240-242). In some ways, fictive Fyodor's essay anticipates the overwrought *baroquisme* of the real-life Nabokov's future fantasy, *Ada*. It is, in short, a text for the Elect: for Nabokov insiders, specialists, and cultists. One does not read "The Life of Chernyshevsky" to find out about the life of Chernyshevsky; one reads it to wade one's way through Nabokov's highly sectarian, idiosyncratic, and extremely personal agenda concerning Chernyshevsky.

To top all this indulgence, chapter 5 of the novel starts out with some eight pages citing *in extenso* the reviews of Fyodor's "book," adding thereby to the self-reflexive—nay, claustrophobic—atmosphere of *The Gift*. Some of those dreamt-up reviews, to Nabokov's credit, do hit the nail on the head. The very first of his fictive critics, for example, describes young Fyodor's alleged biography as "pretentiously capricious" (301) and filled with "all sorts of digressions on the most diversified themes" (302). Perhaps not coincidentally, *Ada*, with which I've already drawn parallels, also ends with a review of itself.

The Gift, appropriately, was Nabokov's last novel in his native tongue. The most specifically Russian and hence most local of all his Russian fictions, it is of interest solely to Russian-literature adepts. Its beautifully crafted, jewel-like prose aside, the book's appeal to any other reading publics is close to negligible. Without the good fortune of being able to ride on *Lolita*'s coat-tails, *The Gift* would exist as little more than one of many lost works of art—good, bad, or uneven—from the 1930s.

*

The connections between Chernyshevsky and Ayn Rand are scarcely known in the U.S., either to fans or critics. His name is virtually absent from the indexes of books dealing with her. The lacuna is understandable. The language, cultural climate, and frame of reference of *What Is to Be Done?* stand so distant from our 20th/21st-century, post-modern, Americanized world as to render any such relationship opaque and elusive. Rand herself rarely alludes to him, just as she seldom would make public reference to Nietzsche, who nonetheless, as we've seen in previous chapters, was a shaping influence that she later concealed. Given the looming presence of Chernyshevsky in the collective mind of educated

---

[4] Adam Ulam, *In the Name of the People*, p. 59.

Russians, pre- as well as post-1917, some degree of exposure of Alyssa
Rosenbaum/Ayn Rand to her precursor's thinking and his work—in
secondary school classrooms; at Petrograd University; and among her
classmates, fellow budding intellects, and kindred friends—would have
been unavoidable.

Not surprisingly, it took a seasoned scholar of Russian literature, D.
Barton Johnson of the University of California-Santa Barbara, to first draw
attention to the many parallels, affinities, linkages, and other ties that bind
the 19th-century Russian polemicist and scribbler to the covertly
influenced 20th-century one. First, Johnson notes in general terms that
"Rand took her utilitarian view of literature (and style) from Chernyshevsky—
although substituting a very different ideological content." As Prof.
Johnson further observes, *WIBD* is "the progenitor of Socialist Realism
and Rand's Capitalist Realism."[5]

The two authors' chosen purposes, moreover, are analogous:
Chernyshevsky wrote first essays and then fiction to oppose feudalism,
religion, and Tsarism, and to imagine a future modernity in Russia; Rand
in turn wrote fiction and then essays to oppose Communism, socialism,
religion, the New Deal, and the welfare state, and to imagine a renewed
future for unfettered capitalism in America. One critic indeed cites her as
desiring to write a novel with the force of *What Is to Be Done?*[6]

In all fairness it must be said that *Atlas* is a more ably crafted and
structured book than is *WIBD*. After all, Rand was no novice, having
accumulated working experience with fiction in the milieu of Hollywood
script departments and from writing her three previous novels. Moreover,
whereas *What Is to Be Done?* was produced under the rush, duress, and
harsh restraints of Tsarist imprisonment even as its author awaited trial,
Rand possessed the good fortune to compose *Atlas* over a twelve-year
period, in the easy comfort of her California home and, subsequently, in
her Manhattan apartment, always accompanied by her husband. *Atlas*, in
sum, is the better book. As with every artistic genre, some works of
propaganda are better than others, just as, in the area of cuisine, junk food
specialty *X* can be better than junk food dish *Y*.

Their genetic and aesthetic differences aside, the parallels between the
two publicist novels are nevertheless striking. Both contain an inordinate
amount of long speeches and expositions of general ideas. Their characters
exist exclusively to embody, in allegorical fashion, either an idea or a

[5] D. Barton Johnson, "Nabokov, Ayn Rand, and Russian-American Literature or,
the Odd Couple," p. 103.
[6] Claudia Roth Pierpont, "Twilight of the Goddess," p. 81.

personality type. In both novels, moreover, the family is an oppressive, controlling institution that is to be fled and rejected; and, not accidentally, in both works, children are conspicuous by their absence.

Vera Pavlovna, with her cooperative of seamstresses who are seen as working solely for themselves, is clearly an early model for Dagny Taggart and her single-minded railroad entrepreneurialism, working only for herself. The frank, proud egoism that we've seen in Chernyshevsky's three main characters is replicated throughout *Atlas*. For example, chapter VIII of Part 3 bears the title "The Egoist." And at one point a contemptible James Taggart (the worthless, altruistic brother of Dagny) snaps at John Galt, "You're an egoist!"—to which the super-hero comes back with the simple, disyllabic riposte, "I am" (1033). Of self-sacrifice, Chernyshevsky's extraordinary exemplar, Rakhmetov, says that it is "all stuff and nonsense" (149). Likewise, *Atlas* is replete with one-liners ridiculing or condemning "self-sacrifice," and Galt singles out "sacrifice" numerous times for attack in his lengthy allocution. Rakhmetov himself can be seen as a vivid, dramatic forebear to Rand's genius extraordinaire, though Nietzsche's *Übermensch* also provided Rand with a generic model.

The rational, unemotional, succinct way in which Lopukhov yields ground so that his spouse Vera can join up with his friend Kirsanov, the man she truly loves, has its exact, if more inflated parallel episode in *Atlas*. Throughout much of the novel, Dagny carries on a passionate, illicit, transcontinental affair with steel magnate Hank Rearden (whose wife, brother, and mother are all despicable, whining moochers). Later, however, Dagny gets romantically involved with the mighty, still elusive John Galt, who becomes to her "the love I had wanted to reach long before he existed, and I think he will remain beyond my reach, but that I love him will be enough to keep my living." When she informs Hank of this drastic change in her affections, the genius industrialist and inventor calmly, manfully accepts this new development, happy for her, and—we are informed— "his face had the serenity of pure strength" (800). Some pages thereafter, Hank will send Dagny a note, its entire text reading, "I have met him. I don't blame you" (930). Thus, as in *What Is to Be Done?*, we have in *Atlas* the proper comportment of a superior, rational being.

In her real-life love life, moreover, Rand emulated the first half of Chernyshevsky's rational paradigm when she entered into her years-long liaison with devoted disciple Nathaniel Branden. Following the *What Is to Be Done?* plotline yet further expanding it to include the two couples, spouse Barbara and spouse Frank were persuaded to calmly accept the situation, in keeping with the high and mighty rational beings the foursome claimed to be. Not for them the emotional shackles of second-handers, collectivists, altruists, looters, moochers, and other infrahuman specimens. *BUT* (background music, fortissimo! trumpets! drums!) when Nathaniel finally informed the philosopher-queen about his ongoing amour with beautiful, youthful model Patrecia Gullison, the goddess of Reason cast aside her official rulebook and erupted into righteous fury. Rather than emulate her own creation Hank Rearden, rather than free Nathaniel of any blame and instead feel happy for her acolyte and thereby demonstrate "the serenity of pure strength" (as Hank Rearden does), she reverted instead to the traditional archetypes of the dreadful Gorgon cum Queen Dido, her titanic jealousy leading not to tragic suicide but to Nathaniel's finding himself vengefully expelled from the Objectivist kingdom, with a personal malediction to boot, transformed, Kremlin-style, into a non-person.

It is in Chernyshevsky's utopian vision, however, that one especially can see the close kinship between the imprisoned Russian and Rand the émigré. The crystal palaces that dot the imagined landscape in Vera's dream are built from the brand-new metal, aluminum. Hank Rearden, in turn, has devised an unprecedented new metal (never described; referred to simply as "Rearden Metal"), to be utilized in Galt's Gulch's industries. In Chernyshevsky's oneiric wonderland much of the work is performed by machines. In Rand's Rocky Mountain enclave, all energy is generated by John Galt's miracle motor (at one-hundredth the cost of conventional sources) together with shale oil, the latter of which the exiled geniuses are readily and most easily extracting from the ground and then refining for use. (Again, Rand merely tells, does not show.) Among the "strikers" is Ellis Wyatt, a petroleum magnate who has left his oil wells behind him to burn, he too in protest against government altruism; and somehow he feels no threat to his own enterprises in the face of these amazing developments in alternative energy.

Finally, each of these utopias portrays its respective residents as living just as they please, without worries or care. In sum, *What Is to Be Done?* can safely be singled out as a major source for the art, the purposes, and the world view of Ayn Rand. It is *the* ultimate template, the narrative model for the thick volume known as *Atlas Shrugged*.

The aesthetics of Soviet Russia, strange though it may seem, also serve as lifeblood for Rand the writer. Soviet propaganda narratives notoriously glorified the heroic, committed worker who—as the *Encyclopedia Britannica* entry on "Russia" puts it—"overcomes various saboteurs, spies, or other obstacles in order to get the factory, farm, or construction site up and running."[7] Rand's "capitalist realist" novels similarly glorify the heroic, committed entrepreneur who overcomes those same obstacles, and, at the end of *Fountainhead*, the Roark construction site is "up and running." The godhead of Objectivism once characterized the aim of her work as "the projection of an ideal man" (RM, 161); for Soviet apparatchiks the explicit goal of art, by the same token, was to foster "the positive hero." As D. Barton Johnson tellingly points out, Rand's formula "sounds quite at home in the context of Socialist Realism."[8] Also says Rand, "Art is the technology of the soul" (RM, 170), a notion uncannily close to Stalin's conception of artists as "engineers of human souls." The breathless descriptions of Hank Rearden's chugging factories in *Atlas Shrugged* are just the sort of thing we might expect to find in Soviet novels or films that mythologized the tempering of steel.

In addition, that primal creation myth of proletarian art and Communist folklore—a workers' strike—is at the very basis of *Atlas*. "We are on strike," says leader John Galt on numerous occasions—at one point three times in succession, in a kind of litany. ("We are on strike against those who believe that one man must exist for the sake of another"—688.) "The Strike" in fact was the original working title Rand's thick opus-in-progress. Significantly, *The Strike* (1925) also happens to be the title of a renowned film by Russian director Sergey Eisenstein, which Rand, as a Soviet film-school student, may well have viewed just before her emigration. Eisenstein, moreover, had directed *Battleship Potemkin* (1925), about a mutiny of sailors against their Tsarist officers that took place on the eponymous craft during the 1905 Revolution. A workers' strike is also the *primum mobile* in the series of events comprising Maxim Gorki's proto-socialist-realist novel *The Mother* (1907) and in Vsevolod Pudovkin's 1926 movie of that name. Not accidentally, many industrialists in *Atlas* vanish on May 1st—the traditional, international workers' holiday and a day of rest and military parades in the USSR.

Meanwhile, back in Rand's novel, the brilliant Argentine businessman Francisco D'Anconia, scion of one of his country's most puissant clans, has launched his very own copper mine in the Rockies. As he proudly informs Dagny, "I did the prospecting. I discovered it. I broke the first excavation … I started it with my own hands" (716). The distinct impression given is that he somehow performs the myriad of necessary labors by himself: riding down into the mineshafts with pick and shovel and protective gear, bringing out the clumps of rock in a wheelbarrow, and

---

[7] "Russia," vol. 26, p. 958.
[8] Johnson, p. 104.

then separating, smelting, and refining the metal, all with no one else's assistance. Except for his passing mention of a superintendent (Question: Is the latter also one of the exiled geniuses on strike?), Francisco does not refer to any work crews, any miners heading down the pit to retrieve en masse those raw materials. Señor D'Anconia thus truly qualifies as a solitary, rugged superman, the world's loneliest yet most productive miner, without either being himself a worker or needing workers.

Even Rand's famous enshrining of the dollar sign is a conscious appropriation of that symbol's use in left-wing cartooning and caricature. As Owen Kellogg, one of the entrepreneurs-on-strike, explains to Dagny, who has asked what the dollar symbol stands for among them:

> "The dollar sign? For a great deal. It stands on the vest of every fat, piglike creature in every cartoon, for the purpose of denoting a crook, a grafter, a scoundrel—as the one sure-fire brand of evil. It stands—as the money of a free country—for achievement, for success, for ability, for man's creative power—and precisely for these reasons, it is used as a brand of infamy... Incidentally, do you know where that sign comes from? It stands for the initials of the United States." (637)

Kellogg's account of the origins of the symbol, incidentally, is here the product of his maker's tendentious imagination and her quasi-nationalist ideology. Many hypotheses exist for the derivation of $, but the most common ones have to do with the plural form of the Spanish word *peso*, which on the peso coin bore a letter "S" juxtaposed with the two pillars of Hercules at Gibraltar. Even for this sort of minutiae, Rand's mythmaking impulse is at work.

At every level, then, Rand took the standard myths and stories, emblems and issues, of Russian, Soviet, Communist, and Western left-wing culture, and with Chernyshevsky himself as a starting point, turned them all inside out in one of the longest and most influential works of right-wing propaganda ever written.

It goes without saying that Communism, Russia, and the Western left are not the sole cultural sources for the approach, vision, and aesthetics of *Atlas*. The self-made man is obviously a bourgeois and peculiarly American mytheme, here taken to extremes. In addition there is revised medieval folklore in the figure of Ragnar Danneskjöld, the reverse Robin Hood who courageously steals from the have-nots to donate to the haves, or, to be exact, "who robs the thieving poor and gives back to the productive rich" (540). More importantly, the Hollywood machinery within which Rand labored provided her with narrative formulas aplenty. At one point a character in *Atlas* is likened to a cowboy with a gun, and among the book's action-packed final episodes is a veritable gunfight between the entrepreneurial white-hats of Galt's Gulch (the place-name is clearly suggestive of titles of horse-operas) and the evil, altruistic, governmental black-hat bad guys, as in many a standard-issue Western flick. At one moment during those scenes, we read, "the window burst into a shower of glass—and from the limb of a tree, as from a catapult, the tall and slender figure of a man flew into the room, landed on its feet and fired at the first guard in reach" (1071). And who is it? Is it Superman? Tarzan? Mighty Mouse? No, dear readers, it's the handsome Viking, Ragnar Dannerskjöld, come to the rescue!

The mark left by *Atlas Shrugged* on susceptible American youths, pro-business ideologues, and the more reactionary elements in North American life, can on several counts be likened to the impact that *What Is to Be Done?* had on the entire spectrum of anti-Tsarist and official Soviet culture. "What would John Galt do?" has served as a common rallying cry for Rand cultists, similar to "What would Jesus do?" among Evangelicals, and similar to the Rakhmetov role model for anti-Czarists in the 19th and 20th centuries. Re-reading *Atlas* is a point of duty among Rand acolytes, much as rereading *WIBD* and studying the Bible has been for their respective parties.[9] Randians of all ages talk and blog about John Galt and Dagny Taggart as if they were living entities, like Rakhmetov or the Lord God or Jesus, and a casual Google search reveals a long list of parents proudly naming their daughters "Dagny." The phrase "Who is John Galt?" crops up here and there on telephone poles, wall graffiti, and Tea Party placards. Lululemon Athletics, a manufacturer of yoga clothing in Vancouver, displays the slogan on its stores' shopping bags; its founder, Chip Wilson, having first read the book at age 18, now wished to "elevate the world from mediocrity to greatness."[10] Perhaps not accidentally, the key quotation in *Atlas Shrugged* is a question, like the title of Chernyshevsky's novel.

*

Nabokov's Russian backgrounds form a commanding part of his oeuvre and personality. Scholars of Nabokov's art, moreover, have explored his complex and palpable debt to the Russian Symbolist movement. Indeed, *Petersburg*, by Andrei Bely, a major participant in that school, was singled out by Nabokov himself as one of the three great novels (along with *In Search of Lost Time* and *Ulysses*) of the twentieth century. His polemic

---

[9] Jeff Walker, *The Ayn Rand Cult*, pp. 37-39.
[10] www.lululemon.com/community/blog/who-is-john-galt/

against Chernyshevsky thus grows out of his allegiance to his Symbolist brethren and to Art for Art's Sake.

The strictly Russian components of Rand *the writer*, by contrast, remain relatively hidden to this day, even as her formative years as a restless, young, middle-class citizen of Russia have at long last undergone exploration by recent biographers and researchers. It is my hope that the connections I have noted here between 19th-century Russian literature and Soviet aesthetics on one hand, and Rand's work on the other, can shed light on this crucial yet scarcely acknowledged aspect of her writing practice.

CHAPTER TWELVE

ON THEIR NASTY SIDE

"Nabokov and Nastiness"

So reads the aggressive, in-your-face title with which the respected literary quarterly, *Hudson Review*, headlined in 1993 its featured review essay, by Smith College professor Dean Flower, on Brian Boyd's monumental two-volume biography of the Russian-American master.

Professor Flower's focus on the nastiness of Nabokov came in response to two things: 1) Boyd's repeated insistence that his biographical subject was a deeply kind, thoughtful, and generous man (an image also propagated by many of the novelist's admiring critics), and 2) Boyd's further contention that the petulant and disagreeable fellow whom we know from the interviews, and from the prefaces to his translated Russian works, is in reality an artifice, a persona constructed by the famed novelist for use in his public appearances.

Not so, argues Professor Flower, who goes on to cite one example after another in which Nabokov was most unpleasant in his dealings with other people—with resident governesses and tutors both foreign and Russian, with friends, and with siblings (whom he largely disregarded). In addition Flower points out the nastiness of Nabokov's leading characters, often identifying their churlish traits with those of their artful progenitor.

Now, it is a simple truism that being a great artist does not necessarily make one a halfway decent, let alone a great and admirable, human being. If anything, the history of the arts shows a fair number of writers, painters, and musicians who were mean-spirited, pettish individuals at best, and destructive, psychopathic monsters at worst. Of course, it should be said in turn that few monsters or psychopaths are artists, at least not in the strict, conventional sense of the word, though some psychopaths may be virtuoso play-actors in the arena of daily life, and many of them are indeed known as "confidence *artists*" or as career criminals. In any case, when legitimate artists have a nasty side, it is only their art that redeems them for posterity.

Neither Nabokov nor Rand is much known for their humane qualities. Still, their respective fans like to assert that the one or the other could be bounteous with friends and even with regular folks. The documentary evidence, however, suggests otherwise. If the reader of these pages happens to be a devoted Randian or Nabokovian, I apologize in advance for dedicating this entire chapter to so disquieting and distasteful a topic.

Observers who held no stake in maintaining warm relations with the Nabokov inner circle have taken note over time of the novelist's less than attractive personal qualities. Already in the 1950s, Nabokov's then-friend Edmund Wilson was confiding such observations to his journal, later published, naturally enough, under the title *The Fifties*. We read of the novelist's enormous vanity, "his impulse to think of himself as the only writer in history equally proficient in Russian, English, and French" (424). Following a visit by the Nabokov couple, Wilson reports a "disagreeable impression," especially Vladimir's "addiction to *Schadenfreude*—everybody is always being humiliated." Summing up Nabokov's divers unlikeable aspects, Wilson remarks, "there is also something in him rather nasty—the cruelty of the arrogant rich man that makes him want to humiliate others, and his characters he has completely at his mercy" (426). The famous rift that took place in 1964, when Wilson penned a negative review of the author's mammoth translation of Pushkin's *Eugene Onegin* in the *New York Review of Books*, was thus probably long simmering. America's leading man of letters had clearly grown tired of the less than admirable traits of what was seen at the time as America's most eminent novelist.

Biographers and memoirists alike, even sympathetic ones like Boyd, have alluded to Nabokov's penchant, at academic social gatherings in his Cambridge, Massachusetts days, for striking up mock-serious conversations about some fictitious literary or historical figure or other, and leading on his interlocutor(s) for a long while, simply for the fun of it. The endless "hoaxing" reached the point where Elena Levin, wife of the prominent Harvard critic Harry Levin, could no longer bring herself to invite the Russian couple to her home. There are enough reports about Nabokov cruelly playing with his real-life listeners, much as he does with his invented literary characters in his prose fiction, to see in this persistent minor vice and "shabby behavior" (Professor Flower's phrase) a symptom of something larger.

In previous chapters we have seen the Nabokov who would habitually dismiss great authors via a clever epithet and shoot down major thinkers with facile name-calling. That intellectual crudity of his is actually part of a broader set of personal and psychological habits. Such meanness crops up repeatedly in Nabokov's life's work, wherein he often presents characters, even fleeting ones, in vicious and sadistic terms. In *Speak,*

Memory, for instance he introduces us briefly to "Hristofor, a blue-faced footman ... with an idiotic smile" (154). Servants and house subordinates are several times subject to this sort of verbal condescension. The Nabokov household's resident foreign-language tutors—its educational servants—are especially subject to routine ridicule. Besides the boy's "myopic little Miss Hunt" and his "pink-nosed Miss Robinson" (87), there is "Mademoiselle O," who stayed seven years with the family, and about whom the author derisively remembers "her prodigious posterior" (96), "her elephantine body" (114), "the shallowness of her culture" and "the banality of her mind" (113), as well as mocking the various slights and hurts the lady endured in the course of her home stay. In recalling his relationship with her—a woman who, after all, was his first major instructor of French—there is scarcely a sign of affection, loyalty, or gratitude, just a cold-hearted superciliousness. One hears here less the nostalgia for a treasured person past than the voice of a spoiled, eleven-year-old brat, poking easy fun at a teacher in her absence.

It is therefore not surprising that an otherwise positively admiring scholar from France, Georges Nivat, speaks of Nabokov the memoirist, as "a strange and not very sympathetic adolescent from a rich family."[1] Moreover, he cites another émigré writer and friend of the Nabokovs, Zinaida Shakhovskaya, who refers with some displeasure to "the snobbish egocentrism of [*Speak, Memory*],... the class pride, the nearly total ignorance of other social worlds, the faceless domestics, the absence of real peasants ..."[2] Of course, the denial of society, we have been seeing throughout this study, is a fundamental in the vision and oeuvre of both Nabokov and Rand.

Far more importantly for our purposes, the nastiness of Nabokov comes through repeatedly within the covers of his fictions. The prefaces added to his earlier works, written at the height of his fame, can be as combative, prickly, and rude as are La Rand's characters (or as Rand reportedly was in real-life appearances). In his "Introduction" to *Bend Sinister*, for instance, the author makes a statement that lies not far from notions found throughout *Atlas Shrugged*. Says Nabokov: "Politics and economics, atomic bombs,... the entire Orient, symptoms of 'thaw' in Soviet Russia, the Future of Mankind, and so on, leave me supremely indifferent" (6).

Moreover, in considering Nabokov's more tendentious novels such as *Glory*, *The Gift*, and *Sebastian Knight*, one encounters exactly the sort of

---

[1] Georges Nivat, "*Speak, Memory*," p. 674.
[2] Cited by Nivat, p. 677.

protagonist—smart, handsome, arrogant, wise, outrageous, courageous, and absolutely right in all his endeavors and opinions—that could have stepped out of the pages of an Ayn Rand novel. Fyodor's father in *The Gift*, for example, is recollected in terms that (the male progenitor's "warmth" aside) seem taken from *Fountainhead* or *Shrugged*: "his live masculinity and independence; the chill and the warmth of his personality; his power over everything he undertook." In Godunov *père*'s reported lepidopteral travels through Asia, moreover, he has no interest in "the natives," shows "no indulgence to mandarins," and feels "total indifference to ethnography" (112). (Rand's indifference to Asia was analogous, if more strident.) Such, then, are Nabokov's positive heroes, the representative characters of his imagined world.

Serving as foils to these high exemplars are many if not most of Nabokov's other characters, frequently rendered in grotesque terms, oftentimes via animal imagery (dogs, frogs, and toads being frequent terms of comparison). Here follows a partial, initial catalogue:

The Real Life of Sebastian Knight. We are introduced to the social-minded literary critic, and hence the villain of the novel—its Ellsworth Toohey, so to speak—Goodman, "whose long, soft, pinkish face was, and is, remarkably like a cow's udder" (50).

King, Queen, Knave. A book filled with grotesques, their aspects and actions mirthfully reported: e.g. "That morning a cripple walking in front of her had slipped on the bare ice. It was frightfully funny to see his wooden stump erect when he sprawled on his stupid back" (126). Martha is described as "a large white toad" (259). The narrative voice in this work is that of a puppet master, reveling in his power over some contemptible non-entities.

Laughter in the Dark. Passing portrait of a cook: "a huge woman with arms like lumps of raw meat" (50).

Pnin. Nabokov here already begins to settle scores with his fellow academics. Virtually every character in this campus novel is a more or less contemptible stick figure and an intellectual fraud. Russian speakers' accents and grammatical errors in English also serve as a source of ethnic humor. Another passing description: "two lumpy old ladies in semitransparent raincoats, like potatoes in cellophane" (438).

The Gift is particularly rife with this sort of thing. The list that follows is, of necessity, selective.

"Lorentz's pug-faced wife" (59)

"a fat lawyer who resembled an overfed turtle" (66)

In Tibet, "one idiot, particularly tiresome, in yellow silk under a red umbrella" (123)

Of Schchyogolev, "a bulky, chubby man whose outline reminded me of a carp" (143)

"an elderly, nosy-faced beggar woman with legs cut off at the pelvis" (163)

"a dreadfully skinny man with ... wrinkles of fastidious distaste around his apish mouth" (166)

"this elderly, fleshy woman with a toad's face" (185)

"The office manager Hammeke (a fat, coarse animal with smelly feet and a perpetually oozing furuncle on the nape...)" (189)

"Gurman's other friend, loose-fleshed, gray-skinned ... his whole aspect resembling a peaceful toad that wants ... to be left in complete peace in a damp place" (332)

Look at the Harlequins! "a particularly stupid baby-sitter" (139); "Mrs. Blogovo was a half-witted cripple" (163)

There are many more like instances I could cite, especially from *Ada*, which is in some ways Nabokov's equivalent—along with *The Gift*—to Rand's *Atlas Shrugged*. But, dear reader, I do not wish to exceed myself here. On a somewhat marginal note, it is significant that such nasty comments do not much stand out in *Despair* and even less so in *Lolita* or *Pale Fire*. Given that, in these novels, the unreliable narrator is already nasty by nature, such perverse verbal sallies belong ipso facto to his overall make-up and their humor is thus intimately bound up with the entire book-length joke.

If Nabokov were a satirical brand of artist, in the vein, say, of Jonathan Swift or the countercultural cartoonist R. Crumb, portrayals such as these could be seen as emanating from, and imbued with, the spirit of a bitter yet sensitive misanthrope, outraged at the morally and socially grotesque nature of his fellow citizens and human brethren. Nabokov, however,

never claimed to be a satirist, and in fact more than once disowned the
rubric. (Thus, from the preface to *Bend Sinister*: "I am not 'satirical.'")
Hence, should any one source be singled out for such nasty depictions, it is
precisely that of Nabokov the aristocrat cum artistic purist and high verbal
artificer, who looks down with uncharitable, mocking disdain at all those
standing below or outside his charmed circle and its happy few.

As a kind of foil-to-these-foils, Nabokov on occasion inserts himself
into the concluding stages of a fiction. Toward the end of *King Queen
Knave*, we are informed of "a remarkably handsome man in an old-
fashioned dinner jacket," whom protagonist Franz sees strolling about,
sometimes carrying "a butterfly net" and generally "contemptuous of
everything on earth" save for the woman accompanying him (254). The
butterfly net, needless to say, makes clear the identity of this comely
fellow. (The approving adjective "contemptuous," incidentally, is one
commonly employed by La Rand in describing her heroes.)

Nabokov's referencing his own good looks merits a brief comment.
The author's oft-voiced scorn, via his narrators, for those who are
allegedly unattractive, seems just too perfect, too predictable, coming from
the pen of a then extremely handsome man. Not a few of us have known
the personality type: a devilishly beautiful, rakish young stud whose luck
with the ladies seems limitless, whose sexual conquests never cease—and
who in the process has acquired a touch of arrogance as well as a disdain
toward others (his conquests included), he finding it all too easy to mock
their corporeal and facial deficiencies. (Perhaps, dear reader, you can
remember some instances thereof; in my college days I knew at least two
of them.) Already in the still-traditionalist Russia of 1916, Nabokov was
carrying on three affairs simultaneously. Of his later sojourn in Yalta,
while his family waited out the Bolsheviks, biographer Boyd sums it up
thus: "sexually ... a rather torrid summer for him" (146). When the
England-bound ship *Nadezhda* made a three-and-a-half week stop in
Athens, the twenty-year-old again juggled three amours at once. At
Cambridge University he was very much the young libertine. (Not
surprisingly, some of his male literary peers would at times express
grudging envy at the author's success with women.) Hence, when
Nabokov's narrators so persistently spoof the plain and the homely, the ill-
favored, the frog-faced, and the ugly, well, the source of it all makes the
spoofing somewhat suspect...

Nabokov toward the end of his campus novel *Pnin* assigns to his own
person a somewhat more extended cameo appearance, this time as "a
prominent Anglo-Russian writer." Even as the pathetic, inept, titular
protagonist—a frequent figure of fun throughout the book—finds himself

being relieved of his duties, the college's English department is making overtures to a certain V.V., whom the Chair describes to Pnin as "one of your most brilliant compatriots, a really fascinating lecturer" (494). V.V. is in fact taking over as narrator of the novel at this point, and actually concedes that he, name of Vladimir Vladimirovich, has been rather "arrogant" (500)—much indeed, as was real-life Anglo-Russian writer Vladimir Vladimirovich Nabokov himself, the model for, and partial namesake of, V.V.. In the 1940s and 40s, of course, Nabokov was often given to quietly inserting himself among Russia's greatest authors via his early pseudonym "Sirin."

Nabokov's arrogance and nastiness constitute an important subtheme in *The Unreal Life of Sergey Nabokov* (2011), by Paul Russell, a novelist who teaches at Vassar College. Russell's book fictionalizes, in first person, the story of Vladimir's eponymous younger brother who ended up staying behind in the Third Reich. Because of his homosexuality and for having criticized the regime, the real-life Sergey died tragically in the Neuengamme labor camp outside Hamburg. After the war, several survivors of the prison looked up other Nabokovs in the telephone book and called them simply to talk about Sergey's extraordinary kindness toward fellow inmates, his having shared clothes and food with those less fortunate than he was.

The flesh-and-blood Vladimir thought little of Sergey, whom, following the latter's death, he described in a letter to Edmund Wilson as "a harmless, indolent, pathetic person who spent his life vaguely shuttling between the Quartier Latin and a castle in Austria." In keeping with the standard prejudices of his time, the novelist thought of homosexuality as a hereditary disease, and referred to gay painters in Taos, New Mexico as "faded pansies."[3]

Throughout Paul Russell's fine novel, Sergey lives, almost invisibly, in the shadow of his talented brother, who in his own scenes does not come off well. When the Russian civil war is raging in the streets, Vladimir, indifferent to anything outside literature and butterflies, lies on the sofa composing a poem. In another episode, when Sergey goes to tell him about the death of a friend, Vladimir doesn't want to be bothered, working as he is on a butterfly. Vladimir routinely condescends to his brother, or is at best indifferent, as he is to most of the rest of his family. Their Uncle Ruka's limping gait "provoked a cruel imitation by my brother" (18),[4]

[3] Quotations and references in these two paragraphs come from Lev Grossman, "The Gay Nabokov," www.salon.com/2000/05/17/Nabokov_5/
[4] Paul Russell, *The Unreal Life of Sergey Nabokov*. Page references to this work will be cited parenthetically within the text.

Sergey remembers. Naturally, the elder sibling is not pleased with Sergey's sexual inclination, and, in comparing him with gay Uncle Ruka, says, "I must confess, Seryosha: I hated seeing you become one of his kind" (330).

Vladimir's summary dismissal of all socially oriented literature, a pattern I noted earlier in my chapter 7, is given flesh in Russell's novel via an exchange in which Sergey praises Balzac's *Splendeurs et misères des courtisanes*, and the elder brother brushes it off as "not literature at all but only a crude attempt at social history" (177). Meanwhile, outside the family, Vladimir is similarly nasty. During his exile in Paris, starting in 1937, we read that "his literary judgments were provoking outrage," and he offends and insults several respected émigré authors to their faces. "The very mention of his name made Nobel laureate Bunin livid" (333). Infant son Dmitri doesn't get off the hook in Russell's recounting, either; the little boy, Sergey says, is "a little terror, and his doting parents did nothing to control his anarchic spirit" (366).[5] Granted, Paul Russell's book is a fiction, but it is fiction strongly based on what many who knew him have recounted about Nabokov as a person.

Though some Nabokov devotees (professional or not) would disagree, many sincere admirers do feel that something went grievously wrong with Nabokov, both the man and the writer, in the wake of the wealth and fame brought to him by *Lolita* and *Pale Fire*. Philosopher Richard Rorty is very polite and discreet in describing *Ada* and *Look at the Harlequins!* (*LATH* for short) as "merely idiosyncratic," and of the former work he says, "[Nabokov] is talking only to himself half the time" (161). Critic Douglas Fowler cautiously characterizes *Ada* as a novel "for the Nabokov specialist" and "a very imperfect book" (177) that is "almost without conflict, naked Nabokoviana" (188). From the start, British reviewers— D.J. Enright, Gillian Tindall, Philip Toynbee—frankly attacked *Ada*, as did Morris Dickstein and former ardent fan Mary McCarthy in the United States.

Nabokov's first, "other" biographer, Andrew Field, in a later book adjudges *Ada* "the weakest novel he ever wrote," and finds it "sprawling and self-indulgent," even "juvenile," "a parody of a parody."[6] For daring to doubt the great man's continuing greatness, Field was excommunicated

---

[5] Dmitri Nabokov as an aging adult apparently followed in his father's footsteps. In his introduction to the posthumous sketch by Nabokov *père*, *The Original of Laura*, he alludes to "the lesser minds among the hordes of letter writers that were to descend upon me" (xvi), as well as the "fashionable morons" out there.
[6] Andrew Field, *VN: The Life and Art of Vladimir Nabokov*, pp. 362-364. Future page references to this book will be cited in parentheses.

from the Nabokovian heights, ridiculed by son Dmitri in public, and banned from the world of Nabokov specialists. And of *Look at the Harlequins!*, even Nabokov's major biographer Brian Boyd more recently remarked, "Its self-referentiality seemed sterile and sour," and confesses that he was "sadly disappointed by" the book, seeing in it "an irreversible decline in Nabokov's powers."[7]

With the latter-day Nabokov, one witnesses the spectacle of a major literary artist, who had achieved undoubted mastery and even greatness, now becoming filled with himself and turning both arrogant and deluded. As Field again remarks, "he wore his fame badly," felt he was "on Olympus and yet had an irritating awareness that not all the world agreed" (362). Summing up, Field observes, "Nabokov/Narcissus wandered away from the perfect pool and turned into a garden-variety egotist" (364). In the process, the nasty side of Nabokov that had once manifested itself only in private and in his interpersonal relationships, in his attacks on most writers and thinkers and in passing characterizations in his previous novels, and finally in parodic form in *Lolita* and *Pale Fire*—in the end the nastiness took over and crystallized as his normal self in those sunset novels, *Ada* and *...Harlequins*, as well as in his interviews, and in the prefaces affixed to his reissued earlier books. In many ways, it seems, Nabokov never outgrew the combination of spoiled brat, semi-feral child, and anti-social snob that he had actually been from early on.

*

Rand never claimed to be a kind or generous woman. In her fiction, moreover, kindness is generally depicted as suspect, even as destructive or downright evil. And her cultists seldom thought it necessary to note any role for kindness in her "philosophy" or her personality. With her abject devotees, Rand was ever the attentive hostess, but it was very much the cordiality of the cult leader and dictator toward their sycophants. (In her relations with her acolytes, one is reminded of Yugoslav dissident Milovan Djilas's bitter remembrances of his conversations with Stalin in his memoir by that name, or the accounts, both fictional and historical, of Dominican dictator Trujillo's treatment of his subordinates at his table talk or cabinet meetings.)[8] At Rand's public presentations, by contrast, when replying to questions she disliked or disagreed with, she was wont to

---

[7] Boyd, *Stalking Nabokov: Selected Essays*, pp. 330 and 287.
[8] Milovan Djilas, *Conversations with Stalin*. For Trujillo, see Mario Vargas Llosa's fine novel, *The Feast of the Goat*.

shouting down the question, and quashing any potential dissent with an insult. (As Carlin Romano notes in his examination of Rand, "she never argued when she could name-call.")[9] If the talk was before a friendly crowd of Objectivists, she might call the inquirer "a person of low self-esteem" or "a cheap fraud,"[10] to which the audience responded with adoring applause. Rand's fans today tend to follow suit and mimic her style in their own intellectual exchanges on the Internet, routinely accusing their interlocutors of being ignorant or stupid.

Much has been said in biographies, memoirs, and polemical works about Rand's cavalier, thoughtless, and *selfish* (ergo, virtuous) treatment of her family members and her husband Frank. One such instance will suffice for now. While the couple was living in California in the 1940s, Frank had developed a thriving business as a horticulturalist and florist—an activity he was forced to abandon when Rand insisted on moving to New York in order to be near her prospective lover, Nathaniel Branden. The affair with the latter, of course, contributed to Frank's deterioration. Barbara Weiss, Rand's secretary for fifteen years, later remarked about her former boss in an interview to Barbara Branden, "She just robbed him of everything," and that she, Weiss, came to "look on [Rand] as a killer of people."[11]

Then there is the quasi-Stalinist spell that La Rand held over her disciples. Libertarian writer Murray Rothbard noted in a letter to Richard Cornuelle that he found Rand's followers to be "almost lifeless, devoid of enthusiasm or spark, and almost completely dependent on Ayn for intellectual sustenance."[12] And she would break with anyone, ranging from small-fry Objectivists to major figures like Ludwig von Mises or Milton Friedman, over the most minute issues (in a bizarre echo of the Communists' sectarian battles, both in and outside of Russia, at the height of the Soviet dictatorship). Rand's view was essentially, "Either you are with me or against me," a sentiment she often expressed in words to that effect. In one unintentionally comical touch, the *Überfrau* expressed her dislike of facial hair, and henceforth no beards or moustaches were to be found among the Rand faithful.

It is in Rand's written works, though, that her nastiness is systematic, a constant, indeed an essential component of her oeuvre.

Simply the way Rand's characters *look* serves as one of the foundations of her world view. Close disciple and early biographer

---

[9] Carlin Romano, *America the Philosophical*, p. 365.
[10] Burns, p. 222.
[11] Cited in Heller, p. 400.
[12] Burns, p. 152.

Barbara Branden recalls, "All her life she was to respond to men and women who had an appearance [that] she believed to be 'the best of the American type:' the tall, blond, long-legged, emotionally reserved men and women who would typify the heroes of her novels."[13] In brief, the strong, silent type, Nordic-featured and preferably high in stature, then the norm for film fame in Hollywood, where Rand had first worked and absorbed this aesthetic-cum-ethics. Or, in Rand's own words, "I fully believed that appearance showed character, that my type of face necessarily showed a good character, my kind of man."[14] An interesting throwback, this, to the early-modern, and now discredited pseudo-science of physiognomy...

Such a conception is applied systematically throughout Rand's works of fiction. Moreover, her protagonists, besides always being strikingly handsome, are invariably described as possessing such traits (in her view, positive) as "arrogance," "contempt," and "scorn." The pattern is already evident in her first novel, *We the Living*, in which Kira, the heroine, is introduced with her "severe, arrogant calm" and her "haughty profile" (12). Of her lover Lev, we read: "His mouth, calm, severe, contemptuous, was that of an ancient chieftain who would order men to die," and his lips are in the shape of "a scornful arc" (53). Later on, from Kira's point of view: his "body was white as marble and hard and straight; the body of a god, she thought" (175). Kira's other mate, Andrei, walks with "his body slender, erect ... the kind of body that in centuries past had worn the armor of a Roman, the mail of a crusader" (297). Later on, depicting Lev once again: "He moved as if his whole body were a living will: straight, arrogant, commanding, as will a body that could never bend because both had been born without the capacity to conceive of bending ... There was a contemptuous tenderness in his movement, and a command, and a hunger; he was not a lover, but *a slave owner*" (132; emphasis added). Rand's early mentor Nietzsche, let us recall, was frankly on the side of the slaveholders.

In *Atlas*, this sort of haughty appearance becomes generalized throughout, as we've already seen in chapter 2. For example, oil magnate Ellis Wyatt is "young, tall, and something about him suggested violence," and has a "quality of self-control that seemed almost arrogant" (82). South American oligarch Francisco D'Anconia's face is "merciless," with a "naked, implacable look" (397). The Nordic visage especially takes on importance in Rand's pop epic. Several times along we are informed about

---

[13] Barbara Branden, p. 23.
[14] Ibid, p. 81.

steel magnate Hank Rearden's eyes of "pale blue ice" along with his
"blond hair," as well as his being, of course, tall, "too tall for those around
him" (34). Like Francisco, he also is "icily implacable" (447). Even Eddie
Willers, the lifelong, loyal, almost feudal retainer of the Taggart
enterprise, has his own eyes of blue with "blond hair and a square face"
(15), though, not being a high-placed genius-hero, he is not granted the
gift of tallness.

Rand's cult of the Nordic countenance comes especially alive in the
various sudden, dramatic entrances put in by the reverse Robin Hood
figure of Ragnar Danneskjöld. At first the Norwegian is remembered by an
anonymous spinster as having "the purest gold hair and the most
frightening face on earth, a face with no sign of any feeling" (148). Later,
Rearden encounters the swashbuckling Nord, and remarks that
"Danneskjöld's face was more than handsome, that it had the startling
beauty of physical perfection—the hard, proud features, the scornful
mouth of a Viking's statue" (539). And again, at Galt's Gulch, Dagny too
will take note of rogue Ragnar's beautiful face and—the phrase
repeated!—his "physical perfection" (704).

Such physically perfect, righteously arrogant, scornful beauty has its
corresponding behavior in its superbly-endowed protagonists, and,
conversely, has the inevitable foils in its second-hand antagonists. The
deeds of Rand's heroes, as we've seen, are always heroic, always right,
always admirable. Their utterances, accordingly, are for the most part
either of two kinds: 1) sententious, abstract speeches in which they
aggressively expound their general principles, or 2) characteristically
brusque, curt statements that are blunt and churlish, even rude and hostile.
Generally, we hear little else. Much of the dialogue in Rand fiction is
adversarial in nature, consisting largely of verbal sparring, permanent
"philosophic" combat. A not uncommon climactic, wrap-up line in her
exchanges is the tart command by a hero to some second-hander, "Get out
of my house/my office."

Not surprisingly, in Rand's vast panoply of personages there is not a
single outstanding figure who could be thought of as a sunny, warm, and
caring, even amicable or benevolent, human being, no one on the order of,
say, Shakespeare's Benvolio or Bassanio or Orlando; or Jane Austen's
Jane Bennett or Mr. Bingley; or Tolstoy's Levin or Bezukhov; or Sonia
(either Dostoevsky's or Chekhov's); or Joyce's Bloom; or many of Anne
Tyler's people. Whatever characters seem to be sunny and caring are
ultimately unmasked as either contemptible fakes or sinister second-
handers, like Peter Keating, or his officious mother, or his dowdy ex-girl
friend Catherine Halsey.

Correspondingly, those who oppose Rand's views, even the most fleeting of characters (as I've also observed above) find themselves regularly portrayed in the most unflattering terms, often as simply ugly. One of the protesters and picketers who cause a hullabaloo in the later scenes of *Fountainhead* is depicted thus: "She was fat and middle-aged. She wore a filthy cotton dress and a crushed hat. She had a pasty, sagging face, and a shapeless mouth … the face of self-righteous evil" (622). Or again, another such lowly she-lout: "Her hips began at her ankles, bulging over … her shoes; she had square shoulders and a long coat of cheap brown tweed over a huge square body … She had an incision for a mouth, without lips, and she waddled as she moved" (643).

In *Atlas*, because of the plethora of spiteful, mean-spirited, malign altruists who hold power, such caricatures abound. A Mr. Potter from the infamous State Science Institute has as "his only mark of distinction … a bulbous nose" (172). Mr. Thompson, none other than the United States President, is "slight," "unintelligent," and "lazy" (499). Wesley Mouch, another government lackey (his surname, one assumes, is pronounced "mooch"), sports a "flat-topped skull," a "petulant bulb" for a lower lip, and "eyes … like the yolks of eggs smeared under the not fully translucent whites" (503). The face of Orren Boyle, rival to Hank Rearden and ally of the worthless James Taggart, features "small slits of pig's eyes" (525).

As I observed in connection with Nabokov, such simplistic caricatures would be appropriate were Rand writing satire or comedy, à la Dickens, for instance. However, in a highly dramatic novel that purports to be a serious literary statement about "Man" (one of Rand's favorite big topics), to so lampoon its designated villains shows a monumental lack of subtlety and suggests a profound poverty of imagination. In many great narratives and tragedies, the evildoers are portrayed not that differently from other characters, and—as often indeed happens in real life—the malefactors can be eloquent, even attractive. As people, there's nothing grotesque or repellent about Goneril or Iago, about either of the Macbeths or Hamlet's stepfather Claudius. (Even Humbert Humbert, let us recall, wields a superb prose style).[15] It is in their choice of actions, not in their physiques or their physiognomies, that these characters' maliciousness becomes manifest. How authors portray their adversarial, negative characters is among the prime tests of their artistry, and Rand in *Atlas* fails that test.

---

[15] Further regarding Shakespeare's villains: Richard III is based on an historical figure, and Caliban has some of the more eloquent speeches in what is basically a fairy tale.

In this regard, there are some memorable moments when Rand as narrator intrudes and frankly, joyfully revels in the death and destruction of her subhuman second-handers. In a notorious disaster episode set exactly halfway through *Atlas Shrugged*, the Taggart Line's Comet train, carrying 300 altruists, sits broken down and stranded in the Rockies. Diesel engines not being available, an ignorant politician on board orders a coal-burning locomotive, even though its fumes would be dangerous when the train goes through a tunnel further ahead. The coal burner is hooked on nonetheless. And now Rand dedicates a paragraph each to sixteen select passengers, all of them contemptible: e.g. a sociology professor, a schoolteacher who trains "miserable cowards," "a worker who believed that he had 'a right' to a job," an economics professor who rejects private property, a mother of two whose unpardonable sin is having a husband employed by the government, an anti-business playwright, and the last one, a "humanitarian." And sure enough, they all die asphyxiated in the tunnel... Inasmuch as, in the judicious words of the narrator, "there was not a man aboard who did not share one or more of their ideas" (567-68), they are all guilty as charged. Rand seems to delight in their demise, for, dear reader, it surely serves them right!

In yet another incident during the final gunfight, Dagny Taggart is confronted by an armed guard who is undecided as to whose orders to follow. So Dagny, giving him his just desserts, "pulled the trigger and fired straight at the heart of a man who had wanted to exist without the responsibility of consciousness" (1066). Melodrama, as we know, can be unintentionally humorous and campy.

Rand goes to even further extremes in an episode in *Fountainhead* in which Ellsworth Toohey convinces a benefactor to endow and build the "Hopton Stoddard Home for Subnormal Children." The author now has a heyday relating the recruitment of "sixty-five children, their ages ranging from three to fifteen," these charges "picked out by zealous ladies who were full of kindness" and who therefore select "only the hopeless cases." And who are these kids?

> a fifteen-year-old boy who had never learned to speak; a grinning child who could not be taught to read or write; a girl born without a nose, whose father was also her grandfather; a person called "Jackie" of whose age or sex nobody could be certain. They marched into their new home, their eyes staring vacantly, the stare of death before which no world existed (378).

La Rand as narrator here, and in the passages that follow, oozes palpable disgust both at these young unfortunates and at the charitable attempts to aid them. The Nazi regime, one might note, would have remedied the problem via their euthanasia policy for the variously disabled, a program that, following some 70,000 deaths (among them at least 5,000 children), was discontinued only after senior members of the Catholic clergy protested against it. Perhaps not accidentally, Whittaker Chambers's famous attack in *National Review* on Rand's *Atlas* had as its resounding climax, "From almost any page ... a voice can be heard ... commanding, 'To a gas chamber—go!'" (Or if not a gas chamber, dear readers, at least to a train tunnel.)[16]

Two other groups earn La Rand's casual but recurring scorn: pre-industrial tribal societies and modern-day social workers. Perhaps surprisingly, in an essay entitled "Racism," Rand condemns this sort of prejudice from the start as "the lowest, most crudely primitive form of collectivism" (VS, 126). When alluding to "primitive," indigenous peoples, however, she unthinkingly resorts to the nineteenth-century Eurocentric, racist mindset whereby only "the West" is civilized and all other cultures as barbarous. She is thus obsessed with the counter-image of "barefoot savages who lived in mudholes" (FNI, 12). In her fiction and essays she routinely employs terms such as "naked savages," "cavemen," and "cannibals."

Hence, in *Atlas*, when Owen Kellogg, an assistant manager for the Taggart empire, quits his job, he feigns the indifference of "a savage who had never heard of railroads" (32). And in *Fountainhead*, Gail Wynand expresses his bafflement at those American travelers who undertake "pilgrimages to some dark pesthole in a jungle... to do homage to a crumbling temple, to a leering stone monster with a pot belly created by some leprous savage" (439). Reflecting Rand's ethnocentrism, nothing of value is to be found outside of Europe or the United States, whether in "the pest holes of Asia" or among "the savages of Asia and Africa" (FNI, 12). In the world according to Rand, neither anthropology nor non-Western history has yet come into existence as a body of knowledge or for understanding and "reason."

Finally, Rand reserves special ammunition for social workers, beings that, in her universe, rate scarcely higher than those naked savages. When Peter Keating in *The Fountainhead* re-encounters his former fiancée Catherine Halsey, who has joined forces with the altruists in Washington D.C., she is now drawn as "completely the spinster, the frustrated social worker" (592). As a telltale sign of her connection to the primitives, she wears "a preposterous ornament—a bow legged Mexican with red ...

[16] Cited in Burns, p. 175.

enamel pants" (587). Later on, among those horrified by Howard Roark's egotistic act of violence (which some might call terrorism), there is [what else?] "the social worker who had found no aim in life and could generate no aim within the sterility of his soul, but basked in virtue ... by grace of his fingers on the wounds of others" (615).

Similarly, in *Atlas Shrugged*, one reads in the long speech by genius-on-strike Dr. Akston a reference to "the simpering social worker incapable of earning a penny" (733). And it is a conniving social worker with "a gray face" who, on the streets one night, runs into a distraught Cherryl Brooks, the wife of slimy James Taggart, and chides her so cruelly for being a "society girl ... drunk as a tramp" and for "living for your own enjoyment" (842) that she, the social worker, drives the poor woman to commit suicide by jumping in the river.

In this regard, I must bring up a personal connection. My younger brother, Kanani Bell, spent two very busy decades as a psychiatric social worker for the Hartford, Connecticut, inner-city, public school system. Over those twenty years he and his colleagues had the job of dealing with a host of social pathologies endemic to poverty in America: among them, hungry school kids and Kanani's helping to secure meals for them; dysfunctional families and domestic violence; angry parents; theft; chronic drug addiction; and a general, pervasive, day-to-day hopelessness and degradation. My brother often found himself on call to serve as an intermediary in interpersonal conflicts. The stresses were persistent and intense; threats to his ordinary well-being were not unheard of. (Kanani likes to quote Gandhi's maxim on the subject: "Poverty is the worst form of violence.") My brother's adequate salary, then, was well-earned, and he entered early retirement, on a public pension, with a great sense of relief. And so, when I read a smug Ayn Rand character in *Atlas Shrugged* blithely deriding "the simpering social worker incapable of earning a penny" (733), my response to such nonsense is sheer revulsion. Needless to say, it is not the sole passage in Rand's thick opus where she happens to be quite mistaken.

CHAPTER THIRTEEN

ON THEIR RESPECTIVE LEGACIES

The twin legacies of the two Russian-American writers go deep, running in parallel if occasionally converging channels. Though differing in their outcomes, their origins are one and the same: to wit, a personal, visceral hatred not only of the Soviet dictatorship, but also of everything that that regime stood for, and then, the subsequent adoption of an extreme opposite position.

Nabokov thus despised the social aesthetic; Rand loathed the social ethic. Nabokov dismissed all social and humanitarian writing as trash; Rand condemned all socially oriented policy, and all humanitarian sentiment and conduct, as evil. Each of these writers believed in an intrinsic, aprioristic, totally self-fashioned individual autonomy, and so both balked at the slightest hint of determinism and denied the very existence of society as an entity with dynamics of its own. Only individual actions and values mattered, in their view. Above all, Nabokov prized absolute freedom of art and the free inventiveness of genius; Rand gave sole credence to absolute freedom of enterprise and to inventors of genius. For Nabokov, the purpose of art is "aesthetic bliss," with no moral, social, or cognitive aims; Rand likewise grants at one point that "the function of art is non-social," that an art work "serves no practical material end, but is an end in itself; it serves no purpose other than contemplation" (RM, 18-19).

Moreover, as noted earlier, the works of both authors overlap in certain significant ways. All four of Rand's novels are fictions with a didactic agenda; and during roughly the same time period that Rand produced them, Nabokov produced ideological fictions of his own. La Rand's *We the Living*, her first and only strictly realist work, was consciously conceived as anti-Soviet propaganda. Her dystopian fantasy, *Anthem*, purports to be "anti-collectivist" but is really anti-Communist. In *Fountainhead* Rand uses architectural design as a weapon with which to do battle against social aesthetics, altruistic values, and—for good measure—public housing. And with *Atlas*, under cover of a 1000-page futuristic narrative, she pours forth a flagrantly full-throttled anti-Communist tract.

Similarly, although Nabokov claimed to loathe what he himself called "publicist fiction," during the 1930s and '40s, contemporaneously with Rand, he himself brought out *The Gift* (in Russian) and *Sebastian Knight* (in English), both of them attacks on social art, with altruism as added target in the second work. In *Invitation to a Beheading*, Nabokov has his own dystopian novel, and he later created a slim, overwrought, yet no less propagandistic anti-Communist tract in *Bend Sinister*. The latter book is five times better than *Atlas Shrugged* if only in that it is five times shorter.

When we speak of a Nabokovian legacy, however, we mean specifically the Nabokov of *Lolita* and *Pale Fire*. By the time he was sculpting those twin pillars, the author had put his publicist phase behind him, and would never admit to having worked in such a lowly genre. Significantly, his other fifteen novels from before and after the two masterpieces (some of them beautiful though limited, others fairly awful) have had no significant impact on the larger literary culture. One reads the rest of Nabokov's fictions *because* of that pair of unique books. With the latter, the former would exist on the distant sidelines at best.

As a writer, Nabokov forged a substantial if idiosyncratic heritage. Quite simply, one cannot *be* a serious literary practitioner or connoisseur of literature without knowing Nabokov. As a casual instance, even a lay figure such as William Weld, Republican governor of Massachusetts in the 1990s, and himself the author of three mass-market fictions, has singled out Nabokov as his favorite novelist. Unlike Rand, however, Nabokov is no writer for adolescents. (Teens need not apply!) To read him adequately requires some level of literary sophistication, some background acquaintance with the Modernist classics—their sensibility, their high artifice, their boundless experiments with language and form, their challenges to past cultural norms and traditions, their tendency toward what the economist Joseph Schumpeter singled out, in capitalism, as "creative destruction." With *Lolita* and especially *Pale Fire*, Nabokov builds on and continues with that practice as he invents new forms, reinvents the novel, and shows that prefaces, verse, and even endnotes can play key roles in shaping narrative.

In addition the perfection of Nabokov's prose style, in which every sentence is something new, distinctive, and virtually unprecedented, serves as model for anyone who values the art of language. For Nabokov, cliché and set phrase are capital sins, and from him one learns to shun them, eschew them, banish them, purge them! Prose should have beauty, should be ever fresh, always striking. One grasps this when one has read and reread the master. And finally, Nabokov as mentor demonstrates to many a writer the sheer difficulty of conveying narrative motion. To move a character from one room to another, from one dwelling or one town to another, from one hour, day, or week to another, is a supreme creative task, and Nabokov's writing suggests as much.

The intricate set of ways in which Nabokov conceived of and patterned his fictions, moreover, posed an artistic challenge to 1950s American realism and its serious, somewhat morose focus on existential subjectivity. With *Lolita* and *Pale Fire*, the gates were opened once again to structural games, formal playfulness, textual humor, and extreme parody. The postmodern fiction movement of the 1970s and '80s (Barthelme, Coover, Pynchon, Federman, Gass, et al.) owes a direct debt to the Russian-American. (Coincidentally, Pynchon at Cornell had taken Nabokov's course on the European Novel.) Novelist John Barth, in his landmark 1967 essay that appeared originally in the *Atlantic Monthly*, "The Literature of Exhaustion," singled out a troika consisting of Nabokov, Beckett, and Borges as models for experimental writers to emulate.[1]

I too must honor the master: despite my many ambivalences and reservations about Nabokov the man and the dogmatist, I must admit that my one published book-length novel, *The Carlos Chadwick Mystery*—itself an assemblage of texts (consisting of a "Foreword to the British Edition," two faux memoirs, a closet play, and a diary) that, in its totality, spoofs American relativisms—could not have been constructed without the originating example provided to me by *Pale Fire*.

Nabokov nonetheless has his limits, as we have seen. His absolutist, purist, individualist aesthetic eventually clashes with those who handle other forms of knowledge and who hold a broader, more ecumenical and inclusive conception of art. The Irish writer John Banville, in an interview with Noah Charney for *The Daily Beast*, gives voice quite aptly to this discomfort: "Nabokov was a great love of my youth, but I find his artistic self-absorption and tone of self-satisfaction increasingly irritating."[2] American novelist Paul Russell also has mixed feelings regarding Nabokov, which he admitted to me in an e-mail message and which presumably had prompted his less than sympathetic portrait of the master-to-be in *The Unreal Life of Sergey Nabokov*. And in the autobiographical portions of this book, I have looked back on my past Nabokovophilia, and my growing disenchantment with him on several fronts.

---

[1] D. Barton Johnson, "Nabokov and the Sixties," p. 145. In addition, see Susan Elizabeth Sweeney, "How Nabokov Rewrote America," especially its final section, "America the Nabokovian," pp. 80-83.

[2] Noah Charney, interview with John Banville, in *The Daily Beast*.

It bears noting that Banville, Russell, and I are not alone in our middle-aged disillusionment. A colleague of mine at Williams College, Stephen Fix, informs me of a similar experience. Steve Fix teaches an English course on Nabokov and Pynchon, in which highly sophisticated seniors read some of the Russian-American's short stories, plus *Pnin*, *Lolita*, and *Pale Fire*. So they come to know Nabokov fairly well. Next, he has the class read *Strong Opinions*. And now, grievously disconcerted, the intelligent, sensitive twenty-somethings invariably ask Professor Fix, "How could so great an author also be the nasty little man of the interviews?", or words to that effect. This happens every time he teaches the course, incidentally. Still more disconcerting is to encounter, in print, some of the commentaries of Nabokov's ardent admirers, who, blinded by his pronunciamientos and prose style, heap praise on even his worst works and parrot his prejudices concerning Freud and Marx, Darwin and Einstein, like the faithful repeating dictates from a high priest, a commissar, or a Fox News presenter. Nabokov has his cultists, too.

Time goes by, however, and new voices, new literary currents emerge, taking their rightful place in the ever-shifting canon. Since the 1960s, Latin American authors have gained world prominence by having found innovative ways to juggle form, expand technique, and chisel language in order to give shape to their rich, ample social and historical vision. The novels of García Márquez, Carpentier, Vargas Llosa, Lispector, and Bolaño, to cite just a few, demonstrate that artistic complexity and a humane, passionate engagement with politics and society are not mutually exclusive projects. In my introduction to this book I noted that Harold Bloom, in *The Western Canon*, makes no mention of Nabokov; on the other hand, among the authors whom the Yale sage does include in his volume are Borges, Neruda, and García Márquez.

I should like to bring to an end my exploration of Nabokoviana with two related anecdotes, each of them involving (what else?) butterflies … but also death.

The first was reported in a memoir by Donald Hall in the *New York Times Book Review*. It seems that sometime in the 1940s, Hall and Nabokov, among others, were guests at the Utah home of James Laughlin, the publisher of New Directions. Nabokov had been out in pursuit of a rare butterfly, and on his return he noted casually that he had heard "someone groaning most piteously down by the stream."

"Did you stop?" Laughlin asked.

"No," Nabokov answered, "I had to get the butterfly."

Next day, the body of an old prospector was found dead in what was subsequently called Dead Man's Gulch, in Nabokov's honor.[3]

The incident poses a perfect conundrum, a point of initial contention for Rand and her devoted scholiasts, who might perhaps argue that Nabokov, in pursuing his butterfly, was actually being selfish and therefore virtuous. It was his free choice; he was not hurting anyone; and it is immoral for someone to be forced into helping others. And so on and so forth. In some ways, one could say that the Randians are right. And yet... Such sophistries go against our very sense of our humanity.

The second anecdote, an almost complete mirror image of the first, could, with its ironies, serve as a fitting finale for a tragic stage drama. In 1975, Nabokov was in Davos, Switzerland, chasing butterflies, where he chanced to fall down a hillside and, in the words of his son Dmitri, found himself "stuck in an odd position on the steep slope." The novelist called out for assistance. Tour buses kept chugging by, and the tourists on board "responded with guffaws, misunderstanding as a holiday prank [Nabokov's] cries for help and waves of a butterfly net." Dmitri does not specify how long the unfortunate situation lasted, but, when the novelist was eventually rescued and taken back to his lodgings, the hotel staff scolded him "for stumbling back into the lobby ... with his shorts in disarray." (OL, xi) The entire nightmare triggered "a period of illness" from which the elderly genius never recovered. Ongoing complications from the ordeal led to his death in 1977.

It is all too easy, dear reader, to feel *Schadenfreude* at Nabokov's fatal (prat)fall, to see in the whole tragicomic sequence his comeuppance some thirty-five years after his ignoring the lone prospector's agonized cries; but we should best put aside such small sentiments. Again, Rand and her advocates here have grist aplenty for their debating mill, with coolly objective reasonings that will exonerate the tourists from any obligation to come to the rescue of an old lepidopterist in distress. Passengers and chauffeurs alike had their selfish tourism activities to tend to, were hurting no one, and were thus being virtuous. Indeed, in *The Fountainhead*, anyone who offered an altruistic helping hand might well have been depicted by Rand in the most despicable of terms (as noted in my previous chapter).

*

This leads us to the matter of Rand's peculiar legacy.

---

[3] Donald Hall, "James Laughlin of New Directions," pp. 22-23.

Rand's work, it should be said, is by and large dispensable to any serious, artful wordsmithing endeavor. She is indeed an example of how *not* to write. The simplistic crudity of her character portrayals, the sheer implausibility of her plotlines, the vulgarity and unsubtlety of her recurrent preachments, the workmanlike nature of her prose—these traits all place her novels and essays well below any legitimate, reputable artistic standard. Hers is an instance of a third-rate or fourth-rate infra-literature commanding a broad readership for reasons thoroughly unliterary.

Of course, high libertarian reasoners without much of a taste for or understanding of art might easily find themselves bowled over by Rand's agenda-driven, propagandistic fairy tales. Professional theorist Murray Rothbard, who frankly had no liking for fiction, in a note to Rand praised *Atlas* as "the greatest novel ever written," because, in his view, she had depicted "persons and their actions in perfect accordance with their principles and their consequences."[4] This is a somewhat ingenuous way of categorizing *Atlas* as the pure allegory it is, one with which Rothbard agrees and whose characters, it goes without saying, embody *his* principles. Libertarian economist Ludwig von Mises, for his part, in his own personal letter to Rand, said of *Atlas* that it "is not merely a novel" but "a cogent analysis of the evils that plague our society ... You have the courage to tell the masses what no politician told them: you [the masses] are inferior and all the improvements in your conditions ... you owe to the efforts of men who are better than you."[5] It is thus perfectly understandable that libertarian thinkers and evangelizers would be pleased to find their doctrines positively dramatized within a hefty, best-selling pop novel. Opinions such as theirs, however, do somewhat suggest that committed, full-time system-builders are not necessarily among those best qualified to make aesthetical judgments.

Still, the fact remains that, over the past few decades, the United States has become something of an "Ayn Rand Nation," in the words of the title sported by Gary Weiss's recent, disturbing book. The query "Who Is John Galt?" can thus be sighted on signs carried at Tea Party rallies, on leaflets affixed to telephone posts, on bumper stickers here and there, even on the occasional bathroom wall. Weiss quotes Tea Party organizer Mark Meckler as seeing in Rand's work his "spiritual books, in addition to Scripture."[6] As Weiss himself observes, "the Republican Party has become

---

[4] Cited in Heller, p. 296.
[5] Cited in ibid., p. 283.
[6] Weiss, p. 148.

more the party of Ayn Rand than the party of Teddy Roosevelt or Abraham Lincoln."[7]

The libertarian view, always there as a constant current in twentieth-century U.S. life, has, since the Reagan years, gathered momentum to become a steadily mounting wave. Rand, needless to say, was already a big fish in that ever-present undertow. As libertarian journalist Jerome Tuccille puts it in his humorously titled 1971 volume, *It Usually Begins with Ayn Rand*... What, prior to La Rand, had existed as a somewhat abstract doctrine, detached from everyday life, within her big novels took on flesh and blood, with dashing heroes and unabashed hero worship, vivid myths and technological magic, page-turning suspense and torrid, heart-throbbing sex. Libertarianism in her hands became a gospel, a story, not just a disembodied, scholastic theory. For every studious college sophomore or curious educated reader who dutifully pores over von Hayek or Milton Friedman, there are dozens of half-formed, still-developing minds who plunge eagerly into *Fountainhead* or *Atlas Shrugged*, living vicariously through her fables. Brian Doherty noted in 2007 that Friedman's *Capitalism and Freedom* had sold a total of a half-million copies. In the wake of the 2008 Wall Street crash, sales of *Atlas* in the year 2009 alone, by contrast, well surpassed that impressive figure.

There are several types of Rand readers and devotees, all of them, needless to say, American, inasmuch as Randianism as a mass phenomenon exists exclusively in the United States. I will focus herewith on a select few.

First, it should come as no surprise that many corporate executives, well-heeled hedge funders, and successful entrepreneurs in Silicon Valley and elsewhere are Rand believers. Her egoist doctrines flatter their sensibilities and justify their mega-millions, making them feel not just smarter and better but also morally righteous in their riches. Right-wing propagandist Dinesh D'Souza has a book actually entitled *The Virtue of Prosperity* (2000), in obvious echo of Rand's *Virtue of Selfishness*. Whereas Sir Isaac Newton is often credited as saying, "I stand on the shoulders of giants," Rand enables her opulent adherents to proclaim, "I stand on the shoulders of no one!" Rand's bad novels serve these business strivers the same purpose that Horatio Alger's pulp fictions, and Napoleon Hill, Bruce Barton, and Norman Vincent Peale's bibles of self-help have done for American business people—whether accomplished or wannabe— in previous decades. In her heroes, they see themselves. (Who is John Galt? Why, *I* am Galt ... Galt is *me*!)

---

[7] Ibid., p. 248.

Next, Rand famously appeals to callow adolescents; entire empirical studies in the sociology of culture could conceivably focus on that trend alone. In the light of such a readership pattern, let us consider briefly a few well-known aspects of post-pubescent psychology. Teen-aged girls are given to speculating on the notion of "ideal men;" and the heroes of La Rand—she whose avowed authorial mission was, in fact, "the projection of an ideal man"—satisfies precisely that wish fulfillment. Many of these American youngsters, moreover, are infatuated with the Harlequin-romance image of a strong, rough, handsome brute; and again Rand plays to that fantasy. Susan Brownmiller, in her well-known encyclopedic study of rape, *Against Our Will*, remarks that, when she borrowed a copy of *Fountainhead* from a public library and cracked it open, the tome's pages automatically flipped onto the infamous Roark-Dominique violation scene, so often had its (presumably youthful) fans turned to that episode.

Teen-aged boys, in turn, might be hearing from their unworldly, horny, male peers the idea of "Treat 'em rough!" and even notions of "Women want to be raped!" Rand's books second such primitive ideas of male-female relations. Moreover, adolescent boys have already found themselves exposed to super-heroes via a diet of comic books, Hollywood movies, and video games. Hence, Rand's best-known novels, which in some ways are comic books without the graphics, segue quite logically from that earlier, juvenile inclination. For a fifteen-year-old innocent who imagines that such men are possible, Rand fills the bill, except that whereas comic-book heroes have rescued helpless victims, La Rand's heroes save only themselves and their fellow *Übermenschen*.

Adolescence, moreover, is a period of great inner turmoil and uncertainty, a time in which parents, teachers, and other authority figures try to inculcate into awkward, as-yet-unsocialized kids the need to be considerate of other people's feelings. Rand's curt, snappish, and often rude protagonists provide convincing counter-examples for teenagers' inchoate attempts at revolt.

Finally, bright adolescents who are just discovering stories of great inventors might be green enough to believe that all inventions spring, like Pallas Athena, from the brains of isolated, unattached geniuses. Over the years I have met the occasional student who was surprised to find out that industrial firms and government agencies keep salaried inventors on their research and development staffs; that many product breakthroughs come not from a single mind but from the cumulative efforts of many, via both the scientific community's inherited knowledge and current teamwork; and that moreover it is mostly the corporations—huge collectives, really—that reap the economic benefits thereof.

Moving from the adolescent phase to the twenty-somethings, there are those bright students in and recent graduates of disciplines that call for highly specialized quantitative skills—engineering and accounting, not to mention mathematics, physical science, and computers—yet for whom the world of verbal traditions, humanistic values and passions, history and society, knowledge and beauty, right and wrong, has been mostly a blank, even a mystery. Enter into their lives La Rand, with her clear-cut, simplistic, unequivocal formulations, and the stage is set for something like a revelation.

In this regard, Rand's best-known disciple, Alan Greenspan, sets forth in his autobiography a narrative that fits the above pattern to a T:

> I was intellectually limited until I met her [Rand]. All of my work had
> been empirical and numbers-based, never values-oriented. I was a talented
> technician, but that was all. My logical positivism had discounted history
> and literature ... Rand persuaded me to look at human beings, their values,
> how they work, what they do and why they do it, and how they think and
> why they think ... She introduced me to a vast realm from which I'd shut
> myself off.[8]

Despite Greenspan's early background as a jazz musician, Rand, it seems, was the first humanist thinker and writer ever encountered by the economist-in-the-making. One wonders if she may have been the last as well.

Expanding neatly on Greenspan's declared apprenticeship with Rand, the libertarian writer and editor Joan Kennedy Taylor, daughter of classical composer and music critic Deems Taylor, remarked rather tellingly in an interview with Brian Doherty that:

> Many of the people attracted to Objectivism were not intellectuals, but
> technicians, engineers—bright, accomplished people ... many [of whom]
> hadn't read at all in philosophy or fiction or the humanities.

Not a few of them, Taylor notes, somehow actually believed that Rand had "invented laissez-faire capitalism."[9] (336). The pull that Rand can exert on intelligent, restless technicians, then, is roughly analogous to the power she has over adolescents. Both groups are cultural demographics whose subjects have not yet located ways of dealing with emotions or ethics or ideals, other than through the standard Judeo-Christian maxims with which they may have been reared in conventional U.S. society.

---

[8] Alan Greenspan, *The Age of Turbulence*, p. 52.
[9] Brian Doherty, *Radicals for Capitalism*, p. 336.

From my limited experience, I've also met or known of mature individuals who, suffering from some sort of long-term ailment yet also possessing a strong will, find inspiration in Rand's indomitable heroes. Such figures of strength serve for them the same function as the lives of saints or of Jesus for Christian ascetics, or of exemplary deities for other religious recluses. There is, as we know, a long history of unfortunates turning to religion as a means of inward consolation. For those who do not, cannot believe in any higher beings yet wish to believe in Man (or Woman), Objectivism provides, in biographer Burns's words, "a substitute, offering a similar regimentation and moralism without a sense of conformity. Rand's ideas allowed students to reject traditional religion without feeling lost in a nihilistic, meaningless universe."[10] A few bookish academics whom I've met have described their relationship to Rand in such terms. One of them was a cancer patient (since deceased), a frank left-winger who nonetheless admitted to concentrating her inner fortitude by reading Ayn Rand.

Finally, among the middle-aged and up, there are those intelligent, secular, rationalistic conservatives without much interest in religion or spirituality, who above all insist on rigor, logic, and principle when grounding their political opinions. People of this type are particularly fond of methodical, Aristotelian, scholastic-style reasoning processes, and are given to spinning out their claims concerning this issue or that on World Wide Web sites and in the "Readers' Comments" sections of online magazines and booksellers. Compulsive argufiers by nature, they want a solid foundation for their non-Christian, non-feudal, non-traditionalist, yet also non-socialist or even non-social-democratic sense of what is right, and just, and true. Rand's prolix, baroque ratiocinations afford them precisely that.

By contrast with Nabokov, whose attractions are strictly literary and for the literati only (whether budding or seasoned), Randianism is a mass phenomenon. Raw, still-developing youths in the U.S. can thus respond to her stuff on an immediate level. It is not for nothing that Jerome Tuccille's volume, in a stroke of inspiration, features the verb "begins" in its telling title. (Rand, in a word, is for beginners.) And so her absolutist thoughts and visions help to shape the minds of millions of Americans from ages 16 through 86. Rand is an opinion-maker and opinion-shaper on a massive level, and her opinions in turn serve as a kind of political unconscious for certain kinds of secular American right-wingers.

---

[10] Burns, p. 203.

In this regard, one can point to direct connections between Rand thought and bricks-and-mortar institutions in the real world. The aptly named *Reason* magazine was launched in 1968 by an Objectivist student from Boston University named Larry Friedlander. Two years later, he sold the journal to Bob Poole, another convinced Randian and also a graduate of M.I.T. and an engineer. Poole's partner in the venture publishing venture, Tibor Machan, a Hungarian emigré and a Rand devotee as well, eventually became a prolific libertarian philosopher. *Reason*, the only specifically libertarian magazine with longevity to its credit, can claim a peak circulation of 40,000.

"No Ayn Rand, no Libertarian Party." So goes the occasionally asserted counter-factual speculation. Politics, of course, is never that simple; yet the case is worth considering. Many early activists for the Libertarian Party (founded in 1970) were indeed Randians of some stripe or other. The first Libertarian presidential candidate, in 1972, the Objectivist theoretician John Hospers, was a tenured philosopher at the University of Southern California. Subsequently, Jerome Tuccille ran for New York governor on the Party ticket in 1974. Edward Crane III, a professional financier, started out as a fan of Goldwater and then shifted to Rand; he later became involved in Libertarian Party organizational matters in its early days and in fact was its Chair from 1974 to 1977. The Party's candidate Ed Clark garnered one million votes in the 1980 presidential election. Among those voters was the *Washington Post*'s left-leaning columnist Nicholas von Hoffman. There is even an Association of Libertarian Feminists, founded in 1975 by journalist Tonie Nathan. Finally, mention is always worth making of the growing number of career government officials—congressmen, governors, the 2012 vice-presidential candidate Paul Ryan—who qualify as Ayn Rand believers.

The Rand legacy can also be discerned in U.S. academic life. Given the existence of Rand's strong-willed female characters (Dominique in *Fountainhead*, Dagny in *Atlas*) on one hand, and the 1970s rise of the left-wing women's movement on the other, it was inevitable that convergence would occur and some intellectual and scholarly attention would be paid to Rand's work from a feminist perspective. Hence, in 1999, Mimi Reisel Gladstein, a noted literary scholar at University of Texas-El Paso, together with Chris Matthew Sciabarra, a "Randologist" at New York University, compiled a collection of nineteen items under the title, *Feminist Interpretations of Ayn Rand* (1999). The book's contents includes items by well-known public feminist intellectuals Susan Brownmiller, Barbara Grizzuti Harrison, and Camille Paglia, along with more strictly academic sorts of contributors. A volume such as this brings to mind the dynamic captured by Corey Robin in his important study, *The Reactionary Mind* (2011), whereby, since 1789, conservative thinkers and right-wing movements have found themselves driven to absorb ideas, phrases, and strategies from the left, as a means of staying on top of things and remaining up to date. (More on this in my next chapter.)

With the quasi "mainstreaming" of libertarianism as an identifiable mass current and ideology in U.S. life, including its own political party, scholarly attention to its foundational figure is inevitably on the increase. Chris Matthew Sciabarra issued in 1995 a volume entitled *Ayn Rand: The Russian Radical*, in which he focuses on the future novelist's background in Russia and on the dialectical methods she was trained in under Soviet education. In 1999, Sciabarra launched the *Journal of Ayn Rand Studies*, a biannual publication featuring academic essays, lively forums, and a book review section. It also runs essays by non-Randians and anti-Randians (including myself), prompting attacks on the magazine by more orthodox Objectivist voices.

Continuing with the trend, the year 2009 saw the issuance of not just one but two full-length, objective Rand biographies. *Ayn Rand and the World She Made*, by journalist and editor Anne Heller, concentrates primarily on the chronology of Rand's life. *Goddess of the Market: Ayn Rand and the American Right*, by Jennifer Burns, a professor of U.S. history at the University of Virginia and later at Stanford, focuses more on Rand's ideas, intellectual evolution, and creative processes, as well as on her important role in separating American conservative thinking from its past ties to religion. Gary Weiss's *Ayn Rand Nation* (2011) takes matters further in tracing the Russian-American's posthumous role in shaping U.S. right-wing sentiment. His book serves as a useful update to the more hostile and acerbic, yet highly informative in-depth survey, *The Ayn Rand Cult* (1999), by Canadian journalist Jeff Walker.

In much of U.S. intellectual life, Rand may be viewed as slightly more suspect than Marx and Engels. Her presence in American political thinking, however, is implicitly acknowledged by these ongoing developments, and makes clear why she is an important focus of study.

*

Ayn Rand lived her last ten years as a classically angry, rancorous, lonely old woman—famed and fêted by her American followers, yet alienated and virtually friendless, having fought bitterly and broken off with most everyone save for a few abject, servile disciples. In the public arena, she attacked feminism as "collectivist." She also anathematized the Libertarian

Party, accusing it of stealing her ideas, and dismissing its members and leaders as "a monstrous, disgusting bunch of people"[11] and "hippies of the right."

The elderly Rand's family ties were also close to nil. She had long ceased to communicate with the Chicago relatives who had first given her entry into American life, and her in-laws harbored little liking for her. (When she died, her acolytes at first claimed that she had no family in America.) Her ties with the old country were also defunct. A six-week visit in 1973 by her sister Nora—Rand's sole surviving Russian kin—along with Nora's husband Fedor Drobyshev, a retired engineer, went terribly as the siblings differed and clashed irreconcilably on every possible political and literary topic. To make matters worse, Nora was unimpressed with Ayn's books, preferring instead Solzhenitsyn, whom Rand despised as a mystic. By the time the Soviet pair returned to the USSR, Ayn was scarcely speaking to them, and she promptly disinherited Nora. Meanwhile Rand's husband Frank was succumbing to drink and dementia—a condition Rand persistently denied, in keeping with her disbelief in illness—and his death in 1979 left her with no immediate relatives. Her own paranoid delusions multiplied, although her outsized sense of her worth as a thinker was unaltered.

Rand's personal fate perhaps says something about the perils of adhering to so absolute and extreme an idea of the free, disconnected individual human being. Just as the aging Nabokov could, for the most part, imagine little outside parodic versions of himself, Rand degenerated into a parody of her own philosophy of the lonely genius, with neither a rising skyscraper nor a Galt's Gulch to serve as her realm. Rand's sole human contact in her final phases was her cook and housekeeper Eloise Huggins, and she was otherwise lacking in anyone else for simple things like solace, companionship, or intimacy. It was the Autumn of the Matriarch, much like García Márquez's aged dictator, or like the legendary Boris Godunov: trapped alone in their palaces, haunted by past ghosts. Ultimately, Rand offers a painful object lesson, a glimpse into the dark side of American individualism. One wonders how many other Randians there are out there, living their final decades in comparably righteous, bilious, hate-filled solitude.

---

[11] Ibid., p. 268.

CHAPTER FOURTEEN

ON THE LIBERTARIAN MIND

Some semantic distinctions are in order.

The Amerenglish word *libertarian* in its current sense—i.e. having to do with the idea of an unfettered, unregulated market, the latter being the key to all other individual freedoms—is a strictly American usage, in the same way that libertarianism itself is fundamentally an American ideology.

By contrast, in Spanish, Italian, and French, the terms *libertario* and *libertaire* are loosely employed as synonyms for those worker-based *anarchist* movements that rose to prominence in nineteenth- and early twentieth-century Europe and the United States. Needless to say, the pro-labor, anti-private property views of Proudhon, Bakunin, Prince Kropotkin, and the IWW are not what the U.S.-based libertarians have in mind. Among Romance speakers, by contrast, when referring to the free-market perspective, *neo-liberal* is currently their term of choice.

The English language, being unique in its twin layers of Anglo-Saxon and Franco-Latinate lexicons, is a special case in having at its disposal the two nouns *freedom* and *liberty*, with their overlapping semantic fields and their subtle differences. To my knowledge, German and Russian—like the Romance languages—have only one such word, *Freiheit* and *svoboda*, respectively. Curiously, there is no English adjective for "liberty" that would correspond to "free <freedom," although the adjectival phrase "at liberty" exists, as well as the slightly pejorative expression, "to take liberties." (*Liberty*, one may also note, is at the root of *libertine* and *libertinism*.) While the two vocables, *freedom* and *liberty*, have political uses, the former possesses by far the broader, more general scope. *Liberty* is narrower and carries more specialized, ideological connotations of *negative* freedom from official coercion, as in "civil *liberties*." One can easily imagine a teen-aged girl, who has been grounded by her parents, exclaiming, "I want my *freedom* back!" yet not "I want my *liberty* back!"

As a revealing instance, in the mid-1930s there emerged a lobbying organization that called itself the American *Liberty* League (emphasis added). Funded in part by the DuPonts and the financier E.F. Hutton, the short-lived group existed specifically to oppose such progressive developments as labor bargaining rights, federal regulations and taxation, New Deal public works, and (way back then) the recently founded Social Security program. More recently, we have the example of *Liberty* University in Lynchburg, Virginia, a prosperous Evangelical institution founded in 1971 by Southern Baptist preacher and activist Jerry Falwell (1933-2007). The choice of name is obviously significant.

The word *liberty*, then, is at the root of the term *libertarian*, the latter of which only started acquiring status as a recognizable lexeme in the 1960s.

An entire essay could be written on the gradual, twentieth-century development and diffusion of this *echt*-American sign, though that is not my aim here. Still, a few references are worth highlighting. The curmudgeonly H. L. Mencken employed the word on occasion in his newspaper columns for the *Baltimore Sun*. Rose Wilder Lane, daughter of best-selling novelist Laura Ingalls Wilder (author of the *Little House on the Prairie* series), is credited with being the first writer to have identified herself with the "libertarian" designation. Economist and political philosopher Friedrich von Hayek, in his well-known essay, "Why I Am Not a Conservative" (originally a talk delivered in Switzerland in 1957) gives the "l-word" brief consideration, yet ultimately rejects it as "singularly unattractive," with "too much the flavor of a manufactured term and of a substitute."[1]

Why, however, would Hayek, a man whose work became intimately associated with the Right, claim *not* to be a conservative? The lecture, it bears pointing out, was indirectly aimed at Russell Kirk, who was present in the audience (though is not mentioned by name in the text), and who had long been associated with a more traditionalist, Burkean doctrine that favored the preservation of a long-standing order of hierarchy, aristocracy, and crown.[2] Hayek's reply thus takes his distance from a brand of conservatism that differed broadly from his own. From the era of the French Revolution on through Hayek's earlier years, what in another context I've called "organic conservatism" had by and large looked back to an integrated system of feudalism, monarchy, and religious traditions as its preferred model.[3] Its original targets of attack were the then-emerging liberal democracy and, in addition, all those who, since 1789, were

---

[1] Hayek, *The Constitution of Liberty*, p. 408. Future page references from this book will be indicated parenthetically in the text.
[2] As summarized in Angus Burgin, *The Great Persuasion*, p. 143.
[3] See Bell-Villada, *Art for Art's Sake and Literary Life*, chapter 9, "The Changing Politics of Art for Art's Sake," pp. 203 ff.

battling for such a new system. The socialist adversary only came later, and gradually, in 1848.

Hence, when liberalism was doing battle against the old order's set hierarchies in Europe, it was a revolutionary force. Meanwhile, with the rise and slow triumph of the industrial bourgeoisie—a process spanning through 1918—liberal capitalism found itself confronting newer structural phenomena of its making: among them, business cycles and recurrent financial panics; a laboring class that demanded shorter work weeks, higher wages, improved working conditions, and countervailing powers of its own; socialist movements representing the latter's demands; governments at times responsive to those subaltern classes and to a greater social good; the direct challenge of a counter-example, beginning in 1917, of an outright Communist state; and in the later twentieth century, protests and legislation over environmental degradation and destruction.

With outright monarchy and feudalism no longer the targets of its larger battles following World War I, nineteenth-century liberalism in its purest form was struggling to retain its autonomy and hegemony against the antagonists that it had spawned. Hayek, then, was a classical, nineteenth-century liberal who indeed frankly identified himself as such. So, for that matter, was Nabokov an instance (though politically uninformed) thereof, whereas Rand's vision was that of a Nietzschean capitalism. "Neo-liberal" is thus a strictly accurate term (even if some libertarians find it pejorative) for denoting the committed, ideological defenders of the free market, just as one might say, e.g. "neo-classical," "neo-feudal," "neo-Marxist" and any other "neo" when referring to latter-day representatives of those ideas and practices.

In the American arena, the terminology became muddled when leaders of the 1930s New Deal started describing themselves as the true "liberals." They thus appropriated for themselves the term that, in much of the rest of the world, is synonymous with the free market. The usage, as we know, has stuck. To this day, *liberal* in U.S. parlance denotes government policies that intervene in the private sector to correct structural flaws and dysfunctions and to prevent social abuses. American liberals thereby serve as the pale local equivalent to social democrats across the Atlantic. In the absence of the kind of mass-based, American Socialist or Communist parties as exist in Western Europe, the Democrats play that role in somewhat attenuated form.

As we've been seeing in the course of this book, the libertarian project had long preceded the coining of the term or the founding of a Party by that name. What we now recognize as "libertarianism" had always been an integral part of pro-business thinking, judging, and lawmaking, not to mention utopian speculation and dreaming, in the U.S.A. The always-present if formerly submerged current was to experience a surge with the presidential election of actor-publicist Ronald Reagan in 1980, an event that put aspects of the libertarian world view at center stage and gave such opinions a renewed visibility and respectability. To cite Reagan's oft-quoted aphorism, "The nine most terrifying words in the English language are: 'I'm from the government and I'm here to help,'" a sentiment that might easily have come from the pages of Ayn Rand.

Previously, at the height of the Cold War, the ideological distinctions between the two parties had been blurred when an aggressive, global anti-Communism became the chief unifying, bipartisan preoccupation of the U.S. government. You know this history, dear reader: major wars in Korea and Indochina (in which millions of Asians and thousands of Americans died); CIA-sponsored coups d'état in Iran, Guatemala, Brazil, Indonesia, and Chile; brushfire military operations throughout the Third World; and bloody, indirect interventions in Central America in the 1980s.

With the totally unexpected collapse of Soviet Communism in 1989-91, and with mainland China's sea-change to Party-directed capitalism in 1988, the libertarian-conservative focus in the U.S. promptly shifted to constant, relentless attack against domestic, government-funded social programs, with the ultimate aim of dismantling a New Deal that they'd openly loathed from the start. These battles were waged (and continue to be waged) under the banner of fighting "Big Government," a phrase that has, for the time being, thoroughly displaced ""Big Business" as a traditional catchword for public enemy number one. Even by 1994 the Republicans had swept Congress via the so-called "Contract with America," with its successful bid to gut welfare benefits and deregulate banking. Then, the Bush II presidency instituted its massive tax cuts during an aggressive oil war; launched a failed attempt to privatize Social Security; and weathered the 2008 Wall Street crash that came dangerously close to being a reprise of 1929. Finally there came the 2012 national elections, featuring as Republican vice-presidential candidate Paul Ryan, an avowed believer in Ayn Rand and with plans to hand over Medicare, Medicaid, and a host of other government programs to the private market.

This rise to prominence (though not yet a majority) of the libertarian right in the U.S. forms part of a broader, long-term tendency ably traced in *The Reactionary Mind*, an insightful study by Brooklyn College professor Corey Robin. Robin notes how, starting with Edmund Burke and Joseph de Maistre in their responses to the events of 1789 and onward, conservatives have felt compelled to assimilate some of the traits of those revolutionary movements to which they were so strenuously opposed. The author cites old-guard traditionalist Russell Kirk's own words in this regard: "the thinking conservative, in truth, must take on some of the outward characteristics of the radical."[4] Fittingly, William F. Buckley Jr. at one point called conservatives "the new radicals;"[5] and some libertarians see themselves as "radicals for capitalism," the title of a book by Brian Doherty. Hence, rather than seeking merely to restore and *conserve* a desired yet defeated status quo ante, they adapt to circumstances by appearing to offer something new. In this complex dialectic, the forces as well as the ideas of the right (and in this I include fascists) exist precisely *because of* the left, in reaction to the left; and in the process they end up stealing language, imagery, tactics, and even an occasional program from the left.

Hence the German fascists appropriated the term "socialist" and "workers" for the official name of their organization, as part of their overall competition with their rivals, the mass-based Communists and Socialists, even as the "National" in their brand name sought to make inroads among followers of the more traditionally conservative National People's Party. At the same time, the Nazis received contributions from a number of domestic and foreign businessmen (including Henry Ford). Revealing his true allegiances, Hitler spoke in 1932 to the Industry Club in Düsseldorf, where he subtly reassured his well-heeled audience by defending private property and the German army, criticizing Communism and democracy, and advocating *Lebensraum* as a policy worthy of the white race.

Once in power, the Nazi regime crushed Socialism while reviving German capitalism through its military rearmament program. Hitler's rapid, destructive blow against the Communist Party shortly after coming into power in 1933, together with his pro-industry policies, earned him admiration and support from conservatives across Europe and the United States. Nazi revolutionary rhetoric and theatrics notwithstanding, the German class structure remained essentially unaltered throughout the entire life of the Reich. Except for confiscated Jewish properties, no major nationalizations took place under the National Socialists—a fact almost totally covered up and denied by subsequent representations of Nazism in the U.S. media. (On the other hand, free-market economist Milton Friedman did retrospectively recognize Nazi Germany as an instance of a capitalist state.)

---

[4] Cited in Robin, *The Reactionary Mind*, p. 24.
[5] Ibid., p. 25.

In 1945, the massive Red Army battlefield victories over Nazi Germany (and over the latter's Hungarian and Rumanian confederates) enabled the imposition of Communist regimes in Soviet-occupied areas and the rise of strong Communist parties in Italy and France (which in turn had grown out of the left-wing underground Resistance movements in those countries). At this point, American conservatives began claiming for themselves the previous mantle of anti-fascism, claiming—quite disingenuously—that they had been anti-"totalitarian" all along, and that they were currently opposing totalitarianism's new embodiment in Communism. Conveniently concealing their previous indifference to and even preference for fascism, U.S. conservatives cast themselves as the standard bearers for the post-war anti-Communist Internationale, fully supporting vast defense expenditures and compulsory military service. As we've seen, Ayn Rand, who in the 1930s had remained steadfastly silent on Nazism and had seen Communism as the greater evil, after 1945 suddenly declared herself against all forms of "collectivism." And Nabokov and his son Dmitri, along with many of Nabokov's ardent fans, would present his anti-Communist novel *Bend Sinister* in an analogous, anti-"totalitarian" light.

Later, in the 1960s and 1970s, in the face of massive protests sparked by the seemingly endless Indochina War, many American conservatives, especially younger ones, came to share in the disaffection with that conflict, and opposed the national military draft that was impinging directly on their lives. Yet they could not bring themselves to make common cause with the anti-war left and its anti-imperialist—often anti-American—positions, nor with the more respectable, liberal peace groups and candidates. The emergence of the Libertarian Party and the movement itself, then, came in great measure as a response to the conflict in Vietnam, with segments of conservative opinion declaring themselves to be against war, though on the basis of "anti-statism," and at times laying the blame on FDR and the New Deal for the rise and continuation of the gargantuan U.S. military machine, rather than on the role played by their Republican brethren in those policies.

Among the major legacies of the slow but steady growth of libertarian anti-war sentiment is the neo-liberal Cato Institute, founded in 1974 in Washington with funding by the Koch brothers. Cato's stated policy on national security is strictly isolationist and anti-interventionist: "The use of U.S. military force should be limited to those occasions when the territorial integrity, national sovereignty, or liberty of the United States is at risk."[6] The think tank actually lost $1 million in donations from the conservative Olin Foundation and other sources as a result of its principled stance against the 1991 Gulf War. (On the other hand, Cato did support Bush II's 2001 invasion and occupation of Afghanistan.) Another example of libertarian anti-war sentiment was congressman Ron Paul (R-Texas), who has maintained absolute opposition to all U.S. military actions abroad, probably among the chief reasons for his appeal to idealistic young voters until his retirement in 2012. Also worth mentioning is the hard-hitting, highly informative website <Antiwar.com>, run by libertarians who mostly keep their ideology under wraps. These of course are positive developments for those who take issue with U.S. militarism overseas, although it is doubtful whether they would have existed without the original example of anti-war activism from the left.

Libertarians, it should be said, are by no means uniformly anti-militarist. As a key counter-instance, their patron saint, Sen. Barry Goldwater, advocated a yet more destructive war in Vietnam, calling for use of atomic weapons in that conflict and for bombing Soviet ships in Haiphong harbor. Goldwater even opposed trade with Communist nations, including selling wheat to Russia. His most famous statement in this regard was, "Extremism in the defense of liberty is no vice." Note again the word "liberty." And in the 2000s, the Ayn Rand Institute in Irvine, California, fervently applauded the Iraq War, calling for direct U.S. seizure of that country's oil resources. Jeff Jacoby, a libertarian columnist for the *Boston Globe*, is likewise an unreconstructed hawk on foreign policy matters.

Starting with the Reagan presidency, grass-roots sorts of libertarian-conservative subgroups began achieving visibility via a selective lifting of words and causes from the cultural left. For instance, the struggle for gay rights had initially emerged as part of the protest waves of the 1960s and 1970s, a development anticipated in *Eros and Civilization*, the legendary work of utopian speculation by Marxist philosopher Herbert Marcuse. In the wake of that upsurge there now emerged gay libertarians, including an organization that calls itself "Log Cabin Republicans." Similarly, thanks to 1960s "Second Wave" feminism, libertarian-conservative feminists exist, too, though with scanty credit given to the earlier battles for gender equality. Significantly, when John McCain's 2008 running mate Sarah Palin (whose vice-presidential candidacy would have been unimaginable without the earlier women's struggles) was subjected to criticism for her astounding ignorance on many key issues, some of her conservative

---

[6] Cited in http://www.cato.org/foreign-policy-national-security

champions cried "Sexism!"—perhaps those eloquent defenders' first public use of that term of opprobrium. In a similar appropriation of language, some libertarians have been inclined to stamp e.g. college professors, environmentalists, and the Public Broadcasting System with the "elitist" label, another byword of the 1960s counter-culture.

The question of access to recreational drugs has, among libertarians, evolved into a hot topic. Drug use, though, had previously been the underground practice of countercultural dissidents and outliers (e.g. the 1950s Beats, jazzmen, rock musicians, hippies, committed hedonists) and a cause for assorted New Left elements (e.g. Yippie activist Jerry Rubin, who in 1966 ran for mayor of Berkeley on a platform that included decriminalizing pot). NORML, the advocacy outfit that aims to legalize the weed, was launched in 1970 by consumer advocate Keith Strup, with initial funding from the Playboy Foundation. (By contrast, it was a mainstream Republican, Richard Nixon, who launched the infamous "War on Drugs" in 1971, a significant aspect of the "culture wars" of the time.) In the years since, the Libertarian Party in its 1972 platform and libertarians in general have yet again followed the lead of those dissenting pioneers and made the freedom to consume drugs one of their stated goals—another likely reason for Ron Paul's sometime popularity among the young. Still, within the neo-liberals' view, drugs are more a matter of individual liberties than of public health. The same libertarians who oppose disaster relief are not likely to favor tax-funded rehabilitation programs for the victims of drug addiction.

On the matter of concentration of power, libertarians and their allies in the public, private, and media sectors have succeeded in thoroughly demonizing "Big Government" and thereby supplanting the old target of Big Business (or even, say, Big Oil) as chief malefactor. At most, they single out "crony capitalism"—alleged special complicity between politicians and corporations—as the prime evil. The Federal Reserve, as the government's central bank, morphs into the role of arch-villain, rather than the banking behemoths and the massive financial deregulations that started in the 1980s and 1990s. Tellingly, Ron Paul at the height of his career published a volume entitled *End the Fed* (2009), along with a campaign book whose title bears two nouns of recognizable leftist pedigree, to wit, *The Revolution: A Manifesto* (2009). Reagan's tenure as president administration, let us recall, was often referred to as "the Reagan Revolution." Gone, then, is the term "counter-revolution" from the libertarian—and American—political lexicon.

*

The libertarian position, as I've been demonstrating in these pages, did not originate with Ayn Rand, though it was she who gave it mass appeal and made it thrilling, compelling, and seemingly new and sexy. Many business people and their voluntary associations previous to Rand had held such views long before the designation "libertarian" even existed. And in turn, pro-business figures in the press and the universities, many of them well-known in their time, had aired this set of views in their writings. From that extensive cast of characters I should like to single out an individual with genuine academic credentials and some standing as an intellectual, the Austrian economist Friedrich von Hayek (1899-1992), born, coincidentally, the same year as Nabokov. The "von" in his family name indicates origins in the landed gentry.

Hayek's ideological lineage is a clear-cut one. In the 1920s he was a direct disciple of neo-liberal economist Ludwig von Mises in Vienna. Following studies and some research and pedagogical duties in the Austrian capital, though, he sensed the incoming fascist tide. A series of lectures he delivered in England in 1931 led to a long-term faculty appointment at the London School of Economics; in time he became a British citizen. Later he held teaching positions at the universities of Chicago, Freiburg, and Salzburg, as well as doing briefer stints at Arkansas and the University of California-Los Angeles.

In the 1920s and 1930s Hayek published specialized theoretical work on savings, prices, and business cycles; these technical investigations earned him, in 1974, the "Swedish State Bank Prize in Economic Science in Memory of Alfred Nobel" (the actual, full name of the award, inasmuch as it is not a "real" Nobel). Hayek shared the honor with Gunnar Myrdal, the widely respected social democrat. It has since been assumed that the prize committee, for the sake of "balance," had decided to recognize two thinkers from opposite ends of the spectrum.

What had originally brought Hayek world attention, however, was *The Road to Serfdom* (1944), an erudite (or perhaps bookish) attack on the concept of a planned economy, an idea that, during those decades, was considered by many to be the optimal arrangement for production of goods and services. Hayek's polemic, ironically, had more local sorts of origins. The author was in reality taking direct issue with Fabian socialists such as Beatrice Webb and Harold Laski, his immediate colleagues at LSE. (Like Rand, Hayek could not abide Laski.) Moreover, with the upcoming elections in UK, Hayek was concerned about a possible victory for the Labour Party, with their announced plans to nationalize major industries. Despite dire warnings from Churchill about "Reds under the beds," the Labourites won, and went on to establish a welfare state, nationalizing utilities, mining, transport, and steel, and, in the medical area, establishing the National Health Service, an institution that remains in place today and is held in high esteem by British public opinion. Contrary to Hayek's harsh admonitions, there was no "serfdom," let alone ongoing domination by the Labour Party, which was voted out of office in 1951.

Much to Hayek's and his British publisher's surprise, *The Road to Serfdom* became a transatlantic success. When the U.S. edition came out from the University of Chicago Press later the same year, critical response, albeit divided, was lively and widespread. As one might expect, the book was recommended by the National Association of Manufacturers and praised by Henry Luce's *Fortune* magazine. A rave review on the front page of the *New York Times Book Review* by libertarian journalist Henry Hazlitt led to a brisk increase in orders in just days, from the initial print run of 2,000 to 10,000 copies. Next, *Reader's Digest*, which at the time commanded a monthly circulation of 10 million, abridged and serialized the work, then gave it further sales of 600,000 in its Condensed Books format through the Book-of-the-Month Club. *Look* magazine even issued a comic-book version that was distributed by General Motors. Much of this took place even as Hayek happened to be on a lecture tour of the United States.

The internal shape and focus of *The Road to Serfdom* has its own history. What had first begun as a critique of government planning eventually grew into an overall attack on the very idea of socialism, period. Indeed, "socialism" in Hayek's tract becomes virtually the cause of all economic and political woes and is employed almost interchangeably with "collectivism," which term kindred spirit Ayn Rand, of course, would make synonymous with evil incarnate.

In equating socialism with any type of collective arrangement, Hayek erects a schematic, mental system that largely disregards historical specificity. As a dramatic instance, in a chapter called "The Socialist Roots of Naziism," Hayek takes an extended look at the writings of German sociologist Werner Sombart, along with a host of (today largely forgotten) left-wing publicists from the first two decades of the twentieth century—this in order to "explain" the rise and implementation of Hitler's régime. Nothing about the role played by the Treaty of Versailles or the 1930s Depression. Nothing about then-actually existing Nazism, with its capitalist combines in steel, chemicals, and weaponry (Thyssen, Farben, Krupp, etc.). Nothing about the prosperous war economy built on plunder and on German *Lebensraum* settlement in the East (in frank emulation of nineteenth-century, U.S. westward expansion). Nothing in this chapter on Hitler himself, who, as we saw above, in *Mein Kampf* had declared a "war to the death on Marxism." Next to nothing about blood-and-soil nationalism, with its racialist, anti-Semitic, anti-democratic and anti-Marxist components, which was part of the turmoil in Central Europe. Hayek does grant that Nazis and Communists had clashed frequently before 1933, yet still sees the two phenomena as "closely… related."[7] Hayek's textual approach to Nazism reminds one of those Cold-War Kremlinologists who used to peruse Marx's *Capital* in order to "understand" Soviet behavior. It would also be akin to reading sixteenth-century Spanish theologians to somehow account for the conquest of Mexico.

Similarly, in the book's one passage that deals with imperialism, Hayek again cites (whom else?) those Fabian socialists, the Webbs, on the Boer War, and George Bernard Shaw on the unviability of small states. And that is all, dear reader! From these meager sources he arrives at the conclusion that "the glorification of power" of a trio of scattered socialists is the prime motive for Empire. Going by Hayek's quickie account one might infer that the wars of conquest of and genocide in the Americas, Britain's takeover of India and its Opium Wars in China, the scramble for Africa, the Spanish-American War, the European domination of the globe, and Japan's "Greater East Asia Co-Prosperity Sphere" were "socialist" undertakings, with no role played in these vast domains by such minor matters as, say, competition for markets, raw materials, and lands.

By targeting "socialism" as the sole and universal enemy, *The Road to Serfdom*, not surprisingly, grew into one of the long-standing bibles (along with *Atlas Shrugged*) of true-believing right-wingers. The book not-so-subtly covered up the role of capitalism's past support of Nazism and of imperialism generally. It soothed the consciences of all those anti-Communist conservatives—whether neo-feudal, religious, or libertarian—who in the 1920s and 1930s had variously defended fascism; and it concealed that darker past from innocent and uninformed future rightists, young or old. Coming out as it did in 1944, Hayek's book was one of the opening salvoes in the cultural and intellectual sectors of the Cold War, and has since become oft-cited as a prime influence by ideologues as diverse as Chief Justice William Rehnquist, comic writer P. J. O'Rourke, and TV host Glenn Beck (whose public endorsement of the book in 2010 catapulted it to the Number 1 spot on Amazon.com).

Still, even in this sacred text, there are suggestions that would not square with the commonly shared goals and dogmas of American libertarianism. Hayek the anti-socialist also believes in a minimum safety

---

[7] Hayek, *The Road to Serfdom*, p. 29.

net that would provide basic food, shelter, and clothing so as to preserve individuals' health and the capacity to work. In addition he sees nothing amiss with regulations that limit working hours and call for sanitary arrangements in the work place. Finally, poisonous substances, deforestation, and factory smoke could be subject to control for their harmful effects. The American vulgarizers of Hayek, who see absolutely no role for government in the market, are therefore in denial of their own spokesman's modest caveats.

It is no doubt because of these cautious proposals that Ayn Rand, in her private letters, dismissed Hayek as a "compromiser" and as a "most pernicious enemy,…. real poison."[8] Owing to his defense of pollution controls and government-built roads, she found him "so saturated with all the bromides of collectivism that it is terrifying," and dismissed him as an "abysmal fool" and "a totally, complete vicious bastard."[9] Hayek, for his part, tried to read *Atlas Shrugged* but could not get through the book "because there was no romance in it," and especially gave up on "that fellow John Galt's hundred-page declaration of independence."[10]

In 1947, Hayek took it upon himself to found the Mount Pelerin Society, with support from the libertarian Volker Charities Fund and other ideologically sympathetic sources. Hayek's original aim was to help acquaint German-speaking economists with neo-liberal thinkers from the West, but the group evolved into an international association of leading, libertarian-minded social scientists and business people, who met regularly at the Swiss mountain resort that bears its name. Hayek served as its president until 1960, remaining thereafter in an honorary capacity until his death in 1992. Eight of the society's members would eventually become Nobel laureates in Economics. Over the years, tensions reportedly arose between the European participants, who saw a positive role for government in dealing with poverty and joblessness in a market economy, and the Americans, purists who spurned such interventionist notions and perceived their European counterparts as "squishy."[11] The organization survives to this day, with an unsavory episode involving the Chilean dictatorship in 1977 (see below), an incident suppressed in the official histories. (Reading about Mont Pelerin, one is reminded vaguely of those imaginary secret societies that hold sway in the fantastical novels of Umberto Eco or Thomas Pynchon.)

---

[8] Cited in Ebenstein, *Friedrich Hayek*, p. 275.

[9] Doherty, p. 653, note 84.

[10] Cited in <http:FTalphaville.ft.com/2012/08/20/112561/paul-ryan-and-hayek-vs-rand>

[11] Doherty, p. 213.

By the 1950s Hayek saw himself as moving away from his economics specialty and taking on an enlarged role as political philosopher. Embarked on this new path, he spent four years writing what he thought of as his magnum opus, *The Constitution of Liberty* (1960), entertaining hopes that it would become a twentieth-century equivalent to Adam Smith's *Wealth of Nations* and be reviewed in *Time* and *Life*. Such hopes did not materialize, but the volume did in time become a standard scholarly source for colleagues and for libertarians who, after the polemical fireworks of *Road to Serfdom*, needed from Hayek a more sober and objectively focused product. However, with its dry, workmanlike prose and its numbered subsections, *Constitution* stood little chance of going beyond a limited circle of convinced cultists. A crabbed, overwrought, withholding, and highly scholastic treatise, its seemingly fair method is to consider a subject (more or less: "I am, in principle, in favor of *X*"), then to raise a vociferous "BUT" in objection and, in the end, explain why *X*, actually, is wrong...

Hence Hayek recognizes, pro forma, the rights of labor unions to organize, yet soon accuses them of having become "uniquely privileged institutions to which the general rules of law do not apply" (267).[12] In his view, "even so called 'peaceful' picketing in numbers is severely coercive" (274), one of the many union tactics that result in "restraint of trade" (275). Indeed, he sees *unions* as the main cause of unemployment. Similarly, unemployment insurance is more "likely in the long run to aggravate the evil it is meant to cure" (302).

In a book that purports to deal with issues of liberty, there is but a brief look at racial segregation in the United States, and this in the schools only. The source of this unfortunate practice, according to Hayek, is "the management of schools by government" (379)—nothing about the restrictions on liberty caused by white racism. Hayek in fact feels that "it is no longer necessary that education be ... financed [and] also provided by the government" (381). Ultimately, "it may be better that some children go without formal education" than that there be battles over the control of education. Hayek's overall stance, in a word, is that the government should be as little involved as possible in schooling. Similar, and by now familiar, arguments (i.e. coercion, inefficiency) are adduced by Hayek against Social Security and universal health care. It is no wonder, then, that at a Conservative Party meeting in 1975, future British head of state Margaret Thatcher held up a copy of *The Constitution of Liberty* to those

---

[12] Friedrich von Hayek, *The Constitution of Liberty*. Page references from this volume will be cited parenthetically within the text.

in attendance, slapped it down onto the table, and announced, "This is what we believe."[13]

In the ensuing years, Hayek's thought became sour and jaundiced, hardening into a kind of parody of itself. Volume 2 of what was supposed to be his next "big" work, *Law, Legislation and Liberty*, bears the truculent, attention-grabbing title, *The Mirage of Social Justice* (1978). Already, in *Constitution...*, the author had alluded to "social justice" in quotation marks, as something essentially objectionable (387). Here in *Mirage* he systematically and relentlessly lets fly at the very notion. Some typical quotations: "The phrase 'social justice' means nothing at all, and to imply it is either thoughtless or fraudulent" (xii).[14] Social justice, says Hayek, is "a superstition," a "will-o'-the-wisp which has lured men to abandon many of the values which in the past have inspired the development of civilization" (67). Again: "In a society of free men (*sic*), the term 'social justice' is mostly devoid of meaning or content" (96). Another: "The term is intellectually disreputable, the mask of demagogy or cheap journalism, which responsible thinkers ought to be ashamed of to use because, once its vanity is recognized, its use is dishonest" (97). Yet another: "Ideals of social justice are an atavism, a vain attempt to impose upon the Open Society the morals of the tribal society, which, if it prevails, must not only destroy society but would also threaten the survival of large numbers of people" (147). In a passage that deals specifically with the right to paid vacations, Hayek makes an attempt at humor (never one of his salient traits), as he asserts, "The conception of a 'universal right' which assures to the peasant, to the Eskimo, and presumably to the Abominable Snowman, 'periodic holidays with pay' shows the absurdity of the whole thing" (105). Very funny...

In his final work, a gathering of essays entitled *The Fatal Conceit: The Errors of Socialism* (1978), Hayek's scattered insights border on the nonsensical, the crackpot, and the grossly mistaken. Regarding the future, he waxes visionary: "Antarctica will enable thousands of miners to earn an ample livelihood" (43).[15] Looking back at earlier times, he asserts, "no advanced civilization has yet developed without a government which saw as its chief aim in the protection of private property" (32), apparently unaware of the civilizations of the Incans and the Mayans, which were destroyed by European imperialism. And my favorite: "I doubt whether

---

[13] Ebenstein, p. 292.
[14] Hayek, *Law, Legislation and Liberty, vol. 2: The Mirage of Social Justice.* Page references from this volume will be cited parenthetically within the text.
[15] Hayek, *The Fatal Conceit.* Page references from this volume will be cited parenthetically within the text.

there exists a single great work of literature which we would not possess had the author been unable to obtain an exclusive copyright" (36). Does Hayek actually believe there were extensive, rigorous copyright laws in the time of Euripides, or Chaucer, or Shakespeare, or Goethe, or Jane Austen? Such seems the case, strangely enough.

In one of Hayek's more sweeping statements, he even declares "the expression 'society' itself" as well as its "adjective 'social'" as "useless as a tool of communication," yet another "weasel word" and indeed "a kind of animism" (114). Like Nabokov and Rand in their later phases, Hayek chooses to deny the very existence of society, along with negating the traditional words ordinarily used to denote it.

As a replacement for "society" and "social," Hayek takes his cue from an obscure nineteenth-century archbishop, Richard Whately (1787-1863), who proposed a word "for the theoretical science explaining the market order"—to wit: *catallactics*. Prompted by Whately's suggestion, Hayek calls for the adoption of "the term *catallaxy* to describe the object of the science we generally call economics" (112). One wonders: on what planet would the professors in Hayek's well-established field agree to say, "I teach *catallaxy*"? What university subdivision would willingly re-baptize itself the "Department of *Catallaxy*"? Can one imagine a primer entitled *Catallaxy for Beginners*? Or introductory courses with the name *Catallaxy 101*? Or a "London School of Catallaxy"? Or a prestigious British weekly called *The Catallactist*? The humorous puns on this neologism (say, *Catastrophics*, or *Cataractics*, not to mention *Scatallaxy*) would proliferate without limit. Dear reader, I can only marvel at the tin ear, the schematic, utopian mind lacking in any sense of beauty, any simple contact with everyday usage, that could dream up so demented a term.

In the long interim since 1944 and *Road to Serfdom* until today, Hayek's quasi-apocalyptic claims about the destructiveness of social justice and the welfare state have simply not been borne out. As Jim Mahon, my colleague at Williams College has observed to me, one of the best refutations of the Austrian school of economics is, in fact, post-war Austria, where social democracy created an enviable standard of living *and* liberal freedoms for all of its citizens, without having had to resort to the tough medicine of a Thatcher or the tyranny of a Pinochet. By contrast, if the Western world had adhered to the harsh beliefs of Hayek and his fellow libertarians, we would still have forced racial segregation, starvation wages, fifteen-hour workdays, six-day work weeks, impoverished retirees, and strictly male professions—not to mention vacations without pay (albeit still none of the latter for the Abominable Snowman).

There is also in this regard a biographical dimension that casts a disquieting shadow on Hayek's principled opposition to government programs. Among the reasons for his moving to Freiburg in 1962 was that his position at the University of Chicago offered no institutional pension benefits, since his salary originated not in the institution's coffers but from the libertarian Volker Charities Fund. A teaching job at Freiburg, a State-run university, by contrast, would eventually provide him a decent pension—from the West German government.[16] The same was the case, presumably, with the Universität Salzburg, to which Hayek moved, yet again, in 1969. Thus, the man who, in *The Constitution of Liberty*, had severely criticized Social Security in the United States, ended up choosing to build up equity toward a couple of *state* pensions in Germany and Austria.

A second anecdote relates to Hayek and medical concerns. Hayek, needless to say, was no proponent of socialized medicine. As it happens, libertarian magnate and patron Charles Koch invited Hayek in 1973 to serve as a "distinguished senior scholar" at the Institute for Humane Studies (IHS), one of several think tanks that Koch Industries supports. Hayek, however, had recently undergone gall bladder surgery in Austria, where there was close to universal health care. Understandably, he was worried about encountering health problems while temporarily stationed, uninsured, in the U.S. His age of 74, moreover, made obtaining private insurance an impossibility.

Enter Yale Brozen, a University of Chicago economics professor and also a libertarian, who looked into Hayek's employment history at that institution and found out that the Austrian had paid into Social Security for the requisite ten years. This would make him eligible for benefit payments and hospital coverage. Koch then sent to Hayek a reassuring letter, on letterhead with his own signature, along with a Social Security pamphlet that explained the necessary registration procedures and mechanics, and moreover encouraged him to apply for routine retirement benefits from the federal program. Hayek eventually did spend the summer of 1975 at IHS in a capacity as "resident scholar." The entire affair harks back to the case of Ayn Rand fiercely attacking Medicare in the 1960s, then depending on that very program to pay for life-saving surgery in the wake of her lung cancer in the 1970s.[17]

---

[16] John Cassidy, *How Markets Fail*, p. 47.

[17] The episode is recounted in Yasha Levine and Mark Ames, "Koch to Hayek: Use Social Security."

In these years a darker side of Hayek came to the fore when, in 1978, he visited Chile, a country then living under the barracks dictatorship of Gen. Augusto Pinochet. Hayek's sojourn took place under the auspices of his own Mont Pelerin Society which, in a symbolic gesture, chose to hold its annual meeting at Viña del Mar, the notorious coastal resort town in which the brutal 1973 military coup had originated. In a letter to the *Times* of London, Hayek went on to claim that he had "not been able to find a single person even in much maligned Chile who did not agree that personal freedom was much greater under Pinochet that it had been under Allende."[18] Later, in an interview in Venezuela in 1981, Hayek would judge Salvador Allende's democratically elected administration as the only "totalitarian" régime in South America.[19]

Moreover, in an interview with *El Mercurio* in 1977, Hayek, on a preliminary mission to the Andean nation, had praised Pinochet's policies as "an example at the global level" for economic development. In that conversation he maintained, somewhat chillingly, that sometimes "democracy needs 'a good cleaning' by strong government," and he is cited in that right-wing daily as saying that "unlimited democracy does not work." Hayek eventually met with Pinochet himself, who requested copies of Hayek's writings. Hayek promptly had his secretary back home mail to the dictator "A Model Constitution," a draft chapter in volume 3 of his upcoming *Law, Legislation and Liberty*, in which he asserts that constitutional freedoms may be suspended if a free society is under threat. The encounter between the Chilean general and the Austrian professor yielded results: a new Chilean constitution, unveiled in September 1980, was actually named after Hayek's own *Constitution of Liberty* and included elements of Hayek's arguments.[20]

Things had thus come full circle. The same Hayek who, in *Road to Serfdom*, had exonerated capitalism from any role in Nazism and who moreover had placed the blame for fascism (and on "totalitarianism") solely and squarely on socialists, was now, in the name of anti-"totalitarianism," *applauding* a military autocracy that was routinely kidnapping, torturing, and killing democratic socialists for the supposed crime of involvement with a legally elected government that, by contrast, had scrupulously respected constitutional liberties. In the later 1970s, one might add, Hayek was to receive honorary doctorates from universities in

---

[18] Cited in Robin, p. 74.
[19] Ebenstein, p. 306.
[20] From Andrew Farrant, Edward McPhail, and Sebastian Berger, "Preventing the 'Abuses' of Democracy." Cited and discussed in http://coreyrobin.com/tag/alan-ebenstein

Guatemala, Argentina, and again Chile, all three of which were then governed by military dictatorships. Subsequently, a private secondary school, the Colegio Preparatorio Friedrich von Hayek, was established in Guatemala.

Still, it bears mention that, in the best specimens of his writing, Hayek is more than just a crude ideologue or a pamphleteer. He is a serious thinker who sets forth some worthy and stimulating arguments about the dynamics of tradition and of knowledge, the emergence of what he calls "spontaneous order," and especially the rule of law. And he writes in the sober, rationalistic style of the pure academic he happens to be, rather than in the white-hot prose of Rand or the nasty, simplistic sloganeering of punster Nabokov. Moreover, hidden in various corners of Hayek's work there are arguments that his neo-liberal champions would prefer to ignore. In *Constitution...*, for instance, he accepts that government can play a role in helping "the indigent, unfortunate, and disabled" (257) and in providing "security against severe physical privation," and "may, usefully and without any harm, assist or lead in such endeavors" (257-59)—a humanitarian function that hard-line American libertarians would relegate exclusively to private charities and individuals. In *Law, Legislation and Liberty* vol. 3, Hayek even defends "restrictions on sales" of firearms; as he elaborates, "it is both desirable and unobjectionable that only persons satisfying certain intellectual and moral qualities should be allowed to practice such trade."[21] Obviously, those who argue for the right of private gun shows, big-box stores, and mail-order houses to sell whatever deadly, high-fire weapons they wish, will not find supporting material in Hayek. He also found taxation and military conscription to be defensible practices.

These caveats and nuances exist, then, in Hayek's work, though they are not exactly conspicuous. In the end, there is something desiccated about Hayek's vision, its nostalgic schemes devised by a learned nobleman in his study, who spins forth theories meant to explain away massive historical changes that he dislikes on principle. (One can imagine him as a character in Voltaire's *Candide* or in Borges's fantastical stories about cloistered scholars.)

*

The libertarian mind—its world view, its interpretation of events, its overall aims—has for some time now figured as a key player in U.S. political debate and public discourse. Suspicion of government programs

---

[21] Cited in ibid., p. 225.

and the very idea that government can do *nothing* right are notions that
have gained considerable traction and have achieved the status of a kind of
shared folklore. Although self-identified "pure" libertarians form only a
select if sizeable minority among those polled (about 15 per cent), chosen
aspects of libertarian thinking are now all but orthodoxy within the ranks
of the Republican Party.

Confusion also plays a part in popular sorts of libertarian attitudes.
Gary Weiss, in his *Ayn Rand Nation*, reports having interviewed Tea Party
participants in the wake of the 2008 financial meltdown. While the
protesters who spoke to him were certainly angry at the banks for the
débacle, in some vague way they mainly blamed the *government* for the
crash.

Hence, with the rise of libertarianism, ideas and practices that, in the
wake of the 1929 financial downturn, the subsequent depression, and the
rise of fascism, had seemingly been discredited, would re-emerge in force
during the Reagan years and after. Yet one aspect of the libertarian agenda
had already been the dominant feature in American political life following
World War II. With the anti-Communist purge at home aimed at
undermining the liberal Democrats and their New Deal programs,
followed by accusations that the Democrats had "lost China" to Mao's
guerrillas, the libertarian Right was setting the rules of the game,
succeeding in making global anti-communism *the* foreign-policy focus of
both parties, including that of Presidents Truman, Kennedy, Johnson, and,
to an extent, Carter. Until 1989, scarcely any mainstream U.S. politician
could have withstood the libertarian Right's continued onslaught on those
it deemed "soft on Communism."

With the end of Communism as a significant ideological challenge on
the world stage, the libertarian mind and its exponents have shifted their
focus to domestic concerns, with "the deficit" and "the debt" as their
prime targets—alarmist terms that mask a tactic of chipping away at social
programs and state regulations, and a long-term goal of doing away with
the New Deal and Great Society legacies, relegating government to its
limited, nineteenth-century, caretaker role. (The battle cry "the Deficit!" is
for enemies of the welfare state what "States' Rights!" was for opponents
of the struggles for racial equality in the 1960s.) Popular books get
written—notably Amity Shlaes's *The Forgotten Man* (2007)—with the
intent to "prove" that FDR's reforms only made the Depression worse.

Meanwhile, since the 1970s, the secular, libertarian sectors of the
Republican Party have made common cause (the famous "Southern
Strategy") with the more traditional, religious, white conservative forces in
the South, the latter of which, for reasons of their own, still harbor

resentments about the 1960s Civil Rights movement and its resulting laws, and in some cases are even angry over the 1865 Confederate defeat and emancipation of the slaves. The alliance between secular libertarians and religious Southern traditionalists has, under the banner of fighting "Big Government," unleashed a mass movement of the Right that, on occasion, assumes disquieting forms—among them the 1990s militias, the terrorist bombing in Oklahoma City in 1995, the war fever of the 2000s, the Tea Party rallies of the 2010s, and renewed talk of outright Secession in Texas and elsewhere. In public discourse, the European welfare states have replaced "Communism" as bogeymen, as instances of what *not* to be. As some libertarian conservatives like to proclaim, "We are not Sweden!" and even "We are not Canada!"

One of the leading characteristics of the libertarian Right—both among individual writers and in the larger coalition movement—has been a broad pattern of denial. Here follow a few instances.

1. Denial of any link between tobacco and lung cancer. (Rand and followers.)
2. Denial of any human instincts. (Rand)
3. Denial of the human unconscious. (Nabokov)
4. Denial of the theory of Relativity. (Nabokov)
5. Denial of the existence of society. (Rand, Nabokov, Hayek, Thatcher.)
6. Denial of any role played by the social environment and physical factors in shaping individuals. (Nabokov. Rand. Standard Libertarian Line.)
7. Denial of the role of sheer blind luck and happenstance in the success and failure of individuals. (Standard Libertarian Line)
8. Denial of mental illness and of the value of therapeutic treatments. (Dr. Thomas Szasz and followers.)
9. Denial of any positive outcomes from the 1964 and 1965 Civil Rights laws. (Rep. Ron Paul)
10. Denial that socialized medicine *anywhere* is effective. (Standard Libertarian Line)
11. Denial that Social Democracy works at all. (Standard Libertarian Line)
12. Denial that Nazi Germany was a capitalist and anti-Communist country. (Hayek. Nabokov. Rand. Standard Libertarian Line.)
13. Total, absolute denial of any past conservative sympathy and praise for fascism. (Rand. Hayek. Standard Libertarian Line.)

14. Denial of the Soviet role in fighting, stopping, and defeating Nazism. (Standard Libertarian Line)
15. Denial of Evolution, and proposing "Creationism" or "Intelligent Design" in its stead. (Many libertarians.)
16. Denial of the viability and value of all public education. (Standard Libertarian Line)
17. Denial of any past or present role played by government in road-building, water supply, sewage disposal, public transportation, public health and sanitation, scientific research, telecommunications, and the Internet. (Standard Libertarian Line)
18. Denial of the role of labor unions in improving the post-war living standards of labor and the middle class. (Standard Libertarian Line)
19. Denial of the value of government regulations in finance, pharmaceuticals, and the environment. (Ayn Rand. Milton Friedman. Standard Libertarian Line.)
20. Denial that the easy availability of guns can lead to exorbitantly high homicide rates and shooting rampages, or that gun control can help prevent crime. (Standard Libertarian Line). And last but not least,
21. Denial of anthropogenic global warming. (Republicans and Standard Libertarian Line.)

Absolute libertarianism is a way of thinking, a conception of life that can only flourish in a country with the philosophy of John Locke as its foundational premise, and with a history of an ever-expanding frontier; a once-new nation whose central government had among its chief functions in its first hundred years to send in the cavalry and clear the land of Indians so as to make way for white settlers. That past frontier is of course central to the national mythology and to the American political unconscious, which is among the reasons for the popular allure of libertarian attitudes in vast, still sparsely inhabited states such as Wyoming, Montana, and Idaho.

As part of the frontier mind, the libertarians have a utopia of their own enshrined in pulp fiction: to wit, the "Galt's Gulch" sections in *Atlas Shrugged*. Rand's expository chapters hold in the libertarian imaginary a place roughly analogous to that of Edward Bellamy's *Looking Backward* for nineteenth-century utopian socialists. Meanwhile, certain other libertarian utopias, as byproducts of the continued growth of the movement, can be found circulating in their mentisphere and blogosphere, some of them more visibly than others. Here follow, in extremely sketchy form, just a few examples:

1. *Crime Prevention.* Let everyone, without exception, carry a firearm! This is the ultimate eschatological vision of America's gun lovers and of the National Rifle Association. Seen on bumper stickers: "AN ARMED SOCIETY IS A POLITE SOCIETY."
2. *Traffic Utopia.* Gary Johnson, ex-governor of New Mexico (1995-2003) and Libertarian Party nominee for President in 2012, believes in abolishing maximum speed limits on roads and in removing "STOP" signs and red lights from intersections.
3. *The Free State Project.* Relocation to the frontier, again. This was a plan launched in the year 2001, to have 20,000 people move to New Hampshire and form a libertarian society, with taxes and regulations at a minimum, a kind of real-life Galt's Gulch. By 2011, some eleven thousand individuals had signed letters of intent, and around nine hundred had actually moved.
4. *"Seasteading."* By analogy with "homesteading," this concept is in part a   brainchild of Peter Thiel, the libertarian co-founder of PayPal. The idea is to create brand-new, sovereign islands 200 miles off the coast of San Francisco and establish on the open seas an entire, independent, libertarian entity.

The libertarian mind exists as a potent, mass-based, self-renewing force in U.S. politics. At the time of this writing, it is arguably the most vocal, visible, and aggressively militant presence on the American socio-political scene. Even when its adherents do not hold state power, the libertarian mind nonetheless sets the terms of political discussion and functions as an obstructive force to its legitimate opponents. The liberal Democrats bear some responsibility for this stand-off as they are too timid to stand their ground and defend their progressive legacy, too frightened and irresolute to reject the libertarians' absolutist demands outright. (As the poet Yeats wrote in another context, "The best lack all conviction, while the worst/Are full of passionate intensity.") Choosing instead to "dialogue" and "compromise" with their libertarian adversaries and enemies, the Democrats in their "bipartisan" faith end up giving the latter slow but steady piecemeal victories that provide further incentive to pursue upcoming battles. Just as, during the Cold War, the Democrats yielded to the libertarian Right on anti-Communism abroad, they yield now subtly to a broad, free-market, libertarian agenda of "limited government" and deregulation at home. Periodic electoral setbacks notwithstanding, the libertarian mind is always with us, sometimes dominant, other times less so, but very much there. It will not be going away for years to come.

CHAPTER FIFTEEN

ON GUNS, FLOOD VICTIMS, LIBERTARIANS, ORWELLIANA, MY FATHER, AND ME

In June 1972, Hurricane Agnes barreled upwards, south to north, battering the bulk of the eastern United States. Among the results: more than 100 deaths, and what was then the costliest and geographically most extensive storm damage in recorded U.S. history. Hardest hit of all were Florida and Pennsylvania; in addition, towns in southern New York State experienced major flooding and devastation, if no loss of life.

At the time I was a novice college instructor residing in Binghamton, New York—this among the communities adversely affected, though not as grievously as Elmira and Corning, to the west. During those years I was a very angry young man, seething in a constant rage over the horrors of the Vietnam War, the tawdry dishonesty of President Nixon, and the overall rightward drift of both the country and the town where I lived. And so, in the aftermath of storm Agnes and the public relief efforts aimed at dealing with its ravages, I penned and sent off to the local newspaper a satirical letter. It read thus:

> To the Editor:
> I'm absolutely sick and tired of reading all these bleeding-heart reports about alleged flood victims. If these people are having such a rough time, they can show some private initiative and rebuild their homes on their own.
> I made everything by my own efforts, and frankly I do not like having to pay taxes out of my hard-earned salary so that these crybabies can mooch off a government handout. All this flood-welfare is a step toward socialism, and I'd just as soon have no part of it.
> (signed)
> JONATHAN SWIFTE
> Binghamton

To my surprise, Swifte's letter elicited a spate of angry responses from area readers. One tender-hearted lady wrote: "I have sat here and read the letter from Jonathan Swifte in disbelief at least five times, and I still can't believe it. I'm sorry, Mr. Swifte, but I can't believe there are such heartless and callous people as you make yourself out to be ... Where is your compassion?"

Another, sterner woman noted: "You are sick and tired? You can bet they're sick and tired of cleaning mud and slime and dirt from their homes ... They should show 'private initiative'? Of course they have private initiative or they would have had nothing to lose in the first place ..."

The most memorable riposte came from a man, who began by saying, "While being a conservative who is opposed to much of the socialism being thrust upon us, I am totally disgusted with the letter written by Jonathan Swifte about flood relief ... I was in Elmira the day after the flood, and in Corning the following day. While I've never met an 'alleged' victim, there are plenty of real ones available." After citing some of the heart-rending losses, the angry conservative summed up with noble indignation, "I applaud any ... efforts made by state and federal governments to assist these people ... along with [funds from] private individuals ... Maybe they should start one for Mr. Swifte so he wouldn't have to pay his share of one for these 'crybabies.' If he is a self-made man, I thank God I was created."

Finding myself caught up in this maelstrom, I drafted a response to my respondents:

> To the Editors:
> I am shocked by the hysteria people have shown in their vicious attacks on me. Isn't this a free country, a democracy? Don't I have the right to say what I want?
> It simply doesn't make sense. Here we spend billions fighting Communism halfway around the globe. And yet we let the Communists sneak in through the back door by allowing tax-funded flood welfare.
> As I see it, if somebody chooses to build his home next to a river and then the river floods, well, that's his problem. Why should I have to pay for his stupid mistakes?
> The attackers and their alleged victims should read American's greatest writer, Ayn Rand. A wise lady, she might teach them a few lessons about what it means to depend on yourself, not on others.
>   JONATHAN SWIFTE

In the end, deciding not to add more fuel to the fire, I chucked Mr. Swifte's second letter, unsent. Still, there I was, already utilizing Ayn Rand as part of my little spoof of American right-wing thinking. In a telling irony, though, a decade or so later I was to find out that—yes! Indeed!—Randian true-believers stood, and still stand, in solid opposition to government relief for the victims of natural disasters ...

Meanwhile, how the larger picture has changed! In 1972, an earnest conservative, in rebutting Jonathan Swifte's complaints, could without hesitation defend government aid to flood victims and not see it as a gateway to socialism.

Rand back then was a fringe phenomenon. In the intervening decades, however, her view has gradually gained something like mainstream respectability, with libertarians openly coming out against any type of public assistance to those fellow citizens who'd had the poor judgment to live in the path of a tropical storm.

Hence, in 2005, Rep. Ron Paul was one of ten congressmen who voted against Federal aid to the victims of Hurricane Katrina, in New Orleans and elsewhere. In Dr. Paul's own words, "Why do people in Arizona have to be robbed in order to support the people from the coast?" Similarly, in 2011, Mitt Romney, just a year before his bid for President, advocated abolishing the Federal Emergency Management Agency (FEMA) and shifting those relief tasks to private charities and local governments. Along the same lines, in 2012, Ron Paul's son Rand, in his capacity as a senator from Kentucky, argued for ending federal disaster assistance, this time to the victims of Hurricane Sandy.

Yet we need not go so far beyond 1972 to find such dismal science. Already in an interview from that very year, economist Milton Friedman offered arguments that seem an echo of my second letter. Historian Angus Burgin sums it up thus:

> [I]n the wake of Hurricane Agnes in 1972, [Friedman] implied that the federal government should not provide aid after a natural disaster. Such aid encourages the inhabitation of unsafe areas, he asserted, and would inevitably lead to a situation in which the government needed to regulate where one would live and not live.[1]

The pattern, as once foreseen by my "Jonathan Swifte" persona in 1972, then, is clear.

Today, at the lower levels of this debate, one encounters on the Internet all sorts of guttersnipe argufiers who opine, roughly, thus: "If people are so stupid as to build their home on a flood plain/in earthquake country/tornado country/blizzard country, well, that's their problem. Using taxes to help them rebuild is akin to theft. " Unlike my much-maligned Letter to the Editor, satires these postings, I should say, are definitely *not*. Here are three representative examples.

---

[1] As paraphrased in Angus Burgin, *The Great Persuasion*, p. 182.

From a regular visitor to the Alternet online news service, who signs with the byline "Prinzowhales:"

> I'm tired of disaster relief for people who live in flood plains and build stick houses in tornado alley,... tired of trying to create designer shores for assholes in ocean front condos every time a hurricane hits...
>
> Anyone willing to trust to Corps of Engineers to maintaining dikes while you live 18 feet below sea level? I'm not ... and I don't want to pay for idiots who do!

Next, two postings from one David Elmore on Amazon.com. The first one contains almost the exact same wording as the above:

> Paul, you're wasting your time on altruistic idiots who think that people who build in front of hurricanes (and reap the consequences of such insanity) deserve booty stolen from people are actually responsible for their lives.
>
> Signed, David Elmore [2]

Another, more convoluted posting from Mr. Elmore, draws on a tortuous analogy from medical needs and theft:

> I have a question for you, Mr. Villada: If a family member (John) tells the rest of his family that they should rob the neighbors across the street to pay for gramma's dialysis, and after the robbery, they all happily pay for the dialysis, should John and his family be tried in a court of law and then imprisoned for the robbery?
>
> If your answer is yes, then please turn yourself in to your local magistrate, because the "government aid" you suggest for flood victims (or whatever altruistic subject de jour you might have) is simply robbery of the rest of us Americans to pay for the plight of whatever Americans you and your altruistic tribe decide upon today or tomorrow. [3]

So, the "Jonathan Swifte" who, in 1972, had lambasted government aid to hapless flood victims, was apparently onto something. He was ahead of his time; curmudgeon though he was, good ol' Swifte had his sights on an attitude that eventually would, as the phrase puts it, "go viral." These days,

---

[2]   http://www.amazon.com/review/R289ZF87I0N4VL/ref=cm_cd_pg_pg3?ie=UTF8&asin=0195324870&cdForum=Fx2Y2EICMRVLWKO&cdPage=3&cdThread=Tx330BHDDUZY9XT&store=books#wasThisHelpful

[33]   http://www.amazon.com/review/R289ZF87I0N4VL/ref=cm_cd_pg_next?ie=UTF8&asin=0195324870&cdForum=Fx2Y2EICMRVLWKO&cdPage=6&cdThread=Tx330BHDDUZY9XT&store=books#wasThisHelpful

when I publish similar satirical Letters to the Editor in which (under other monikers) I skewer disaster relief, approximately one-third of the responses are from online readers who are in frank *agreement* with such sentiments!

*

To my dismay, over the years I've racked up something of a history of anticipating libertarian developments. As early as 1970, I had a brief article in *Boston after Dark* (later *The Boston Phoenix*) wherein I conjectured that, in 1976, Ronald Reagan could well be elected to chief executive. Friends of mine who read the item thought my prediction to be slightly daffy. The piece, I later realized, was not of high caliber, and my forecast, moreover, was off by a good four years. And yet ... I had intuited something that lay in store for the political future ...

My next venture, post-Agnes, into such political speculation was a talk I gave at the December 1983 conference of the Modern Language association, the near-midpoint of the Reagan era, on a panel called "Orwell's *1984* on the Eve of 1984." Following a summary review of the background to that iconic book, I posed the question, in echo of the title of Sinclair Lewis's own speculative novel, "Can *1984* happen here?" And I answered thus:

> Perhaps, but with a difference. In the West, or the Americas at least, Orwell's nightmare seems more likely to come from the libertarian-capitalist right than from the Stalinist-socialist left. The Chilean and Argentine *militares* have already proved as much; and the extent of U.S. domestic surveillance, revealed during the Watergate hearings, is "Orwellian" enough in its implications (27).[4]

In this regard, the direct support given by the United States government and corporations, as well as by libertarian economists (Hayek, Friedman et al.) to the Chilean military dictatorship, is now established fact. In the more mundane realms of everyday economic life, moreover, I noted the "Orwellian" prophecy:

> Orwell imagines an economy largely centralized under Party control, yet with a rundown private sector of dreary shops and pubs persisting in sad brown slums north of London. Those slums bring to mind, if anything, the inner core of our own cities, abandoned by a highly centralized *corporate*

---

[4] Bell-Villada, "*1984*: Looking Backward at Orwell's Novel of the 1940s." Page references from this article will be cited parenthetically within the text.

economy, those private conglomerates whose interlocking interests include telecommunications, hotels, publishers, bakeries, baseball teams, parking lots, and insurance. It's an open secret in the business press that the biggest rewards today are in buying up and selling of other firms (27).

Then there is the matter of how Orwell envisioned the relationships between reality, thought, and language in his dystopia:

> In his climactic confrontation with Winston Smith, high Party dogmatist O'Brien preaches a kind of collective solipsism that denies objective truth and places reality "in the human mind, and nowhere else. Not in the individual mind, which can make mistakes...; only in the name of the Party, which is ... immortal." For a common-sense empiricist like Orwell this clearly represents madness in high places. Alas, intellectual history has played him a trick. Real party Marxism has remained obstinately nineteenth-century materialist, even positivist, in outlook, whereas solipsist notions are now commonplace in the liberal West and the United States in particular. "Reality" as something shadowy and irrelevant, vague, insubstantial, something malleable to human manipulation—this is the world view of media men, public-relations whiz kids, and *Advertising Age* editorialists, who believe less in truth than in "creative approaches," "stories" to be attractively packaged and marketed. It is the ideology of center-right, post-modernist authors like Nabokov, for whom "reality" was a word that belonged in quotation marks. It is the doctrine of infinite pluralism, taught by virtuoso humanists at Yale and Johns Hopkins universities, whose baroque ahistoricism and overwrought relativism pay highest respects to believing in nothing at all. *History is a fiction, reality is a fiction*: these are the fashionable buzzwords today in upper academe and vanguard lit. crit. (27-28).

Well, in an astounding instance of political life imitating satirical fiction, there is the famous statement made in 2004 to journalist Ron Susskind by an aide to Pres. Bush II, an individual later identified as political advisor and boss Karl Rove. In a riposte to the journalists and their so-called "reality-based community," Rove baldly announced as follows: "That's not the way the world works anymore. We're an empire now, and when we act, we create our own reality. And while you're studying that reality ... we'll act again, creating another new reality, which you can study too, and that's how things will sort out. We're history's actors... and you, all of you, will be left to just study what we do."[5] Rove's words could have come straight from the lips of Orwell's reality-denying Party ideologue.

---

[5] Cited in "Reality-based Community," http://en.wikipedia.org.wiki/reality-based-community

Regarding the use and misuse of language, I observed the following in my MLA talk:

> Painfully conscious of good language, clear thinking, and political malpractices, Orwell in *1984* invented and diagnosed two now-proverbial psycho-linguistic disorders, Doublethink and Newspeak. Earlier, in 1946, he had examined the malady in his lucid and renowned essay, "Politics and the English Language." Today he has an entire new set of patients on the libertarian right, with …their attacks on *big government*, a tangled code meaning (1) big business gets carte blanche, (2) "small" government builds vast weaponry, and (3) the army and spies get enlarged assignments. *Liberty* and *free choice* are principles evoked in defense of polluters, sweatshop operators, and the statecraft of General Pinochet. Traditionally positive adjectives have become drastically narrowed in actual semantic practice: *balanced, flexible,* and *open-minded* now usually signify a readiness to honor the ideas of the libertarian Right, while pejoratives such as *biased, dogmatic, one-sided,* and *fanatical* are invariably applied to any group opposing racism, militarism, exploitation, or any other such injustices (28).

As we know, "balanced" has become part of the company slogan of the Fox News network. And on the practical, foreign-policy applications of Doublethink:

> Cold War theory builds its premises on a chronic condition of Doublethink: Communist Russia, laughable and pathetically inefficient, can't get anything done right; but Communist Russia is also capable of, and is embarked on, world conquest. The suffering peoples of Warsaw, Prague, etc., hate their oppressor, Muscovy; but the Warsaw Pact, comprising those very same people of Warsaw, Prague, etc., is a mighty force that is soon to storm across Europe, all for Muscovy. Russians are brainwashed by Marxist thought control, but they're also cynical, disbelieve everything their government tells them, and are ripe for revolt! (29)

Summing up, I conjectured once again:

> It is not idle to speculate on a fully "Orwellian" situation imposed by the libertarian Right. Looking backward from our 1984, one finds a consistent record largely exorcised from the textbooks—such as a favorable and "open-minded" attitude toward European fascism during the 1930s; anti-left repression in the 1940s and '50s; staunch opposition to Civil Rights laws as tyrannical threats to individual "liberty" in the 1960s; expansion of surveillance here and abroad; vocal defense of military dictatorships in Spain, Greece, and Central America; and active aid for the most murderous regime in Chile's history. Looking to the future, the libertarian

Right has ample cultural support from Evangelical anti-eroticism and creationist neo-Lysenkoism (29).

And, rather than the specter of a "Big Brother Watching You," I took note of the ever-growing media society:

> Meanwhile the mega-apparatus of consumerism, with its infinite array of manufactured sounds, colors, and pretty faces watching you, and its constant production of fantasy wishes and dreams—fast thrills and cool sex for one market, smiling nuclear families for another, and a multitude of special-interest images in stock—serves as a perfect substitute for Big Brother, enticing and seemingly gratifying rather than terrorizing the individual imagination (29).

Such, then, was my prognosis.

To my surprise, the panel in which I'd participated was written up—my own talk included—in a *New York Times* news story by their arts critic-at-large Walter Goodman. As a result of this unexpected exposure, I received some congratulatory phone calls from friends, as well as hate mail from a few strangers out there—an Army captain, a rabbi, a Williams College alumnus from the 1950s. None of the poison-pensters took the trouble to deal with my arguments about a possible "Orwellian" future from the libertarian Right. Instead, the rabbi attacked me for speaking ill about "the freest country the world has ever seen," and ended his missive with the words, "P.S. I pity your students." According to the military man, Bell-Villada in his paper had said, "America stinks."

In the years following my talk (later published as an essay), some unforeseen, truly astounding events would lead to wholesale revisions and additions to the "Orwellian" paradigm that, in the American political imaginary, stands as the ultimate, primal evil. At the end of that same decade, the Soviet Union, a state and system that, by "totalitarian" theorists and U.S. policy makers alike, had been deemed an eternal, inexorable, cosmic threat of near-mythic proportions, suddenly began to unravel and finally collapsed, almost peacefully, with scarcely a shot fired. (One wonders: *this* was the mighty juggernaut that, in libertarian-conservative Senator Goldwater's phrase, was poised to "conquer the world"?)

Shortly thereafter, in the United States, rather than the emergence of a yearned-for "peace dividend," there arose some ominous, extreme-libertarian stirrings: First, the 1994 elections, with a right-wing congressional sweep in both houses, spearheaded by libertarian Representative Newt Gingrich, and similar victories at the local and state levels as well, announced a new libertarian "Contract with America" of tax cuts, small government, and deregulation. Second, in a kind of informal alliance, armed militias emerged in the southern and middle states, with their heated, vulgar-libertarian rhetoric. This double wave crested in the 1995 detonation of the Federal Building in Oklahoma City, the work of two libertarian-minded militia members. With its 168 dead and more than 600 wounded, it was the largest act of terrorism in U.S. history up to that date. The mutually complementary twin movements, electoral cum paramilitary, did peter out, temporarily discredited, by the year 2000. However, in the governmental arena we saw the constant Doublethink of "the Deficit," whereby the dire, oh so dire fiscal shortfall was to be solved by *cutting* rather than raising taxes and, somehow, by upping military expenditures, too.

Then, the earth shifted once again. The Islamic fundamentalists in Afghanistan, who had been enthusiastically praised by President Reagan as noble "freedom fighters" and given generous U.S. military assistance by his administration when they'd resisted the Russians, now turned against the United States with the triple attack of 11 September 2001, an atrocity that surpassed the Oklahoma bombing. The so-called "Global War on Terror" and its concomitant of fear have thence come to dominate most U.S. foreign policy, obscuring most all other debate and leading to increased state surveillance and to far more deaths than had been caused by 9/11. Fittingly, instead of the "Two Minutes of Hate" to which the inhabitants of Orwell's world are subject every day, there are now weekly TV serials such as the Fox network's *24*, in which torture is routinely depicted as a positive and effective force, as employed by a heroic Jack Bauer against hateful Muslims.

In addition, the libertarian Right now has at its disposal a vast array of muscular, well-funded institutional entities—giant media combines and think tanks, along with a cadre of strident, bellicose, individual spokespeople, all of which comprise a multiple, hydra-headed, decentralized propaganda system, the libertarian equivalent to Orwell's unitary "Ministry of Truth." The organizations almost all bear neutral, bland-sounding names that aim to conceal their right-wing agenda. Here follows a selective list:

Fox News
The Heritage Foundation
The American Enterprise Institute
The Cato Institute
The Hoover Institution on War, Revolution, and Peace
Americans for Prosperity
The American Legislative Exchange Council (ALEC)

The Foundation for Economic Education
The Heartland Institute
The Discovery Institute
The Hudson Institute
The Manhattan Institute
The Competitive Enterprise Institute
The Peterson Institute for International Economics
Mercatus Institute
The American Council on Science and Health
The Club for Growth
Frontiers of Freedom
FreedomWorks
Institute for Humane Studies
National Center for Policy Analysis
Advancement of Sound Science Coalition (now defunct)
Sarah Scaife Foundation
John Locke Foundation

and also….

Rush Limbaugh
Glenn Beck
Ann Coulter
Et Cetera

Libertarians are in many ways the mirror image of Stalinism. They are the Stalinists of 19th-century liberal capitalism today.

Stalinists and their successors saw private property as the root of all evil, and attacked social democracy as an inauthentic and false socialism. Libertarians, likewise, view government as the source of all evil, and attack social democracy as not only inefficient but destructive and immoral.

Stalinists believed that Communism by itself would eradicate racial prejudice, with no grass-roots initiatives necessary. Libertarians likewise believe that the market and money-making activities will bring an end to racism, with no grass-roots actions or governmental directives necessary.

Soviet-style Stalinists were against independent labor unions because, in their view, under socialism, workers don't need them. Libertarians are against independent labor unions because, in their view, in a free-market system, workers don't need them.

Stalinism generated the phenomenon of Lysenkoism, named after

Trofim Lysenko (1898-1976), the Soviet science bureaucrat who rejected genetics as "bourgeois" and consequently set back Russian research in biology for decades. Libertarians, on the other hand, have their own answer to Lysenkoism in the deniers of Evolution and in those who declare global warming "a hoax."

Stalinists believed that the Soviet way was the only way, and that any "third way" was imperialism. (These were the exact words of a preachy female guide for the Intourist agency, with whom my traveling group and I chatted in Kharkov, USSR, in 1969.) Libertarians, for their part, believe the absolute free market is the only way ("There is no alternative"— Margaret Thatcher's slogan), and that any third way, as we have seen, is "the road to serfdom."

*

In the 1980s and '90s, I took to writing a series of send-ups of libertarianism that appeared in local newspapers. Among the topics I dealt with were "the deficit" (of course), "limited government," the positive value of greed, anti-Soviet obsessions (still alive in 1986), a "balanced" look at Nazism, the uselessness of government programs, and—that mass mainstay of grass-roots libertarian politics—"gun rights." Several of these spoofs have remained even more relevant today, two or three decades later, and so I have included them in Appendix B of this volume. One piece in particular, having to do with the matter of "the right to bear arms," drew a brief but disquieting response, and, alas, has become eerily apposite for our time.

First, however, some background.

In 1993, in a car of the Long Island Railroad, there occurred one of those killing rampages that flare up with almost pathological regularity on the American stage. At the Merillon Station stop in Garden City, a Jamaican immigrant by the name of Colin Ferguson pulled out a pistol and started coolly, randomly shooting passengers, emptying out two fifteen-round magazines in the process. Six people were dead and nineteen were wounded by the time three male passengers succeeded in overpowering the gunman. In the media aftermath, many conservatives subsequently invoked this horrific incident as an argument for allowing ordinary citizens to carry firearms, anywhere and anytime, for the purpose of self-defense.

Coincidentally, a few months later, prompted by the report of a teacher who'd been punched on the face by a student, a lead editorial appeared in our local daily, *The Berkshire Eagle*, deploring the fact of everyday school violence.

In a gust of inspiration, I dashed off a deadpan satire in which both these events were fused. With a cold, calm, rigorous logic, I argued that the best way to prevent future classroom violence was to let teachers and pupils carry firearms in schools. Parodying a well-known slogan, I noted, "If you outlaw guns for children, only outlaw children will have guns." The spoof (see "Arm the Teachers and Students" in Appendix B) ran in *The Transcript*, another area newspaper. A few days later, what should I receive but ... a personal letter from the owner of a friendly neighborhood gun shop! The surprise fan warmly praised my arguments; he further informed me of his intention to send my article on to our then-governor, Jane Swift, and urge her to promulgate precisely such legislation.

The gun merchant, it appears, had taken my joke seriously.

And indeed, in the two decades that have since elapsed, my original satire has begun to resemble reality. With every U.S. school shooting since my little squib, libertarian conservatives routinely and vociferously argue that the solution to such violence in schools is ... allowing guns in schools. (In fact, in August 2008, the town of Harrold, Texas, began letting teachers and employees at its public schools carry concealed weapons on the job.)[6] Schools at every level, too. In fact, each year, more and more state governments open up college campuses to legal carrying of weapons—200 such institutions at the time of this writing, including the University of Colorado. There are even pro-gun initiatives to *force* schools and universities to permit guns on the premises, to disallow "gun-free" locations. (According to Wayne Lapierre, president of the NRA, gun-free schools are the *cause* of school shootings.)

Hence, in the wake of the massacre at the Sandy Hook school in Newtown, Connecticut, on 14 December 2012, in which a troubled 20-year-old Adam Lanza mowed down twenty small children, four teachers, the principal, a counselor, and finally himself, "gun rights" advocates were crying out for the arming of teachers and administrators in response. Indeed, the day before the shooting, the Republican-dominated state legislature in Michigan presented a bill calling for guns in schools *and day-care centers*; the Republican governor, Tim Snyder, vetoed the bill on grounds that such institutions were not being given the choice to opt out of the measure.

To this "debate" there is no end in sight. It is entirely conceivable that the weapons manufacturers, professional gun activists, and their broader libertarian supporters will one day get firearms accepted, by law, into

---

[6] Angela K. Brown (for the Associate Press), "Texas Education: Teachers Pack Heat?"

schools, stores, bars, restaurants, offices, buses, churches, and (why not?) airplanes across the land. In an ever-growing armed camp, one is less at the mercy of a remote Big Brother than at the whims of one's neighbor or of any fellow citizen. It's not so much the state or Big Government that controls the means of violence, but rather your schoolmate, your student, a fellow passenger, a co-worker, a co-parishioner, your own son or father, a total stranger in a crowd. In this proverbial war of all versus all, Thomas Hobbes meets George Orwell.

Meanwhile, in a dynamic well captured by Corey Robin in his book on the reactionary mind, the right-wing National Rifle Association utilizes the language of resistance to government tyranny in its call to legalize possession of fire arms for all...

*

But, returning to La Rand ...

I have binged on the work of the goddess of libertarianism on two lengthy occasions. First, when preparing to create my novella, "The Pianist Who Liked Ayn Rand," I perused, pen in hand, all of Rand's fiction and major nonfiction, for the ad hoc purpose of dramatizing her ideas and giving them flesh and blood via my cast of youthful characters.

Twenty years later, in the interests of refreshing my memory for the writing of this study, I carefully *re*-read, again with pen in hand, much of that oeuvre, including *Fountainhead* and *Atlas*, along with the rest of her thought pieces (I resist calling them "essays"), a great deal of her personal correspondence, and numerous, newly published scholarly works about her.

The second reading experience was something of a dark revelation. During my first such exposure, my mind had alighted on Rand's fanciful heroics; on her cult of superiority and genius; on her lofty talk about individual grandeur and the greatness of Man; and so forth. During my recent re-encounter, by contrast, being already well-acquainted with her positive figures and her rhetoric, I found my reader's focus falling rather on Rand's negative, nasty side: to wit, her implacable rage against the most simple, fundamental, affective human ties and family relations (mothers, wives, uncles, siblings); her loathing of almost all the ordinary people who must struggle just to get by, whom she dismisses without respite as "second-handers" and "looters and moochers"; her manifest disgust at social workers or at anyone who assumes the task of caring about others—about one's son, about disabled or subnormal children, or about the poor or about any less than privileged, less than fortunate folk;

her frank cult of cold-heartedness in males; and finally, her chronic, relentless romanticizing of physically violent sex between men and women.

So shaken was I by Rand's unsavory, unseemly contents that at one point my research labors actually gave me nightmares, a bad dream in which I found myself holed up in some dreary, isolated Hitchcockian motel room, with naught available for distraction save for a frayed, grimy, well-thumbed, drugstore-paperback edition of *Atlas Shrugged*.

I had been doing my homework, and it was not fun. I love reading, but not all reading is enjoyable.

Defenders of La Rand are wont to argue that she arrived at her uncompromising stance as a result of her bitter experiences with the Soviet system. It is only too obvious to point out that, in fact, she had simply moved from one absolute position to another, in the same way that some émigré Tsarists in Germany, notably those who assassinated Nabokov's father, became fascists under Nazism. Such an extreme pilgrimage, needless to say, is not the only path available. Not all Russian expatriates have ended up despising family life, social workers, charitable works, philanthropy, public housing, and disaster relief, just for starters. They don't even all argue that Nazism was less evil than Communism.

Still, inasmuch as Randians deploy that environmental argument in support of her drastic reaction to her past, I should like to offer a counter-example of my own. In many respects I grew up in circumstances that, in my upbringing under my father, much resembled the capitalist utopia envisioned by Rand. Though I doubt that my dad ever had occasion to come across the market diva's name or her writings, a smaller version of him could easily be imagined in the pages of her novels, could have been modeled after Madame Rand herself.

My father was a man for whom virtually nothing mattered except making money,   lots and lots and lots of money. The hundreds of letters he wrote to my mother, first from Asia and later from across the Caribbean, focus on two topics: 1) his then-love of her, effusively expressed, and 2) his money matters, business matters, transactions completed or to be done, deals past or present or to become, and dreams of cornering this market or that. There is in his missives precious little about anything else—about books or movies, places or politics. Every sale he makes is going to be the "big" one that will bring him wealth aplenty. His treasured reading at the time was Napoleon Hill's *Think and Grow Rich*, one of those classic American self-help manuals of the philosophy of success, at the time a commanding best-seller and still a popular title today.

During all these years, my mom was doing his bidding, contributing from her own savings some of the seed money for his initial investments in Hawaii and Haiti, and later, when in Puerto Rico, answering his business mail and phone calls, essentially minding the store, uncompensated, during his many extended absences. Like many a white man in the U.S. who would later seek a Pacific, "Cherry-Blossom," mail-order bride (I now realize), my father had found a compliant, devoted Asian wife who would do his will and support him through his far-flung money-making schemes. When he was "at home" at all, it was mostly to sack out. Otherwise he was either at the office or at the port with his cargo ships all day, every day.

In his role as a father, I have no memory of his playing, romping, biking, or chatting with my brother and me, or of him teaching us, or doing yard work with us, or taking us to cultural or sporting events. I have only a recollection or two of his going for family strolls with us. In Puerto Rico and later in Cuba, both my brother and I were good students who got excellent grades, making Honor Roll numerous times. Yet my father never offered any congratulations for our achievements. In fact, I cannot recall his demonstrating any pride or pleasure in his children at all. And of course he never refers to us in his many letters. Not believing that the environment shapes a human being, he took next to no interest in creating a suitable environment for his offspring. Meanwhile, as noted in chapter 3, I showed an exceptional sensitivity to and talent for music; my dad did nothing about it, indeed did everything possible to discourage it, deny it, crush it, trying to make me into an apprentice salesman or mechanic instead. He cultivated no relationships with the Puerto Rican community, with the neighbors, with fellow parents of any nationality, or with our teachers at any of the three schools where we attended. His sole ties were with his business associates and his entrepreneurial and adventurer peers—his own little "Galt's Gulch."

My father, then, shared with Ayn Rand, and with her business heroes Hank Rearden, Dagny Taggart, and John Galt, the ideal of a selfish pursuit of individual wealth, together with a studied indifference toward others and a concomitant lack of interest in nurturing or loving his own blood-kin. At home and elsewhere, he lived by Galt's dictum: "Do you ask what moral obligation I owe to my fellow man? None—except the obligation I owe to myself." If one adds the words "and family" after "fellow man," the Galtian statement of principles fits my male progenitor perfectly. And again, like Rand herself receiving crucial help from all sorts of people throughout her life, while asserting apodictically that no one had helped her along the way, my father too claimed to be "self-made" and to have earned everything, in his familiar words, "from the sweat of my brow."

After dumping my mother in San Juan and starting over with a new wife in Caracas, my father put my brother and me into the Havana Military Academy a thousand miles away, thereby gaining control over the two of us without having to deal with us on a daily basis. Years later, in a letter to me, he would pat himself on the back for having paid the tuition there and at other "private schools, costing money," in his righteous words. During my college years, although his financial aid was sporadic, with each occasional check that he sent in he'd express great pride in himself as he presented me with those fitful cash outlays. When, decades hence, in the 1990s, in a brief exchange of letters, I stated to him that he had not been a good father, he replied saying, "I don't think I was the worst father in the world," and once more took credit for his tuition payments at those schools.

Some earnest defenders of my father—Randian or otherwise—might argue, "Your dad gave you guys food, plus a roof over your heads, plus an education." Hard-line Stalinists could in fact rightfully say precisely that about their own system; and the anti-Communists could just as rightfully counter-argue, "That's not enough." Whatever the case, a middle-class parent assuming special commendation for providing room and board to his kids is a bit like a bricklayer taking credit for laying bricks, a wheat farmer for harvesting wheat, or a historian for getting his facts right. Quality concerns aside, it simply goes with the job.

Besides being an inadvertent product of a "Randian" household, I am an offshoot of the dynamic of frontier-imperialism that, as I noted in my previous chapter, has been historically linked with the libertarian mind. The 18-year-old Bell Sr. left behind his parental home in the 19th-century border state of Missouri, first moving in with his older brother in Los Angeles to enroll in the (State-supported) UCLA campus there; next, going on to the then-colony of Hawaii (annexed by the U.S. in 1898), nominally for studies at the territorial university, but really to check out the money-making opportunities throughout Asia. Already as a student he was starting ventures in magazine subscriptions and private mailboxes. Around the campus hangouts he met my mother Carmen, a sophomore. During their courtship he often asked the fresh, young Honolulu native if her parents might lend him several thousand dollars in order to launch a business, or to purchase a house or car. (How this request was received is something I have never found out.) And then there were those savings of hers, some of which he would use as capital.

After the couple was married, they shipped off to the Caribbean, first, to Haiti (occupied by the U.S. Marines, 1915-34), where I was born; then on to Puerto Rico (also annexed in 1898), where Kanani and I would spend our childhood. From there, my father went on to do deals in Cuba (occupied by U.S. Marines, 1906-09 and 1917-22, and permanently in Guantánamo), site of the military school where my brother and I lived for two years; and to conduct business in Venezuela (then under a U.S.-supported dictatorship), Florida, and other areas of the American lagoon.

Hence, my father took full advantage of the constantly expanding frontier—an ever-shifting zone backed by American military, economic, and political power—and claimed for himself the title of self-made man. And his son, this scribbler—a sort of American counterpart to George Orwell, who'd been born in British India and later served a stint there in the colonial police force—is a by-product of American empire and its hidden history of settlers, adventurers, and seekers of fortune, who justify their unrooted, restless quest for money on grounds of "liberty" and "individual rights," and who have in dime-store philosopher Ayn Rand a vulgar-libertarian legitimization for their actions. Howard Roark in his courtroom speech describes the United States as "the noblest country in the history of man" (676). Rand, for her part, in her introduction to *For the New Intellectual*, speaks of "America, the greatest, noblest, freest country on earth" (11). Such nationalist-cum-ideological rhetoric was a standard ingredient in Bell *père*'s preachments.

In sum, during much of my first quarter-century of earthly existence, I lived a real-life version of Rand's dream of pure selfishness within a John-Galt utopia of greed. And years later I would realize just how close that desolate experience had come to destroying my mother, my two siblings, myself, our family, and my own personal sense of family. I also now know that Randianism is no way to live a sane or fulfilling life, and that (as conservatives are wont to say about communism) Rand's vision goes against, violates, is contrary to simple, ordinary "human nature."

*

In leaving Russia, Rand was not fleeing for her life. Her trajectory can rather be described as that of an expatriate or émigrée, much like that of millions of migrants from elsewhere, who, putting poverty and uncertainty behind them, come to America in search of an improved existence—and, in the case of Rand, to become rich and famous. Granted, back in the USSR, Rand's father's pharmacy had been nationalized, the family thus losing its wealth and, along the way, descending into deprivation (a process partly evoked in her first novel, *We, the Living*). Yet, neither she nor her relatives ever endured physical violence or torture, Gulag imprisonment or state execution. Ironically, it was the invading armies of Nazi Germany—a country that, in a letter from 1941, Rand had characterized as the lesser menace in comparison to Communism and the New Deal—that would lead directly to the deaths of two of her blood kin.

Nabokov, on the other hand, does qualify as a refugee, one whose father had been murdered in Germany by Russian fascists, whose wife and son would surely have been sent to a death camp had the threesome stayed on in occupied France, and whose brother Sergey died because of his homosexuality as well as his anti-fascism. For Nabokov, fleeing to the United States turned out to be literally a life-saving measure.

Every period in history has its best and worst, its cultural products good, bad or indifferent. Under the long reign of Queen Elizabeth I, for instance, hundreds, perhaps thousands of plays were written and staged, ranging from the anonymous, crude, and grisly *Gorboduc* to a sublime and magisterial *King Lear*. Similarly, America's Cold War 1950s gave us both *Atlas Shrugged* and *Lolita*. Each of their two authors clung to nineteenth-century ideologies (Nietzsche and free-market capitalism for the former, classical liberalism and aestheticism for the latter) that, through much of the twentieth century, were on the defensive. And of course they were both of them Russian exiles whose writings were products of that displacement.

Nabokov, however, had the good fortune to grow artistically, transcending and sublimating his array of manias in two great novels, *Lolita* and *Pale Fire*. Rand, by contrast, poured her primal obsessions into *Fountainhead* partly, and into *Atlas* fully and beyond. Although she remained fundamentally "stuck," her verbal overflow gave a clangorous voice to a certain subjacent American world-view that, in her hands, took on a larger-than-life existence of its own. That utopian vision now motivates many an American public figure and moves and inspires millions of susceptible American reader-followers. Its future effects are uncertain—perhaps disturbing and dangerous, perhaps in the long run ephemeral. Great art works like *Lolita* can survive; propaganda art, but seldom.

There is to Nabokov's art, moreover, a concealed side that even his most devoted exegetes appear largely to have missed. Such an undercurrent is expertly brought out by journalist Andrea Pitzer in *The Secret History of Vladimir Nabokov*, a remarkable and aptly titled study that breaks new ground in our assessment and understanding of the Russian-American (and that appeared only in the final months of my writing this book). Through a deft combination of detailed historical sleuthing and close attention to certain key works of the master, Pitzer shows that Nabokov's fiction is significantly more attuned to issues of historical conflict and repression, of destructive prejudice and ordinary bigotry, than is commonly thought, and that also, in almost indiscernible ways, he captures the damage and suffering that these forces can inflict on the human psyche.

As an instance, early on during the First World War, in each of the belligerent nations, thousands of resident aliens whom governments deemed suspicious were interned in concentration camps across Europe. Accordingly, a young Hermann in *Despair*, being part-German and studying in St. Petersburg in 1914, was relocated to an internment camp in Astrakhan, in southern Russia, to be released only in 1919, i.e. by the Bolsheviks. Without going deeply into the psychological, Hermann's experience can be seen as a source of the mental derangement that will later lead him to his crazed delusions and strange crime. It also explains Hermann's positive disposition toward a regime that had, after all, freed him from imprisonment. In chapter 2 of the novel, Hermann spends an entire paragraph praising Communism as "a great and necessary thing" that "was producing wonderful values" (20), though, of course, for Nabokov, this in itself may perhaps be interpreted as yet another sign of the protagonist's madness.

Thicker and more varied backgrounds go into the "secret history" imbedded in *Lolita*. Pitzer adduces the following:

1) The Greek island of Corfu was a major League of Nations center for refugees of recent wars and of the Armenian genocide. Many of its internees perished from the widespread epidemics there. Annabel Leigh, Humbert's first love, had died of typhus in Corfu in 1923. (AL, 13)

2) At the height of World War II, Great Britain, finding itself swamped with Jewish and other refugees, enemy aliens, and military POWs, proceeded to ship thousands of them overseas to relocation camps in Canada. Pitzer raises the speculation that Humbert's mysterious sojourn in northern Ontario may have been a political internment. In Nabokov's own renowned essay on *Lolita* (later appended as an afterword), he describes Humbert as "a foreigner and an anarchist" (AL, 315).

3) "NO DOGS, JEWS, OR NEGROES ALLOWED." When these words were no longer considered acceptable on hotel signs or advertisements, many establishments took instead to utilizing coded messages saying "NEAR CHURCHES" and "NO DOGS." In their travels across the U.S., Nabokov and his wife and child encountered a good number of places that requested "Christian clientele" and that frankly discriminated against Jews, or whose employees would make casual anti-

Semitic slurs. Whereupon the Nabokovs would promptly withdraw and move on. Humbert, too, comes across such placards in his own travels, and he notes people who are on the verge of making anti-Semitic comments.

Pitzer in fact makes a strong case for "the possibility that Nabokov intended Humbert Humbert to be Jewish,"[7] even though the words "Jew" or "Jewish" never once appear in the work. Several textual facts point subtly in that direction. Family occupations on Humbert's father's side include commerce in wines, jewelry, and silk—traditionally Jewish trades. Charlotte Haze, Humbert's second wife, worries about "a certain strange strain" in his ancestry, and she confesses that if he "did not believe in our Christian God, she would commit suicide" (AL, 74-75). Humbert pays special empathetic note to Lolita's peers who seem Jewish. On seeing the list of her classmates at Ramsdale, he reflects on pupil Irving Flashman, "for whom I am sorry" (AL, 53). (In this regard, Alfred Appel reports Nabokov saying to him, "Poor Irving; he is the only Jew among all those Gentiles." [AL, 363, 53/3]) We are also informed of Lolita's friend Eva Rosen, "a displaced little person from France" who speaks English "with a slight Brooklyn accent" that at one time was the mark of Jews from New York (AL, 190).

Later, after Humbert has lost Lolita and is depicted wandering about alone, he mentions to us his many nightmares, including one about "the brown wigs of tragic old women who had been gassed" (AL, 254)—an unmistakable allusion to the Orthodox Jewish women whose hair pieces, following their deaths in the crematoria, were piled up along with other personal effects of murdered Jews such as eyeglasses. Finally, when Humbert confronts Clare Quilty in his rival's house, Quilty informs him, "this is a Gentile's home, you know" (AL, 297)—a statement that would be made only to a Jewish antagonist by some sort of anti-Semite.

In all these cases and more, the Jewish-specific content is never foregrounded but rather mingles with the plethora of narrative and descriptive detail. They will be visible only to a reader who sets out to watch for them, as Andrea Pitzer has done. Nabokov presumably hides these needles in his novelistic haystack in order that the book will not be perceived as being "about" a Jew.

In addition, a few of Nabokov's finest short fictions deal quite artfully with the "social" subject of ethnic suffering and victimization. "Cloud, Castle, Lake," written in his native tongue in 1937, tells about a Russian refugee in Berlin who, at a charity ball, wins a vacation in the countryside with an undetermined group of Germans (perhaps representatives of the

---

[7] Andrea Pitzer, *The Secret History of Vladimir Nabokov*, p. 251.

"Strength through Joy" movement, though the narrator never says so). On the idyllic holiday journey, however, the unnamed protagonist finds himself subjected increasingly to sadistic abuse and torture by the vicious four men and four women who accompany him, and who, short of being actual Nazis, come across as vulgar, brutish sorts.

More dramatic still is "Signs and Symbols," composed in English in 1946, characterized by biographer Brian Boyd as "one of the greatest short stories ever written," and certainly a beautifully suggestive tale.[8] Its elderly Russian-Jewish couple languishes in refugee poverty in New York. Meanwhile their son, "incurably deranged" as a result of their horrific experiences and family losses back in Europe, is institutionalized at a "miserably understaffed" sanitarium. The boy has attempted suicide more than once; at the end, he may or may not have taken the fatal step... By contrast, "Conversation Piece, 1945" (also known as "Double Talk") is more of a satire in which the Russian narrator is accidentally invited to a soirée in Boston, where an émigré German named Dr. Shoe holds forth to a gathering of naively Germanophile ladies about the model behavior of his original country's fighting forces in the recent war; Dr. Shoe attributes "those so-called atrocities" to the work of a few madmen such as Hitler himself or to propaganda by Jews.

Nabokov in his public statements, we have seen, steadfastly dismissed the use of social conflict, current affairs, and other "human interest" concerns in literature. "Topical trash" was his oft-cited epithet for such writing. And yet, in these superb stories he engages precisely such topics: Russian and Jewish victimization, Jewish suffering in the aftermath of fascist persecution, and Nazi apologetics. How works such as these were meant to fit in with his aloof aesthetic is anyone's guess.

What is interesting for our purposes, however, is that Nabokov wrote the above fictions at all. Their plots provide striking instances of the "hidden history" that is buried discreetly in his work and is imparted obliquely rather than placed at center-stage, is an orchestral part rather than a vocal solo. Nabokov's fans of every stripe—the uncritical admirers as well as the admiringly critical—have Andrea Pitzer to thank for her fresh look at his oeuvre.

On the other hand, in the world according to compatriot Ayn Rand, the only victims and sufferers in her novels are the geniuses, inventors, and capitalists, who are in fact the targets of hateful altruists and do-gooders. The weak, the dispossessed, and the otherwise disadvantaged have no place in her cosmos, and Jews are never even mentioned in her fiction, her

---

[8] Boyd, *The American Years*, p. 117.

own background notwithstanding. And aid to any "moochers" only compounds the alleged evil.

*

And so, ladies and gentlemen, we have completed our chronicle of the parallel lives, our travels through the overlapping universes of our two Russian-American imaginers! Let's hear it for the odd pair, Vladimir Nabokov and Ayn Rand! (APPLAUSE)

We have come to know both of them better. The Olympian and the didact. The aristocrat and the bourgeoise. The virtuoso artificer and the campaigning publicist. The master sensorialist and the abstracted, system-building megathinker. The ivory-tower aesthete and the Nietzschean, free-market crusader. ([*Aside, with a smile and a wink at the audience.*] Though, as we've seen, friends, Nabokov likewise had his crusading, publicist phrase and even tried his hand at juggling with ideas, too... While Rand herself fashioned towering peaks and a Rocky-Mountain Olympus for her conquering heroes...)

They differ from yet mirror each other. They're both the creators of alternate, ideal realms in which countless reader-fans—some young, others less so; some sedate professionals, others ardent amateurs—-have found themselves and staked their claims, erecting a personal verbal fortress against other worlds, somewhere, that may not be to their liking. They're united, the odd pair, in their absolute anti-communism. Moreover, in resolutely denying the existence of society and its class structure, they are both libertarians of some sort. And finally, both of them are born-again Americans, whose life-paths stand as *echt*-instances of the twentieth-century, immigrant-American success story.

Each of these writers has his/her corresponding, iconic associations. To wit: Berlin, funny motels, comical colleges and schools, Zembla, and Ardis Hall; New York, chugging factories, formidable building sites, an ailing railroad, and salvation at Galt's Gulch... Travels across America's highways (Humbert and Lolita; Dagny and Hank)... Aesthetic quests and missions (Count Fyodor, Sebastian); a motor to end all motors (Galt) and an analogous super-metal (Rearden)... "Socially" minded sermonizers (Goodman, Albinus, and Chernyshevsky; Toohey and hundreds of "People's-State" do-gooders) who rail either against pure artists (Rex, Udo Conrad, and Sebastian) or against heroic builders (Roark) and inventors (Galt, Rearden)...

Plus butterflies, pure beauty, lost Russia, and a lush, elaborate prose; cigarette holders, pure greed, dollar signs, and ever-longer speeches. All this, ladies and gentlemen, and much, much more!

From there we've made the leap to the bigger picture, have placed the twosome within the larger libertarian mind (the "oversoul," let's call it) and noted that mind's incarnation in a loosely aggregated yet real libertarian movement that, in its ebb and flow, features energy extractors and industrial manufacturers in the production sphere; bankers, financiers, and hedge-funders in the areas of exchange; governmental figures believing strongly in the libertarian project, or pragmatists willing to "compromise" with it; well-funded information and propaganda organs that spread the libertarian creed; bright, innocent youths who are susceptible to persuasion by libertarian preachments and can thus bring constant infusions of "new blood" to the demographic; and, in matters of security, the informal alliance of gun makers, grass-roots gun lovers, recurrent militias, the NRA, and other entities making up the libertarians' paramilitary sector, exerting pressures without respite on civilian leaders, high-level and low!

But more's to come. Turn the page, dear readers, and you will come upon the luminous retrospective look at Nabokov's memoirs, by eminent novelist and essayist Louis Begley. Here again you will see some familiar subjects, now filtered through the wise evocations of a more recent literary master—the sumptuous, ancestral manor in North Russia; the warm family fold; Uncle Ruka and brother Sergey; young Vladimir's first loves and losses; Nabokov's prose style; and the inevitable comparisons to Proust.

In the meantime, dear readers, you have been bearing witness to the complex, writerly relationship that yours truly, your host, had developed over the years with each of these Russian-Americans… That, along with his own experiences of the libertarian mind, starting with childhood and teenhood and life with father; on through the Cold War and the 1960s; the Vietnam War and the Libertarian Party; Reagan and the Afghan mujahedeen; Hayek and Mt. Pelerin and General Pinochet; guns in schools and elsewhere; a long-buried (yet here descried) history involving proto-libertarians and Hitler and Mussolini, anti-communism and the 1930s; and disaster relief, for and against.

Nabokov and Rand have thus functioned as points of departure, as a means of access to the broader question of libertarianism itself and its modes of perceiving and dealing with our world. In the process of anatomizing these two literati, I believe I've gained not only a more thorough grasp of them as authors and ideologues but also a stronger sense of the libertarianism that has shaped them, and that they, in turn, have shaped. Finally, in the encounters with libertarians that follow herewith in Appendix B, I aim to capture the standard discourse, the rhetorical ploys, and even the set phrases that are generated by the libertarians' inner grammars and style of thought. In sum, my conjuring up and then reinventing these personal demons, has served, paradoxically, as my indirect way of exorcising them!

And thus, in the end, rather than glimpses of a latticed gallery, a painted ceiling, marble steps, or an ancestral park, you will share in your host's very own chance meetings with a series of colorful libertarians. The repertoire of well-rehearsed dialectics wielded by these debate-prone souls may ring a bell with those among you who've known such exchanges with flesh-and-blood libertarian acquaintances, past and present.

Hoping these encores will please our audience members, we bid you good luck and good night! (APPLAUSE)

APPENDIX A

A SUPPRESSED ESSAY

[Louis Begley is the noted American novelist and essayist. His critically acclaimed novel, About Schmidt, *was a finalist for the 1997 National Book Critics Circle Award and served as basis for the 2002 film directed by Alexander Payne, with Jack Nicholson in the title role.*

As reported in my Preface and in chapter 10, the following item was commissioned in the 1990s by Random House for their projected new edition of Nabokov's Speak, Memory. *Nabokov's son Dmitri, however, read the essay in proofs and was displeased with Begley's polite criticisms of Nabokov's indifference to politics. Dmitri then demanded changes that Begley thought inappropriate; the essay was eventually scratched.*

There was a strange follow-up to this incident. As recently as 2009, Everyman's Library in the UK was advertising its own edition of Nabokov's memoir as containing an introduction by Louis Begley. Mr. Begley and I both ordered and received copies of the volume, only to find in it … a Foreword by biographer Brian Boyd! The entire odd episode is suggestive of some fantastical story by Jorge Luis Borges.

I am grateful to Mr. Begley for retrieving the text and relaying to me its curious history, as well as for giving me permission to publish it in these pages, where it is available for the first time. GB-V]

INTRODUCTION
[TO VLADIMIR NABOKOV'S *SPEAK, MEMORY*]

BY LOUIS BEGLEY

Fortunate indeed is the reader of *Speak, Memory* for whom this is the initiatory voyage to the least oblique and most loving of Nabokov's recreations of his North Russian childhood and early youth: a world blown apart by the Bolshevik Revolution, shards of which, hoarded with a "hypertrophied sense of a lost childhood," he recombined nostalgically, but often with wild, self-lacerating irony, on page after page of his fiction. But the erudite reader, who returns to this ingenious and lovely book after an absence, with "a thrill of gratitude to whom it may concern," ready to linger over its pages, is even more to be envied. Written in pellucid prose, its structure ostensibly symmetrical like the façade of a gleaming Palladian villa, Nabokov's autobiography is a work of labyrinthine intricacy. Nabokov began to write his novel, *Ada, or Ardor*, subtitled "A Family Chronicle," in 1967 and published it in 1969, almost twenty years after the present autobiography appeared in book form. Transported to the imaginary planet of Antiterra, the subject matter of *Speak, Memory* is decomposed and jumbled, as though Nabokov had stood the autobiography on its head. In the middle of the twentieth century, *Ada*'s protagonist, Van Veen, a cross between Nabokov and an erudite James Bond, undertakes to reconstruct *his* "deepest past." Soon, he notices

> that such details of his infancy as really mattered ... could be best treated, could not seldom be *only* treated, when reappearing at various later stages of his boyhood and youth, as sudden juxtapositions that revived the part while vivifying the whole.

Nabokov's treatment of the past here in this work is not dissimilar. In *Speak, Memory*, family secrets are hinted at through moments of near silence, or in sentences that open certain essential vistas only upon a second or third reading of the entire text; never-to-be-healed wounds remain decorously concealed behind the gorgeous screen of a master stylist's prose; and the horrors and bestiality of the first half of this century are held up for view with a mixture of a humanist's compassion and the disdain of an aristocrat who does not dislike to strike, when it suits him, the pose of a consummate dandy. Nabokov's autobiography is anything but a confession: we could not be farther from Jean-Jacques Rousseau and his ambition to show a man in the total truth of his nature. Rather, the reader should think of *Speak, Memory* as the meticulously posed, composed, and retouched self-portrait of a writer who held that "art at its greatest is fantastically deceitful and complex."

Nabokov devoted a prodigious amount of time during the first twenty years of his exile to making up chess problems—because he was obsessed by these "fanciful, stylish riddles," and to earn money; he continued that occupation when money no longer mattered. Experts distinguish among "several schools of the chess-problem art." In the problems he invented, "Deceit, to the point of diabolism, and originality, verging upon the grotesque, were my notions of strategy." The "notion of strategy" he applied to his fiction and to *Speak, Memory*, is the same, reinforced by the conviction that:

> in a first-rate work of fiction the real clash is not between the characters but between the author and the world ... a great part of a problem's value is due to the number of "tries"—delusive opening moves, false scents, specious lines of play, astutely and lovingly prepared to lead the would-be solver astray.

The reader will do well to keep these principles in mind—at the same time remembering that they too and their disclosure in *Speak, Memory*, are part of Nabokov's triumphant confidence game.

The text reproduced here is the revised 1966 edition. It includes Nabokov's important Foreword, written in January of that year, in which he states that:

> The present work is a systematically correlated assemblage of personal recollections ranging geographically from St Petersburg to St Nazaire, and covering thirty-seven years, from August 1903 [when Nabokov was four and acquired "the inner knowledge that I was I and that my parents were my parents"] to May 1940 [the departure of Nabokov with his wife Véra and their six-year-old son Dmitri from France for the United States], with only a few sallies into later space-time.

As the Foreword makes clear, the fifteen chapters that constitute *Speak, Memory* were originally published as separate memoirs over a period stretching from 1936 to 1951, in the sequence they were written (which was quite different from the one we find here). For instance, the story of Nabokov's governess, "Mademoiselle," Chapter Five of the present volume, in fact came first. Written in French, it appeared in Paris, in a magazine called *Mesures*. Nabokov wrote the remaining chapters in English. They were published in American periodicals, principally *The New Yorker*. In 1951, Nabokov put the chapters in the present order and, as so arranged, they came out in book form as *Conclusive Evidence*—"of my having existed," according to a later Nabokovian quip. *Speak, Memory*, that Nabokovian gem of a title was found for the British edition that appeared in the same year.

Two years later, Nabokov translated *Speak, Memory* into Russian:

> I revised many passages and tried to do something about the amnesic defects of the original—blank spots, blurry areas, domains of dimness. I discovered that sometimes, by means of intense concentration, the neutral smudge might be forced to come into beautiful focus so that the sudden view could be identified, and the anonymous servant named.

And for the "final" 1966 edition of the work,

> I have not only introduced basic changes and copious additions into the initial English texts, but I have availed myself of the corrections I made while turning it into Russian.

According to the Foreword, the corrections were of errors due to unavailability of source materials, and Nabokov's separation, since before World War II, from family members living in Europe, who subsequently questioned certain recollections; the additions consisted of material supplied by Nabokov's cousin and sisters, and new information that had come to light about certain personages mentioned in the work. Nevertheless, a comparison of the 1951 and 1966 editions shows that neither the point of view nor the narrative was substantially altered. The order of the chapters remained the same.

The Foreword (which, as noted above, dates from 1966), stakes out the gallant claim that the chapters, written and published in "erratic sequence,"

> had been neatly filling numbered gaps in my mind which followed the present order of chapters. That order had been established in 1936, at the placing of the cornerstone which already held in its hidden hollow various maps, timetables, a collection of matchboxes, a chip of ruby glass, and even—as I now realize—the view from my balcony of Geneva lake, of its ripples and glades of light, black-dotted today, at teatime, with coots and tufted ducks.

I am inclined to think that the very elegance of this passage signals, and perhaps was intended to signal a glorious fib—of the sort Nabokov warns about:

> I confess I do not believe in time. I like to fold my magic carpet after use, in such a way as to superimpose one part of the pattern upon another. Let visitors trip.

Fib or a queer result of Nabokov's intellectual as well as artistic mastery, the insistence on the preordained design of the work, even when it is difficult to avoid the conclusion that the arrangement of the chapters must have been dictated retrospectively by a practical concern—the need for a degree of coherence in the narrative—and the pains taken to remind the reader that the author is always right there, omnipresent as stage manager and master puppeteer, are characteristic of Nabokov's manner. They are an example of the devices Nabokov used to hold the action and characters of his fiction at a distance, as an artifact to be examined dispassionately. An important aspect of Nabokov's personality, which marks *Speak, Memory* and the entire oeuvre, is revealed by them. A pedant cohabited with the dandy and the artist inside Nabokov. Just like the esoterica of entomology, the transliterated snatches of Russian that may bring an occasional tear to the eye of a Slav, but are served up relentlessly, as accompaniment to perfectly adequate English renditions of the very same phrases, for the uncomprehending rest of the world, and, of course, the poker-faced technical discussion of chess problems—all of which, together with their analogues, abound in *Speak, Memory* and in Nabokov's fiction—these are the marks left by the literary dandy and, most often, by the irrepressible pedant.

The possibility that the exigencies of writing for magazines had a greater influence on the form and content of *Speak, Memory* than a design completely conceived in 1936 may explain certain lacunae in the autobiography. A case in point is how little Nabokov says in this volume about Véra or what it was like to live in the thirties in Berlin with a Jewish wife and a half-Jewish child. Chapters Fourteen and Fifteen simply weren't about *that*, but had a different, specific focus, and needed to be confined to a prescribed maximum number of words.

Who was the puzzling subject of this autobiography that stops when the life is only half over, the haughty intellectual unafraid to assert "I think like a genius," the great writer best known for having made Lolita and other nymphets totems of modern popular culture?

"The cradle rocks above an abyss..." *Speak, Memory* opens with this majestic phrase. Grandson of a Minister of Justice to Tsars Alexander II

and III, and son of Vladimir Dmitrievich Nabokov, a distinguished jurist
indefatigable and courageous in his commitment to liberal and constitutional
causes, our author, Vladimir Vladimirovich Nabokov (writing in English
he did not use the patronymic), was born in St. Petersburg on 23 April
1899, just as this century was about to open. His mother was Elena
Rukavishnikov. The Nabokovs entered history as substantial landowners;
in time, there were generals and court officials among them. By marriage
they acquired even grander aristocratic connections, as to the Sayn-
Wittgensteins. The social standing of the Rukavishnikovs was lower, but
they were fabulously rich, and Elena was an important heiress. Her
personal fortune made possible the haunting opulence of Vladimir's
childhood.

Until the flight from St. Petersburg at the end of 1917, unless it was
traveling abroad, in Italy, France, and Germany—for instance, the crucial
encounter with Colegge is on a beach in Biarritz, and Nabokov and his
brother were sent with a tutor to stay in Berlin to have braces put on their
teeth—the family divided its time between an imposing house on
Morskaya Street, one of the city's most elegant addresses, and an estate,
south of Petersburg, called Vyra. That property, together with the
adjoining Batovo, which belonged to Vladimir's maternal grandmother,
and the Rukavishnikovs' Rozhestvento, became in Nabokov's memory a
magical domain of which he was the prince. The present volume includes
a map of the three estates that Nabokov prepared for the 1966 edition and
embellished by the drawing of a butterfly. Indeed when he was seventeen,
Vladimir inherited Rozhestveno, and a very large sum of money, from his
uncle Ruka, "a slender, neat little man" with "small, mincing feet in high-
heeled shoes." Oddly, Nabokov sees to it that the uncle's inversion cannot
be ignored:

> When I was eight or nine, he would invariably take me upon his knee after
> lunch and (while two young footmen were clearing the table in the empty
> dining room) fondle me, with crooning sounds and fancy endearments, and
> I felt embarrassed for my uncle by the presence of the servants and
> relieved when my father called him from the veranda, *"Basile, on vous
> attend."*

Vladimir Dmitrievich's and Elena's first child, a boy, was stillborn. Of
the living children, Vladimir Vladimirovich was the eldest, followed by
Sergey, born less than eleven months later, and another brother and two
sisters, all three of whom were much younger. In 1964, Nabokov told an
interviewer that

I could always tell when a sentence I compose happens to resemble in cut
and intonation that of any of the writers I loved or detested half a century
ago.

In another interview, given in 1965, he put "the first half of Proust's
fairy tale, *In Search of Lost Time*," in the last place among "*my*
masterpieces of twentieth-century prose." (We learn in *Ada* that Van, "In
later years ... had never been able to reread Proust ... without a roll-wave
of surfeit and a rasp of gravelly heart burn; yet his favorite passage
remained the one concerning the name 'Guermantes.'") The other three
were, in that order, by Joyce, Kafka, and Bely. One may, therefore,
assume that when Nabokov in *Speak, Memory* gave Sergey a walk-on role,
he was not unconscious of how Proust had handled *his* younger brother—
although, perhaps because he was writing memoirs and not fiction, he did
not follow that example to the very end, Proust having made the Narrator
an only child, thus expunging the annoying sibling from the
autobiographical *Remembrances of Things Past*—or without hope that his
readers might catch on. Nabokov was also fond of laying a "false scent":
In contrast to the treatment of Ruka, which leaves no doubt about his
sexual orientation, or Proust's unequivocal decision to present the Narrator
as a lover of women, Nabokov tells an anecdote about Sergey that is a
perfect example of the Proustian gaffe—a blunder, the comic or cruel
effect of which depends on the witnesses of the gaffe and the reader
having the information that the gaffe's perpetrator lacks. What happened is
that Nabokov showed "in stupid wonder" to his and Sergey's tutor a page
from Sergey's diary which "abruptly provided retroactive clarification of
certain oddities of behavior on his part", and the tutor "promptly" carried
to their father. The punchline—which Nabokov never gives—is that the
particular page referred to a homosexual romance of Sergey's. That crucial
piece of information the reader has to learn from someone other than
Nabokov. Proust would have told the reader all he needed to know, unless
the effect he was seeking required him to assume that the reader's
knowledge of the ways of the world and good manners made explanation
unnecessary.

In 1919, the family left Russia from the Crimean port of Sebastopol
and paused momentarily in London. With the help of scholarships
available to émigré Russians, Vladimir and Sergey both went to
Cambridge University although to different Colleges; the rest of the family
settled in Berlin. From great wealth they had sunk to a form of destitution
well known to refugees: They made ends meet by selling jewelry Elena
had smuggled out of Russia in a talcum powder container held in her
elegant traveling necessaire, and accepted more or less official forms of

subventions and discreet alms. His studies completed in 1922, Nabokov joined them, and, in August of that year, in Berlin, occurred the greatest tragedy of Nabokov's life—the assassination of his father by a thug of the White Russian extreme right, an event that Nabokov hints at repeatedly and with increasing distress, as in the celebrated scene in Chapter One, where we see grateful peasants joyfully tossing the father in the air, according to Russian custom:

> and then there he would be, on his last and loftiest flight, reclining as if for good, against the cobalt blue of the summer noon, like one of those paradisiac personages who comfortably soar, with such a wealth of folds in their garments, on the vaulted ceiling of a church while below, one by one, the wax tapers in mortal hands light up to make a swarm of minute flames in the mist of incense, and the priest chants of eternal repose, and funeral lilies conceal the face of whoever lies there, among the swimming lights, in the open coffin.

A year later, Elena and one of Nabokov's sisters moved to Prague, where one could live more cheaply and the government paid pensions of widows of former Russian officials. The other sister followed. Soon, the family was dispersed. In 1925, after a liaison of some two years, Nabokov married Véra Slonim, the daughter of cultivated and formerly rich St. Petersburg Jews. They remained in Berlin until 1937. Nabokov earned his living at first by giving language and tennis lessons; eventually, he began to earn fees and royalties for his Russian language poetry and fiction published by émigré presses, and for translations of his work. This income was tiny; Véra supplemented it, working variously as a secretary, translator and tourist guide. Their son, Dmitri, was born in 1934.

Under the Nuremberg racial laws, which went into effect in 1935, Dmitri as well as Véra was a Jew. Life for Jews in Germany became intolerable at an accelerating pace. *Speak, Memory* leaves one with the impression that Nabokov's ability, during those "secluded years in Germany," to distance himself from everything but his writing and personal concerns was almost total. As a boy, he had been "intently averse to joining movements or associations of any kind." He recalls that

> The constant pressure upon me to belong to some group or other never broke my resistance but led to a state of tension that was hardly alleviated by everybody harping on the example set by my father.

And later, in Cambridge, to some extent in reaction to the sympathy for Bolsheviks and especially Lenin prevalent among his fellow students, he had "turned away from politics and concentrated on literature." In this instance, however, given the impact of "politics" on his family's immediate situation, the contrast between Nabokov's aloofness and the "example" of his father, who was stripped of his court title of Junior Gentleman of the Chamber as punishment for an article in which he condemned the part played by the Tsarist policy in promoting a pogrom, is prodigious. It is fair to note that Nabokov's turned up nose is less repugnant than the callow incomprehension that afflicted in the late thirties such politically engaged writers as Sartre and Beauvoir.

Nabokov writes eloquently of his own and other Russians' isolation—another consequence of the loss of fatherland—from "spectral Germans and Frenchmen in whose more or less illusory cities, we, émigrés, happened to dwell." But Nabokov's solipsism is also a literary dandy's pose of choice. As he explains in Chapter Fourteen, with irony and acuity that are exquisite (but impenetrable to readers who don't happen to know that Sirin was the pseudonym Nabokov adopted to distinguish his writings from those of his eminent and prolific father, a circumstance mentioned in *Speak, Memory*), during those years,

> the author that interested me most was naturally Sirin. He belonged to my generation. Among the young writers produced in exile he was the loneliest and most arrogant one. Beginning with the appearance of his first novel in 1925 and throughout the next fifteen years, until he vanished as strangely as he had come [Nabokov stopped using Sirin as a pen name], his work kept provoking an acute and rather morbid interest on the part of critics ... the mystagogues of émigré letters deplored his lack of religious insight and of moral preoccupation ... Russian readers who had been raised on the sturdy straightforwardness of Russian realism and had called the bluff of decadent cheats, were impressed by the mirror-like angles of his clear but weirdly misleading sentences and by the fact that the real life of his books flowed in his figures of speech, which one critic has compared to "windows giving upon a contiguous world ... a rolling corollary, the shadow of a train of thought." Across the dark sky of exile, Sirin passed, to use a simile of more conservative nature, like a meteor, and disappeared, leaving nothing much else behind him than a vague sense of uneasiness.

This *boutade*, a fine example of Nabokovian mystification, has also a serious purpose, which is to remind the reader of Nabokov's position as man of letters. Unlike Conrad who had never written any fiction in Polish, by the time Nabokov composed *The Real Life of Sebastian Knight*, his first novel in English, he had behind him a full career as an important writer of Russian language poetry and fiction, including the novels *The Defense*, *Laughter in the Dark*, *Invitation to a Beheading*, and *the Gift*, at least two of which equal in quality his best work in English.

As a result of public readings for Russian-speaking audiences and contacts with French publishers, from 1932 Nabokov began to spend considerable periods of time in Paris. Véra and Dmitri joined him in 1938. But two years later, France was defeated by Germany, and it was time for the cellular Nabokov family to flee again. The forty-one-year-old penniless refugee writer and his wife and child walked across the flowered square of a provincial French city to board the ocean liner *Champlain*, which would carry them to the New World. Nabokov had intended to write about his American existence in a second autobiography, to be called *Speak On, Memory*. That project was not completed, but readers interested in Nabokov's vision of the United States will find its reflection in the magnificently cracked and distorting mirrors of *Lolita, Pnin, Pale Fire*, and *Ada*.

The exploration of the self, of the "individual mystery," is inevitably the great subject of autobiography. In Nabokov's case, "lost childhood," Vyra and the house on Morskaya, his mother and his father, and family traits and history all seem inseparable from the self. Obsessively re-examined, with the catastrophe of the Russian diaspora as an overlay, they are the building blocks of *Speak, Memory* and, indeed, of all his fiction. It is, therefore, a piquant measure of Nabokov's Luciferian pride (or his intermittent need for quasi-scientific precision) to find, at the end of Section 2 of Chapter One, that:

> Neither in environment nor in heredity can I find the exact instrument that fashioned me, the anonymous roller that pressed upon my life a certain intricate watermark whose unique design becomes visible when the lamp of art is make to shine through life's foolscap.

What might be a partial retraction appears in Chapter Three:

> The act of vividly recalling a patch of the past is something that I seem to have been performing with the utmost zeal all my life, and I have reason to believe that this almost pathological keenness of the retrospective faculty is a hereditary trait.

There are others. But Chapter Three dates from the summer of 1947, while Chapter One was written in the spring of 1950, and perhaps, on the contrary, Chapter One is the correction of an earlier view.

Given Nabokov's insistence on the conscious control he exercised over each detail of his artistic creation, and his corollary contempt for most modern art and literature, it is not surprising that Nabokov's search for "the instrument that fashioned me" is resolutely and comically anti-Freudian.

> I reject completely the vulgar, shabby, fundamentally medieval world of
> Freud, with its crankish quest for sexual symbols (something like
> searching for Baconian acrostics in Shakespeare's work) and its bitter little
> embryos, spying from their natural nooks, upon the love life of their
> parents.

The vehemence of the invective Nabokov directed, often gratuitously,
in book after book, at the "Viennese Quack" is another story. It makes one
wonder what mischief might have been afoot in that paradisal childhood
Nabokov evoked so unforgettably, over and over, as in this image of a
schoolroom.

> I see again my schoolroom in Vyra, the blue roses of the wallpaper, the
> open window. Its reflection fills the oval mirror above the leather couch
> where my uncle sits, gloating over a tattered book. A sense of security, of
> well-being, of summer warmth pervades my memory. That robust reality
> makes a ghost of the present. Everything is as it should be, nothing will
> ever change, nobody will ever die.

None at all would seem to be the stubborn answer. The premonitory
hints of mortality and lurking disaster are to be seen as such only in
hindsight, or indeed as painted in longer afterward, over the varnish, after
"the shadow of fool-made history vitiated even the exactitude of sundials."

In the depiction of Nabokov's immediate family, only his uncle Ruka
and his brother Sergey fail to attain sunlit perfection. And yet, as the world
goes, the lot of the artistic and high-strung eldest son of a man as famous,
accomplished and handsome, and frankly fond of the good things in life as
Nabokov *père*, is seldom easy. This ordinary rule did not apply in the zone
bounded by Vyra and Morskaya; love and good manners always prevailed.
For all his occasional harshness of tongue ("he was extremely strict in
matters of conduct and given to biting remarks when cross with a child or
a servant"), prowess as an athlete and former butterfly collector (a passion
he passed on to our author), his physical courage, and distinction as
statesman and writer, the father did not weigh too heavily on Nabokov.
Nabokov's admiration for him is shown as unstinting, and the feelings of
"tender friendship" and "the charm of our perfect accord" somehow
withstood even such perils as joint father-and-son boxing lessons.

A special and untroubled affinity bound Nabokov to his mother; she
understood his "confessions of a synesthete" at once. They "discovered …
that some of her letters had the same tint" as Nabokov's; if he mentioned
an unusual sensation, her answer would be, "Yes, I know all that." She
painted endless aquarelles for her son, let him play with her "tiaras,
chokers and rings," some of which would all too soon sustain the family in

exile; admired and coddled him, and kept elaborate albums of his juvenile verse. Nabokov lets us sense that she was difficult—perhaps to the point of brittleness; but such recollections as of her refusal to have anything to do with the management of the Nabokovs' elaborate household, while the chauffeur waited "in the relentless frost of an unending night", only add to her glamour. And the relationship between the mother and father appears to have been no different in its well-bred placidity from what one might infer examining the photograph of the couple, included in this volume [*Speak, Memory*], that was taken one year after Nabokov was born. Every inch a Petrogradian swell, grave, solid almost to the point of corpulence, and impeccable in his summer coat and knickers, the father gazes at us calmly from the rattan chair on which he sits cross-legged. Elena stands at his side, slightly to the rear. Her ample bosom is pressed against his shoulder, her hands are draped affectionately over his arms.

Only once are we given a concrete reason to suspect—over Nabokov's immediate denial—that the serpent has slithered into the family Eden: The mother used to "refer with amusement to a flame she had kindled," and Nabokov remembers, although his recollection wavers,

> a door ajar into a drawing room, and there, in the middle of the floor, Ordo, our Ordo [the children's tutor], crouching on his knees and wringing his hands in front of my young, beautiful, and dumb-founded mother. The fact that I seem to see, out of the corner of my mind's eye, the undulations of a romantic cloak around Ordo's heaving shoulders suggests my having transferred something of the earlier forest dance [in the Batovo woods, for the entertainment of Nabokov and his brother, Ordo "would slowly cavort around a lugubrious aspen"] to that blurred room in our Biarritz apartment (under the windows of which, in a roped-off section of the square, a huge custard-colored balloon was being inflated by Sigismond Lejoyeux, a local aeronaut).

Shame on the reader who thinks he sees evil, is the portent of the concluding pun that side-swipes Freud. But why does Nabokov mention the recollection if it was so confused? To provide an occasion for the pun? To show how a menial's unwanted advances were dealt with by a good-humored and utterly respectable Russian matron? Or is it possible that, for once, Nabokov let his guard down, that his defense was as imperfect as that of his creature, the chess-master Luzhin, that he was under a compulsion to tell?

Nabokov consistently refuted attempts of critics and interviewers to identify ways in which other masters had influenced him. Thus, when asked what he had learned from Joyce, whose *Ulysses* he admired without reserve and taught for many years in his courses on the novel, he replied

"Nothing." Allusions to the work of other writers, and the use Nabokov made of them as foils for his inventions, or as interlocutors, are another matter. In *Speak, Memory* the presence of Proust, the elder who redefined for twentieth-century readers the relationship between memory and art, is to be taken for granted, as is that of Chateaubriand, the greatest memoirist of emigration and exile. It is in the best literary tradition that Nabokov should challenge Proust by certain correspondences and divergences between childhood scenes in *Speak, Memory* and the childhood remembered by Proust's narrator. Chateaubriand's search for the Sylphide in the abandoned and overgrown park of the chateau of Combourg is similarly invoked and challenged when, in a birch grove somewhere in Vyra, Batovo or Rozhestveno, sixteen-year-old Nabokov discovers Tamara. More will be said of her later.

Proust's Narrator too had an eminent father much admired by others. That father, unlike Nabokov's, on occasion differed with the mother about their only son's upbringing. There was a particular complicity between that mother and the precocious, sickly son. Photographs of young Marcel have the same quality of ineffable self-satisfaction that we may observe in this volume in the picture of Nabokov as a sixteen-year-old fop. Living in unostentatious, solid comfort, typical of rich French bourgeoisie, very different from the Russian splendor of the Nabokovs, the Narrator's family spent winters in Paris and long summer holidays in Combray, an imaginary and idealized version of the town of Proust's childhood vacations. Nabokov roamed, on foot or by bicycle, from Vyra to its allied estates. The Narrator's family promenades had destinations whose names his memory clothed with unequalled enchantment: the property of his grandfather's friend, Charles Swann, where the Narrator glimpsed, beyond a hedge, his first love, Gilberte, and the astonishing dark figure of the Baron de Charlus, or the chateau of the Guermantes.

In a celebrated episode in Proust's novel, on a summer evening the family is still gathered around the table in the Combray garden when Swann comes to call. It is already the Narrator's bedtime; he is sent to his room knowing that the presence of a guest will prevent his mother from coming to bestow the goodnight kiss that is the sacred part of their compact. An insomniac, like Nabokov, facing the torment of the night without the appeasement of the mother's embrace, the Narrator invents a stratagem that must bring her to him. The lie is discovered, but good resolutions and discipline are breached by a whim of the father, for whom consistency is not an imperative. Instead of becoming angry, he encourages the mother to spend the night in the Narrator's room, just for once, as a special treat. Thus are shown the seeds of a lifetime of neurasthenia. Here is how Nabokov was put to bed on summer evenings, a scene that seems designed to show that things were managed better in Vyra:

> The final stage in the course of my vague navigation would come when I reached the island of my bed. From the veranda or drawing room, where life was going on without me, my mother would come up for the warm murmur of her good-night kiss. Closed inside shutters, a lighted candle, Gentle Jesus, meek and mild, something-something little child, the child kneeling on the pillow that presently would engulf his humming head. English prayers and the little icon featuring a sun-tanned Greek Catholic saint formed an innocent association upon which I look back with pleasure … I knelt on my pillow in a mist of drowsiness and talc-powdered well-being …

Unclouded childhood bliss, a special relationship with the "ecological niche" of Vyra and Northern Russia, heightened by Nabokov's passion for butterfly collecting, the rituals of the well-ordered life or a rich and harmonious large family, two beautiful houses endowed with a perfection that could not be found elsewhere, were transformed into recollections like this one:

> A large, alabaster-based kerosene lamp is steered into the gloaming. Gently it floats and comes down; the hand of memory, now in a footman's white glove, places it in the center of a round table. The flame is nicely adjusted … Revealed: a warm, bright stylish ("Russian Empire") drawing room in a snow-muffled house …

Like Proust's novel, *Speak, Memory* is an intrepid bet on the power of art to restore everything that has been lost irretrievably except in memory; it is a prayer book of exile. And we cannot escape the conclusion that dispossession and displacement were the forces that pressed upon Nabokov the "intricate watermark" of a very great writer. Certainly, they concerned "intangible property and unreal estate," and not lost bank-notes. Nabokov makes clear, and we must not for a moment doubt his word, his "contempt for the émigré who 'hates the Reds' because they 'stole' his money and land." But the contrast between the remembered past perfect and the "large, gloomy, eminently bourgeois apartments that I have let to so many émigré families in my novels and short stories," accounts for the bitterness—perceptible, for all Nabokov's devil-may-care gaiety and irony of a *grand seigneur*—and the withering scorn always present under the surface of his descriptions of the years of exile. In a 1964 interview, he offered a forthright explanation for having never owned a home in

America, and camping instead with his wife and child impermanently in motels, cabins, furnished apartments and houses of professors on leave:

> The main reason, the background reason, is, I suppose that nothing short of a replica of my childhood surroundings would have satisfied me...

Speak, Memory is dedicated to Nabokov's wife, Véra. She is the "You" addressed for the first time in Chapter Ten, and then invoked in the lovely sentences that open Chapter Fifteen, the book's last:

> They are passing, posthaste, posthaste, the gliding years—to use a soul-rending Horatian inflection. The years are passing by, my dear, and presently nobody will know what you and I know.

As it turns out, however, Chapter Fifteen is not an ode to Véra or even to conjugal love: it celebrates, instead, the author's overwhelming and minutely observed love for Dmitri as a baby and as a little boy. The importance of the couple, Véra and Nabokov, is that they are the lonely, unbowed and vulnerable defenders of Dmitri's right to a happy childhood even in "Hitler's Germany and Maginot's France." Chapter Fifteen, with its "infant's journey into the next dimension" of the outside world, thus closes the cycle begun by the exploration in Chapter One of the awakening of Nabokov's own consciousness in a world made of gentle certainties. In place of the sun-flecked "alley of ornamental oaklings" in Vyra, Nabokov inventories a succession of alien parks and gardens where

> you and I did our best to encompass with vigilant tenderness the trustful tenderness of our child but were inevitably confronted by the fact that the filth left by hoodlums in a sandbox on a playground was the least serious of possible offenses, and that the horrors which former generations had mentally dismissed as anachronisms or things occurring only in remote khanates and mandarinates, were all around us.

Loss of material possessions can be borne with stoical calm until one is obliged to observe its effect on those whom one loves the most. Nabokov's detachment cracks when he sees in Prague his mother's "pitiable lodgings," and how albums in which she had copied out her favorite poems "lay around her on odds and ends of decrepit, secondhand furniture," and a "soapbox covered with green cloth supported the dim little photographs in crumbling frames she liked to have near her couch." The cracks are wider in Chapter Fifteen, because, while his mother "had with her all that her soul had stored," Dmitri had nothing and no one except Nabokov and Véra to watch, in Yeats's phrase, "the uncertainty of his setting forth:"

> We were more or less constantly hard up ... Although powerless to do much about it, you and I jointly kept a jealous eye on any possible rift between his childhood and our own incunabula in the opulent past ...

Chapter Fifteen glows with Nabokov's intensely physical descriptions of Dmitri, Véra is almost discarnate. We see her only twice, and even then the focus is on the child. She holds him, "replete with his warm formula and grave as an idol." On cold days, we are told

> he wore a lambskin coat, with a similar cap, both a brownish color mottled with rime-like gray, and these, and mittens, and the fervency of his faith kept him glowing, and kept *you* warm too, since all you had to do to prevent your delicate fingers from freezing was to hold one of his hands alternately in your right and left, switching every minute or so, and marveling at the incredible amount of heat generated by a big baby's body.

A gentleman's reserve about his wife and the mother of his child, so complete that a show of affection more specific to Véra's "delicate fingers" is unthinkable, or a chasm between reasonable love and love of the senses? Whatever may be the answer, not a trace of sexual attraction, never mind passion, or the desire to pierce the mystery of the other is to be found in Nabokov's relation of Véra. These are reserved for Lolita's and the young Ada's riveting precursors: Colette, the peasant girl Polenka, and Tamara, Nabokov's acknowledged first love. (One supposes, perhaps unkindly, that a good deal of Véra and of the way she and Nabokov lived together are to be found in the portrayal of Ada when old!)

Nabokov met Colette on the beach at Biarritz when they were both ten. *Her* forerunner had been Zina,

> Lovely, sun-tanned, bad-tempered little daughter of a Serbian naturopath—she had, I rememver (absurdly, for she and I were only eight at the time), a *grain de beauté* on her apricot skin just below the heart ...

About Colette, he acquired "the feeling that she was less happy than I, less loved. A bruise on her delicate, downy forearm gave rise to awful conjectures ..." Soon, "my passion for [her] all but surpassed my passion for Cleopatra." He thought of her constantly, althought they met only at the beach. As in the case of Tamara, she was not of his class; "my parents were not keen to meet hers." Typically, pathos and imperfection acted on him powerfully:

> If I noticed she had been crying, I felt a surge of helpless anguish that brought tears to my own eyes. I could not destroy the mosquitoes that had left their bites on her frail neck ... One day, as we were bending together

over a starfish, and Colette's ringlets were tickling my ear, she suddenly turned toward me and kissed me on the cheek. So great was my emotion that all I could think of saying was, "You little monkey."

Here is stuff that went into making both Lolita and Annabel, the nymphet who bent Humbert's taste forever, encountered on a Riviera beach when they were thirteen, and also Ada. Take, for instance, Lolita, before her mother becomes Mrs. Humbert:

She was barefooted; her toenails showed remnants of cherry-red polish and there was a bit of adhesive tape across her big toe; and, God what I would not have given to kiss them then and there, those delicate-boned, long-toed, monkeyish feet!

And Lolita, again:

The day before she had collided with the heavy chest in the hall and— "Look, look!" I gasped—"look what you have done, what you have done to yourself, ah, look:" for there was, I swear, a yellowish-violet bruise on her lovely nymphet thigh which my huge hair hand massaged and slowly enveloped ...

Or twelve-year-old Ada (incidentally, Van Veen, through whose head these thoughts are passing, is fifteen):

Her poor pretty hands—one could not help cooing with pity over them— rosy in comparison to the translucent skin of the arm, rosier than the elbow that seemed to be blushing for the state of her nails; she bit them so thoroughly that all vestige of free margin was replaced by a groove cutting into the flesh with the tightness of wire and lending an additional spatule of length to her naked fingertips.

The description of Polenka gives the reader a sample of Nabokov's *gout de la canaille*, which is also at the core of his sensuality. Polenka was thirteen, the same age as he, the daughter of the Nabokovs' head coachman. He would see when he rode out on horseback,

leaning against the jamb, her bare arms folded on her breast in a soft, comfortable manner peculiar to rural Russia. She would watch the approach with a wonderful welcoming radiance on her face, but as I rode nearer, this would dwindle to a half smile, then to a faint light at the corners of her compressed lips, and, finally, this too would fade, so that when I reached her, there would be no expression at all on her round, pretty face. As soon as I had passed, however, and had turned my head for an instant ... the dimple would be back, the enigmatic light would be playing again on her dear features.

Their "ocular relationship" spanned two or three summers. He notes how she would appear "always barefoot," and,

> Strange to say, she was the first to have the poignant power, by merely *not* letting her smile fade, of burning a hole in my sleep and jolting me into clammy consciousness, whenever I dreamed of her, although in real life I was even more afraid of being revolted by her dirt-caked feet and stale-smelling clothes than of insulting her by the triteness of quasi-seigniorial advances.

There was more to the "nymphean incarnations of her pitiful beauty." Once the hunt for butterflies led Nabokov to the edge of the river. Some peasant children were bathing, naked, and he was able to see her

> gasping, one nostril of her snub nose running, the ribs of her adolescent body arched under her pale, goose-pimpled skin, her calves flecked with black mud ... for a second or two—before I crept away in a dismal haze of disgust and desire—I saw a strange Polenka shiver and squat on the boards of the half-broken wharf, covering her breasts against the east wind with her crossed arms ...

Chapter Twelve of *Speak, Memory* is the exquisitely told, romantic, wistful, and fundamentally tragic story of Nabokov's love for Tamara, an invented name itself, changed to Mary in the eponymous novel written in Russian that was Nabokov's first. He possessed her when she was thirteen, one year younger than he: "In one particular pine grove everything fell into place, I parted the fabric of fancy, I tasted reality ..." The affair continued that winter in St. Petersburg, in museums and movie houses, and when all else failed they were "reduced to exploring the wilderness of the world's most gaunt and enigmatic city," and during the next summer. Then some months passed when he did not see her at all, "engrossed as I was in the kind of varied experience which I thought an elegant *littérateur* should seek."

In 1917, after a winter of "incomprehensible separation," he met her by chance on a suburban train. And that was their last encounter: "Thenceforth, for several years, until the writing of a novel relieved me of that fertile emotion, the loss of my country was equated for me with the loss of my love." Read in conjunction with another passage, in Chapter Five, in which Nabokov tells how he has "distributed among the characters in my books to keep fictitious children busy" fragments of his life, until "Few things are left, many have been squandered," this last phrase has a heart-breaking significance, one that I was able to understand only when I too wrote a novel out of my own experience.

It is, therefore, surprising to find Tamara outside the canon of Nabokov's sensuality: the only characteristic Tamara shares with Zina, Colette, and Polenka, and the later creatures of Nabokov's erotic imagination, is her possibly indispensable inferior social status—she was a "dachnik" living in a house near Vyra rented for the summer, the "mother's first name and patronymic ... had merchant-class or clerical connotations," the father was "the steward of a large estate somewhere in the south." There was nothing of the nymphet in this "adorable girl:"

> She was short and a trifle on the plump side but very graceful, with her slim ankles and supple waist. A drop of Tatar or Circassian blood might have accounted for the slight slant of her merry dark eye and the duskiness of her blooming cheek. A light down, akin to that found on fruit of the almond group, lined her profile with a fine rim of radiance. She accused her rich-brown hair of being unruly and oppressive and threatened to have it bobbed, and did have it bobbed a year later, but I always recall it as it looked first, fiercely braided into a thick plait that was looped up at the back of her head and tied there with a big blow of black silk. Her lovely neck was always bare, even in winter in St. Petersburg ...

Ah, the fears that haunted Humbert when he imagined how nymphal Lolita would change into a pupa!

A great deal has been written about Nabokov's mastery of English prose style; the use I have made of quotations will have given a preview of its beauty and power. The reader will discover other pearls of intelligence and expression, as well as infelicities or marks of a pedant I have referred to, be they words anyone not writing instructions on the use of insecticides would take pains to avoid or heavy and difficult constructions. It doesn't matter. Each great master invents his own language; Nabokov had to make that miracle happen twice, in Russian and in English. *The Real Life of Sebastian Knight* is the first novel Nabokov wrote in English. Its Russian narrator tells in English the story of his dead elder novelist half-brother, born speaking Russian, who wrote in English. *Sebastian Knight* was composed before Nabokov knew how far his gift would take him in the new medium. Here is the judgment the narrator passes on the brother's English style:

> I know, I know as definitely as I know we had the same father, I know Sebastian's Russian was better and more natural to him than his English ... I have in my possession a letter written by him not long before his death. And that short letter is couched in a Russian purer and richer than his English was, no matter what beauty of expression he attained in his books.

I am certain that Nabokov wrote differently in Russian, but it is difficult to believe that he wrote better.

In Chapter Fourteen of *Speak, Memory* Nabokov puts the question that is the hardest, because it requires setting a price on the lives of others. Yet, it is a question that each exile who has survived a calamitous upheaval has to contend with at one time or other, as he ponders Fortune's jokes:

> I wonder ... whether there is really much to be said for more anesthetic destinies, for, let us say, a smooth, safe, small-town continuity of time, with its primitive absence of perspective, when, at fifty, one is still dwelling in the clapboard house of one's childhood, so that every time one cleans the attic one comes across the same pile of old brown schoolbooks, still together among later accumulations of dead objects, and where, on summery Sunday mornings, one's wife stops on the sidewalk to endure for a minute or two that terrible, garrulous, dyed, church-bound McGee woman, who way back in 1915, used to be pretty Margaret Ann of the mint-flavored mouth and nimble fingers.

I rejoice in his answer, one that probably only a genius, supremely confident of his power, could dare to give aloud: "The break in my own destiny affords me in retrospect a syncopal kick I would not have missed for words." Brazenly selfish, it faces the tragic truth that broken destinies make the fertile soil from which grows the greatest art.

APPENDIX B

MY ENCOUNTERS WITH LIBERTARIANS

BY GENE H. BELL-VILLADA

[The following pieces first appeared in various venues—newspapers, a campus magazine, a book of stories, an alternative online news service— between 1985 and 2012. They are reprinted here in virtually the same form as in their initial appearance. The few changes made in content have to do with topical references, which have been either deleted or updated for the sake of clarity.

"Arm the Teachers and Students," the fifth item in this selection, prompted a personal letter from the owner of a local gun shop, who, after praising my ideas, informed me of his intention to forward the article to our state governor, Jane Swift, and urge her to put through such legislation.]

LARRY'S UNMODEST PROPOSAL:
"IT'LL BRING DOWN THE DEFICIT!"

WILLIAMSTOWN

BIG government. Gargantuan deficits. These are the central dilemmas of our time. And the Big Question cries out: What is to be done? At a high-glitz cocktail party, hosted by a happy pair of Harvard yuppies in Boston's Back Bay, I recently heard out somebody's revolutionary fix, and something in my mind whispered "Eureka!" Readers should know about this.

There I was, standing all alone by the maplewood wet bar, taking a first sip of my Bloody Mary. As I surveyed the overpopulated parlor, seeking a familiar face, who should I see propped up wearily against the wall, eyes half-shut, martini in hand, but Larry (horn-rimmed glasses, short blond hair), my old neighbor from college freshmen days. Larry Z. was his name, but back then, he humorously and affectionately dubbed himself Larry the Libertarian. Nowadays he flaunts the label triumphantly.

"Larry, old boy, how's it goin'?"

"Hey, what's up?"

"I wish it was me, Larry, but it's the deficit that's up instead! Larry, you always used to be morally incensed at those profligate spenders in government. Today, though, not even the sky's the limit! Really, what's to be done?"

"Yeah, it's gotten serious, I'll grant you that. But I've hit upon the ultimate solution. In fact I'm flying down to Washington later this week to (ahem) discuss it with high government officials." He leaned over momentarily and patted his Gucci briefcase.

"Aha. So let's hear it."

"Well, we all agree that the executive branch has grown too fat."

"Right. I'll drink to that." My Bloody Mary dwindled by a quarter of an inch.

"The truly cost-effective thing would be to pare down the cabinet. So I say, abolish every department, save for Defense."

Very novel, I thought. "But will it work?"

"It's got to work. In fact, it's the only workable solution."

"But what about all those other federal programs? Like, for instance, Social Security?"

He shrugged his broad shoulders. "Turn it over to the investment banks and brokers. They'd do a better job anyhow. They know where to put your money."

Yeah, that's true, I thought. I remembered those big killings they'd made with derivatives and credit default swaps. Still, I felt uncomfortable. "Larry, how 'bout the departments of the Interior, Agriculture, Commerce, and Labor? Or Medicare?"

"We spend too much money on useless things like national parks. My view is, unleash the developers. And those farmers can fend for themselves! Really, why should some dame in Lexington pay for some guy's corn drought in Kansas? Government-in-commerce is a contradiction in terms, the Labor Department folks are too pro-labor union, and anybody who turns 65 and hasn't invested in enough stocks and bonds to cover his medical costs must be lazy or stupid or both."

"The Environmental Protection Agency?"

"Who needs it? Industry can regulate itself just fine!"

"Gee, but, I don't know, Larry ... What if some factory pollutes the local drinking water? Or makes a medicine that turns out to be toxic?"

"So then you can sue the bastards! Better that than being told what to do by the government. And with a gun pointed at your head!"

"What about some sort of financial regulation?"

He shrugged his shoulders once again. "For your information, old man, the FDIC and all those other bank regulations are what leads to bank failures."

"Amtrak?"

"Hey, what've we all got cars for? This is America, not some dippy little European country. Besides, trains are collectivist."

"Unemployment compensation?"

"Sorry, but you've got it backwards. Unemployment compensation is the prime *cause* of unemployment!"

"Disaster relief?"

"Repeat after me: Disaster relief makes people move to areas that are disaster prone. Period. Again? It's because of disaster relief that people live in disaster-prone areas."

"Gee, Larry, I mean, if the deficit is the biggest problem we face, then why not raise taxes, like on the rich?"

"You've got to be kidding. That would surely lead to another depression. Or inflation. Or both! No way, man."

Yes, there certainly was a revolution brewing in Larry's briefcase. Occam the Razor could have been his other nickname. "OK, Larry, everything you say makes sense. But what about the State Department?"

Larry's free hand made a dismissive gesture, then adjusted his glasses. "Diplomacy is a waste of time. You get nowhere dealing with Marxist countries or other fanatics. And as far as our allies are concerned, well, if they're on our side, do we need embassies? Why bother? Let's face it, ambassadors' fat-cat salaries are a drain on the budget. Oh, sure, what the heck, those Europeans, Asians, and Latinos can maintain embassies in Washington if they so wish." He pointed toward Washington. "Brings in hard currency at least."

"So who should handle foreign policy?"

"The White House, what else? With minimal government, the national security advisor could do the entire job, along with the Pentagon."

Drastic, yet beautifully simple, and I said so. "Still, Larry, how d'you justify those cuts? I mean, what d'you see as the proper role of government?"

Larry was almost yawning now. "Look, I always said it back in college, and I still do: the sole legitimate function of government is to fight communism. Plus crime. Neither more nor less."

So pure a logic could only strike me as, well, awesome. But I had my reservations. "Larry, do you think government has no other obligations to its citizenry?"

"None at all. If anything, government intervention in health, disability, disaster relief, old-age pensions, and all those other high-cost frills— they're only the first step toward communism. And under communism, *everybody* suffers. Look, Gene—that's your name, right?—it's either the free market, or Marxist serfdom. Hey, haven't you read our greatest thinkers, Milton Friedman and Ayn Rand? Anyway, cutting government down to the essential DOD would be *fighting* communism."

At this point a tall dapper fellow whose chin and coiffure were vaguely suggestive of the Buckley clan's look started approaching us. I realized Larry had much bigger fish to fry than yours truly, and I took my silent leave. But any day now I expect Larry's plan to become the biggest sweep yet in the Reagan Revolution's good fight against big government deficits.

[1985]

LARRY THE LIBERTARIAN A HARD LINER ON SOVIET NEGOTIATIONS

WILLIAMSTOWN

THE Soviet Union! That strange, mysterious country whose ways defy all human logic. Only in the Kremlin's peculiar empire can contradictory truths reign equal and supreme. Such is the logic of Communism, however.

These bewildering thoughts well up in the wake of my latest encounter with that brilliant old college neighbor of mine, Larry Z., affectionately known to his friends as Larry the Libertarian. During those distant days as a freshman, Larry used to argue fiercely against having talks with the Soviets.

"Hey, look, man, those guys're completely closed to our views," he'd say, swilling a 3.2 beer. "What's there to negotiate?"

So the other day I'm on break at our local super-deli, pastrami-on-rye in my left hand and *New York Times* in my right. I'm savoring somebody-or-other's comments on Reagan-Gorbachev when I suddenly hear a familiar clipped baritone voice exclaiming, "Look at that evil creep!"

"What do you mean, Larry?"

"I mean, how can the President of the United States even share a picture with that vicious tyrant?"

"Well, Larry, can we really cut ourselves off? There's 280 million Soviet citizens, remember."

Looking pained, Larry exhales a gust of air. "Yes, every one of them suffering under the most horrendous tyranny known to man. 280 million folks who hate Communism and are dying to get out. And yet, there's President Reagan, beaming at their oppressor."

I took a bite of some dangling pastrami. "Oh, Larry, well, I see it this way. Maybe the talks could be of help to those 280 million people."

He plopped into the chair opposite me and donned his most disdainful smirk. "What help can we offer to robots who've been brainwashed by Kremlin bellicosity?" (The latter being one of Larry's favorite words.)

Puzzled, I bit my lower lip. "You say they're brainwashed, Larry. Fine. But how come they also hate Communism?"

He drummed impatiently on his bulging portfolio. "It's elementary, old boy. The Kremlin bosses are notorious for their messianic ideology. They pump Marxist doctrine into people's brains, and nobody's allowed to believe anything else."

I nodded earnestly as I picked up Part 2 of my sandwich. "Oh, sure, Larry, I know, it's Orwellian, folks being forced to love 'Big Brother.' Why do they also want to get out, though?"

"Hey, don't play dumb. You know it's because Communism doesn't work and nobody believes in it. You think anybody over there takes Karl Marx seriously? There's 280 million folks yawning at Marxy's phony-baloney balderdash."

I chewed at my dill pickle. "Oh, I agree, Larry, there's nothing deadlier than Marxist slogans. Give me Civics anytime! But can 280 million bored Soviets pose a threat to us?"

Larry's ordinary correct speech turns edgy now. "Good golly, old man, don't you understand the relentless and demonic drive of Communism? Russia is the most powerful nation on earth, and they've got their people whipped up for global expansion and enslavement."

"It's fearsome, I know. But, Larry, tell me, can your average Ivan fight for a system he hates?"

"Geez, old sport, you can't follow a simple argument." (Good old Larry, always saying just what he thinks.) "They hate that backward, primitive system that can't feed its own people, where everything from winter boots to jet travel is third-rate."

"I know, Larry, President Reagan's said it many times. The Soviets are on the verge of collapse."

He smiled and nodded. "You're catching on."

"But I still don't understand, Larry. If they're on the verge of collapse, then how can they conquer the world?"

With a broad gesture he delved into his portfolio and out came a legal-size map of Europe, complete with arrows and X's. He pointed at Poland. "See that? That's where the infamous Warsaw Pact was signed. World's biggest concentration of military might. They've got twice as many tanks as Western Europe does."

I shuddered at the thought of all those Russian tanks parading through the Champs-Elysées. "Yeah, it's awful, those loyal puppet countries, ready to jump when the Russian bear says 'Jump!'"

Larry was silent for a moment or two. "Loyal puppets? Where'd you get that idea?"

"Well, you said it, Larry. The Warsaw Pact nations are the biggest war machine on earth. Moscow's faithful puppets, ready to push West."

"You are naïve. You've got it wrong. The Poles won't fight for Moscow, and the Czechs aren't too lovey-dovey toward the Russkies either. I mean, look, Romania openly defies Russian pressures. You should get informed, uh …" He snapped his fingers.

"How quickly you forget, Larry. Gene's the name."

"Right. No, old man, you don't seem aware of how profoundly the people in the satellite countries loathe their Russian masters."

Confused, I took a last chomp of rye crust. "But Larry, if those East Europeans all hate Russia, then how is the Warsaw Pact this monolithic force?"

Larry's sleek hands manifested his impatience. "I've told you already, there's those Soviet tanks, plus demonic Communism."

"Well, Larry, how 'bout the view that Russians are afraid of war 'cause of the twenty-five million people they lost to Hitler?"

"Vastly exaggerated." He stood up, snatched his portfolio and said, "It was only twenty million. And besides, maybe that's the one good thing Hitler did." Larry always prided himself on thinking about the unthinkable.

I expressed my admiration. "You're your own mind, Larry. I must grant you that."

"Well, let's face it, anybody who fought the Russkies can't be completely bad." He winked, buttoned up his trench coat, and gave me a devilish grin as he waved good-bye.

I washed my dill pickle down with diet soda, and pondered the USSR, that bizarre place where folks are brainwashed by Marxism, yet don't buy Marxism, where inefficiency is the rule and yet they're ready for global conquest, where everybody's famished and super-strong both, fanatical and cynical at the same time. And then the Poles and Romanians resist Kremlin decrees while serving as canon fodder for the hated Warsaw Pact empire. My innocent mind just can't grasp it all…

What can we say? Communism and Russian tanks simply operate by rules all their own. It's like a remote planet hopelessly beyond the ken of straight-thinking Americans. Larry comes bearing a truth that is indeed stranger than science fiction…

[First printed in The North Adams Transcript, *January 25, 1986]*

FOR LARRY THE LIBERTARIAN, GREED CAN BE GOOD, EVEN BEAUTIFUL

WILLIAMSTOWN

GREED is generosity. Selfishness is altruism. And egotism really means concern for other folks. These are the revolutionary new principles I've picked up in my latest and most informative encounter with my old college chum Larry the Libertarian.

Through Boston there runs a river, and on the banks of that river there sit some of our top graduate schools of business. At Larry's suggestion I recently took a long drive to Charles Polytechnic Institute (CPI) to hear an unforgettable lecture by Dr. Hugh Maylove Gaines, the famed economic writer whose blockbuster book, *The Bottom Line Is Your Best Friend*, is in its 66th week on the best-seller list. The title of his scheduled talk was "Help Thy Neighbor. Get Rich Now!"

So as my yellow Honda crosses the river, I glimpse the spires and arches of Charles Poly's enchanted world, and at a neighboring 10-story parking lot I pay my $20 for the right to take up three hours' worth of prime pavement. As I step into those green groves, however, I feel like the first earthly visitor to planet Pluto. Lecture was announced as taking place at Fortune Hall, and, not knowing the whereabouts of anything whatsoever, I approached a tall young man very much in a hurry, so busy he's carrying both attaché case and portfolio. Because he appears to be a native I ask the speed walker, "Excuse me, sir, which way to Fortune Hall?" But he says nothing and just rushes right on, and I know he's got something truly important to get to.

And as I stroll timidly along the birch-lined paths I ask two more men and a woman, and regularly elicit the same silent response, until I happen luckily upon a sheet-white modernist building with slender columns, stained-glass windows, and **FORTUNE HALL** written in golden letters across the façade. I mount the marble steps. Wondering if I'm late, I see a crisp Nordic beauty in her Oscar de la Renta pants suit descending those same milky steps, and I ask, "Pardon me, miss, do you have the exact time?" But she gazes straight ahead, her regal carriage undisturbed, and I'm reminded of just how precious a commodity is time, something you don't simply dole out. Time is money.

But—thank God!—there's Larry standing outside the auditorium in his $1,000 spring attire. "Boy, Larry, is it a relief to see you."

In his right hand he's clutching a copy of Dr. Gaines's book. "Hey, old sport, you look frazzled."

"Well, Larry, it's upsetting, I ask for directions here and people won't even give me the time of day ..."

With his free hand he gave me his classic dismissive gesture. "You've got to understand, old boy, this is a school of business administration, and we firmly believe people should find things out on their own. Self-reliance, you know. Hey, if you start dishing out freebies to any Joe that comes your way, you'll never get anything done." The crowd is swelling now. "We'd better move, though. Everybody wants ringside. And folks here like spreading themselves over two seats each."

Well, I felt cowed by the very air in that teak-paneled hall. The men had thin tight lips and eyelids that never batted, and ditto for the women, whose glances were few and frosty. And their spit-shine combination-lock briefcases on adjoining seats all seemed to bulge with deals in 8 figures. As Dr. Gaines strutted out onto the podium, even their applause dripped icy power.

In just under 50 minutes a rotund and bespectacled Dr. Gaines gave eloquent solutions for everything. "Get rich, and the poor will grow rich with you." "The best way to assist others is to look out for number one." "With every million you make and every yacht you buy, you're helping to create jobs for workers." "Want to be of service to the community? Buy stocks!" "Your computerized 10-room house will do more for the homeless than any HUD programs ever did." "Following this lecture I'm going to have the $99 lobster special at the Ritz-Carlton, and that, my friends, is the answer to the world hunger problem!" (Voluminous applause greeted this one.)

In his final peroration Dr. Gaines thundered out, "For far too long, Greed has been thought of as a deadly sin. Well, it's time to decertify Greed. It's time to be frank and say, 'Greed is Good. Greed is Beautiful.' And yes, 'Greed is Love.'" (Tumultuous applause.)

I'm feeling simply dazzled by Dr. Gaines's oratory, and as we get up I say so to Larry, who seems moved nearly to tears. Still, I thought "Greed is Generosity" might be sort of Orwellian, like "War is peace," and said so.

Larry looked terribly offended. "No way. Orwell was attacking communist slavery. Greed is freedom. It's the basis of our free society."

I felt confused. "Well, Larry, not too long ago we were furious at those OPEC oil sheiks. And they were really greedy."

Vigorously he shook his head. "That's completely different. OPEC was lining the pockets of those governments, not individuals, and that was evil."

I sigh as we amble out of our row. "How 'bout right-wing governments, like Ferdinand Marcos in the Philippines? He made billions."

"Marcos was a good businessman who just happened to be president. Better him than some commie bureaucrat who'll steal everything from the people."

"Larry, you're so true to your convictions, it's admirable. But then, what about labor unions demanding higher wages? Don't they have their own right to greed?"

"No, no, no, you don't follow me." (Actually I'm walking right behind him.) "Unions are group-oriented, and that's collectivism. Greed is good only when it's individual."

As we jostle through the crowd I marvel at his quick and ready replies. And so I finally resort to that trite, contemptible, discredited, bleeding-heart question, "OK, Larry, I see the value of greed. But where does compassion fit into your world scheme?"

His smile was almost sly. "Oh, I feel lots of compassion—for myself, for our overtaxed billionaires, for the businessmen being hurt by environmental regulations and by Jap imports ..."

Now I've got him, I though. "Aha. So the Japanese are too greedy for you?"

Moral indignation flashed over his face. "No, man, it's not that way. The Japs don't play fair. Greed has rules, and the Japs aren't following the rules."

I don't like being manipulative, but I felt it's time to touch my old buddy's inner heartstrings. "Well, Larry, don't you feel compassion for all the homeless in America?"

His face showed absolutely no expression. "What homeless? There's only people who choose to sleep outdoors." But then he turns softer, "Hell, I feel more compassion for little Feefah."

After breathing the fresher air in the lobby, I bite Larry's bait. "Who, pray tell, is Feefah?"

"My Persian cat. Now she really suffers." And he proceeds to give me a long catalog of Feefah's woes. As his voice becomes more charged with emotion, however, we see Dr. Gaines emerging through the doorway, surrounded by an admiring throng. And Larry cuts his speech short. Hand outstretched, he rushes over to the happy crowd, beaming warmly at the great thinker.

Meanwhile I'd had the most enlightening afternoon of my life. And as I drove back to the Berkshires that night I felt damned proud whenever I hogged the narrow road. No wimpy pedestrian at a yellow light got so much as a chance to cut into my path or my precious time, and not once did I deign to dim my lights for any of those faceless twits honking angrily at me in the opposite lane.

[First printed in The North Adams Transcript, *May 7, 1986]*
[1986]

A DAY IN THE LIFE OF A RUGGED
INDIVIDUALIST

SUBURBAN LOS ANGELES

AWAKENED by his clock radio, he crawls out of his bed and heads for his state-of-the-art bathroom, where, with water piped in from a faraway Colorado River by the Metropolitan Water district, he lazily indulges in a long morning shower. In the meantime his wife prepares for him a large glass of freshly-squeezed orange juice, made from succulent citrus grown on Imperial Valley farms irrigated by Boulder Dam projects.

Showing up all fresh and clean in his thick, white bathrobe, he savors the pulpy liquid and consumes his toast and coffee. Silently, he and his wife look out the picture window onto their resplendent green lawn and kidney-shaped swimming pool—replenished by waters from the federally funded Parker Dam—and feel some pride at what they have achieved by their own efforts. He has only dimmest recollections of fleeing the Dust Bowl with his parents and migrating across the desert to California in the remote 1930s—all ancient history to him.

Now dressed for work, he ambles toward the door, and she kisses him goodbye. Ever since their twin boys graduated from medical school at UCLA (one of the top campuses in California's huge state-university system), she has had considerably less to do with her day. She does not regret having stayed at home to concentrate on bringing up their children, however ("Parenting is a full-time job," she likes to say with a smile), given the long hours her husband regularly puts in at his dental practice. They both often deplore the millions of unmarried welfare mothers who shamelessly raise kids on taxpayers' money and refuse to work for their living.

He drives with ease on the massive, eight-lane freeway constructed, expanded, and then renovated with federal funds. He relishes the strength and power of his Imperial—his sixth consecutive one—and still looks back with relief at the 1979 government bailout of Chrysler Corporation. (He simply does not like the look either of Cadillacs or Continentals. Plus of course there were his long-standing investments in Chrysler preferred stock...) He approaches the building where he works, a handsome, neo-classical structure built decades ago under WPA auspices. As he enters his elegant office and greets his smiling young blonde receptionist, he stares just beyond her at his conspicuously displayed B.S. and D.D.S. degrees, both of them earned—following his overseas stint as an Army artilleryman—with G.I. Bill aid at UCLA. Toward mid-morning the friendly mail carrier from the U.S. Postal service drops in and leaves the day's delivery, which the brunette secretary cheerfully opens, placing the checks for fee-for-service in the in-box.

Several of his patients that day are retirees, and he envies his sons who have clients on Medicare, wishing the program applied to dental work as well. He nonetheless provides them with the full treatment, pausing as they rinse their mouths with water piped in from the Owens River, 215 miles away. His staff includes four dental hygienists, to whom he relegates the more mundane tasks, such as teeth-cleaning. Off and on throughout the day he will indulge his sense of satisfaction at the practice he has built up completely on his own, with no help from anyone but himself.

As he gets into his Chrysler Imperial late in the afternoon, he looks up at the sky, coughs, and notes that pollution levels have fallen over the last few years. He revs up the engine, turns on the radio, and hears an unidentified politician lambasting the environmental laws that are wrecking America. The doctor nods in approval. "Government just can't do anything right!" he remarks bitterly. On the way home he drives by Arcadia Park, made by the WPA into a golf course in 1938, and where he and his wife often play golf on weekends. He thinks back on the passage of Proposition 13, the tax-cutting measure on which, in 1978, he and his family all voted a resounding "Yes!" Retirement is not that far off, he muses as he waits at a long stop light, and he mentally calculates how much of a supplement he might count on from Social Security, a government program he nonetheless has always felt should be privatized and passed on to the banks.

He parks in front of his spacious, prairie-style home, built on a Veterans Administration loan in the '50s. His wife has just returned from an afternoon of playing bridge with her lady friends at Griffith Park Clubhouse, rebuilt by the WPA after it had been destroyed by fire. Their modest dinner starts out with salad greens and finishes with fresh fruit grown in the Central Valley on farms watered by the U.S. Bureau of Reclamation. Their dishes will be automatically washed with water brought in from sources more than 500 miles away, in Nevada. Following dinner, they watch the evening news on TV, with many items beamed direct by NASA satellite. He looks forward to having electronic mail access in his office, made possible by the federal Internet services.

As they sip their coffee, they fret over the immigrants who are unfairly taking advantage of America's social services.

"Why can't others do it on their own?" he asks. "I made it by my own efforts. No one helped me."

"That's right, dear."

"And all those people depending on government handouts. Really, it's time to get government out of our lives."

"No question, dear."

A couple of hours later, under a full moon barely visible through the L.A. smog, they will go for a short dip in the cool, crystalline waters of their swimming pool.

(1994)

ARM THE TEACHERS AND THE STUDENTS

LAST October, a 10-year-old schoolboy in Cheshire, Mass. beat up a classmate and punched his fifth-grade teacher on her lip. School authorities promptly responded by expelling the youth and eliminating the morning recess period. And this was in an idyllic, small town that could have been invented by Norman Rockwell. The situation, of course, is incomparably worse in the cesspool of our inner cities, where teachers routinely use grim phrases like "hardship pay" and "combat duty."

At the national level, violence among minors has been escalating dramatically. A recent editorial in the *Berkshire Eagle* notes that, from 1985 to 1991, the teen homicide rate went up by a whopping 127 per cent. "Nearly all of those killings of children are by other children, and 97 per cent are carried out by guns." What is tragic is that this pathology of intra-youth violence has spilled over into our school halls. And no one—neither teachers nor students—is safe.

What, then, can be done? Half-measures like expelling violent pupils won't achieve much of anything. The kids will only take their bad behavior out onto the streets or bring it home. There is, however, a simple, sure-fire solution (no pun intended) to the problem of school violence, and I should like to air it for the benefit of every normal American.

My proposal comes in three parts. First, I believe schools should adopt a policy of allowing teachers regularly to bear arms whenever they're on duty in the classrooms, hallways, and playgrounds. The number of guns per teacher might be limited to one, perhaps two, while the type of weapons would be a matter of individual choice. This will serve as a deterrent to any sullen and resentful pupils who, having overdosed on "The Simpsons" or reading about Evolution, seek to take their frustrations out onto their teachers.

I anticipate the inevitable objection from the hordes of do-gooders and well-meaning anti-gun lobbyists out there: Wouldn't this be potentially dangerous to the students? Suppose a teacher, in a fit of blind rage, resorted not to her roll book but her Magnum and unwillingly shot one of her youngsters dead? Clearly, this would amount to a senseless and tragic turn of events that might best be avoided. And it can be done.

Here I arrive at Part 2 of my proposal. As a counter-deterrent against abuses by their teachers, pupils should also be allowed—nay, encouraged—to bear arms on the school premises. Besides protecting them from attacks by adults as well as by their immediate peers, such a measure would introduce our young scholars to key Constitutional principles in a manner far more effective than all their liberal, homosexual-influenced classes put together. And finally there is the pay-off that will come from learning by doing: By exercising their Second Amendment rights, our youthful charges will acquire the necessary hands-on experience of living, day by day, in a society where the freedom to possess sophisticated weapons has become as essential to all of us as is the right to spend entire weekends at the mall or surf through 500 TV channels every night.

Most of us remember the blood-curdling incident in the fall of 1993, when a lone gunman named Colin Ferguson shot and killed six people, randomly and point-blank, in a jam-packed commuter train on the Long Island Railroad. Such a massive horror could have been easily prevented from the start, were it not for gun-control laws. How so? Dedicated NRA activists have eloquently made the case that, if every passenger in that rail car had packed a pistol, the man would have been quickly "outgunned" and shot dead long before he had murdered his sixth victim.

The same argument, I maintain, should be applied, mutatis mutandis, to our schools. Would that 10-year-old have punched his teacher's face had she been brandishing so much as a Colt, let alone an AK-47? Most probably not. On the other hand, concerning the rights of schoolchildren to bear arms, there are those who insist on there being an age minimum for gun ownership. And to them I only say for the thousandth time: if you outlaw guns for children, only outlaw children will have guns.

Other extremists make the claim that some places are sacred and should be off-limits to guns—schools being a prime example. And to such discredited liberals I reply that imposing such limits would only be the first step toward total gun control in every corner of our society, leading ultimately to a totalitarian state. One day it's the schools, next day it'll be house-to-house searches. As NRA publicists like to note, a 1928 gun-control law in Weimar Germany paved the way for Hitler's takeover in 1933. And besides, gun control simply doesn't work, as everyone knows. Japan has gun-control statutes that all but suffocate its citizens' basic freedoms, and yet last year, in Tokyo alone, there were at least six reported murders.

Still, if guns are to be allowed in public schools, then what is to prevent the occasional verbal spat from degenerating into a shootout? That is a profound and legitimate concern—which brings me to Part 3 of my proposal. I have a simple, old-fashioned solution: school prayer. Daily morning prayers in the classroom will serve as an effective means of keeping the violent side of young people firmly in control, however armed they may be. With the GOP now fully in the saddle in both House and Senate, it is to be hoped not only that unconstitutional limits on the right to bear assault weapons in the schools will be lifted, but also that a new Amendment mandating school prayer will become law by next summer. A 10-year-old delinquent who has recited the "Our Father" and communed with the Creator will surely never feel moved to punch his teacher's face or pump lead into his fellow classmates any time.

[First printed in The North Adams Transcript, *March 8, 1995]*
[1995]

HITLER RECONSIDERED*[1]

HITLER RECONSIDERED: AN AMERICAN CONSERVATIVE TAKES A BALANCED LOOK AT THE THIRD REICH, AND FINDS MORE THAN A FEW THINGS TO RECOMMEND. By Will E. McPazzo. Washington, D.C: Adroit Ventures Institute, 1988. 200 pp. $19.50

Reviewed by Gene H. Bell-Villada

COUNTLESS sacred cows have been gored by the Reagan Revolution, and many liberal dogmas have been consigned to history's scrap heap. But then, wasn't it about time sensible Americans asked if environmental regulations might be *harmful* to the environment, or labor unions bad for labor? Or Affirmative Action actually hazardous to blacks and Civil Rights laws a pox on all concerned? In sum, after five decades of profligate New Deal, Fair Deal, and Great Society spending, the American people are finally seeing the light and realizing that government meddling in the economy only makes things worse, period.

Such at least has long been the contention of Dr. Will E. McPazzo, scion of a renowned conservative clan and Director of the Adroit Ventures Institute, a respected conservative think tank in Washington D.C. On more than one occasion Dr. McPazzo has been known to quip, "I was against the New Deal then; I still am now."

One large liberal totem, though, still remains: the so-called "Good War" and "Grande Alliance" that FDR made with the Soviets against Hitler. Here especially McPazzo brings fresh thinking with his highly polemical book (and runaway best-seller), *Hitler Reconsidered: An American Conservative Takes a Balanced Look at the Third Reich, and Finds More than a Few Things to Recommend.* As one might expect, McPazzo's open-minded approach has elicited harsh debate among the pundits. A lead editorial in *Commentary* speculated that "there can be such a thing as excessive anti-communism, and McPazzo's bizarre book

---

[1] An earlier version of this book review originally appeared in *The Gharial,* Williams College. It is now included in the collection *The Pianist Who Liked Ayn Rand: A Novella and 13 Stories.* All of the historical data cited in this piece are true; and all of the attributed quotations are accurate.

suggests as much." The curmudgeonly *American Nationalist*, by contrast, gave McPazzo warm if cautious praise, while *U.S. News and World Report* broke with tradition and ran its first book review ever, noting that "McPazzo has raised some hard-nosed if troubling questions for our time." On the other hand the London *Economist* haughtily dismissed *Hitler Reconsidered* as "a perfectly silly book" and judged "*signor*" McPazzo "a disgrace to Anglo-Saxon conservativism."

With his crackling, whip-like prose that rivals Bill Buckley's or William Safire's or Pat Buchanan's, Dr. McPazzo forcefully argues that siding with the Soviets against Germany in 1942 was "an incalculable mistake, the start of a fifty-year disaster" whose consequences we are still paying for today. While solidly deploring the "stupid anti-Semitism of Adolf Hitler and his cronies," McPazzo finds this "heart-rending minus" largely balanced out by a substantial if oft-ignored plus, namely, Hitler's staunch anti-communism.

McPazzo marshals ample data on this score, reminding us, for example, that just two months after taking office in 1933, the Nazi government wiped out the German Communist Party and "carted off its leaders to Dachau," thereby smashing the biggest Marxist party in Europe. "Only a bleeding-heart liberal would see much wrong with *that!*" McPazzo wryly reflects, noting that, throughout Europe and America, the business communities and conservative press gallantly praised Hitler for his "war to the death on Marxism."

McPazzo's "second look" next zeroes in on crucial Nazi support in helping General Francisco Franco ("a great man" warmly admired by Patrick Buchanan's father as well as by the entire McPazzo family) overthrow Spain's "Red Republic" in 1936-39; and he is so bold, moreover, as to dismiss the "so-called French Resistance" as "Moscow-directed" and "communist-tainted," and hence fair game for Hitler's objectives. What McPazzo finds most laudable in Hitler, however, was his "anti-Bolshevik crusade to the East" and the death-blow it dealt to 20 million Soviets. "Can anybody who killed 20 million Soviets be all that bad?" McPazzo ventures to speculate. In this regard, he quotes—music and all—a song sung by the Young Americans for Freedom in the wake of President Reagan's 1980 electoral triumph:

> Deck the halls with commie corpses/ Fa la la la lah, la lah la lah!
> Tis the time to be remorseless/Fa la la la lah, la lah la lah!
> Now we wield our sharp stiletti/Fa la la la lah, la lah la lah!
> Carve the pinks into confettti/Fa la la la lah, la lah la lah!

Alas, we know the outcome: the Soviets in 1944 proceeded to embark on their war of westward expansion, invading Germany "without provocation" even as the liberal West stood idly by and appeased Moscow instead. The naked Soviet conquest of East Europe and Eastern Germany in the 1940s provides clear proof that, if anything, "we in the West strongly needed Hitler's anti-Bolshevist bulwark," McPazzo concludes.

German capitalism and its great strides in the 1930s and early '40s also earn high marks in McPazzo's book. By 1940 the German economy was Europe's most developed and prosperous, a classic "miracle." Growth in the corporate sector from 1933 to 1941, particularly in steel and chemicals, surpassed growth in all previous fifty years combined. Moreover, McPazzo points out, in contrast with Communist states, Hitler never confiscated U.S. business investments in Germany, which in 1940 stood at half a billion dollars.[2]

Indeed, Dr. McPazzo asserts, GM, Ford, and IT & T made large amounts of money in their German truck, tank, and fighter aircraft divisions during the Nazi period. In a supreme irony, it was American aerial bombardment that reduced those firms' German plants to rubble, a violation of property rights for which a contrite U.S. government later paid millions of dollars in damages to its corporate victims.

Nevertheless McPazzo forcefully rejects the anti-Semitism of the Nazi leaders, which he finds "quite abhorrent." Dr. McPazzo, it should be said, has become highly sensitive to allegations that his "balanced look" at Nazism somehow stems from ethnic prejudice on his part. And in order to quell such rumors he recently published in the Adroit Ventures monthly magazine, *Objectives*, a hard-hitting essay entitled "The Case against Nazi anti-Semitism." Invoking libertarian philosopher Ayn Rand, he strenuously repudiates as "emotional, not rational" the "primitive, quasi-African collectivism" that led Germany to treat Jews not as individuals but as members of a group. (As Dr. McPazzo emphatically asserted on Buckley's "Firing Line," long before Margaret Thatcher later did on British television, "Groups don't exist, societies don't exist, I would even say that Jews do not exist. Only individuals do, and their families.") And McPazzo has consistently opposed all state collectivisms, whether they take the form of Nuremberg Laws or Affirmative Action programs.[3]

---

[2] On this basis, Dr. McPazzo applies Professor Jeanne Kirkpatrick's renowned model and places the Nazi system in the "authoritarian" rather than "totalitarian" category. He concludes, moreover, that "the only truly 'totalitarian regimes' have been Communist ones."

[3] In this connection, McPazzo has gone on record as being against the category of "Crimes against Humanity" that was applied at the Nuremberg Trials. For future use

And yet even in Hitler's camps McPazzo finds silver linings. He observes with almost childlike glee that "professional Communists" from all over Europe, including 3 million Red Army soldiers, died in the camps too. ("And I'll drink to that, by jingo!") In addition there were the half-million Gypsies, "notorious for their criminal element"—in McPazzo's own words—and hence their liquidation was Hitler's way of "getting tough on crime." And he is overt in his praise of Hitler's decisive action against the growing problem of homosexuality. He forcefully cites Norman Podhoretz, who in *Harper's* in 1977 singled out the gay subculture as the chief cause of malignant "pacifism," of "hostility to one's country," of an "appeasement" mentality that has long been weakening the West in its battle against Soviet expansionism.[4] "You just can't say that *everybody* in the camps was absolutely innocent," McPazzo soberly reflects. "Would that life were that simple."

Not that everything Nazi, however, looks rosy to Will McPazzo—far from it. His concluding chapter makes a point of confronting Nazism's ugliest flaws, for example the restraints on freedom of expression. ("Few things are as sacred," McPazzo remarks, "as the right to speak our minds, to talk back and say whatever it is we think"—a right that, he observes, is currently "under siege from campus leftists, multiculturalists and feminists.") And the absence of elections under Nazi rule inspires some almost dizzyingly eloquent words of condemnation from McPazzo's able pen.

His very harshest terms, however, are reserved for the Reich's byzantine fiscal policies, particularly its governmental price controls ("arguably among the most repellent features of fascism," McPazzo angrily notes). Above all he singles out "the heavy hand of government regulation" that straitjacketed countless German businessmen, each one of which, McPazzo insists in a paraphrase from Ayn Rand, "probably suffered more than all of the world's alleged underdogs put together." This brings us to what have become the most controversial portions of *Hitler Reconsidered*, namely, McPazzo's paradoxical argument that, though German capitalism prospered under the Reich, Germany's businessmen actually deserve to be memorialized along with the other victims of Nazism. He has, as we know, recently launched a tireless campaign to have monuments and statues erected in Germany, Poland, and Washington

---

he proposes in its stead the concept of "Crimes against the Individual." "I don't give a hoot about humanity," he states frankly in that article; "I care only about the individual."

[4] Norman Podhoretz, "The Culture of Appeasement," *Harper's*, October 1977, pp. 25-32.

D.C, in remembrance of what he calls "the Unknown German Businessman, 1933-1945."

Still, in the balance, Dr. McPazzo believes Nazi Germany to have been a safer bet for America than was Communist Russia. In this regard he notes, "Hitler built the camps, yet he never erected a Berlin Wall." Or in the words he quotes from literary critic Diana Trilling, "More people died under Stalin than under Hitler," and the conclusion to be drawn is obvious. Had America encouraged a healthily capitalist and anti-communist Nazi Germany, we would not have spent the following four decades fighting off Russian proxy troops in Korea, Cuba, Indochina ("Sovietnam," as Vladimir Nabokov so wittily dubbed it), Chile, Libya, Angola, Grenada, Nicaragua, and a host of other Soviet colonies.

McPazzo's closing reflections in his "Epilogue" remind us that, throughout the 1930s, Western conservatives "found *much* to recommend" in European fascism. And the time may have come, he quietly argues, for U.S. conservatives to reclaim that long-forgotten legacy. He brings up the little known fact that fewer Americans died fighting in Hitler's Germany (50 thousand) than were to perish in holding off Soviet expansionism in Korea and Indochina (100 thousand). "Who, then, was America's real enemy?" Dr. McPazzo darkly asks.

McPazzo's book ends with the words, "I was against Roosevelt's war on Germany then. I still am now. And if it ever comes down once again to choosing between Nazism and Liberal-Communism, I'll take Nazism." *Hitler Reconsidered* is surely fated to become a key document of our time.

[1990; 1998]

SHOOTING RAMPAGES:
AN AMERICAN TRADITION

BY GENE H. BELL-VILLADA

THE shooting rampages at a movie theater, at a Sikh temple, at the Empire State Building, and at an elementary school this past year are only the latest in a series of incidents that occur with numbing frequency on the American social landscape. So regularly do they crop up that the time may have come to examine these events through anthropological lenses as a kind of routine social practice, lamented by many, perplexing to all, yet perhaps secretly accepted by some. It is a tradition, albeit a bad tradition, like, say, racism, or wife-beating, or human sacrifice. But a tradition all the same.

Shooting rampages have a set of constants. They always involve a heavily armed individual who sets out to vent his frustrations on whoever happens to be in his gun sights. They flare up in public places: schoolyards, classrooms, churches, bars, movie houses. Numbers of dead and wounded are somewhere in the low double digits. Next, a suspect is either apprehended, or he commits suicide. (Seldom is it a "she.") Then the pundits deplore it. Informal members of the NRA sect engage in all sorts of logical legerdemain to rationalize it. Liberal politicians, out of fear of being attacked or losing votes, remain silent about it. NRA officials issue no comment on it. In short, the same components are to be found solidly in place, time after time. And one simply waits and watches for the next episode of this sort. Such are the elements, then, of a recurring ritual behavior.

Random shootings, I might add, have become such a commonplace feature of American life that only those large-scale rampages that claim multiple lives attract much attention. Whenever a "mere" one or two or three individuals end up killed in an analogous episode in, say, Iowa or Nevada, the incident rates barely a sidebar in the national press.

Shooting rampages in America are by now so strangely *normal* acts of human violence that one might begin to tentatively place them within a larger historical framework. For instance, the Aztecs practiced human sacrifice. The Spanish Inquisition held public burnings. Russia's Tsars encouraged pogroms. The white South had its history of lynchings of African-Americans. Islamic extremists stage suicide bombings. And modern America has its random shooting rampages.

Of course, essential differences separate these phenomena. The violence of Aztec priests, Spanish Inquisitors, and Russian Cossacks was state-sanctioned. Southern lynch mobs were racially motivated, and their local laws both prodded and exonerated them. Suicide bombers, in turn, seek religious salvation. By contrast, in keeping with America's long-standing, free-wheeling, anything-goes, individualistic traditions, shooting rampages take place via the spontaneous will of a free individual, whose arsenal has been enabled by NRA lobbyists, Second-Amendment exegetes and purists, powerful gun manufacturers, widespread gun shows, and friendly gun salesmen. Its wellsprings, then, are private, even though its consequences are public. It is also a form of perverse therapy, of catharsis, of asserting one's individuality when things might not be going well for some lonely, troubled, demented fellow. As in all the above practices, somewhere someone—the gods, the State, white pride, the soul, a guy's irrational thirst for dignity or revenge—gains, while others die.

Shooting rampages, then, are the violence resulting from modern-day, extreme libertarian practices and traditions. They are—to recall the immortal words of 1960s black activist H. Rap Brown—"as American as cherry pie." There is no sign that this tradition is going to recede in our lifetime. Perhaps some anthropologists from the Middle East and the Muslim world could come to America and study this signature ritual practice of ours, and compare it to their suicide bombings. It is a wide-open, virgin field for future researchers.

[2012]

BIBIOGRAPHY

1. Works by Vladimir Nabokov

Ada, or Ardor: A Family Chronicle. [1969] New York: Fawcett, 1970

The Annotated Lolita. Edited, with preface, introduction, and notes by Alfred Appel, Jr. Revised and updated edition. New York: Random House, 1991

Bend Sinister. [1947] London: Penguin Books, 1974

The Defense [1930; 1964] Translated by Michael Scammell in collaboration with the author. London: Granada Publishing, 1967

Despair. [1936; 1966] New York: Vintage International (Random House), 1989

Despair. [1978] Film. Directed by Rainer Werner Fassbinder. New Line Cinema, 1979

The Gift. [1938; 1963] Translated by Michael Scammell with the collaboration of the author. New York: Vintage International, Random House, 1991

Invitation to a Beheading. [1935] Translated by Dmitri Nabokov in collaboration with the author. London: Penguin Books, 1963

King, Queen, Knave. [1928] Translated by Dmitri Nabokov in collaboration with the author. New York: McGraw-Hill, 1968

Laughter in the Dark [1932, orig. *Kamera Obscura*]. Translated by the author. London: Penguin Books, 1963

Laughter in the Dark. Film. Directed by Tony Richardson. Woodfall Film Productions, 1969

Lectures on Literature. Edited by Fredson Bowers. Introduction by John Updike. New York: Harcourt Brace Jovanovich, 1980

Lolita. [1957] (See under *The Annotated Lolita*.)

Lolita. Film. Directed by Stanley Kubrick. Screenplay credited to Nabokov. MGM Studios, 1962

Lolita. Film. Directed by Adrian Lyne. Samuel Goldwyn Company, 1997

Look at the Harlequins! New York: McGraw-Hill, 1974

The Luzhin Defence. Film. Directed by Marleen Gorris. IMDb, 2000

The Original of Laura (Dying Is Fun). Edited by Dmitri Nabokov. New York: Knopf, 2009

Pale Fire. [1962] New York: Vintage Books (Random House), 1989

Pnin. [1957] In Page Stegner, ed., *Nabokov's Congeries*, pp. 362-514.
  New York: Viking, 1968
The Real Life of Sebastian Knight. [1941]. London: Penguin Books, 1964
Short Stories. New York: Vintage, 1995
Speak, Memory: An Autobiography Revisited. [1947] New York: Vintage
  International Random House, 1989
Strong Opinions. New York: McGraw-Hill, 1973

2. Works by Ayn Rand

Anthem. [1946] New York: New American Library, N.D.
Atlas Shrugged [1957]. New York: New American Library, 1959
Atlas Shrugged. Part 1. Film. Directed by Paul Johansson. 20th Century
  Fox, 2011
Atlas Shrugged. Part 2. Film. Directed by John Putch. Atlas Productions,
  2012
Capitalism: The Unknown Ideal. New York: New American Library, 1967
For the New Intellectual [1961]. New York: New American Library, 1963
The Fountainhead [1943]. New York: New American Library, N.D.
The Fountainhead. Film. King Vidor, director. Screenplay by Ayn Rand.
  Warner Bros., 1949
Night of January 16th. [1963] New York: Penguin, 1987
"*Playboy* Interview: Ayn Rand." With Alvin Toffler. *Playboy* March
  1964, pp. 35-43, 64
Romantic Manifesto. [1969] New York: New American Library, 1971
The Virtue of Selfishness: A New Concept of Egoism. [1963] New York:
  New American Library, 1964
We the Living. [1936] New York: New American Library, 1959 (?)

3. Works on Vladimir Nabokov

Alexandrov, Vladimir E., ed. *The Garland Companion to Vladimir
  Nabokov.* New York: Garland Publishing, 1995
Bell-Villada, Gene H. "Nabokov and Rand: Kindred Ideological Spirits,
  Divergent Literary Aims." *Journal of Ayn Rand Studies*, vol. 3, no. 1
  (Fall 2001), pp. 181-94
—. "On the Cold War, American Aestheticism, the Nabokov Problem—
  and Me." In Kelly Comfort. ed., *Art and Life in Aestheticism: De-
  humanizing Art, the Artist, and the Artistic Receptor*, pp. 159-79. New
  York: Palgrave Macmillan, 2008
—. Review of *Strong Opinions. The Nation*, 31 May 1975

—. Combined review of *Look at the Harlequins!* and *Tyrants Destroyed.* *Commonweal*, 13 February 1976

Boyd, Brian. *Stalking Nabokov: Selected Essays.* New York: Columbia University Press, 2011

—. *Vladimir Nabokov: The American Years.* Princeton: Princeton University Press, 1991

—. *Vladimir Nabokov: The Russian Years.* Princeton: Princeton University Press, 1990

Connolly, Julian W., ed. *The Cambridge Companion to Nabokov.* Cambridge and New York: Cambridge University Press, 2005

—. *Nabokov and His Fiction: New Perspectives.* Cambridge and New York: Cambridge University Press, 1999

Field, Andrew. *Nabokov: His Life in Art.* Boston: Little, Brown, 1967

___ . *Nabokov: His Life in Part.* New York: Viking, 1977

—. *VN: The Life and Art of Vladimir Nabokov.* New York: Crown, 1986

Flower, Dean. "Nabokov and Nastiness." Review of Brian Boyd's two-volume biography of Nabokov. *Hudson Review* vol. 45 no. 4 (Winter 1993), pp. 573-82

Foster, John Burt, Jr. *Nabokov's Art of Memory and European Modernism.* Princeton: Princeton University Press, 1993

Fowler, Douglas. [1974] *Reading Nabokov.* Washington, D.C.: University Press of America, 1982. (Reprint)

Grossman, Lev. "The Gay Nabokov," www.salon.com/2000/05/17/Nabokov_5/

Johnson, D. Barton. "Nabokov, Ayn Rand, and Russian-American Literature or, the Odd Couple." *Cycnos* vol. 12 no. 2 (1995), pp. 101-08. Expanded and reprinted as "Strange Bedfellows: Ayn Rand and Vladimir Nabokov." *Journal of Ayn Rand Studies*, Fall 2000, pp. 47-67

—. "Nabokov and the Sixties." In David H. J. Larmour, ed., *Discourse and Ideology in Nabokov's Prose* (q.v.), pp. 139-49

—. *Worlds in Regression: Some Novels of Vladimir Nabokov.* Ann Arbor: Ardis, 1985

Karlinsky, Simon. *Dear Bunny, Dear Volodya: The Nabokov-Wilson Letters, 1940-1971.* Revised and expanded. Berkeley: University of California Press, 2001

Khrushscheva, Nina L. *Imagining Nabokov; Russia between Art and Politics.* New Haven: Yale University Press, 2007

Larmour, David H. J., ed. *Discourse and Ideology in Nabokov's Prose.* New York: Routledge, 2002

Nabokov, Dmitri. "On Returning to Ithaca." In Gavriel Shapiro, ed., *Nabokov at Cornell*, pp. 277-84. Ithaca: Cornell University Press, 1999

Nafisi, Azar. *Reading* Lolita *in Tehran: A Memoir in Books*. New York: Random House, 2000

Nivat, Georges. "*Speak, Memory*." In Vladimir E. Alexandrov, ed., *The Garland Companion to Vladimir Nabokov*, pp. 672-85. New York: Garland Publlishers, 1995

Patnoe, Elizabeth. "Discourse, Ideology, and Hegemony: The Double Drama in and around *Lolita*." In David H. J. Larmour, *Discourse and Ideology in Nabokov's Prose* (q.v.), pp. 111-36

Pitzer, Andrea. *The Secret History of Vladimir Nabokov*. New York: Pegasus Books, 2012

Rampton, David. *Vladimir Nabokov: A Critical Study of the Novels*. New York: Cambridge University Press, 1984

Rorty, Richard. "The Barber of Kasbeam: Nabokov on Cruelty." In *Contingency, Irony, and Solidarity*, pp. 141-68. New York: Cambridge University Press, 1989

Russell, Paul. *The Unreal Life of Sergey Nabokov*. Berkeley: Cleis Press, 2011

Schiff, Stacy. [1999] *Véra (Mrs. Vladimir Nabokov)*. New York: Modern Library, 2000

Shrayer, Maxim. "Jewish Questions in Nabokov's Art and Life." In Julian W. Connolly, ed., *Nabokov and His Fiction: New Perspectives* (q.v), 73-91

Stegner, Page. *Escape into Aesthetics: The Art of Vladimir Nabokov*. New York: Dial Press, 1966

Stringer-Hye, Suellen. "Vladimir Nabokov and Popular Culture." In David H. J. Larmour, ed., *Discourse and Ideology in Nabokov's Prose* (q.v.), pp. 150-59

Sweeney, Susan Elizabeth. "'By Some Sleight of *Land:*' How Nabokov Rewrote America." In Julian W. Connolly, ed., *The Cambridge Companion to Nabokov* (q.v.) ,pp. 65-84.

Wilson, Edmund. *The Fifties: From Notebooks and Diaries of the Period*. Ed. with an Introduction by Leon Edel. New York: Farrar, Straus Giroux, 1986

4. Works on Ayn Rand

Ayn Rand: A Sense of Life. [1997] Documentary film. Written and directed by Michael Paxton. Image Entertainment DVD, 1999

Bell-Villada, Gene H. *The Pianist Who Liked Ayn Rand: A Novella & 13 Stories*. Albuquerque, New Mexico: Amador Publishers, 1998

__. "Who Was Ayn Rand?" *Salmagundi* nos. 111-112 (Winter-Spring 2004), pp. 227-42

Berliner, Michael. *Letters of Ayn Rand.* New York: Dutton, 1995

Branden, Barbara. *The Passion of Ayn Rand.* New York: Doubleday, 1986

Burns, Jennifer. *Goddess of the Market: Ayn Rand and the American Right.* New York: Oxford University Press, 2009

Gaitskill, Mary. *Two Girls. Fat and Thin.* New York: Bantam Books, 1992

García, Cardiff. "Paul Ryan and Hayek vs. Rand." http:FTalphaville.ft.com/2012/08/20/1125611/paul-ryan-and-hayek-vs-rand/

Gladstein, Mimi Reisel, and Chris Matthew Sciabarra, eds. *Feminist Interpretations of Ayn Rand.* University Park: Pennsylvania State University Press, 1999

Heller, Anne C. *Ayn Rand and the World She Made.* New York: Random House, 2009

Johnson, D. Barton. See under "Works on Nabokov."

Mallon, Thomas. "Possessed: Did Ayn Rand's Cult Outstrip Her Canon?" *The New Yorker,* 9 November 2009, pp. 61-67

McConnell, Scott. *100 Voices: An Oral History of Ayn Rand.* New York: New American Library, 2010

Merrill, Ronald E. *Ayn Rand Explained: From Tyranny to Tea Party.* Revised and Updated by Marsha Familaro Enright. Chicago: Open Court, 2013

The Passion of Ayn Rand. TV film. Directed by Christopher Menaul. Producers Entertainment Group, 1999

Pierpont, Claudia Roth. "Twilight of the Goddess." *The New Yorker*, 24 July 1996, pp. 70-81

Sciabarra, Chris Matthew. *Ayn Rand: The Russian Radical.* University Park: Pennsylvania State University Press, 1993

Torres, Louis, and Michelle Marder Kamhi. *What Art Is: The Esthetic Theory of Ayn Rand.* Chicago: Open Court, 2000

Walker, Jeff. *The Ayn Rand Cult.* Chicago: Open Court, 1999

Weiss, Gary. *Ayn Rand Nation: The Hidden Struggle for America's Soul.* New York: St. Martin's Press, 2012

"Who Is John Galt?" www.lululemon.com/community/blog/who-is-john-galt/

5. General Works

Banville, John. "How I Write: John Banville on 'Ancient Light,' Nabokov, and Dublin." Interview with Noah Charney in *The Daily Beast*. www/thedailybeast.com/articles/2012/10/03/how-i-write-john-banville-on-ancient-light-nabokov-and-dublin.html

Bell-Villada, Gene H. *Art for Art's Sake & Literary Life: How Politics & Markets Helped Shape the Ideology & Culture of Aestheticism, 1790-1990*. Lincoln: University of Nebraska Press, 1996

—. *The Carlos Chadwick Mystery: A Novel of College Life and Political Terror*. Albuquerque, New Mexico: Amador Publishers, 1990

—. "*1984*: Looking Backward at Orwell's Novel of the 1940s." *Monthly Review*, vol. 36, no. 1 (May 1984), pp. 22-30

—. *Overseas American: Growing up Gringo in the Tropics*. Jackson: University Press of Mississippi, 2005

—. "On Jean Rhys, Barbara Kingsolver and Myself: Reflections on a Problem that Has No Set Name." In Gene H. Bell-Villada and Nina Sichel, eds., *Writing Out of Limbo: International Childhoods, Global Nomads and Third Culture Kids*, pp. 411-25. Newcastle-upon-Tyne: Cambridge Scholars Publishing, 2011

Berman, Jeffrey. *The Talking Cure: Literary Representations of Psychoanalysis*. New York: New York University Press, 1985

Bloom, Harold. *The Western Canon: The Books and School of the Ages*. New York: Harcourt Brace, 1995

Bracher, Karl Dietrich. *The German Dictatorship. The Origins, Structure, and Effects of National Socialism*. Trans. Jean Steinberg. New York: Praeger, 1970

Broken Flowers. Film. Directed by Jim Jarmusch. Focus Features, 2005

Brown, Angela K. "Texas Education: Teachers Pack Heat?" (For Associated Press) *Berkshire Eagle*, 26 August 2008, pp. A1, A5

Burgin, Angus. *The Great Persuasion: Reinventing Free Markets since the Depression*. Cambridge, Mass.: Harvard University Press, 2012

Byrne, Rhonda. *The Secret*. New York: Atria Books of Simon & Schuster, 2006

Cassidy, John. *How Markets Fail: The Logic of Economic Calamities*. New York: Farrar Straus Giroux, 2009

Charney, Noah. See under "Banville, John."

Chernyshevsky, Nikolai. *What Is to Be Done?* Translated by Michael Katz; annotated by William Wagner. Ithaca: Cornell University Press, 1989

Coll, Steve. "Gusher: The Power of Exxon Mobil." *The New Yorker*, 9 April 2012, pp. 28-37

Davidson, Eugene. *The Trial of the Germans: An Account of the Twenty-two Defendants before the International Military Trial at Nuremberg.* New York: Macmillan, 1966

Dickens, Charles. *Hard Times.* [1854] New York: Everyman's Library, 1992

Dickstein, Morris. *Gates of Eden: American Culture in the Sixties.* Second edition. Cambridge: Harvard University Press, 1997

Diggins, John P. *Mussolini and Fascism: The View from America.* Princeton: Princeton University Press, 1972

Dirty Dancing. Film. Directed by Emile Ardolino. Vestron Pictures, 1987

Djilas, Milovan. *Conversations with Stalin.* Translated by Michael B. Petrovich. New York: Harcourt Brace, 1962

Doherty, Brian. *Radicals for Capitalism: A Freewheeling History of the Modern American Libertarian Movement.* New York: Public Affairs, 2007

D'Souza, Dinesh. *The Virtue of Prosperity: Finding Values in an Age of Techno-Affluence.* New York: The Free Press, 2000

Ebenstein, Alan. *Friedrich Hayek: A Biography.* New York: Palgrave St. Martin's, 2001

Editorials, *Saturday Evening Post.* 3 June 1933; 2 June 1934; 9 June 1934

Elmore, David. Comment against disaster relief. http://www.amazon.com/review/R289ZF87I0N4VL/ref=cm_cd_pg_pg 3?ie=UTF8&asin=0195324870&cdForum=Fx2Y2EICMRVLWKO&c dPage=3&cdThread=Tx330BHDDUZY9XT&store=books#wasThisH elpful

—. Comment against disaster relief. http://www.amazon.com/review/R289ZF87I0N4VL/ref=cm_cd_pg_ne xt?ie=UTF8&asin=0195324870&cdForum=Fx2Y2EICMRVLWKO& cdPage=6&cdThread=Tx330qBHDDUZY9XT&store=books#wasThis Helpful

Farrant, Andrew, Edward McPhail, and Sebastian Berger. "Preventing the 'Abuses' of Democracy: Hayek, the 'Military Usurper' and Transitional Dictatorship in Chile?" *American Journal of Economics & Sociology,* vol. 71 no. 3 (July 2012), pp. 513-58

Frye, Northrop. [1957 *Anatomy of Criticism: Four Essays.* New York: Atheneum, 1968

Gannon, Franklin Reid. *The British Press & Germany, 1936-39.* New York: Oxford University Press, 1971

Gay, Peter. *Modernism: The Lure of Heresy: From Baudelaire to Beckett and Beyond*. New York: W. W. Norton, 2008

Gerard, James W. Review of Adolf Hitler's *My Battle*. *New York Times Book Review*, 15 October 1993, pp. 1, 24. Reprinted in issue for 6 October 1996, p. 42

Greenspan, Alan. *The Age of Turbulence* New York: Penguin Press, 2007

"'Greenspan Shrugged:' When Greed Was a Virtue and Regulation Was the Enemy." *New York Times* Sunday Week in Review section, 21 July 2002, p. 3

Grunberger, Richard. *The 12-Year Reich: A Social History of Germany, 1933-1945*. New York: Holt, Rinehart & Winston, 1971

Guilbaut, Serge. *How New York Stole the Idea of Modern Art: Abstract Expressionism, Freedom, and the Cold War*. Trans. Arthur Goldhammer. Chicago: University of Chicago Press, 1983

Hall, Donald. "James Laughlin of New Directions: Ezra Pound Said Be a Publisher." *The New York Times Book Review*, 23 August 1981, pp. 13, 22-23

Hartz, Louis. *The Liberal Tradition in America: An Interpretation of American Political Thought Since the Revolution*. New York: Harcourt Brace, 1955

Hayek, Friedrich A. *The Constitution of Liberty*. Chicago: University of Chicago Press, 1960

—. *The Fatal Conceit: The Errors of Socialism*. Ed. W. W. Bartley III. Chicago: University of Chicago Press, 1988

—. *Law, Legislation and Liberty*. Vol. 2: *The Mirage of Social Justice*. Chicago: University of Chicago Press, 1976

—. *The Road to Serfdom*. Chicago: University of Chicago Press, 1944

Higham, Charles. *Trading with the Enemy: An Exposé of the Nazi-American Money Plot, 1933-1949*. New York: Delacorte, 1983

Hitler, Adolf. [1925-27] *Mein Kampf*. Trans. Ralph Mannheim. Boston: Houghton Mifflin, 1943

Kelly, Aileen. "Introduction" to Isaiah Berlin, *Russian Thinkers*. London: Hogarth Press, 1978

Levine, Yasha, and Mark Ames. "Koch to Hayek: Use Social Security." *The Nation* Vol. 293 no. 16 (17 October 2011), pp. 18, 20

Martin, Andrew. "Give Him Liberty, But Not a Bailout." *New York Times*, Sunday Business section, 2 August 2009, pp. 1-6

Nietzsche, Friedrich. *Beyond Good and Evil*. Trans. R. J. Hollingdale. New York: Penguin, 2003

Novick, Peter. *The Holocaust in American Life*. Boston: Houghton Mifflin, 1999

Ortega y Gasset, José. *The Dehumanization of Art*. Trans. Helene Weyl. New York: P. Smith, 1951

Paperno, Irina. *Chernyshevsky and the Age of Realism*. Stanford: Stanford University Press, 1988

"Reality-based Community." In http://en.wikipedia.org.wiki/reality-based-community

Roberts, Kenneth. "Hitler Youth." *Saturday Evening Post*, CCVI (26 May 1934), pp. 8- 9, 98-104

Robin, Corey. *The Reactionary Mind: Conservatism from Edmund Burke to Sarah Palin*. New York: Oxford University Press, 2011

Romano, Carlin. *America the Philosophical*. New York: Alfred A. Knopf, 2012

"Russia." *Encyclopedia Britannica*, fifteenth edition, vol. 26, pp. 943-98

Sampson, Anthony. *The Sovereign State of ITT*. New York: Stein & Day, 1973

Saunders, Frances Stonor. *The Cultural Cold War: The CIA and the World of Arts and Letters*. New York: The New Press, 1999

Schoenbaum, David. *Hitler's Social Revolution: Class & Status in Nazi Germany, 1933-1939*. Garden City, NY: Doubleday, 1966

Shlaes, Amity. *The Forgotten Man: A New History of the Great Depression*. New York: HarperCollins, 2007

Swanberg, W. A. *Luce and His Empire*. New York: Scribner, 1972

Szasz, Thomas S. *The Myth of Mental Illness*. New York: Harper & Row, 1974

Thompson, Laurence V. *The Greatest Treason: The Untold Story of Munich*. New York: William Morrow, 1968

Toobin, Jeffrey. "The Absolutist: Don't Underestimate Ted Cruz." *The New Yorker*, June 30, 2014, pp. 35-45

Tuccille, Jerome. *Alan Shrugged: The Life & Times of Alan Greenspan, the World's Most Powerful Banker*. New York: John Wiley & Sons, 2002

—. [1971] *It Usually Begins with Ayn Rand*. San Francisco: Fox & Wilkes, 1997

Ulam, Adam. *In the Name of the People: Prophets and Conspirators in Prerevolutionary Russia*. New York: Viking, 1977

Vargas Llosa, Mario. *The Feast of the Goat*. Translated by Edith Grossman. New York: Farrar, Straus, and Giroux, 2001

Vidal, Gore. "Comment." *Esquire*, July 1961

Wilde, Oscar. "Preface" to *The Picture of Dorian Gray*. New York: Penguin Books, 1985

INDEX